Microsoft® Office Access 2003: Essentials Course

MICHELLE MAROTTI

BRIAN FAVRO

LABYRINTH
PUBLICATIONS®

El Sobrante, CA

Microsoft Office Access 2003: Essentials Course
by Michelle Marotti and Brian Favro

Copyright © 2004 by Labyrinth Publications

LABYRINTH
PUBLICATIONS®

Labyrinth Publications
P.O. Box 20820
El Sobrante, California 94803
800.522.9746
On the Web at labpub.com

President and Publisher:
Brian Favro

Series Editor:
Russel Stolins

Managing Editor:
Laura A. Lionello

Production Manager:
Rad Proctor

Editorial/Production Team:
Holly Hammond, Nancy Logan,
Nancy Roberts

Indexing: Joanne Sprott

Cover and Interior Design:
Seventeenth Street Studios

Labyrinth Publications® and the Labyrinth
Publications logo are registered trademarks of
Labyrinth Publications. Microsoft®, Outlook®,
PowerPoint®, and Windows® are registered
trademarks of Microsoft Corporation. Other product
and company names mentioned herein may be the
trademarks of their respective owners.

The example companies, organizations, products,
people, and events depicted herein are fictitious.

No association with any real company, organization,
product, person, or event is intended or should be
inferred.

Screen shots reprinted with permission from
Microsoft Corporation.

ISBN 1-59136-030-7
ISBN 1-59136-053-6 (perfect)

Manufactured in the United States of America.

10 9 8 7 6   R

Microsoft Office Specialist Program

What Does This Logo Mean?

It means this courseware has been approved by the Microsoft Office Specialist program to be among the finest available for learning Access 2003. It also means that upon completion of this courseware, you may be prepared to become a Microsoft Office Specialist.

What Is a Microsoft Office Specialist?

A Microsoft Office Specialist is an individual who has certified skills in one or more Microsoft Office desktop applications such as Microsoft Word, Microsoft Excel, Microsoft Access, Microsoft PowerPoint®, or Microsoft Project. The Microsoft Office Specialist program typically offers certification exams at different skill levels.* The Microsoft Office Specialist program is the only Microsoft-approved program in the world for certifying proficiency in Microsoft Office desktop applications and Microsoft Project. This certification can be a valuable asset in any job search or career advancement.

Which Exam(s) Will This Publication Prepare You to Take?

Microsoft Office Access 2003: Essentials Course has been approved by Microsoft as courseware for the Microsoft Office Specialist program. After completing this course, students will be prepared to take the Microsoft Office Access 2003 exam.

For more information:

- To learn more about becoming a Microsoft Office Specialist, visit www.microsoft.com/officespecialist/.

- To purchase a Microsoft Office Specialist certification exam, visit www.microsoft.com/officespecialist/.

- To learn about other Microsoft Office Specialist approved courseware from Labyrinth Publications, visit labpub.com/mos/.

Microsoft Office Access 2003 objectives covered in this book

Objective Number	Skill Sets and Skills	Concept Page References	Exercise Page References
AC03S-1	**Structuring Databases**		
AC03S-1-1	Create Access databases	7–8	8–9, 28
AC03S-1-2	Create and modify tables	10, 36, 43	12–15, 25, 27, 36–38, 44–46
AC03S-1-3	Define and modify field types	11–12, 52	52–54
AC03S-1-4	Modify field properties	46–47	47–49
AC03S-1-5	Create and modify one-to-many relationships	122	123–124, 145–146
AC03S-1-6	Enforce referential integrity	123	125
AC03S-1-7	Create and modify queries	137–138	134–135, 137–139, 155–157
AC03S-1-8	Create forms	66, 71	67, 72, 80, 82, 202–203
AC03S-1-9	Add and modify form controls and properties	184, 186, 188, 232–236, 240	185, 188–190, 236–244, 300, 306–309, 317, 323
AC03S-1-10	Create reports	73	74–77, 83–84, 151–152
AC03S-1-11	Add and modify report control properties	277–279	279–283, 288–289
AC03S-1-12	Create a data access page	344–345	345–347, 357–358
AC03S-2	**Entering Data**		
AC03S-2-1	Enter, edit, and delete records	18	18–20
AC03S-2-2	Find and move among records	38–39, 67	39–41, 68–69
AC03S-2-3	Import data to Access	268	269–272
AC03S-3	**Organizing Data**		
AC03S-3-1	Create and modify calculated fields and aggregate functions	127–128, 131	128–129, 131–132, 147–149, 153
AC03S-3-2	Modify form layout	177–180	177–178, 181–184, 206–209
AC03S-3-3	Modify report layout and page setup	276–279	281–283
AC03S-3-4	Format datasheets	22, 109	22–23, 110
AC03S-3-5	Sort records	97, 99, 272	98–100, 272
AC03S-3-6	Filter records	42	42–43
AC03S-4	**Managing Databases**		
AC03S-4-1	Identify object dependencies	348	349
AC03S-4-2	View objects and object data in other views	21, 348	21
AC03S-4-3	Print database objects and data	20–21	23, 27
AC03S-4-4	Export data from Access	342–343	342–344
AC03S-4-5	Back up a database	350	
AC03S-4-6	Compact and repair databases	350	351

Microsoft Office Access 2003: Essentials Course

Contents in Brief

UNIT 3 CUSTOMIZATION AND INTEGRATION

Contents

Index of Quick Reference Tables

List of Keyboard Shortcuts

Editing Commands

Ctrl + C to copy

Ctrl + V to paste

Delete to delete selected object

Enter to open selected object

Design Commands

Ctrl + Enter to open selected object in Design view

F2 to edit object name

F6 to go back to Field Descriptor area

F6 to go to Field Properties area

Document Commands

Ctrl + K to display Insert Hyperlink box

Ctrl + P to display Print dialog box

Ctrl + S to save open object

Preface

Microsoft Office Access 2003: Essentials Course provides an introductory course in Microsoft Access 2003. The text prepares students for the Microsoft Office Access 2003 exam offered through the Microsoft Office Specialist program.

This newest edition of Labyrinth's Microsoft Access book has been reorganized into three units and includes a significant amount of new subject matter. Unit 1: Basic Skills has students design and create a new database, enter data, query the database, and generate reports. Unit 2: Forms and Queries introduces more advanced topics including relationships, advanced querying, subforms, and calculated controls. New subject matter in Unit 2 (not included in the previous edition) includes many-to-many relationships, crosstab queries, and action queries. Unit 3: Customization and Integration teaches students how to customize reports, create switchboards, and integrate Access with other Office programs and the Web. This book boasts brilliantly crafted case studies and end-of-lesson exercises that engage students with sophisticated databases that are developed throughout the course. Students have an opportunity to develop databases from initial planning through Web integration. This book assumes that students understand the basic concepts of using a mouse and drop-down menus, saving files to some type of storage media, and other basic skills required to run Windows programs.

Over the last 10 years of writing and publishing Microsoft Office courses, Labyrinth has developed a unique instructional design that makes learning faster and easier for students at all skill levels. Teachers have found that the Labyrinth model provides effective learning for students in both self-paced and instructor-led learning environments. The material is carefully written and built around compelling case studies that demonstrate the relevance of all subject matter. Mastery of subject matter is ensured through the use of multiple levels of carefully crafted exercises. The text includes Concepts Review questions and Hands-On, Skill Builder, Assessment, and Critical Thinking exercises.

Microsoft Office Access 2003: Essentials Course is also supported on the Labyrinth Website with a comprehensive instructor support package that includes a printable solutions guide, detailed lesson plans, PowerPoint presentations, a course syllabus, extensive test banks, and more.

We are grateful to the many teachers who have used Labyrinth titles and suggested improvements to us during the 10 years we have been writing and publishing Office books. *Microsoft Office Access 2003: Essentials Course* has benefited from the reviewing and suggestions of Joanne Flood of Onondaga-Cortland Madison BOCES, in Liverpool, NY.

About the Authors

Michelle Marotti (BS, Computer Science; MS, Education) earned her degrees from Southern Oregon University. While at Southern Oregon, she began teaching seminars for Word, Excel, and Access, helping the staff migrate to these new applications. After receiving her teaching certificate, she went on to teach high school computer classes. Since June of 2000, she has taught at DeKalb Technical College near Atlanta, Georgia, as a computer instructor. Michelle is a coauthor of *Microsoft Office 2003: Essentials Course*.

Brian Favro (BSc, Computer Engineering) began teaching adult education classes in Richmond, California, in 1991. He found that few books on computer applications met the needs of students and began writing materials to meet those needs. From this experience, he launched Labyrinth Publications and developed the "ease of understanding" format that evolved, with the help of Russel Stolins, into the instructional model that makes Labyrinth books so unique. Other instructors liked what he was doing and soon Brian was selling his books to them, and Labyrinth Publications was born.

Introduction

Welcome to Labyrinth Publications, where you'll find your course to success. Our real world, project-based approach to education helps students grasp concepts, not just read about them, and prepares them for success in the workplace. Our straightforward, easy-to-follow language is ideal for both instructor-led classes and self-paced labs. At Labyrinth, we're dedicated to one purpose: delivering quality courseware that is comprehensive yet concise, effective, and affordable. It's no wonder that Labyrinth is a recognized leader in Microsoft Office and operating system courseware.

More than a million users have learned Office our way. At Labyrinth, we believe that successful teaching begins with exceptional courseware. That's why we've made it our goal to develop innovative texts that empower both teachers and students. We give educators the necessary resources to deliver clear, relevant instruction and students the power to take their new skills far beyond the classroom.

Labyrinth Series Give You More Choices

Labyrinth offers seven exceptionally priced series to meet your needs:

- Microsoft Office 2003 Series—These full-length, full-featured texts explore applications in the Office 2003 system. All application specific books in this series are Microsoft Office Specialist approved for the Microsoft Office 2003 certification exams and the Word and Excel books are also approved for the Microsoft Office 2003 Expert certification exams.

- Silver™ Series—Designed especially for adult learners, seniors, and non-native speakers, this series includes larger fonts and screens, our unmistakable straightforward design, and fun hands-on projects.

- ProStart Foundations™ Series—These full-length, full-featured texts for operating systems and applications include the new Microsoft Windows titles and are designed to lay a solid foundation for students.

- ProStart™ Series for Office XP—These full-length, full-featured texts walk students through the basic and advanced skills of the primary Office XP applications. Most are Microsoft Office Specialist approved. The Office XP Essentials and Comprehensive courses offer surveys of all the primary Office XP applications.

- Briefcase™ Series for Office XP—The popular and inexpensive choice for short classes, self-paced courses, and accelerated workshops (or mix and match for longer classes), these concise texts provide quick access to key concepts. Most are Microsoft Office Specialist approved.

- Off to Work™ Series for Office 2000—Full-length, full-featured texts set the standard for clarity and ease of use in this series. All books in this series are Microsoft Office Specialist approved.

- Briefcase Series for Office 2000—Designed for short classes, self-paced courses, and accelerated workshops, each lesson in this series is broken down into subtopics that provide quick access to key concepts. All books in this series are Microsoft Office Specialist approved.

Microsoft Office 2003 Series Teaching Resources

Instructor Support Material

To help you be more successful, Labyrinth provides a comprehensive instructor support package that includes the following:

Teaching Tools

- Detailed lesson plans, including a topic sequence and suggested classroom demonstrations

- PowerPoint presentations that give an overview of key concepts for each lesson (also available online for students)

- Answer keys for the Concepts Review questions in each lesson

- Comprehensive classroom setup instructions

- A customizable sample syllabus

- A teacher-customizable background knowledge survey to gather information on student needs and experience at the beginning of the course

Testing Tools

- Printer-friendly exercise solution guides and solution files for Hands-On, Skill Builder, Assessment, and Critical Thinking exercises

- Teacher-customizable, project-based Assessment exercises

- Teacher-customizable test banks of objective questions for each lesson and unit

- TestComposer™ test generator for editing test banks with Microsoft Word (and for creating new question banks and online tests)

These resources are available on our Website at labpub.com and on our instructor support CD, which you can obtain by calling our customer service staff at 800.522.9746.

Website

The Website labpub.com/learn/access03/ features content designed to support the lessons and provide additional learning resources for this book. This main page contains links to individual lesson pages. Some of the items you will find at this site are described below.

PowerPoint Presentations The same presentations available to instructors are accessible online. This makes an excellent tool for review, particularly for students who miss a class session.

Downloads Required course files can be downloaded on the lesson pages.

Student Exercise Files The student files needed to complete certain Hands-On, Skill Builder, Assessment, and Critical Thinking exercises are available for download at labpub.com/students/fdmso2003.asp.

Labyrinth's Successful Instructional Design

In conjunction with our straightforward writing style, Labyrinth books feature a proven instructional design. The following pages point out the carefully crafted design elements that build student confidence and ensure success.

Lesson introductions present clear learning objectives.

Case studies introduce a practical application that integrates topics presented in each lesson.

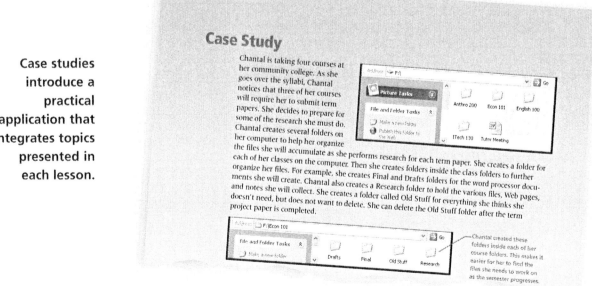

Concepts discussions are kept concise and use illustrations for added clarity and to help students understand the material introduced.

Quick Reference tables provide generic procedures for key tasks that work outside the context of the lesson.

Hands-On exercises are detailed tutorials that help students master the skills introduced in the concepts discussions. The illustrations provide clear instruction and allow unparalleled ease of use.

The Help Window Toolbar

You will encounter this toolbar when viewing Help topics in the Microsoft Word Help Window.

The Auto Tile button displays the Word window and the Help window tiled. If the window is already tiled, the button name changes to Untile. Clicking it causes the Help window to float over the Word window.

Move back one topic.

Move forward one topic.

Print the topic.

QUICK REFERENCE: MOUSE MOTIONS

Motion	How to Do It	This motion is used...
Click	Gently tap and immediately to release the left mouse button.	to "press" a button or select a menu option or object on the screen.
Double-click	Click twice in rapid succession.	as a shortcut for many types of common commands.
Drag	Press and hold down the left mouse button while sliding the mouse. Release the mouse button when you reach your destination.	to move an object, select several objects, draw lines, and select text.
Right-click	Gently tap and immediately release the right mouse button.	to display a context-sensitive menu for the object at which you are pointing.
Point	Slide the mouse without pressing a button until the pointer is in the desired location.	to position the pointer before using one of the four motions above, to select an object on the screen, or to get a menu to appear.

Hands-On 2.7 Move and Size the WordPad Window

In this exercise, you will move the WordPad window to a different location on the Desktop, then change the size of the window.

1. Follow these steps to move the WordPad window:

Ⓐ Click the Save in drop-down list, and choose the 3½ Floppy (A:) drive.

Ⓑ Notice that WordPad proposes the name Document (or Document.doc) in the filename field.

Ⓒ The Hibernation option replaces Stand By in the Windows XP **shutdown** window when you press the (SHIFT) key.

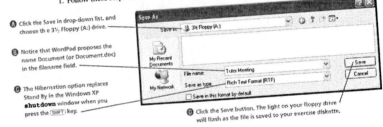

Ⓓ Click the Save button. The light on your floppy drive will flash as the file is saved to your exercise diskette.

The Concepts Review section at the end of each lesson includes both true/false and multiple choice questions.

Concepts Review

True/False Questions

1. A Contents (or Home in Windows XP) search of online Help lets you locate Help topics by typing keywords.   TRUE   FALSE

2. A My Computer window lets you view the files and folders on the computer.   TRUE   FALSE

3. Windows organizes drives and folders in a hierarchy.   TRUE   FALSE

4. You can use the CTRL key to randomly select a group of files.   TRUE   FALSE

5. Folders can have subfolders within them.   TRUE   FALSE

6. You can use the Cut and Paste commands to move files.   TRUE   FALSE

7. Files are sent to the Recycle Bin when they are deleted from floppy disks.   TRUE   FALSE

8. The Properties command displays how much space is left on a floppy disk.   TRUE   FALSE

9. An Exploring window gives you a two-panel view of files and folder.   TRUE   FALSE

10. A quick way to open a file is to double-click on it in a My Computer windows.   TRUE   FALSE

Multiple Choice Questions

1. Which of the following methods would you use to view files and folders on the computer:
   a. Open a My Computer Window

3. Which command is used to create a new folder?
   a. File→Folder→Create
   b. File→New→Folder

Skill Builders, Assessments, and Critical Thinking exercises provide fun, hands-on projects with reduced levels of detailed instruction so students can develop and test their mastery of the material.

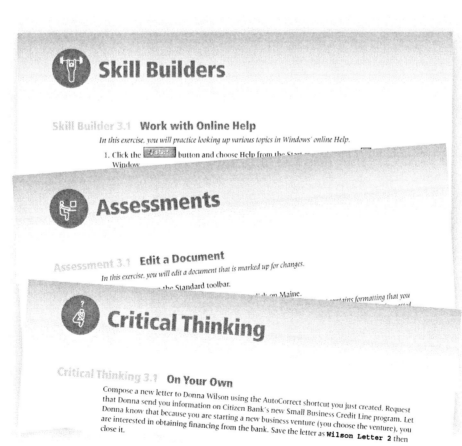

Skill Builders

Skill Builder 3.1   Work with Online Help

In this exercise, you will practice looking up various topics in Windows' online Help.

1. Click the [Start] button and choose Help from the Start menu
   Window

Assessments

Assessment 3.1   Edit a Document

In this exercise, you will edit a document that is marked up for changes.

...the Standard toolbar.

...ick on Maine.

...contains formatting that you

Critical Thinking

Critical Thinking 3.1   On Your Own

Compose a new letter to Donna Wilson using the AutoCorrect shortcut you just created. Request that Donna send you information on Citizen Bank's new Small Business Credit Line program. Let Donna know that because you are starting a new business venture (you choose the venture), you are interested in obtaining financing from the bank. Save the letter as **Wilson Letter 2** then close it.

How This Book is Organized

The information in this book is presented so that you master the fundamental skills first, then build on those skills as you work with the more comprehensive topics.

Visual Conventions

This book uses many visual and typographic cues to guide you through the lessons. These pages provide examples and describe the function of each cue.

Type this text

Anything you should type at the keyboard is printed in this typeface.

Tips, Notes, and Warnings are used throughout the text to draw attention to certain topics.

Command→Command

This convention indicates multiple selections to be made from a menu bar. For example, File→Save means to select File then select Save.

These margin notes indicate shortcut keys for executing a task described in the text.

Quick Reference tables provide generic instructions for key tasks. Only perform these tasks if you are instructed to in an exercise.

Hands-On exercises are introduced immediately after concept discussions. They provide detailed, step-by-step tutorials so you can master the skills presented.

Concepts discussions that deal with the Microsoft Office Specialist Program exam objectives are marked with one of these icons.

The Concepts Review section includes both true/false and multiple choice questions designed to gauge your understanding of concepts.

Skill Builder exercises provide additional hands-on practice with moderate assistance.

Assessment exercises test your skills by describing the correct results without providing specific instructions on how to achieve them.

Critical Thinking exercises are the most challenging. They provide general instructions, allowing you to use your skills and creativity to achieve the result you envision.

Microsoft Office Access 2003: Essentials Course

Unit 1

Access Basics

The lessons in this unit give you solid basics for designing and creating Access databases. By mastering the techniques in this unit, you will be able to create effective databases. You will be introduced to techniques that allow you to create and modify a table design, and you will create forms that help users enter and retrieve data. You will also learn how to structure a query to retrieve only the records you desire from the database. To finish off the basics, you will learn how to create reports to present data in a variety of ways.

Lesson 1: Creating Tables and Entering Data

Lesson 2: Modifying and Maintaining Tables

Lesson 3: Working with Forms and Reports

Lesson 4: Getting Answers with Queries

LESSON 1

Creating Tables and Entering Data

In this lesson, you will begin developing a database for the Pinnacle Pet Care clinic. You will set up one Access table and enter data in it. All data in an Access database is stored in tables. You will learn how to widen table columns, change the margins and page orientation, and print the contents of tables. The Pinnacle Pet Care database will continue to be developed in later lessons.

Microsoft Office Access 2003 objectives covered in this lesson

Objective Number	Skill Sets and Skills	Concept Page References	Exercise Page References
AC03S-1-1	Create Access databases	7–8	8–9, 28
AC03S-1-2	Create and modify tables	10	12–15, 25, 27
AC03S-1-3	Define and modify field types	11–12	
AC03S-2-1	Enter, edit, and delete records	18	18–20
AC03S-3-4	Format datasheets	22	22–23
AC03S-4-2	View objects and object data in other views	21	21
AC03S-4-3	Print database objects and data	20–21	23, 27

Additional learning resources are available at labpub.com/learn/access03/

Case Study

Al Smith is a veterinarian and owner of the Pinnacle Pet Care clinic. Al recently contracted with Penny Johnson, a freelance programmer and Microsoft Access database developer, to develop an order entry system using Access 2003. Al wants to improve customer service by giving the office staff instant access to customer account information. Al chooses Access as his database tool because of its customization capabilities and its integration with other Office applications. Al hopes Access and the other Office applications will make Pinnacle Pet Care's customer service equitable to the excellent care provided to pets.

You can use forms to enter data into tables and to display records.

In Access, all data is stored in tables.

Customer ID	Firstname	Lastname	Address	City	State	Zip	Phone	Last Visit	Current Balance
1	Mark	Roth	760 Maple Avenue	Fremont	CA	94538-	(510) 234-9090	7/7/2003	$235.00
2	Tony	Simpson	312 York Lane	Richmond	CA	94804-	(510) 238-2233	9/7/2003	$185.00
3	Jason	Jones	2233 Crystal Street	San Mateo	CA	94403-	(415) 312-2312	7/15/2003	$48.00

You can create reports using data from your tables.

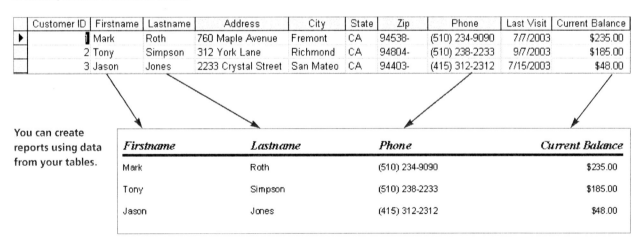

Introducing Access

A database is a collection of information. Microsoft Access is a relational database management system that lets you store, organize, and manage information such as customers, products, employees, and projects. Access is a powerful and flexible program that can handle virtually any data management task. For example, you can use Access to keep a simple contact list or you can develop a full-featured order entry and database management system. Access gives anyone with a personal computer the ability to organize and manage data in a sophisticated manner.

Access is an integral part of the Office 2003 suite of software tools because it is the data storage and management tool. You can share Access data with Word, Excel, PowerPoint, and Outlook. For example, you can merge a Word form letter with an Access database to produce a mass mailing. You can also export Access data to Excel then use Excel's calculating and charting capabilities to analyze the data.

⚠ TIP! Starting Access

In older versions of Windows, the command on the Start Menu is Programs. This text will use (All) Programs to cover all versions of Windows.

The method you use to start Access depends on whether you intend to create a new database or use an existing database. If you are creating a new database, use one of the following methods to start Access:

- Click the button and choose Microsoft Access from the (All) Programs menu.
- Click the button, choose New Office Document, choose the General tab, and double-click the Blank Database icon.

Once Access is started, you can create a new database by choosing the Create a New File option in the Task Pane then choosing the Blank Database option. Access will prompt you to save the new database and give it a name. Name the file at this time because you won't be given the option again.

Use one of the following methods if you intend to open an existing Access database:

- Navigate to the desired database using Windows Explorer or My Computer and double-click the database.
- Click the button and choose Microsoft Access from the (All) Programs menu.

Once Access is started, you may see the file you intend to open listed under Open on the task pane. If you don't, you can open an existing file by choosing the More option and navigating to the desired file.

Hands-On 1.1   Start Access

In this exercise, you will start the Access program.

1. Start your computer and the Windows Desktop will appear.

2. Click the button and choose (All) Programs.

3. Choose Microsoft Access from the (All) Programs menu.
   Access will start and the Access window will appear.

Creating a New Database

You can create a new, blank Access database from scratch or you can use Access's Database Wizard to help you build a database. The task pane that appears on the right side of the Access window gives you several choices. The task pane can be displayed or hidden using the View→Task Pane command.

You open a recently used database or search for an existing database using this section of the task pane.

You create a new database using this section.

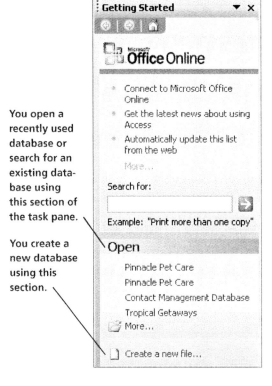

You can create a blank database, a data Access page, or a project using this section of the task pane.

If you choose the On My Computer option then choose one of Access' built-in database templates, the Database Wizard is initiated and guides you step-by-step through the creation of a new database.

The Database Wizard

The Database Wizard lets you choose one of Access's built-in database templates as the basis for your new database. The Database Wizard takes you step-by-step through a series of screens that lets you customize a built-in template to suit your needs. The resulting database is often sufficient to meet the needs of most individuals and some small businesses and organizations. A database created with the wizard can also be used as a foundation from which a more sophisticated database can be developed.

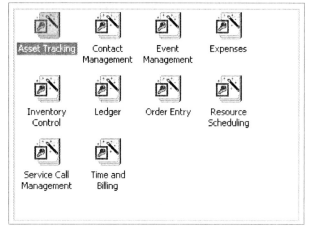

Built-in database templates

Working with Blank Databases

You can also start with a blank database and add objects to it as needed. An Access database is composed of various objects including tables, queries, forms, and reports. Each object type can be created from scratch using a Design view for the particular type of object. Access also provides wizards to help you set up individual objects. You will use both of these techniques as you develop the Pinnacle Pet Care database throughout this course.

Understanding Database Design

The first step in designing any database is to determine the type of information you will need to keep in your database. Examples of data include the name, address, telephone number, and email address of customers or contacts. Once the needed information has been determined, you can design the database to accommodate it. A database structure can be changed but it is more complicated after data has been entered. Sometimes changing the structure can corrupt or delete data that has already been entered. That is why it is important to begin with a good design.

Storing Your Exercise Files

Throughout this book you will be referred to files in your "file storage location." You can store your exercise files on various media such as a floppy disk, a USB flash drive, the My Documents folder, or on a network drive at a school or company. While many figures in the exercises may display files in the 3½ Floppy (A:) drive, it is assumed that you will substitute your own location for that shown in the figure. See the appendix for additional information on alternative file storage media.

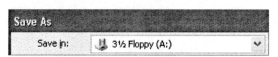

The Save In box as it appears in the book

The Save In box as it might appear if you are saving your files to a USB flash drive

 Hands-On 1.2   Create a Blank Database

In this exercise, you will create a new Access database and explore its components.

Before You Begin: If you have not done so already, please turn to Downloading the Student Exercise Files section of the appendix (page 365) for instructions on how to retrieve the student exercise files for this book from the Labyrinth Website, and to copy the files to your file storage location for use in this and future lessons. See also pages 367–371 for additional details about using this book with a floppy disk, USB flash drive, the My Documents folder, and a folder on a network drive.

1. Make sure the task pane is displayed on the right side of the Access window. If it isn't, use the View→Task Pane command to display it.

2. Choose the Create a New File option.

3. Choose the Blank Database option and notice that the File New Database box appears.

4. Follow these steps to save the new database to your file storage location:

Ⓐ Click here and choose your file storage location. It is most likely the 3½ Floppy (A:) drive.

Ⓑ Notice that Access proposes a name, such as db1, in the File Name box.

Ⓒ Type the name **Pinnacle Pet Care** to replace the proposed name. (If you switched disk drives then you may need to click in the File Name box, delete the name in the box with the ⌈Delete⌉ or ⌈Backspace⌋ keys and type the new name.)

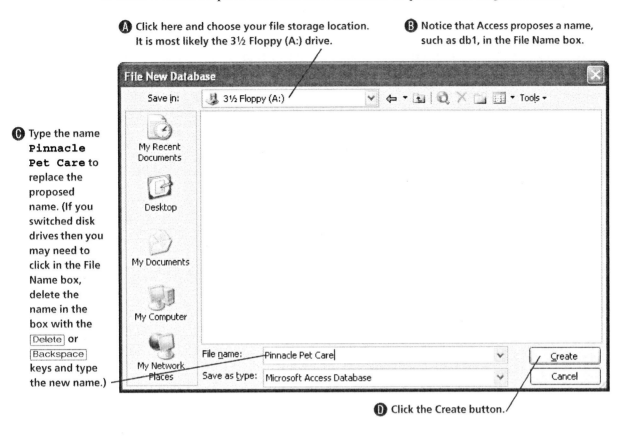

Ⓓ Click the Create button.

5. Follow these steps to explore the Access database window:

Ⓐ Notice the various object buttons displayed on the Objects bar. An Access database is composed of objects. You can create new objects in Design view or with wizards by choosing one of the Create options displayed in the window. Objects you create are also displayed in the database window.

Ⓑ Try clicking the various object buttons.

Ⓒ Click the Tables button when you have finished exploring.

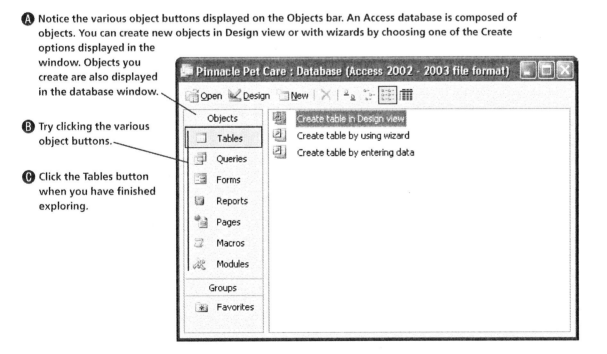

Notice the title bar in the preceding illustration. The text on your title bar may differ; do not be concerned with this.

Introducing Access Tables

In Access, data are stored in tables. Tables organize data so that it can easily be output at a later time. A simple database may have one or two tables while a sophisticated database may have dozens or even hundreds of tables. A separate table is used for each type of related data. For example, your Pinnacle Pet Care database will initially have a table for customers and a table for pets.

Records

Tables are composed of rows and each row is known as a record. For example, your Pinnacle Pet Care database will have a Customers table that stores all of the customer information. All information for one customer is a record. You will have as many records in your database as you have customers.

Fields

Each record is divided into fields. A record can have many fields. For example, the Customers table will have fields for the Customer ID, name, address, telephone number, etc. In Access, each column in a table is a field. Take a few moments to study the following illustration, which shows the first two tables you will create in the Pinnacle Pet Care database.

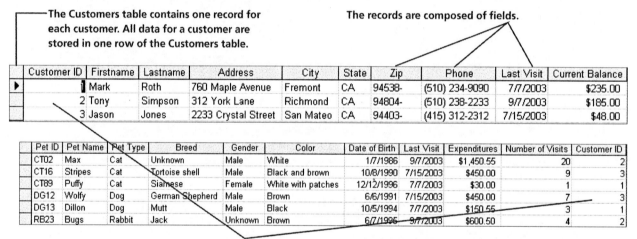

The Customers table contains one record for each customer. All data for a customer are stored in one row of the Customers table.

The records are composed of fields.

Customer ID	Firstname	Lastname	Address	City	State	Zip	Phone	Last Visit	Current Balance
1	Mark	Roth	760 Maple Avenue	Fremont	CA	94538-	(510) 234-9090	7/7/2003	$235.00
2	Tony	Simpson	312 York Lane	Richmond	CA	94804-	(510) 238-2233	9/7/2003	$185.00
3	Jason	Jones	2233 Crystal Street	San Mateo	CA	94403-	(415) 312-2312	7/15/2003	$48.00

Pet ID	Pet Name	Pet Type	Breed	Gender	Color	Date of Birth	Last Visit	Expenditures	Number of Visits	Customer ID
CT02	Max	Cat	Unknown	Male	White	1/7/1986	9/7/2003	$1,450.55	20	2
CT16	Stripes	Cat	Tortoise shell	Male	Black and brown	10/8/1990	7/15/2003	$450.00	9	3
CT89	Puffy	Cat	Siamese	Female	White with patches	12/12/1996	7/7/2003	$30.00	1	1
DG12	Wolfy	Dog	German Shepherd	Male	Brown	6/6/1991	7/15/2003	$450.00	7	3
DG13	Dillon	Dog	Mutt	Male	Black	10/5/1994	7/7/2003	$150.55	3	1
RB23	Bugs	Rabbit	Jack	Unknown	Brown	6/7/1995	9/7/2003	$600.50	4	2

Notice that the Customer ID field appears in both the Customers and Pets tables. Eventually, this field will be used to establish a relationship between the two tables. Establishing relationships between tables is what gives Access and other relational database systems their power and flexibility.

Working with Table Structure

In Access, you can set up tables in Design view or with the Table Wizard. In Design view, you specify the field names, the data type of each field, and any other parameters as needed. Design view lets you precisely determine the characteristics of each field. The Table Wizard automates the process of creating a table by letting you choose from a set of predefined fields. The Table Wizard lacks the flexibility of Design view; however, it is often useful to beginning Access users. Besides, you can always switch to Design view to modify a table that has been set up with the Table Wizard. Access gives you complete control in setting up and modifying tables and other Access objects.

Field Names

Each field in an Access table is identified by a unique name. The name can be up to 64 characters in length and can contain letters, numbers, spaces, and most punctuation marks. Field names cannot contain periods, exclamation marks, or square brackets [ ]. Some examples of field names from the Pinnacle Pet Care Customers table are Firstname, Lastname, Address, City, State, and Zip.

Data Types

Each field is assigned a data type that determines the type of data the field may contain. The most common data types are text, number, currency, and date/time.

- Text—Text fields can contain any type of character. The default size of text fields is 50 characters; however, you can increase or decrease the size as desired.

- Number—Number fields can only contain numbers and typically used in calculations. Therefore, you should use the Text data type if a field will contain a combination of text and numbers or if you are entering phone numbers or zip codes.

- Currency—Currency fields can be used in calculations. Access formats the numbers in a currency field with dollar signs, commas, decimal points, and digits following the decimal point.

- Date/Time—Date/Time fields can contain dates and times. Dates can be used in calculations. For example, you can subtract two dates to determine the number of days between the dates.

- Memo—Memo fields can hold up to 65,536 characters. Use this field when you need to enter lengthy text such as comments or notes.

- AutoNumber—AutoNumber assigns an automatic sequential number to each record. This works well for something like a customer or account number. Using this data type will ensure that no two records have the same number.

- Yes/No—Yes/No fields can contain only one of two values; for example Yes/No, On/Off, or True/False.

- OLE Object—OLE object fields are used to store pictures, sound clips, other documents, or spreadsheets.

- Hyperlink—Hyperlinks are links to another location, such as the Web or another file.

- List—The List field brings up a wizard that walks you through setting up a field that contains list items. It helps you create a drop-down list from which the user can pick. Use this data type when there are certain values that should be entered into the field; for example, a part number or a day of the week.

Field Properties

Each data type has several field properties that can be used to customize the field. For example, you can change the Field Size property for text fields to increase or decrease the maximum number of characters allowed in the field. The field properties can be modified for each field in a table when the table is displayed in Design view.

QUICK REFERENCE: SETTING UP TABLES IN DESIGN VIEW

Task	Procedure
Set up a table in Design view	■ Click the Tables button on the Objects bar in the Access Database window.
	■ Double-click the Create Table in Design View option.
	■ Type a field name in the Field Name column of the table that appears.
	■ Choose a data type for the new field and type a description if desired.
	■ If necessary, modify the field properties at the bottom of the dialog box.
	■ Repeat the previous three steps for all desired fields.
	■ Close the table and give it a name when you have finished.

 Hands-On 1.3   **Set Up a Table in Design View**

FROM THE KEYBOARD
[F6] to go to Field Properties area
[F6] to go back to Field Descriptor area

In this exercise, you will begin setting up the Pets table for the Pinnacle Pet Care database.

Define Text Fields

1. Follow these steps to display a new table in Design view:

Ⓐ Make sure the Tables button is chosen on the Objects bar. ——

Ⓑ Double-click the Create Table in Design View option.

2. If necessary, maximize ▣ both the Access program window and the Table Design window within the Access window.

3. Follow these steps to define a text field:

Ⓐ Type **Pet ID** as the field name.

Ⓑ Tap the [Tab] key to move to the Data Type box. Notice the Data Type is set to Text. This is correct because the Pet ID will be composed of letters and numbers. The Text data type is used if the field contains text or a combination of text and numbers.

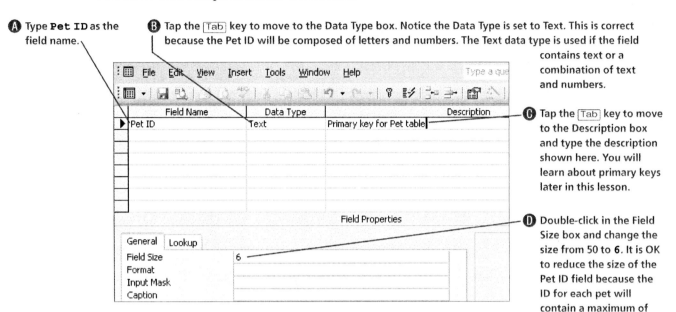

Ⓒ Tap the [Tab] key to move to the Description box and type the description shown here. You will learn about primary keys later in this lesson.

Ⓓ Double-click in the Field Size box and change the size from 50 to **6**. It is OK to reduce the size of the Pet ID field because the ID for each pet will contain a maximum of six characters. The Field Properties section of the dialog box reflects the properties of the current field (Pet ID). You will learn more about these properties as you progress through this course.

You have just defined a field in your database. You will enter data into this field and other fields later in this lesson. You will use a data entry mode known as Datasheet view to enter the data. Currently, you are working in Design view, which allows you to define a table. The Text field type that you chose for the Pet ID field will allow you to enter any type of data in the field. However, the Pet ID for each pet will be restricted to six characters.

4. Follow these steps to define another text field:

Ⓐ Click in the next Field Name box and type **Pet Name**. The Pet Name field will contain the names of the pets.

Ⓑ Tap the [Tab] key and Text will appear as the default Data Type. Leave the Data Type set to Text and do not enter a description for this field. Descriptions are optional and are only used when necessary.

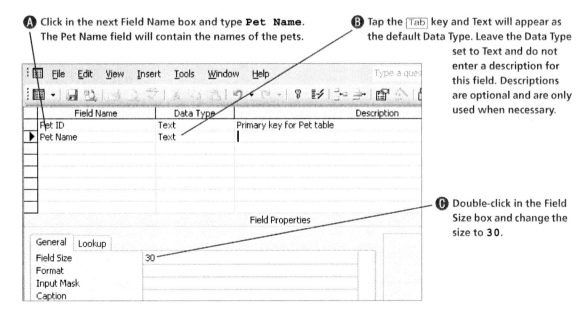

Ⓒ Double-click in the Field Size box and change the size to **30**.

5. Follow the same procedure you used in step 4 to create the next four fields shown in the following illustration. Set the Field Size to **30** for all of the fields except the Gender field. Set the size of the Gender field to **10**.

Field Name	Data Type	Description
Pet ID	Text	Primary key for Pet table
Pet Name	Text	
Pet Type	Text	
Breed	Text	
Gender	Text	
Color	Text	

Define Date Fields

In the next few steps, you will define two fields that will eventually contain dates. You will set the Data Type to Date/Time for these fields. This is useful because Access will identify the contents of the fields as dates. Dates can be used in calculations. For example, you can have Access calculate the number of days an account is past due by subtracting the invoice date from the current date.

6. Follow these steps to define a date field:

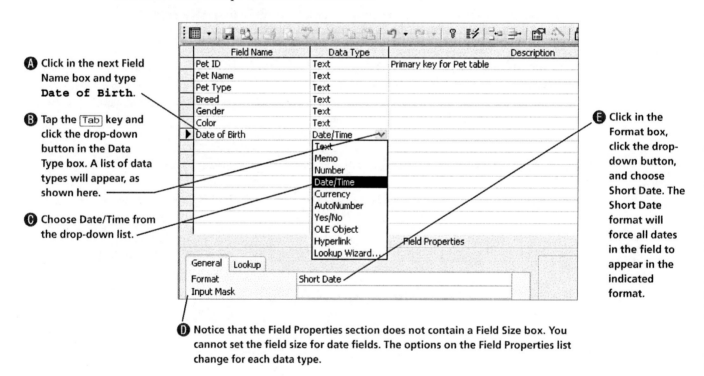

A Click in the next Field Name box and type **Date of Birth**.

B Tap the Tab key and click the drop-down button in the Data Type box. A list of data types will appear, as shown here.

C Choose Date/Time from the drop-down list.

E Click in the Format box, click the drop-down button, and choose Short Date. The Short Date format will force all dates in the field to appear in the indicated format.

D Notice that the Field Properties section does not contain a Field Size box. You cannot set the field size for date fields. The options on the Field Properties list change for each data type.

7. Now define another date field named **Last Visit**, as shown in the following illustration. Set the Format to Short Date, as shown at the bottom of the illustration.

Field Name	Data Type	Descri
Pet ID	Text	Primary key for Pet table
Pet Name	Text	
Pet Type	Text	
Breed	Text	
Gender	Text	
Color	Text	
Date of Birth	Date/Time	
▶ Last Visit	Date/Time	

Field Properties

General | Lookup

Format	Short Date
Input Mask	

Define Currency and Number Fields

In the next few steps, you will define two more fields. You will set the Data Type to Currency for one of the fields and Number for the other. Currency and number fields can be used in calculations. Furthermore, fields formatted with the Currency data type will display a dollar sign, a decimal point, and two decimal places whenever you enter data into the fields.

8. Define the Expenditures and Number of Visits fields as shown in the following illustration:

Ⓐ Set the Data Types and enter the descriptions as shown. Leave the Field Properties at the bottom of the dialog box with the default settings. Number fields normally have a Field Size of Long Integer, as shown here. Keep in mind that choosing Field Properties can be an involved process that often requires extensive knowledge of Access.

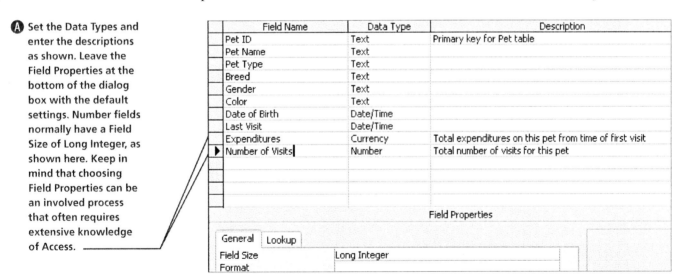

Field Name	Data Type	Description
Pet ID	Text	Primary key for Pet table
Pet Name	Text	
Pet Type	Text	
Breed	Text	
Gender	Text	
Color	Text	
Date of Birth	Date/Time	
Last Visit	Date/Time	
Expenditures	Currency	Total expenditures on this pet from time of first visit
▶ Number of Visits	Number	Total number of visits for this pet

Field Properties

General | Lookup

Field Size	Long Integer
Format	

9. Now continue with the next topic, in which you will define a primary key for the table.

Working with Primary Keys

Most Access tables have one field defined as the primary key. The field chosen to be the primary key field must contain unique data; for example, numbers or codes. The Pet ID field will be the primary key in the Pets table. A unique Pet ID will identify each pet and no two pets can have the same ID. You can't designate a field like Name as the primary key because than one person can have the same name. In Table Design view, you specify a primary key by clicking in the desired field and clicking the Primary Key button on the Access toolbar. Access will also prompt you to choose a primary key field if you close a table that has not been assigned one. If you allow Access to choose your primary key for you, it will create a new field called ID, which will be defined as an AutoNumber so that each record will have unique data in that field. Most often this is not what we want from our databases, so it is best to choose your own primary key. Your tables will be automatically sorted on the field you designate as the primary key.

 Hands-On 1.4 **Choose a Primary Key**

In this exercise, you will choose a primary key for your database.

1. Follow these steps to choose a primary key:

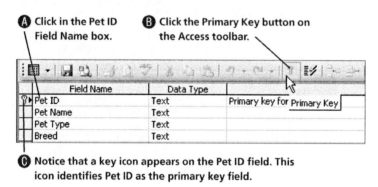

Ⓐ Click in the Pet ID Field Name box.   Ⓑ Click the Primary Key button on the Access toolbar.

Ⓒ Notice that a key icon appears on the Pet ID field. This icon identifies Pet ID as the primary key field.

Saving Database Objects

An Access database is a container that holds tables and other types of objects. The entire database is saved as a single file onto a hard disk or diskette. However, you must also save the objects within the database. Database objects are assigned names when they are saved. This allows you to identify the objects at a later time. Like fields, a database object name can be up to 64 characters in length and may contain letters, numbers, spaces, and other types of characters.

FROM THE KEYBOARD

Ctrl+S to save open object

You save an open object by clicking the Save 🖫 button on the Access toolbar. Access will also prompt you to save an object if you attempt to close the object without saving the changes.

Hands-On 1.5 **Save the Table**

In this exercise, you will save the table to your database.

1. Click the Save 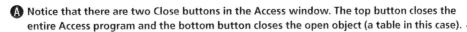 button on the Access toolbar.

2. Type the name **Pets** in the Save As box and click OK.

3. Follow these steps to close the table:

Ⓐ Notice that there are two Close buttons in the Access window. The top button closes the entire Access program and the bottom button closes the open object (a table in this case).

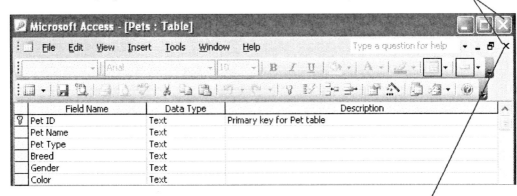

Ⓑ Click the bottom Close button and the table will close.

A Pets icon will appear in the Tables section of the Access window. You have completed the process of setting up a table! At this point, you could set up additional tables or other types of objects. Instead, in Hands-On 1.6, you will enter data into the Pets table. To accomplish this, you will use Datasheet view.

Opening Objects

The Database window provides access to all database objects. You can select any object by clicking the appropriate objects button then clicking the desired object. Once you select an object, you can open the object or display it in Design view.

FROM THE KEYBOARD

Enter to open selected object

Ctrl+Enter to open selected object in Design view

You can open a selected object by double-clicking it or single-clicking the Open button.

You select an object by clicking an object button and choosing the desired object.

You use this button to display a selected object in Design view.

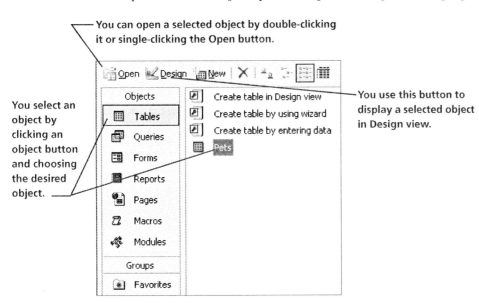

Entering Data in Datasheet View

Microsoft Office Specialist

In Hands-On 1.3 you used Design view to set up the Pets table. Design view lets you set up or modify the structure of tables. However, to enter data into a table, you must display the table in Datasheet view. Remember, you can open a table in Datasheet view from the Access Database window. Once a table is opened in Datasheet view, you can enter data the same way it is entered into an Excel worksheet. The [Tab] key can be used to move forward one table cell and [Shift]+[Tab] can be used to move back one cell. You can also click in any cell and enter new data or edit existing data.

Hands-On 1.6   Enter Data

In this exercise, you will enter data into the Pets table.

1. Follow these steps to open the Pets table in Datasheet view:

Ⓐ Make sure the Tables button is chosen then click the Pets table icon.

Ⓑ Click the Open button. You could also have opened the Pets table by double-clicking the Pets icon.

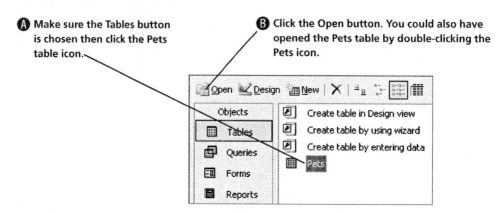

2. Follow these steps to explore the Datasheet view window:
   Keep in mind that your window may have different dimensions than shown here.

Ⓐ Notice that many of the toolbar buttons are different from those in the Design view window.

Ⓑ Notice that the field names are displayed as column headings.

Ⓒ Data are entered into the rows (although you only see one row at this point). Each row is a record. For example, each row will contain all of the data for one pet. You use the [Tab] key to move from one field to the next within a row (or you can click in the desired row or field).

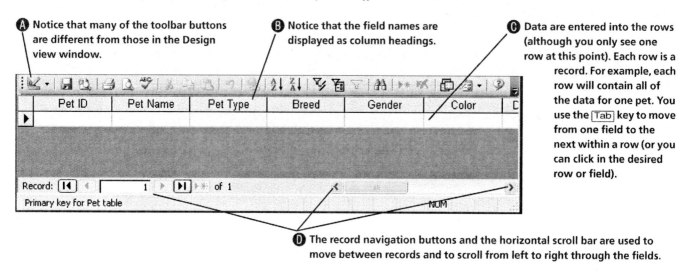

Ⓓ The record navigation buttons and the horizontal scroll bar are used to move between records and to scroll from left to right through the fields.

3. Follow these steps to begin entering a record:

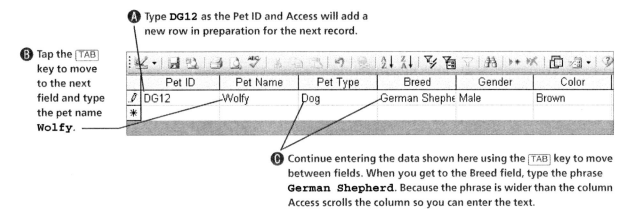

Ⓐ Type **DG12** as the Pet ID and Access will add a new row in preparation for the next record.

Ⓑ Tap the ⌜TAB⌝ key to move to the next field and type the pet name **Wolfy**.

Ⓒ Continue entering the data shown here using the ⌜TAB⌝ key to move between fields. When you get to the Breed field, type the phrase **German Shepherd**. Because the phrase is wider than the column Access scrolls the column so you can enter the text.

4. If necessary, use the horizontal scroll bar to scroll to the right until the fields shown here are visible.

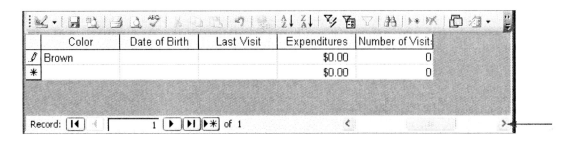

5. Follow these steps to enter data in the remaining fields:

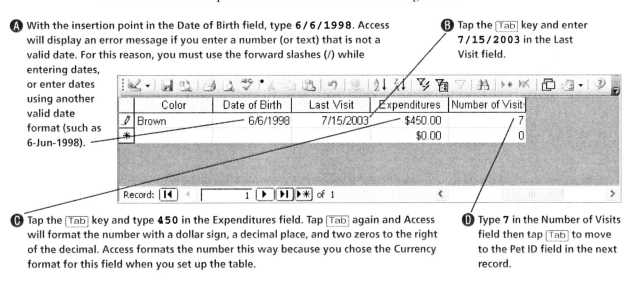

Ⓐ With the insertion point in the Date of Birth field, type **6/6/1998**. Access will display an error message if you enter a number (or text) that is not a valid date. For this reason, you must use the forward slashes (/) while entering dates, or enter dates using another valid date format (such as 6-Jun-1998).

Ⓑ Tap the ⌜Tab⌝ key and enter **7/15/2003** in the Last Visit field.

Ⓒ Tap the ⌜Tab⌝ key and type **450** in the Expenditures field. Tap ⌜Tab⌝ again and Access will format the number with a dollar sign, a decimal place, and two zeros to the right of the decimal. Access formats the number this way because you chose the Currency format for this field when you set up the table.

Ⓓ Type **7** in the Number of Visits field then tap ⌜Tab⌝ to move to the Pet ID field in the next record.

Notice that Access right-aligns the dates and numbers in the last four fields. Access always right-aligns entries that can be used in calculations.

6. Use these guidelines to enter the following records into the table:

- Use the ⌐Tab⌐ key to move between fields.
- Make sure to use forward slashes (/) when entering the dates.
- Do not type dollar signs when entering numbers in the Expenditures field. However, do type a decimal point followed by the indicated decimals.
- Do not try to stack the words under Breed or Color as they appear here. For example, "White with patches" should appear on the same line in your datasheet.

Pet ID	Pet Name	Pet Type	Breed	Gender	Color	Date of Birth	Last Visit	Expenditures	Number of Visits
DG13	Dillon	Dog	Mutt	Male	Black	10/5/2001	7/7/2003	150.55	3
CT89	Puffy	Cat	Siamese	Female	White with patches	12/12/2000	7/7/2003	30.00	1
RB23	Bugs	Rabbit	Jack	Unknown	Brown	6/7/1999	9/7/2003	600.50	4
CT02	Max	Cat	Unknown	Male	White	1/7/1996	9/7/2003	1450.55	20
CT16	Stripes	Cat	Tortoise shell	Male	Black and brown	10/8/2000	7/15/2003	450.00	9
DG14	Fetch	Dog	German Sheperd	Male	Black and brown	8/12/1999	9/10/2003	345.00	3

7. Check your data carefully to make sure it is error free. Accuracy is extremely important when entering data.

8. When you have finished checking your work, choose File→Close from the menu bar. *Access will close the table and the Database window will be displayed. You can close objects with either the File→Close command or by clicking the Close button (as you did earlier). Notice that Access did not prompt you to save the table. Access automatically saves data entered into a table. In fact, it saves the data one record at a time as you enter it.*

Printing Tables

Microsoft Office
Specialist It is very important that you enter data accurately. There are few things more upsetting to customers and other business contacts than seeing their names misspelled and careless data entry errors. For this reason, you should check your data for accuracy after it has been entered. Perhaps the best way to check data accuracy is to print the contents of your tables. Proofreading hard copy (paper printout) is usually the best way to spot errors.

FROM THE KEYBOARD

⌐Ctrl⌐+⌐P⌐ to display
Print dialog box The Print 🖨 button on the Access toolbar sends the entire contents of a table open in Datasheet view to the current printer. You must display the Print dialog box if you want to change printers, adjust the number of copies to be printed, or set other printing options. You display the Print dialog box with the File→Print command. The following illustration highlights the most frequently used options available in the Print dialog box.

You choose printers from this drop-down list.

You specify the number of copies here. The Collate option is useful when you are printing more than one copy of a multi-page table. If the Collate box is checked, all pages of the first copy are printed before the second copy begins printing, etc.

You can choose to print all pages, a range of pages, or selected records.

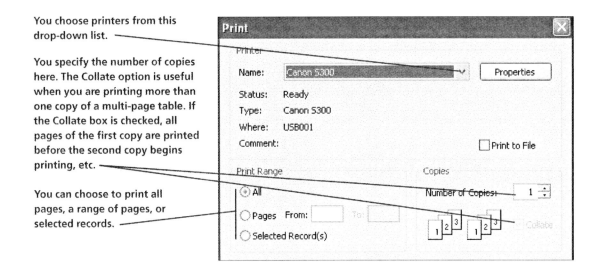

Working with Print Preview

Microsoft Office
Specialist

The Print Preview button on the Access toolbar displays the Print Preview window. Print Preview lets you see exactly how a table will look when printed. Print Preview can save time, paper, and wear-and-tear on your printer. Print Preview is especially useful when printing a table with a large number of records. It is always wise to preview a large table before sending it to the printer. When you display the Print Preview window, the Access toolbar is replaced by the Print Preview toolbar.

 Hands-On 1.7   Use Print Preview

In this exercise, you will see how your table would look if printed.

1. Click the Pets 🔲 **Pets** button in the Access window then click the 📂 **Open** button on the Database toolbar. The Database toolbar is located just above the Objects bar.
   The Pets table will open in Datasheet view.

2. Click the Print Preview 🔍 button on the Access toolbar.

3. Zoom in by clicking anywhere on the table.

4. Zoom out by clicking anywhere on the table.
   Notice that only six of the table's columns are visible in the Print Preview window. It is a good thing that you used Print Preview before printing the table! You should hold off on printing the table until you change the page orientation and margins.

5. Click the Close button on the Print Preview toolbar to exit without printing.

Adjusting Column Widths

You may need to adjust table column widths so you can see the entire contents of table cells on a printout. In Datasheet view, you can use several techniques to adjust column widths, as described in the following Quick Reference table.

QUICK REFERENCE: ADJUSTING COLUMN WIDTHS

Adjustment Technique	Procedure
AutoFit a column to fit the widest entry in the column	Double-click the border between two column headings or choose Format→Column Width and click Best Fit.
Set a precise column width	Choose Format→Column Width and enter the desired width.
Set column widths to the default standard width	Choose Format→Column Width, check the Standard Width box, and click OK.

Hands-On 1.8   Adjust Column Widths

In this exercise, you will adjust the column widths in the table so you can see the full contents of the cells.

1. Follow these steps to manually adjust the width of the Pet ID column:

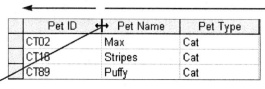

Ⓐ Position the mouse pointer on the border between the Pet ID and Pet Name column headings. Notice that the Adjust pointer appears.

Ⓑ Drag the border to the left until the Pet ID column is just wide enough to display the column heading (Pet ID).

2. Position the mouse pointer on the border between the Pet Name and Pet Type columns. Double-click when the adjust pointer appears.
   This technique can be tricky so keep trying until the Pet Name column shrinks to the width of the heading. If the column has entries wider than the heading, the width will adjust to fit the widest entry in the column.

	Pet ID	Pet Name	Pet Type
	CT02	Max	Cat
	CT16	Stripes	Cat
	CT89	Puffy	Cat

3. Follow these steps to AutoFit the width of all columns:

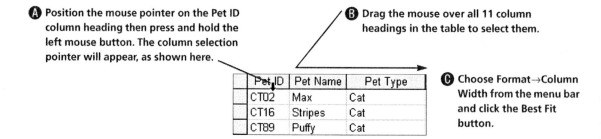

Ⓐ Position the mouse pointer on the Pet ID column heading then press and hold the left mouse button. The column selection pointer will appear, as shown here.

Ⓑ Drag the mouse over all 11 column headings in the table to select them.

Ⓒ Choose Format→Column Width from the menu bar and click the Best Fit button.

4. Click anywhere in the table to deselect the columns.

5. Scroll to the left and notice that all column widths fit the widest entry (or heading) in the columns.

Working with Margins and Page Orientation

Many tables are quite wide and may not fit on a single printed page. Fortunately, most printers can print text both vertically in Portrait orientation and horizontally in Landscape orientation. Landscape orientation may allow a wide table (such as the Pets table) to print on a single page. You can set the orientation of a page by issuing the File→Page Setup command, clicking the Page tab, and choosing the desired orientation. The margins can also be adjusted in the Page Setup dialog box.

 Hands-On 1.9   **Set Page Orientation and Margins, and Print**

In this exercise, you will adjust the page orientation and margins of the table. Then you will print the table.

1. Choose File→Page Setup from the Access menu bar.

2. On the Margins tab, set all four margins to **0.25** (that's 0.25 not 25).

3. Click the Page tab and choose the Landscape option.

4. Click OK to complete the changes.

5. Click the Print Preview 🔍 button on the Access toolbar.

6. If necessary, zoom in by clicking anywhere on the table. Scroll left or right to view all columns in the table.
   Notice that the page orientation is now horizontal (Landscape). All columns should be visible on the page.

7. Print the table by clicking the Print 🖨 button on the Print Preview toolbar.

8. Click the Close button on the Print Preview toolbar when you have finished.

9. Now close the table by choosing File→Close from the Access menu bar.

10. Click the Yes button when Access asks if you want to save the changes.

11. Close Access by choosing File→Exit from the Access menu bar.

12. Now continue with the end-of-lesson questions and exercises.

Concepts Review

True/False Questions

1.	An Access database can have a maximum of one table.	TRUE	FALSE
2.	Datasheet view is used to set up the structure of tables.	TRUE	FALSE
3.	You cannot modify the size of a field in Design view.	TRUE	FALSE
4.	A database is like a container because it can hold several types of objects, including tables.	TRUE	FALSE
5.	The Format→Column Width command can be used to set precise column widths.	TRUE	FALSE
6.	The page orientation can be changed with the File→Print command.	TRUE	FALSE
7.	Portrait orientation causes a table to print horizontally on a page.	TRUE	FALSE
8.	Tables are composed of records.	TRUE	FALSE
9.	Text, Number, and Currency are examples of data types.	TRUE	FALSE
10.	You can enter data into a table in Design view.	TRUE	FALSE

Multiple Choice Questions

1. What is the maximum number of characters that a field name may contain?
   a. 8
   b. 32
   c. 64
   d. 255

2. Which of the following are examples of data types?
   a. Text
   b. Number
   c. Currency
   d. All of the above

3. Which of the following commands is used to change the page orientation?
   a. File→Print
   b. File→Page Setup
   c. Format→Page Orientation
   d. Format→Print Preview

4. What happens when you double-click the border between two column headings in Datasheet view?
   a. The table is closed
   b. The column width is set to the default column width
   c. A new column is inserted
   d. The column width is AutoFit to the widest entry

Skill Builders

Set Up a Table in Design View

In this exercise, you will set up a new database for the Tropical Getaways travel company. Tropical Getaways is an exciting new travel company that specializes in inexpensive vacations to tropical locations worldwide. You have been asked to set up a database to track clients and trips. You will begin by creating the first table for the database.

1. Start Access, choose Create a New File, and then choose Blank Database from the Task Pane.

2. Assign the name **Tropical Getaways** to your new database and save it to your file storage location.
   The Tables object list should be displayed in the Access Database window.

3. Double-click the Create Table in Design View option to begin setting up a new table in Design view.

4. Type **Customer ID** as the first field name and tap the ⌈Tab⌉ key.

5. Click the drop-down ⏷ button in the Data Type box and choose AutoNumber.
   Access will automatically assign sequential Customer IDs when you enter data in this table.

6. Click the Primary Key ⏾ button on the toolbar to make Customer ID the primary key.

7. Set up the remainder of this table using the field names, data types, and options shown in the following table. Keep in mind that you have already set up the Customer ID field.

Field Name	Data Type	Field Size	Primary Key	Description
Customer ID	AutoNumber	Long Integer	Yes	
Firstname	Text	30		
Lastname	Text	30		
Address	Text	50		
City	Text	30		
State	Text	2		
Zip	Text	9		
Profile	Text	20		The profile indicates the category of trips the customer prefers

8. When you have finished, click the Datasheet ▦ view button on the left end of the Access toolbar.
   The veiw button can be used to switch between various views.

9. Click Yes when Access asks if you wish to save the table.

10. Type **Customers** as the table name, click OK, and enter the following four records. The Customer ID numbers should be entered automatically because Customer ID has an AutoNumber data type. Customer ID will be entered automatically after you type the data into the FirstName field.

Customer ID	Firstname	Lastname	Address	City	State	Zip	Profile
1	Debbie	Thomas	450 Crestwood Lane	Austin	TX	78752	Adventure
2	Wilma	Boyd	855 State Street	Richmond	NY	12954	Leisure
3	Ted	Wilkins	900 C Street	Fort Worth	TX	76104	Adventure
4	Alice	Simpson	2450 Ridge Road	Fort Worth	TX	76105	Family

11. When you have finished, choose File→Close from the Access menu bar to close the table. *Access automatically saves the data you entered. You will set up another table in the next Skill Builder exercise.*

Skill Builder 1.2   Set Up a Table in Design View

In this exercise, you will set up another table for the Tropical Getaways database.

1. Double-click the Create Table in Design View option to begin setting up a new table in Design view.

2. Set up the table using the following structure:

Field Name	Data Type	Field Size/Format	Primary Key	Description
Trip ID	Text	8	Yes	Four- to eight-character unique identifier for each trip
Customer ID	Number	Long Integer		ID number from Customers table
Destination	Text	50		
Category	Text	30		All trips have a category such as Adventure, Leisure, etc.
Departure Date	Date/Time	Short Date		
Return Date	Date/Time	Short Date		
Cost	Currency			

3. Close and save the table as **Trips**.

4. Double-click the icon for the Trips table in the Access database window and enter the following data. Do not type the dollar signs and commas when entering the Cost numbers. Access will add these for you because you chose the Auto Number data type when you set up the Cost field.

Trip ID	Customer ID	Destination	Category	Departure Date	Return Date	Cost
Adv01	1	Kenyan Safari	Adventure	8/5/04	9/4/04	$6,600
Lei01	2	Caribbean Cruise	Leisure	9/19/04	9/28/04	$2,390
Adv02	1	Amazon Jungle Trek	Adventure	8/7/04	9/14/04	$7,765
Fam01	4	Orlando	Family	3/4/04	3/10/04	$3,400

5. Close the Trips table when you have finished.
The Tables objects list should now display both the Customers and Trips table icons.

Skill Builder 1.3 Print the Table

In this exercise, you will print the Customers table. The Tropical Getaways database should be open, and the Customers and Trips tables should be visible in the Access Database window.

1. Double-click the Customers table to open it in Datasheet view.
   You can always open a table in Datasheet view by double-clicking it.

2. Adjust the widths of all columns to display the widest entries in the columns.

3. Use the Print Preview [icon] button to preview the table.

4. Zoom in on the table by clicking anywhere on it.

5. Feel free to print the table and check your data for accuracy.

6. Close Print Preview when you have finished.

7. Close the table and choose Yes when Access asks if you want to save the changes.

8. Now open the Trips table and adjust the column widths to fit the widest entries in the columns.
   Notice that the records in the Trips table are now sorted by Trip ID since that is the primary key.

9. Print the table and check your data for accuracy.

10. Close the table and save the changes when you have finished.

11. Exit from Access by choosing File→Exit from the menu bar.

Skill Builder 1.4   Use the Database Wizard

In this exercise, you will use the Database Wizard to set up a database.

1. Start Access and the task pane will appear. If the task pane is not displayed, use the View→Task Pane command to display it.

2. Choose the Create a New File option in the task pane.

3. Under Templates, choose the On My Computer option.

4. Click the Databases tab in the Templates box to view the available predefined databases.
   The Database Wizard is initiated when you choose any of these predefined databases.

5. Double-click the Contact Management database and save it to your file storage location as **Contact Management Database**.

6. Click Next to bypass the first wizard screen.
   The second wizard screen displays the predefined tables in the Contact Management database and the fields in each table. You remove fields by unchecking them or add additional fields by scrolling through the field list and checking the desired additional fields (shown in italics).

7. Click Next to bypass the screen and accept the default fields.

8. Continue to click the Next button on the next few screens. You will be offered various forms and report formats; feel free to choose any options you desire.

9. Click the Finish button when you have finished choosing options.
   The wizard will create the database.

10. Feel free to use your new database. You will be exposed to features that you have not learned about yet, and will certainly be impressed with the database the wizard has created.
    At this point, you could add tables, fields, and other objects to your database or modify the objects already in the database.

11. When you have finished examining your database, close it, and exit from Access.

 **Assessments**

Create a Table

In this exercise, you will begin creating a database for Classic Cars. Classic Cars is an organization devoted to tracking, categorizing, and preserving classic automobiles. You will begin by creating tables to track collectors and cars.

1. Start Access and create a new database named **Classic Cars**.

2. Create a new table with the following structure:

Field Name	Data Type	Field Size	Primary Key	Description
Collector ID	AutoNumber	Long Integer	Yes	
Firstname	Text	30		
Lastname	Text	30		
Address	Text	50		
City	Text	30		
State	Text	2		
Zip	Text	9		
Era of Interest	Text	20		This field identifies the time period that the collector is most interested in
Collection Size	Number	Long Integer		Number of cars in collection

3. Click the Datasheet ⊞ view button and save the table with the name **Collectors**.

4. Enter the following records into the table:

Collector ID	Firstname	Lastname	Address	City	State	Zip	Era of Interest	Collection size
1	Cindy	Johnson	4220 Edward Street	Northlake	IL	60164	1950s	42
2	Tammy	Olson	1200 Big Pine Drive	Moses Lake	WA	98837	1960s	6
3	Ed	Larkson	2300 Watson Street	Cainesville	OH	43701	Early 1900s	34
4	Bob	Barker	6340 Palm Drive	Rockridge	FL	32955	1950s	7

5. AutoFit the width of all columns to fit the largest entry/heading in the columns.

6. Use Print Preview to preview the table. If necessary, switch the orientation to Landscape and reduce the margins until the table fits on one page.

7. Print the table.

8. Close the table when you have finished and save any changes.

9. Create another new table with the following structure:

Field Name	Data Type	Field Size/Format	Primary Key	Description
Car ID	Text	15	Yes	Up to 15 characters to uniquely identify each car
Collector ID	Number	Long Integer		ID number from Collectors table
Year	Text	20		
Make	Text	30		
Model	Text	50		
Color	Text	30		
Condition	Text	30		
Value	Currency			Estimated value

10. Click the Datasheet ▦ view button and save the table with the name **Cars**.

11. Enter the following records into the table:

Car ID	CollectorID	Year	Make	Model	Color	Condition	Value
CJ01	1	58	Chevrolet	Corvette	Red and white	Mint	$65,000
TO05	2	62	Chevrolet	Corvette	Blue	Excellent	$30,000
CJ22	1	59	Ford	Thunderbird	Tan	Good	$20,000
BB03	4	58	Chevrolet	Corvette	Black	Excellent	$35,000

12. AutoFit the width of all columns to fit the largest entry/heading in the columns.

13. Use Print Preview to preview the table.

14. Print the table.

15. Close the table when you have finished and save any changes.

16. Exit from Access when you have finished.

Critical Thinking

Critical Thinking 1.1   Create Tables

Linda Holmes is a real estate agent specializing in investment properties. She needs database software to help her manage her business. She has reviewed commercially available software but has found it inadequate for her needs. Instead, Linda has hired you to create a customized Access database.

Create a new, blank database for Linda named **Holmestead Realty**. The first two categories of information Linda wants to track are contact information for sellers and listing information for the properties they wish to sell. Follow these guidelines to set up two tables in your new database:

- Name the first table **Contacts** and the second table **Listings**.
- Use the field names, data types, and field properties listed in the following table.
- Leave all other field properties set to their default values.

Contacts Table

Field Name	Data Type	Field Properties
Seller ID	Auto Number	Primary key
FirstName	Text	
LastName	Text	
SpouseName	Text	Field size 30
Address	Text	
City	Text	
State	Text	
Zip	Text	
Phone	Text	
Contact Type	Text	

Listings Table

Field Name	Data Type	Field Properties
MLS#	Number	Primary key
Street#	Number	
Address	Text	
Price	Currency	
Listing Date	Date	Short Date format
Expiration Date	Date	Short Date format
Commission Rate	Number	Field Size: Decimal, Format: Percent, Precision: 18, Scale: 3, Decimal Places: 1
Seller ID	Number	

Enter the following data into your completed tables. Be sure to check the data carefully when finished. Adjust all column widths to fit the widest entry in each column. Print copies of both tables when you have finished.

Contacts

Seller ID	FirstName	LastName	Spouse Name	Address	City	ST	Zip	Phone	Contact Type
1	John	Desmond	Lydia	1020 Brevard Road	Asheville	NC	28801	(828) 298-5698	Investor
2	David	Armstrong		15 Dover Street	Swannanoa	NC	28778	(828) 669-8579	Investor
3	Sharon	Carter		9 Forest Pine Circle	Asheville	NC	28803	(828) 277-3658	Investor
4	Jeff	Jones	Susan	107 Glen Meadows Place	Arden	NC	28704	(828) 687-5786	Investor
5	Jamie	Stevens		10 Knollwood Drive	Asheville	NC	28804	(828) 274-6643	Investor
6	Phil	Wallace	Jennifer	1571 Brannon Road	Asheville	NC	28801	(828) 252-2365	Investor

Listings

MLS #	Street #	Address	Price	Listing Date	Expiration Date	Commission Rate	Seller ID
52236	1132	Richwood Road	$55,000	1/14/04	7/14/04	6.0%	4
52358	14	Dover Street	$70,000	5/30/03	11/30/03	7.0%	2
52369	6	Thoroughbred Lane	$125,000	9/25/03	3/25/04	6.0%	1
52425	218	Wildflower Road	$329,500	6/2/03	12/2/03	4.5%	2
52511	403	Hawks Landing	$150,000	9/23/03	3/23/04	6.0%	3
52524	64	Hastings Street	$112,000	4/6/04	10/6/04	4.5%	6
52526	137	Woodbridge Lane	$80,000	3/21/04	9/21/04	4.5%	6
52649	23	Edwards Avenue	$70,000	7/15/03	1/15/04	6.0%	5
52650	24	Edwards Avenue	$75,000	7/15/03	1/15/04	6.0%	5

LESSON 2

Modifying and Maintaining Tables

In this lesson, you will make changes to the tables in the Pinnacle Pet Care database. You will learn how to change the structure of tables and edit records within a database. You will create a table using the Table Wizard and set up validation rules to ensure that users enter valid data.

IN THIS LESSON

Microsoft Office Access 2003 objectives covered in this lesson

Additional learning resources are available at labpub.com/learn/access03/

Case Study

Sometimes after the initial tables in Access have been created, it's necessary to make changes to them. It is also important to ensure that the minimum of errors occur when people enter data into the tables. Penny Johnson has created two of the tables for the database and will now go through modifying them, using validation rules and input masks to minimize entry error. Penny has also talked with some of the employees and has decided to add additional tables and modify the existing tables to hold more information that will be needed by Pinnacle Pet Care. She would also like to show employees how to find certain records and to sort through the data using filters.

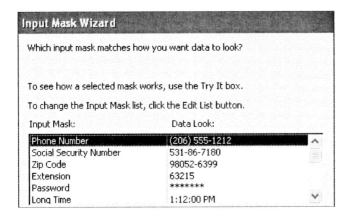

Penny uses the Input Mask Wizard to set up the phone number.

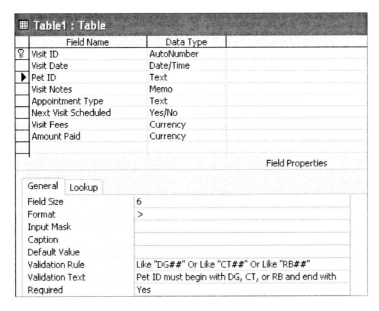

Many data entry errors can be eliminated by using Validation Rules in the Table Design.

Changing the Structure of a Table

You can change the structure of a table after it has been created. For example, you may need to change the size or name of a field, or add a new field. Structural changes are made to a table in Design view.

How Changing the Structure Can Impact Data

You must be careful when changing the structure of a table, especially if data has already been entered. For example, imagine that a field has a length of 30 and you have already entered records into the table. If you reduce the field length to 20, you may delete up to 10 characters from some records. Access will usually provide a warning message if you attempt to make a change that has the potential of destroying data in a field.

Switching between Object Views

The Datasheet ▦ view button appears on the left end of the Access toolbar whenever you are in Design view. You can switch from Design view to Datasheet view by clicking the Datasheet view button.

Likewise, the Design ⬓ view button appears on the left end of the Access toolbar when you are in Datasheet view. You can switch to Design view by clicking the Design view button.

Setting the Default Value of Fields

Access lets you set default values for fields. The default value is automatically entered in new records when you enter data in Datasheet view. This can be convenient if a field is typically set to a certain value. For example, you will set the default value of the Number of Visits field to 1. Pets will be entered into the database when they make their first visit to the clinic. By setting the Number of Visits field to 1, you can skip the Number of Visits field when entering data for a new pet. In Design view, default values are set in the Field Properties area at the bottom of the dialog box.

⚠ **TIP!** *Only set a default value if the field will have that value the majority of the time.*

 Hands-On 2.1   Change the Table Structure

In this exercise, you will open the Pinnacle Pet Care database you created in Lesson 1, Creating Tables and Entering Data and change the structure of the table.

Change a Field's Properties

1. Start Access and open the Pinnacle Pet Care database.

2. Click the ▦ icon in the Access window then click the ⬓ Design button on the Database toolbar.
   The Pets table will open in Design view.

3. Follow these steps to change the default value for the Number of Visits field:

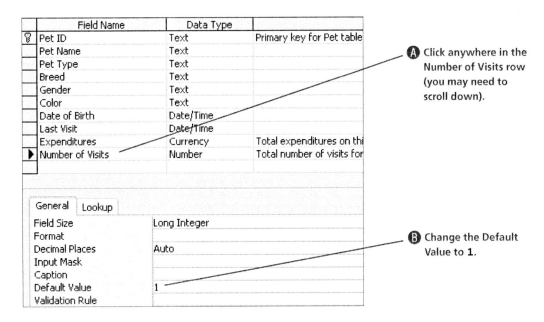

A Click anywhere in the Number of Visits row (you may need to scroll down).

B Change the Default Value to **1**.

Add a Field

In the next few steps, you will add a Customer ID field to the table. The Customer ID field will eventually link the Pets table to the Customers table.

4. Follow these steps to add the Customer ID field:

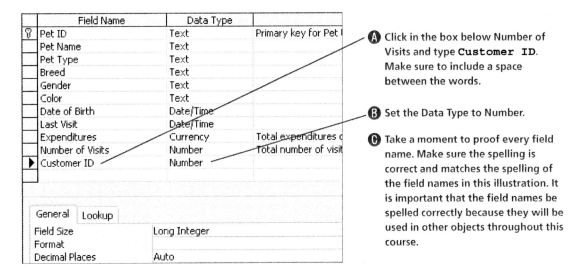

A Click in the box below Number of Visits and type **Customer ID**. Make sure to include a space between the words.

B Set the Data Type to Number.

C Take a moment to proof every field name. Make sure the spelling is correct and matches the spelling of the field names in this illustration. It is important that the field names be spelled correctly because they will be used in other objects throughout this course.

Switch Views and Add Customer IDs

5. Click the Datasheet 🔲 view button on the left end of the Access toolbar and click Yes when Access asks if you want to save the table.
Notice that the order of the records has changed in the table. The records should now be sorted in alphabetical order based on the primary key field. The records were sorted when you closed the table and then reopened it. One of the benefits of choosing a primary key field (such as Pet ID) is that Access will sort the records based on the primary key field.

6. Now add the following Customer IDs into the table. Make sure you enter the correct Customer ID in each record. You may need to scroll to the left and right in the table to ensure that the correct Customer ID has been entered for each Pet ID. As you can see from this example, it can be difficult to add data to records after changing the structure of a table. For this reason, you should spend as much time as necessary designing and planning a database to minimize the number of changes required.

Make sure each Pet ID has the correct Customer ID.

Pet ID	Pet Name	Pet Type	Breed	Gender		Date of Birth	Last Visit	Expenditures	Number of Visits	Customer ID
CT02	Max	Cat	Unknown	Male	V	1/7/1996	9/7/2003	$1,450.55	20	2
CT16	Stripes	Cat	Tortoise shell	Female	Bla	8/2000	7/15/2003	$450.00	9	3
CT89	Puffy	Cat	Siamese	Female	W	2/2000	7/7/2003	$30.00	1	1
DG12	Wolfy	Dog	German Shepherd	Male		6/6/1998	7/15/2003	$450.00	7	3
DG13	Dillon	Dog	Mutt	Male		10/5/2001	7/7/2003	$150.55	3	1
DG14	Fetch	Dog	German Shepherd	Male		8/12/1999	9/10/2003	$345.00	3	3
RB23	Bugs	Rabbit	Jack	Unknown	B	6/7/1999	9/7/2003	$600.50	4	2

7. Leave the table in Datasheet view and continue with the next topic.
You will add a record and make other changes in Hands-On 2.2.

Understanding Record Management

In Datasheet view, the Access toolbar has several buttons that let you manage records. The following table defines four of these buttons.

RECORD MANAGEMENT BUTTONS

Button	Function
🔍 Find	Lets you locate a record by searching for a word or phrase (Replace lets you replace a word or phrase with another word or phrase)
▶ New Record	Adds a new record at the end of the table
▶✕ Delete Record	Deletes the current record
Filter by Selection	Lets you retrieve only records that contain the selected value

Navigating within a Table

Microsoft Office Specialist

In Datasheet view, a record navigation bar appears at the bottom of the Access program window. The following illustration defines the buttons on the navigation bar.

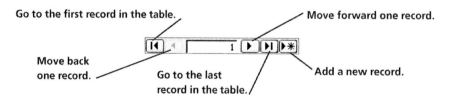

Go to the first record in the table.

Move forward one record.

Move back one record.

Go to the last record in the table.

Add a new record.

Notice that the Back One Record button is "grayed out" in this illustration. This is because the insertion point is in the first record, as shown in the center of the navigation bar. In other words, there is no record to move back to.

 Hands-On 2.2   Manage Records

In this exercise, you will add data to the new record and navigate around the table. The Pets table should be in Datasheet view from the previous exercise.

Add a Record

1. Click the New Record ▶※ button on the Access toolbar.
   The insertion point will move to a new record at the bottom of the table.

2. Enter the following data into the new record:

Pet ID	Pet Name	Pet Type	Breed	Pet Gender	Color	Date of Birth
CT92	Tony	Cat	Unknown	Male	Brown with black stripes	4/3/99

Last Visit	Expenditures	Number of Visits	Customer ID
7/7/2003	145	6	1

Navigate to Records

3. Follow these steps to navigate to various records:

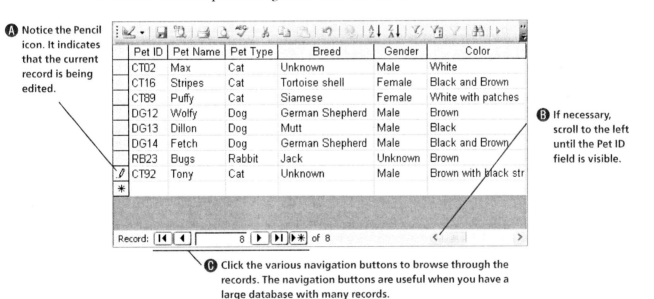

Ⓐ Notice the Pencil icon. It indicates that the current record is being edited.

Ⓑ If necessary, scroll to the left until the Pet ID field is visible.

Ⓒ Click the various navigation buttons to browse through the records. The navigation buttons are useful when you have a large database with many records.

Delete a Record

4. Follow these steps to delete a record:

Ⓐ Click the record selector (square box) to the left of the CT89 record to select the entire record. The vertical column of boxes to the left of the records is called the Selection bar.

Ⓑ Click the Delete Record button on the Access toolbar.

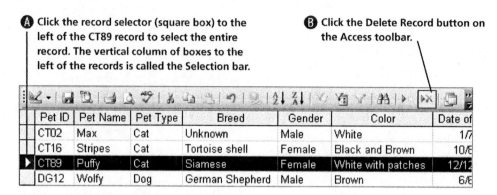

Pet ID	Pet Name	Pet Type	Breed	Gender	Color	Date of
CT02	Max	Cat	Unknown	Male	White	1/7
CT16	Stripes	Cat	Tortoise shell	Female	Black and Brown	10/8
CT89	Puffy	Cat	Siamese	Female	White with patches	12/12
DG12	Wolfy	Dog	German Shepherd	Male	Brown	6/8

Ⓒ Click the Yes button on the warning box that appears to confirm the deletion.

In the preceding steps, you selected the CT89 record prior to deleting it. You could actually have deleted the record by clicking anywhere in the CT89 row and clicking the Delete Record button. The Selection bar is most useful when you want to delete several records. You can select several records by dragging the mouse down the Selection bar.

Find Records

5. Click on any Pet ID in the Pet ID column.
In the following steps, you will search for Pet IDs. You must position the insertion point somewhere in the column that you wish to search prior to initiating the search.

6. Click the Find 🔍 button on the Access toolbar.

7. Follow these steps to conduct the search:

Ⓐ Type **ct92** in the Find What box.

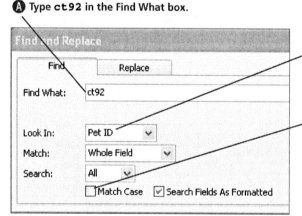

Ⓑ Notice that the Look In field indicates that you are searching for a Pet ID. In a large database, narrowing the search to a particular field can speed up the search.

Ⓒ Notice the Match Case box. It should be unchecked for the current search as shown here. This is because you typed the search string in lowercase (ct92) but the actual Pet ID in the database is in uppercase (CT92). Access will still find the Pet ID because the Match Case box is unchecked.

Ⓓ Click the Find Next button and the Pet ID CT92 will become selected.

8. Use the preceding steps to find Pet ID DG12.
   Keep in mind that the Find feature is most useful when you have a large database and the item you are searching for is not visible on the screen.

9. Click the Cancel button to close the dialog box.

Check Out the Replace Option

10. Click any record in the Gender column.

11. Click the Find 🔍 button on the Access toolbar.

12. Follow these steps to find and replace data:

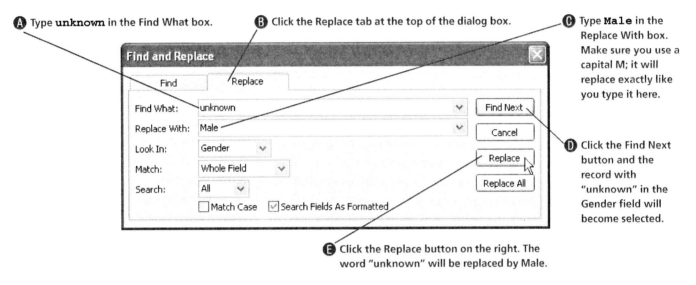

🅐 Type **unknown** in the Find What box.

🅑 Click the Replace tab at the top of the dialog box.

🅒 Type **Male** in the Replace With box. Make sure you use a capital M; it will replace exactly like you type it here.

🅓 Click the Find Next button and the record with "unknown" in the Gender field will become selected.

🅔 Click the Replace button on the right. The word "unknown" will be replaced by Male.

13. Click the Cancel button to close the dialog box.

14. Leave the table open in Datasheet view and continue with the next topic.

Filtering Records in a Datasheet

Microsoft Office Specialist

Filters are used with datasheets and forms to let you temporarily view only those records that meet the criteria specified in the filter. The two most common types of filtering are filtering by selection and filtering by form. In both cases, the end result of applying a filter is that certain records are filtered out, leaving only those records that meet the filter criteria. The difference between the two filter types is the method that is used to apply the filter.

- Filter by Selection ⊘—To filter by selection, you navigate to a record and click in a field that has the desired filter value. For example, if you are interested in seeing only records where the pet type is equal to dog, you should navigate to a record where the pet type is dog and click in the Pet Type field. When you click the Filter by Selection button, Access will only display records where the pet type is equal to dog.

- Filter by Form ⊞—To filter by form, you first click the Filter by Form button and Access displays a form with blank fields. Then, type the desired filter value(s) into the blank field(s). You can also click in the blank fields and choose the desired values from drop-down lists. Access applies the filter when you click the Apply/Remove Filter button.

- Apply Filter ▽—With this button you can apply filters. In addition, you can remove filters by clicking the Remove Filter button. Access then redisplays all records once a filter has been removed.

 Hands-On 2.3   Apply and Remove Filters

In this exercise, you will practice applying and removing filters.

Filter by Selection

1. Click in the Pet Type field on any record where the Pet Type is dog.

2. Click the Filter by Selection ⊘ button on the Access toolbar.
   Notice the navigation bar now indicates that you are viewing record 1 of 3 (Filtered).

3. Notice that only records with a Pet Type of dog are visible.

4. Click the Remove Filter ▽ button.
   The Navigation bar should once again indicate that seven records are available.

Add a Filter to a Filter

You can use the Filter by Selection button to filter records that have already been filtered.

5. Click in the Pet Type field on any record where the Pet Type is cat.

6. Click the Filter by Selection ⊘ button.

7. Notice that only three cat records are visible.

8. If necessary, click a record where "unknown" appears in the Breed field.

9. Click in the Breed field and click the Filter by Selection ⊘ button.
   Only two filtered records should now be available.

10. Click the Remove Filter ▽ button to remove the filtering.

Filter by Form

11. Click the Filter by Form ⊞ button.

12. Follow these steps to enter the desired criteria in the Filter by Form box:

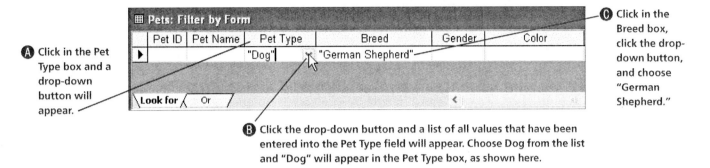

A Click in the Pet Type box and a drop-down button will appear.

C Click in the Breed box, click the drop-down button, and choose "German Shepherd."

B Click the drop-down button and a list of all values that have been entered into the Pet Type field will appear. Choose Dog from the list and "Dog" will appear in the Pet Type box, as shown here.

13. Click the Apply Filter ▽ button.
Browse through the filtered records and notice that they both have a Pet Type of "Dog" and Breed of "German Shepherd". Entering two values in the Filter by Form box has the same effect as applying a filter to a filter using the Filter by Selection tool.

14. Click the Remove Filter ▽ button to remove the filter.

15. Feel free to experiment with filters. Remove all filtering when you have finished.

16. Close and Save the table when finished.

Using the Table Wizard

Microsoft Office Specialist

Access provides a Table Wizard to help you set up common tables. The Table Wizard provides a variety of sample tables and fields for each table. You can choose the sample fields to include in a table and the wizard will then build the table for you. In Hands-On 2.4, you will use the Table Wizard to set up a Customers table. Thus, you will have experience setting up tables in Design view and with the Table Wizard. In the future, you can use whichever method you prefer.

To start the Table Wizard, you click the ⊞ New button on the Access Database toolbar and choose Table Wizard from the New Table box. You can also double-click the Create Table by Using Wizard option that appears in the Tables section of the Access Database window.

Hands-On 2.4   Use the Table Wizard

In this exercise, you will use the Table Wizard to create a new table.

Use the Table Wizard to Create a New Table

1. Click the [New] button on the Access Database toolbar (located just above the Objects bar).

2. Choose Table Wizard and click OK.

3. Follow these steps to begin setting up a table:

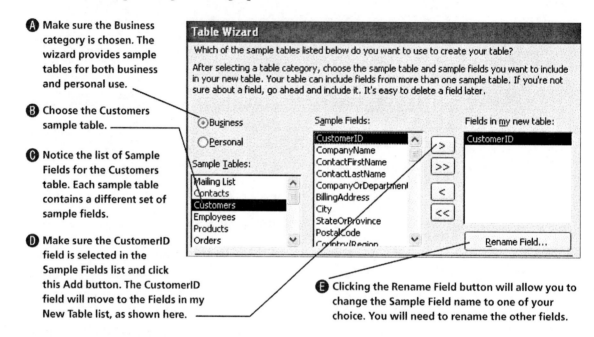

Ⓐ Make sure the Business category is chosen. The wizard provides sample tables for both business and personal use.

Ⓑ Choose the Customers sample table.

Ⓒ Notice the list of Sample Fields for the Customers table. Each sample table contains a different set of sample fields.

Ⓓ Make sure the CustomerID field is selected in the Sample Fields list and click this Add button. The CustomerID field will move to the Fields in my New Table list, as shown here.

Ⓔ Clicking the Rename Field button will allow you to change the Sample Field name to one of your choice. You will need to rename the other fields.

4. Now add the ContactFirstName, ContactLastname, BillingAddress, City, StateOrProvince, PostalCode, and PhoneNumber fields by choosing them one at a time and clicking the Add button. Change the names of the fields as you add them, as shown in the following table.

!TIP! *You can add a field by double-clicking it.*

Change this Field Name . . .	to this Name
ContactFirstName	FirstName
ContactLastName	LastName
BillingAddress	Address
City	*Leave as is*
StateOrProvince	State
PostalCode	Zip
PhoneNumber	Phone

5. Use the Remove Field `<` button if you mistakenly added a field and wish to remove it. Your completed Fields in My New Table list should match the example shown to the right (although your Phone field should be completely visible).

6. Click the Next button at the bottom of the dialog box.
   The next screen will propose the table name Customers and offer to set the primary key for you.

7. Leave the options set as they are by clicking the Next button.
   The next screen will ask you about relationships between tables.

8. Leave the option set to Not Related to Pets by clicking the Next button.
   The next screen will ask how you wish to display the completed table.

9. Choose the Modify the Table Design option and click the Finish button.
   Access will create the table for you and display it in Design view.

Modify the Table Structure

You may find Access wizards most useful for setting up tables and other objects. Once objects are set up, you can modify them to suit your particular needs. In the next few steps, you will use this approach by modifying the structure of the Customers table.

10. Follow these steps to explore the table you just created:

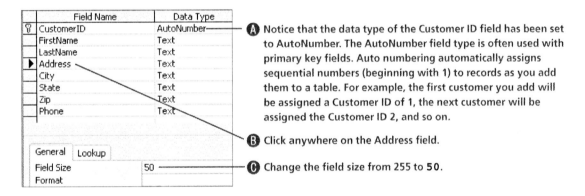

Ⓐ Notice that the data type of the Customer ID field has been set to AutoNumber. The AutoNumber field type is often used with primary key fields. Auto numbering automatically assigns sequential numbers (beginning with 1) to records as you add them to a table. For example, the first customer you add will be assigned a Customer ID of 1, the next customer will be assigned the Customer ID 2, and so on.

Ⓑ Click anywhere on the Address field.

Ⓒ Change the field size from 255 to **50**.

11. Follow these steps to change the default value of the State field:

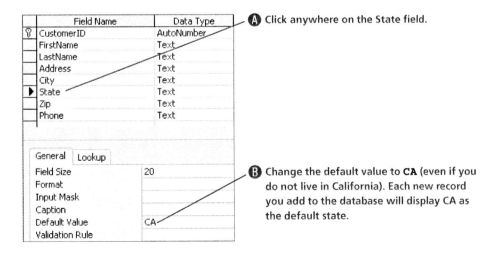

Ⓐ Click anywhere on the State field.

Ⓑ Change the default value to **CA** (even if you do not live in California). Each new record you add to the database will display CA as the default state.

Add New Fields

12. Follow these steps to insert a new date field:

A Click below the Phone field and type **Last Visit**.   **B** Click in the Data Type box and choose Date/Time from the drop down list.

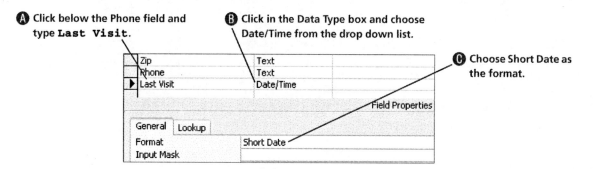

C Choose Short Date as the format.

Zip	Text
Phone	Text
Last Visit	Date/Time

Field Properties

General	Lookup
Format	Short Date
Input Mask	

13. Now add a field named **Current Balance** and set the Data Type to Currency. Continue with the next topic, in which you will create an input mask for the phone field.

Working with Input Masks

Microsoft Office
Specialist

Access lets you define input masks to help you enter formatted data. An input mask consists of a series of characters that define how the data is to be formatted. Input masks can be used for a variety of formatting tasks. For example, you can use an input mask to force all characters entered to be in uppercase or to automatically insert parenthesis and dashes in phone numbers. The input masks character string is entered in the Input Mask field property in Table Design view. Once an input mask is set up in a table, the mask formats display data in queries, forms, and reports.

The Input Mask Wizard

Setting up an input mask can be a tedious process. Fortunately, Access provides an Input Mask Wizard to help you set up common input mask formats. The following illustration discusses the process of setting up an input mask using the Input Mask Wizard.

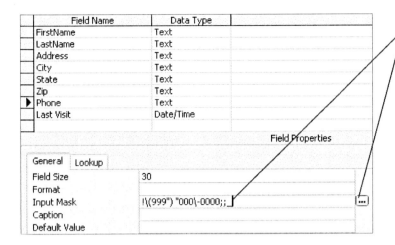

A Build button appears when you click in the Input Mask field property box. The Build button initiates the Input Mask Wizard. This input mask character string formats telephone numbers with parenthesis and dashes. The Input Mask Wizard can only be used with fields that have a Text or Date data type.

The Input Mask Wizard lets you choose common mask formats.

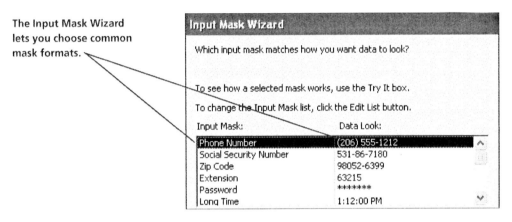

 Hands-On 2.5   **Use the Input Mask Wizard and Complete the Table**

In this exercise, you will set up two input masks and complete the table.

Set Up an Input Mask for the Phone Field

1. Click in the Phone field then click the Input Mask box in the Field Properties section of the window.

2. Click the Build [...] button on the right side of the Input Mask box and choose Yes to save the table.

3. Make sure the Phone Number mask is chosen in the first wizard screen and click Next.

4. Click Next on the second wizard screen to accept the proposed mask format.

5. Make sure the Without the Symbols option is chosen in the third screen and click Next.

6. Click the Finish button to complete the input mask.
   Access will display the input mask characters !(999) 000-0000;;_ in the Input Mask box.

Set Up an Input Mask for the Zip Field

7. Click in the Zip field then click in the Input Mask box.

8. Click the Build ⟨...⟩ button and choose Yes to save the table.

9. Choose the Zip Code mask and click the Finish button to accept the default options.
   You can click the Finish button at any time while using a wizard to accept the remaining default settings. Access will display the input mask characters 00000-9999;;_ in the Input Mask box.

Add Data to the Table

10. Click the Datasheet ⟨▦⟩ view button on the Access toolbar.

11. Click Yes when Access asks if you wish to save the table.
    Notice that the word AutoNumber is selected in the first empty record. This field is formatted with the AutoNumber data type so you will bypass it in the next step. Access will automatically assign the number 1 to the record when you begin entering data in the Firstname field.

12. Tap the ⟨Tab⟩ key to bypass the Customer ID field.

13. Type the name **Mark** in the Firstname field and the number 1 will appear in the Customer ID field.

14. Tap ⟨Tab⟩ and type **Roth** in the Lastname field.

15. Tap ⟨Tab⟩ and type **760 Maple Avenue** in the Address field.

16. Tap ⟨Tab⟩ and type **Fremont** in the City field.

17. Tap ⟨Tab⟩ and notice that the State field is set to CA.
    This is because you set CA as the default value for this field.

18. Tap ⟨Tab⟩ to bypass the State field (CA is correct) and type **94538** in the Zip field.
    You will notice that a hyphen appears to the right of the digits. This is because the Zip field has also been formatted with an input mask. The input mask inserts a hyphen between the first five and last four digits (if you use nine digits) of a zip code.

19. Tap ⟨Tab⟩ to bypass the last four digits of the zip code.

20. Type the area code **510** in the Phone field and the input mask will surround the number with parenthesis.

21. Complete the phone number by typing **2349090**.
    Access will format the number by inserting a hyphen between the 4 and the 9.

22. Tap ⟨Tab⟩ and type **7/7/03** in the Last Visit field.

23. Tap ⟨Tab⟩ and type **235** in the Current Balance field.

24. Now add the following two records to the table:
    The AutoNumber feature will insert numbers in the Customer ID field so just tap ⟨Tab⟩ when you reach that field. Also, do not type parenthesis in the phone numbers because the input mask will automatically apply them for you.

Customer ID	Firstname	Lastname	Address	City	State	Zip	Phone	Last Visit	Current Balance
2	Tony	Simpson	312 York Lane	Richmond	CA	94804	(510) 238-2233	9/7/03	185
3	Jason	Jones	2233 Crystal Street	San Mateo	CA	94403	(415) 312-2312	7/15/03	48

Print the Table

25. Adjust the width of all columns to fit the widest entry/heading in the columns. You can accomplish this by double-clicking the borders between the column headings. You can also select all of the columns by dragging the mouse pointer across the column headings and double-clicking the border between the column headings of any two selected columns. Finally, you can also select all columns and use the Format→Column Width command then click the Best Fit button.

26. Use the File→Page Setup command to set all four margins to **0.5**.

27. Notice that the Print Headings box is checked on the Margins tab.
In a moment, when you preview the table, you will notice a header and footer at the top and bottom of the page. The Print Headings box displays the header and footer. The Table Wizard turned on this option.

28. Set the orientation to Landscape using the Page tab in the Page Setup dialog box then click OK.

29. Use Print Preview to preview the table. Print the table if desired.

30. Close Print Preview and feel free to experiment with any of the topics you have learned so far in this lesson.

31. Save any changes to the table when you have finished experimenting then close it.

Creating Validation Rules

You have now set up and modified tables and entered, deleted, and filtered records. Nothing you have done so far will ensure that users enter valid data. Creating validation rules for data entry that the user must follow will do just that. Access will prevent data from being entered that does not follow these rules.

Understanding Validation Rules

- Specifying a specific range—You can set a specific range of values that are allowed in a field. For example the Visit Date would not be a valid date after today's date. (When you are entering a record of a customer's visit into the database, it would be for today's date or a date previous to today).

- Specifying a required field—A required field is one in which the user must enter data. This field cannot be left blank. The Pet ID is a field that should not be left blank.

- Specifying a default value—A default value is one that will appear in the field if the user does not enter anything in that field.

- Specifying a collection of legal values—A collection of legal values are the acceptable values to be entered into a specific field.

- Specifying format—To make data entry consistent, you can set the field so all text entered is displayed automatically in upper- or lowercase. Another example of a format is to set the number of characters necessary. If the Pet ID must be four characters, you can set it up so the user cannot enter any less than four characters.

- Validation text—Validation text is a message displayed when the user enters data that violates the rules set for that field.

Working with Wildcards

Wildcard characters are symbols that substitute for other characters when using the Find feature, in Queries, and in Table Design (validation rules). You use wildcards if you know only part of the value you are looking for or if you want to find values that begin with a specific letter or that match a certain pattern. For example, to find any word that begins with the letter B, you would type B*.

Three of the wildcard characters are the asterisk (*), which represents more than one character; the question mark (?), which represents only one character; and the pound symbol (#), which represents a single numeric value. In Hands-On 2.6, you will use wildcards because we want to identify values that begin with certain characters. You will set the validation rule for Pet ID, specify a collection of legal values, and set one value to DG##. This indicates that the value must begin with DG but can have any two numeric values after it. Using the wildcard characters allows you to access a number of values without having to name each one separately.

Set Up a New Table and Add Validation Rules

In this exercise, you will set up a new table in the Pinnacle Pet Care database. The new table will record pet visits to the clinic. The table will contain various fields that record visit information. You will set validation rules for several of the fields to ensure accurate data entry. You will also create a Lookup Wizard field to make data entry easier.

1. Click the Tables button on the Objects bar and double-click the Create Table in Design View option.

2. Follow these steps to set up the Visits table:

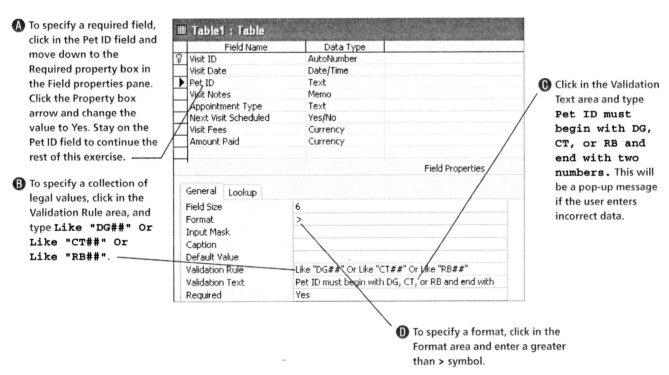

A Type the field names shown here and choose the data types shown for each field name. Make sure you spell the field names correctly.

B Click in the Pet ID row and set the Field Size to **6** in the Field Properties section at the bottom of the dialog box.

C Set the Appointment Type Field Size to **25**.

Field Name	Data Type
Visit ID	AutoNumber
Visit Date	Date/Time
Pet ID	Text
Visit Notes	Memo
Appointment Type	Text
Next Visit Scheduled	Yes/No
Visit Fees	Currency
Amount Paid	Currency

E Click in the Visit Date row and set the Format option in the Field Properties section at the bottom of the dialog box to Short Date.

D Click in the Visit ID row then click the Primary Key button on the Access toolbar. A key icon will appear indicating that Visit ID is the primary key. The primary key uniquely identifies each record in the table.

3. Follow these steps to set up validation rules:

A To specify a required field, click in the Pet ID field and move down to the Required property box in the Field properties pane. Click the Property box arrow and change the value to Yes. Stay on the Pet ID field to continue the rest of this exercise.

B To specify a collection of legal values, click in the Validation Rule area, and type **Like "DG##" Or Like "CT##" Or Like "RB##"**.

C Click in the Validation Text area and type **Pet ID must begin with DG, CT, or RB and end with two numbers.** This will be a pop-up message if the user enters incorrect data.

D To specify a format, click in the Format area and enter a greater than > symbol.

Table1 : Table

Field Name	Data Type	
Visit ID	AutoNumber	
Visit Date	Date/Time	
Pet ID	Text	
Visit Notes	Memo	
Appointment Type	Text	
Next Visit Scheduled	Yes/No	
Visit Fees	Currency	
Amount Paid	Currency	

Field Properties

General | Lookup

Field Size	6
Format	>
Input Mask	
Caption	
Default Value	
Validation Rule	Like "DG##" Or Like "CT##" Or Like "RB##"
Validation Text	Pet ID must begin with DG, CT, or RB and end with
Required	Yes

4. Make sure your table is set up properly then switch to Datasheet view.

5. Click Yes to save the table, type the name **Visits** in the Save As box, and click OK.

Working with the Lookup Wizard

Microsoft Office Specialist A Lookup Wizard field allows the user to pick from a set of values. This reduces errors because the user isn't entering data. The wizard will walk you through the process of building the list from which the user to pick items.

 Hands-On 2.7   Create a Lookup Wizard Field

In this exercise, you will experiment with the Lookup Wizard.

1. Click the Design View button to switch to Design View.

2. Follow these steps to set up a Lookup Wizard field:

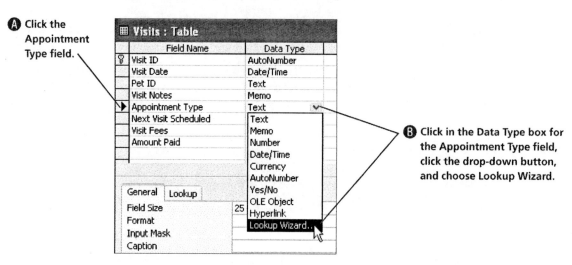

Ⓐ Click the Appointment Type field.

Ⓑ Click in the Data Type box for the Appointment Type field, click the drop-down button, and choose Lookup Wizard.

The Lookup Wizard begins.

3. Click on the I Will Type in the Values I Want option button.

4. Click the Next button to move to the next screen.

5. Follow these steps to specify the values for your lookup field:

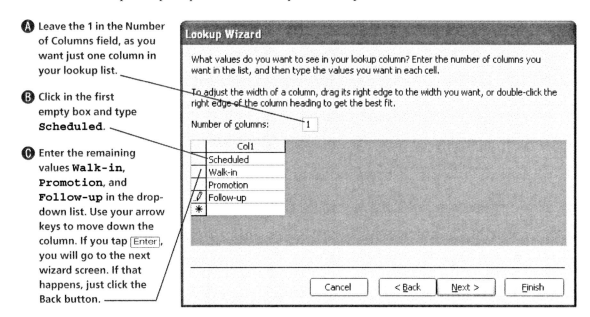

A Leave the 1 in the Number of Columns field, as you want just one column in your lookup list.

B Click in the first empty box and type **Scheduled.**

C Enter the remaining values **Walk-in,** **Promotion,** and **Follow-up** in the drop-down list. Use your arrow keys to move down the column. If you tap ⌈Enter⌉, you will go to the next wizard screen. If that happens, just click the Back button.

6. Click the Next button to move to the next screen. Make sure Appointment Type is listed in the window and click Finish.

7. Switch to Datasheet view and click Yes to save.

8. Tap the ⌈Tab⌉ key to bypass the Visit ID field.
   You don't need to enter the Visit IDs since the Visit ID AutoNumber data type will automatically number the records as you enter data in the other fields.

9. Type **1/09/04** in the Visit Date field.

10. Tap the ⌈Tab⌉ key and type **gd13** in the Pet ID field.

11. Tap the ⌈Tab⌉ key and your message will pop up because you entered an invalid Pet ID. The message tells you how the Pet ID should look. Go back and change the Pet ID to be **dg13.**
    If you typed the letters in lowercase, notice that they automatically changed to uppercase because of the format property you placed on that field.

12. Type **Dillon's owner stopped in to purchase flea treatment and schedule advanced obedience training** in the Visit Notes field.

13. Tap ⌈Tab⌉. In the Appointment Type field you simply need to click the arrow to drop down a list of appointment types to choose from. Choose Walk-In from the list.

14. Tap ⌈Tab⌉ and place a checkmark in the box in the Next Visit Scheduled field.

15. Notice that you check the Next Visit Scheduled box to set that field to Yes and leave the box unchecked to set that field to No.

16. Tap ⌈Tab⌉ and type **60** in the Visit Fees field.

17. Tap ⌈Tab⌉ and type **60** in the Amount Paid field.

Enter Additional Records into the Visits Table

18. Enter the following visit records:

Visit ID	Visit Date	Pet ID	Visit Notes	Appointment Type	Next Visit Scheduled	Visit Fees	Amount Paid
2	1/10/04	RB23	Bugs came by for the grooming promotion	Promotion	No	45	45
3	1/10/04	CT02	Max came by for the grooming promotion	Promotion	No	45	45
4	1/11/04	CT16	Stripes was suffering from a virus	Walk-in	Yes	78	20
5	1/12/04	DG12	Wolfy came in for yearly shots	Scheduled	No	135	50
6	1/12/04	CT16	Stripes viral infection seems to have been cured	Follow-up	No	20	20
7	1/15/04	DG13	First day of obedience training	Follow-up	Yes	25	25
8	1/15/04	DG24	First day of obedience training	Follow-up	Yes	25	0
9	1/15/04	DG25	First day of obedience training	Follow-up	Yes	25	25
10	1/16/04	CT92	New patient, set up appointment for check up	Walk-in	Yes	0	0

19. Close the Visits table, saving any changes if necessary, and close Access.

20. Now continue with the end-of-lesson questions and exercises.

Concepts Review

True/False Questions

1. Filters are a temporary way to view records that meet specific criteria.   TRUE   FALSE

2. To select an entire record, click anywhere in the record.   TRUE   FALSE

3. An input mask can automatically enter parenthesis ( ) around the area code of a phone number.   TRUE   FALSE

4. Changing the structure of a table will never result in lost data.   TRUE   FALSE

5. The Table Wizard is used to automate data entry in a table.   TRUE   FALSE

6. A pencil icon in the row selector indicates a new record in which you can type.   TRUE   FALSE

7. Once you are in Datasheet view, you cannot go back to the Table Design view.   TRUE   FALSE

8. To use Filter by Form you must first click on the field that contains the desired value.   TRUE   FALSE

9. The Table Wizard provides a variety of sample fields to use in a table.   TRUE   FALSE

10. Using validation rules, you can set a specific range of values allowed in the field.   TRUE   FALSE

Multiple Choice Questions

1. What is the first step you should take when deleting a record?
   a. Click in the desired record or select the record.
   b. Click the Delete Record button on the toolbar.
   c. Narrow the column width.
   d. Delete all text from the cells.

2. What is the purpose of setting a default value for a field?
   a. Data integrity—users are not allowed to enter any other value
   b. Saves time—the default value is automatically entered in new records
   c. Data entry simplification—the default value is easily entered by double-clicking
   d. None of the above

3. Filters are used to _____.
   a. establish relationships
   b. view a subset of records in a table
   c. view a list of fields in a table
   d. None of the above

4. Lookup Wizard fields help ensure data integrity by _____.
   a. automatically correcting spelling mistakes
   b. automatically capitalizing entries
   c. forcing users to choose from a list
   d. All of the above

Skill Builders

Skill Builder 2.1   Set Up a New Table

In this exercise, you will set up a new table in the Tropical Getaways database. The managers at Tropical Getaways need a table for the new Custom Travel Packages program. The table will record important information about the packages. Later you will create a form that displays information from both the Customers table and the Custom Packages table.

1. Start Access and open the Tropical Getaways database.

2. Click the Tables button on the Objects bar.

3. Double-click the Create Table in Design View option.

4. Follow these steps to set up the Custom Packages table:

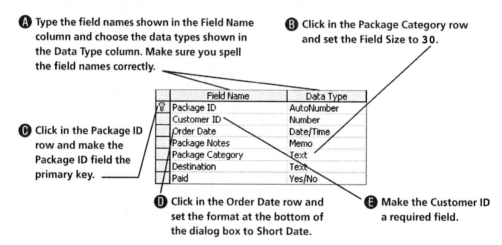

A Type the field names shown in the Field Name column and choose the data types shown in the Data Type column. Make sure you spell the field names correctly.

B Click in the Package Category row and set the Field Size to **30**.

C Click in the Package ID row and make the Package ID field the primary key.

D Click in the Order Date row and set the format at the bottom of the dialog box to Short Date.

E Make the Customer ID a required field.

5. Close the table and save it as **Custom Packages**.

Skill Builder 2.2   Use the Lookup Wizard

In this exercise, you will create a lookup field.

1. Click the Tables button on the Objects bar in the Access database window.

2. Click the Trips Table icon and open in Design View by clicking the Design button in the toolbar.

3. Click the Data type column for the Category field, click the drop-down arrow, and choose Lookup Wizard.

4. Choose I Will Type in the Values that I Want and click Next.

5. Leave the Column number as 1 then enter the values shown to the right into Column 1.

Col1
Adventure
Family
Leisure
Singles

6. Click Next then click Finish.

7. Click the Datasheet 🔲 view button and save the table.

8. Enter the following four records into the table using the drop-down list you just created for the Category field items:

Trip ID	Customer ID	Destination	Category	Departure Date	Return Date	Cost
Fam02	4	Hawaii	Family	7/15/04	7/20/04	$3,250
Lei02	2	Swiss Alps	Leisure	5/05/04	5/23/04	$5,980
Adv03	1	Baja California	Adventure	4/17/04	4/22/04	$1,750

9. Close the table when you have finished.

Skill Builder 2.3 Experiment with the Input Mask and Validation Rules

In this exercise, you will modify a table with an input mask and you will set a format property that will function like a validation rule.

1. Open the Customers table in Design View.

2. Click on the Zip field, go down to Field Properties in the Input Mask area, and click the Build 🔳 button.
   This will open the Input Mask Wizard.

3. Choose Zip Code from the choices and click Next.

4. Click Next two more times then click Finish.

5. Click in the State field then click the Format property box and type **>** to convert all text entered in that field to capital letters.

6. Switch to Datasheet view and save the table.

7. Enter the following records. Try out your validation rule by entering the states in lowercase letters.

Customer ID	Firstname	Lastname	Address	City	State	Zip	Profile
5	Rita	Bailey	1625 Palm Street	Portland	OR	97240	Family
6	Cheryl	DeMarco	1250 Sandy Plains	Atlanta	GA	30062	Singles

8. Close the table and the database when you have finished.

 **Assessments**

Assessment 2.1   Create the Events Table

In this exercise, you will create a new table in the Classic Cars database. You will add input masks and a lookup field.

1. Open the Classic Cars database.

2. Follow these guidelines to set up a new table with the structure shown in step 3:

   - Leave the field lengths of the Event Title, Sponsor, and Location fields set to 50.
   - Set the number of decimal places for the Entrance Fee field to **2**. You can do this in the Decimal Places box at the bottom of the dialog box after setting the Data type to Currency.
   - Make the Event ID field with an AutoNumber data type and designate it as the primary key.
   - Assign the name **Events** to the table.

3. Switch to Datasheet view, save the table, and enter the following records:

Event ID	Collector ID	Event Title	Event Date	Sponsor	Location	Entrance Fee	Mailing Sent	Notes
1	4	1950's Classic Chevys	9/1/04	Classic Cars Bay Chapter	San Francisco	$50	`Yes	
2	3	Early American Automobiles	10/18/04	American Collector's Association	Columbus	$25	Yes	
3	2	Classic Cars - Annual Auto Show	2/1/04	Classic Cars	Los Angeles	$10	Yes	

4. AutoFit the width of all columns and print the table.

5. Close the table when finished.

6. Open the Collectors table in Design view.

7. Place an input mask on the Zip Code field.

8. Format the State field so all characters typed into the field will convert to uppercase letters.

9. Switch to Datasheet view, save the table, and add the following records to the Collectors table:

Collector ID	Firstname	Lastname	Address	City	State	Zip	Era of Interest	Collection Size
5	Isaac	Williams	2684 Curtis Street	Denver	CO	80209	1940s	6
6	Angela	Hall	159 SW Taylor Street	Portland	OR	97205	1960s	12
7	Anthony	Jeffers	6583 F Street	San Diego	CA	92101	1930s	3

10. AutoFit the width of all columns and print the table.

11. Close table when finished.

12. Open the Cars table in Design view.

13. Create a Lookup Wizard field on the Condition field. Add the values in the example to the right to the Lookup Wizard:

Col1
Mint
Excellent
Good
Fair
Poor

14. Switch to Datasheet view, save the table, and add the following records:

Car ID	Collector ID	Year	Make	Model	Color	Condition	Value
FD02	7	30	Ford	Tudor	Black	Excellent	$35,000
CC03	6	68	Chevrolet	Camaro	Blue	Mint	$27,500
DS02	5	41	Dodge	Sedan	Maroon	Fair	$4,900

15. AutoFit the columns and print the table.

16. Close the table when you are finished.

17. Exit from Access.

Critical Thinking

Critical Thinking 2.1   Update Tables

Linda received the printed copies of the database tables and was quite satisfied; however, she has requested some changes. Open the Holmestead Realty database and update it with the following changes:

■ Sharon Carter was recently married to Greg Collins. On the Contacts table, locate Sharon, change her last name, and add Greg to the spouse field.

■ David Armstrong's mother is moving into the house on 14 Dover Street. Delete that listing from the Listings table.

■ The Wallace's bought a new investment property at 17 Keyway Avenue. Add the property to the Listings table using the following information:

MLS #: 52912

Price: $175,000

Commission Rate: 6%

Listing Date: Today's date

Expiration Date: 6 months from today

■ Linda also wants to track the style of each home. Add a field named Style to the Listings table and enter the data in the Style column to the listings currently in the Listings table:

MLS #	Street #	Address	Style
52236	1132	Richwood Road	Bungalow
52369	6	Thoroughbred Lane	Ranch
52425	218	Wildflower Road	Contemporary
52511	403	Hawks Landing	Ranch
52524	64	Hastings Street	2 Story
52526	137	Woodbridge Lane	1 Story w/basement
52649	23	Edwards Avenue	Duplex
52650	24	Edwards Avenue	Duplex
52912	17	Keyway Avenue	2 Story

Add and Modify Tables

Linda Holmes understands that houses sell better when they feel more like homes, so she develops the Feels Like Home service. The Feels Like Home service provides maintenance, cleaning, and other services to owners who list properties with Holmestead Realty. While this service generates additional income for Linda, expenses are also involved. Linda needs to modify the Holmestead Realty database to keep track of houses that receive the Feels Like Home service, and the specific type of service they receive. Follow these guidelines to set up a table to meet these needs:

■ Create a new table named **Feels Like Home**.

■ Use the following field names, data types, and field properties:

Feels Like Home Table Structure

Field Name	Data Type	Field Properties
Service ID	Auto Number	Primary key
Plan	Text	
Special Instructions	Memo	
Invoice	Yes/No	
MLS #	Number	

■ Save your table.

Ensure Data Integrity

Linda employs her nephew to complete data entry work for Holmestead Realty. He is a good worker but he sometimes makes errors. Linda decides to add Lookup Wizard fields to the Feels Like Home Data Entry table to help reduce data entry errors.

Follow these guidelines to create a Lookup Wizard field:

■ Open the Feels Like Home table, go to the Plan field data type, and begin the Lookup Wizard. Enter the following items into the wizard to create a drop-down list:

Table Wizard Values
Plan
Set-up
Winter
Summer
Check-up

Critical Thinking 2.4   Data Entry

Use the Feels Like Home table in Datasheet view to enter the following data into the database:

Service ID	Plan	Special Instructions	Invoice	MLS #
1	Set-up	House had dogs, so clean carpet well	Y	52236
2	Set-up	Take down curtains and wash	Y	52425
3	Check-up	Check basement	Y	52236
4	Set-up	Construction debris, clean up	Y	52511

LESSON 3

Working with Forms and Reports

In this lesson, you will enhance the Pinnacle Pet Care database with forms and reports. You will create forms that will allow you to easily view, enter, and edit data in the Customers and Pets tables. You will also create reports to present your data in a variety of ways.

IN THIS LESSON

Microsoft Office Access 2003 objectives covered in this lesson

Objective Number	Skill Sets and Skills	Concept Page References	Exercise Page References
AC03S-1-8	Create forms	66, 71	67, 72, 80, 82
AC03S-1-10	Create reports	73	74–77, 83–84
AC03S-2-2	Find and move among records	67	68–69

Case Study

Most of the employees at Pinnacle Pet Care have little computer experience, and they have even less experience using Microsoft Access. For this reason, Penny Johnson must make it easy for her employees to enter and extract data from the database. Penny decides to set up data entry forms that let employees enter customer and pet information. Penny also works closely with her employees to determine the types of reports they require. Penny realizes that her employees require an outstanding customer balance report that includes the customer names and telephone numbers. Another report should list the expenditures and number of visits for each pet. This report will be sorted by expenditures so customers spending the most on their pets will appear at the top of the report.

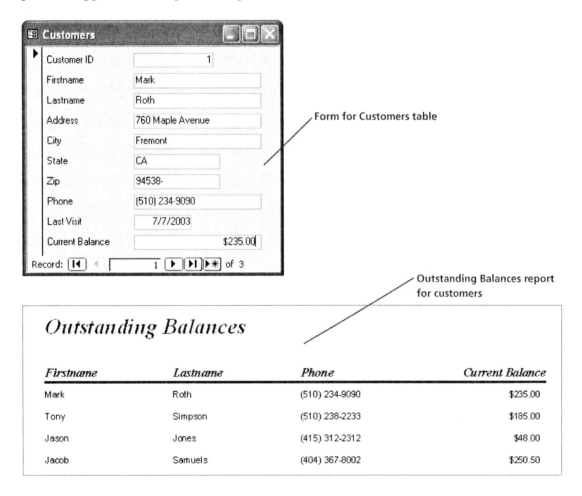

Form for Customers table

Outstanding Balances report for customers

Using Forms

In Lesson 1, Creating Tables and Entering Data and Lesson 2, Modifying and Maintaining Tables, you learned that an Access database is composed of various objects. A form is a type of object that lets you view, edit, and enter data. The benefit of a form is that it allows you to focus on a single record in the database. This is in contrast to Datasheet view, in which you can view many records at the same time. Forms are also used to create the user interface for a database. Using a form for the user to enter data allows the user to see only the record on which they are working. The following illustration shows a form for the Customers table in the Pinnacle Pet Care database.

Notice that the form displays one complete record from the database. Forms let you focus on a single customer, pet, etc.

Fields such as Phone, Last Visit, and Current Balance are automatically formatted with symbols (as they are in Datasheet view).

The form also contains navigation buttons to let you browse through the database.

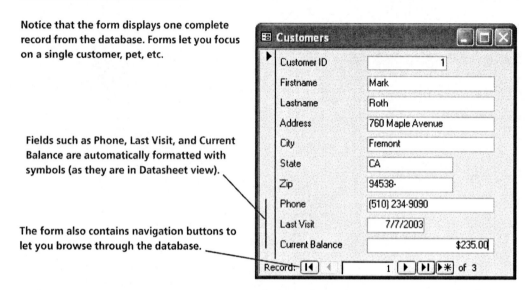

Creating Forms with AutoForm

Microsoft Office Specialist

You can use AutoForm to automatically create simple forms. AutoForm creates a form that displays all fields from a particular table. The form in the preceding illustration was created from the Customers table using AutoForm. More complex forms can be created using Form Design view or the Form Wizard.

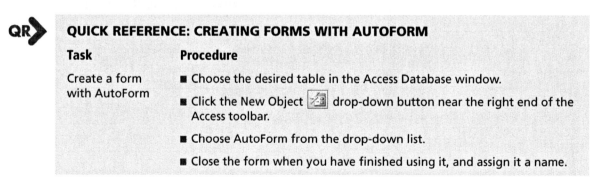

QR

QUICK REFERENCE: CREATING FORMS WITH AUTOFORM

Task	Procedure
Create a form with AutoForm	■ Choose the desired table in the Access Database window.
	■ Click the New Object [icon] drop-down button near the right end of the Access toolbar.
	■ Choose AutoForm from the drop-down list.
	■ Close the form when you have finished using it, and assign it a name.

In this exercise, you will open the Pinnacle Pet Care database you developed in Lesson 2, Modifying and Maintaining Tables.

1. Start Access and open the Pinnacle Pet Care database.

2. Follow these steps to create a form for the Customers table:

A Choose the Customers table from the list of tables. You must choose the desired table before creating a form.

B Click the drop-down button on the New Object button and choose Auto-Form, as shown here.

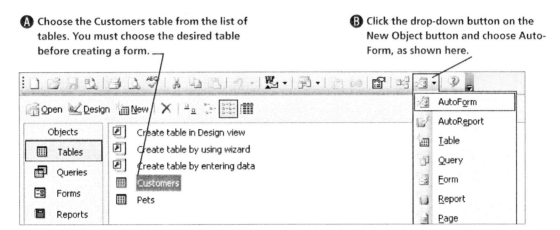

Access will create the form and display the Mark Roth record. This is because the Mark Roth record is the first record in the table.

Entering Data and Navigating Records in Forms

Microsoft Office Specialist

Forms are used for viewing and entering data one record at a time. When you enter data using a form, the data is stored in the underlying table on which that the form is based. Forms also make it easy to navigate to various records. The navigation bar at the bottom of a form lets you navigate to records in the underlying table. The form navigation bar has the same buttons that appear on the navigation bar in Datasheet view.

Go to the first record in the table.   Move forward one record.

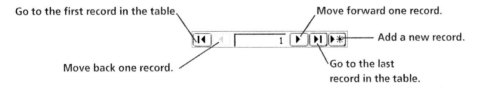
                                                        Add a new record.

Move back one record.   Go to the last record in the table.

In this exercise, you will enter new data and practice navigating through the data.

1. Follow these steps to prepare to enter a new record:

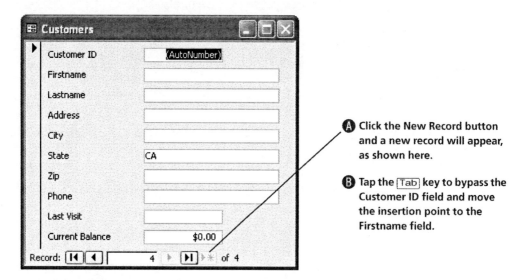

A Click the New Record button and a new record will appear, as shown here.

B Tap the Tab key to bypass the Customer ID field and move the insertion point to the Firstname field.

2. Enter the data shown here, using the Tab key to move from one field to the next:
   Notice that you must change the entry in the State field from CA to GA. You can always change the default value for a record by typing a new value. You set the default value to CA when you created the table in Lesson 2, Modifying and Maintaining Tables. Also, the dollar sign will not appear in the Current Balance field until you go to another field or record after typing the entry in the Current Balance field.

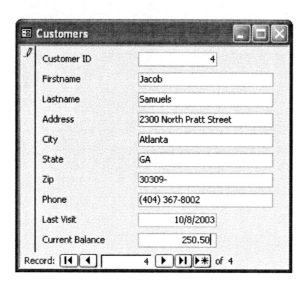

In the next few steps, you will close the form and assign a name to it. Forms use the same naming conventions as tables and all other database objects.

3. Click the Close button on the form.

Access will ask if you want to save the form.

4. Click the Yes button and Access will propose the name Customers.

5. Click OK to accept the proposed name.

6. Follow these steps to confirm that the form has been created and to reopen the form:

A Click the Forms button on the Objects bar and the Customers icon will appear, as shown here.

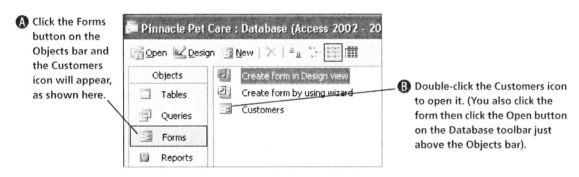

B Double-click the Customers icon to open it. (You also click the form then click the Open button on the Database toolbar just above the Objects bar).

7. Use the navigation bar at the bottom of the form to browse through the records.
Notice that the Jacob Samuels record you just added is visible as the last record. The data you entered for Jacob Samuels has been added to the Customers table.

8. Now close the Customers form again by clicking its Close ☒ button.

Deleting and Editing Records with Forms

The Delete Record ▶☒ button on the Access toolbar deletes the current record displayed in a form. The record is deleted from the underlying table. You can also use a form to edit data in an underlying table. Keep in mind that you must first navigate to a record before you can edit the data or delete the record.

Hands-On 3.3   Create a New Form and Work with Records

In this exercise, you will create a new form for the Pets table. You will also navigate through the table and delete a record.

1. Follow these steps to create a new form for the Pets table:

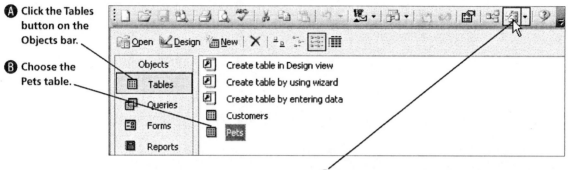

Ⓐ Click the Tables button on the Objects bar.

Ⓑ Choose the Pets table.

Ⓒ Click the AutoForm button (not the drop-down button) to create the form. The New Objects button always displays the most recent object type created on the face of the button.

Notice that the new form is based on the fields in the Pets table.

2. Click the New Record ⏵፧ button on the navigation bar at the bottom of the form.

3. Enter the following records, stopping at the Breed field for Slinky the Snake:

Pet ID	Pet Name	Pet Type	Breed	Gender	Color	Date of Birth	Last Visit	Expenditures	Number of Visits	Customer ID
DG24	Ben	Dog	Terrier	Male	Black	6/1/02	10/8/03	480	3	4
DG25	Spike	Dog	Chow	Male	Brown	4/3/98	10/8/03	890	12	4
SN01	Slinky	Snake								

4. It turns out that snakes are not welcome at Pinnacle Pets so click the Delete Record ⏵✕ button on the Access toolbar.

5. Click Yes to confirm the deletion of Slinky the Snake.

6. Use the navigation bar to navigate back through the records. Notice that the Ben the Dog and Spike the Dog records are still there.

7. Click the Close ✕ button on the form.

8. Click Yes when Access asks if you want to save the form.

9. Click OK on the Save As box to accept the name Pets.

10. Click the Forms button on the Objects bar to see both the Customers and Pets form icons you created.

Printing Forms

You can print the records in a table by clicking the Print button from an open form. Access will print a copy of the form with displayed data for each record in the database. This technique can be useful if you have a large number of fields in a table. Printing a datasheet with a large number of fields is often difficult because the fields can't be displayed on a single page. A form, however, will often fit on a single page. On the other hand, printing forms may not be wise if the table has a large number of records. Forms typically take a large amount of space on the printed page, and you will use a lot of paper if you print a table with many records.

 Hands-On 3.4   **Preview the Pets Form**

In this exercise, you will use Print Preview to see how the Pets form will look if printed.

1. Click the Forms button on the Objects bar.

2. Double-click the Pets icon in the Forms section of the database window.

3. Click the Print Preview button on the Access toolbar.

4. If necessary, maximize the Print Preview window.

5. Click anywhere on the page in the Print Preview window to zoom in.
   Notice that a copy of the form is displayed for each record in the Pets table.

6. Use the navigation bar at the bottom of the Print Preview window to browse through the pages.
   As you can see, printing data via a form may require a lot of paper.

7. Close the Print Preview window without printing.

8. Click the Restore button near the top-right corner of the window to restore the Pets form (not the Access program window).

9. Click the Close button on the Pets form.

Working with the Form Wizard

Microsoft Office Specialist

The Form Wizard guides you step by step through the creation of a form. You can choose the fields to include, various layout options, and a design style for the form. Unlike the AutoForm tool, the Form Wizard gives you flexibility when setting up a form. The Form Wizard is initiated by choosing the Create Form by Using Wizard option in the Forms section of the Access database window.

Hands-On 3.5 **Create a Form Using the Form Wizard**

In this exercise, you will create a new Pets form that includes only some of the fields in the database. The Pinnacle Pet Care database window should be displayed.

1. Click the Forms button on the Objects bar.

2. Double-click the Create Form by Using Wizard option.
   In the next few steps, you will choose the fields that will be displayed on the form. It is important that you choose the fields in the order specified in this exercise.

3. Follow these steps to add fields from the Pets table:

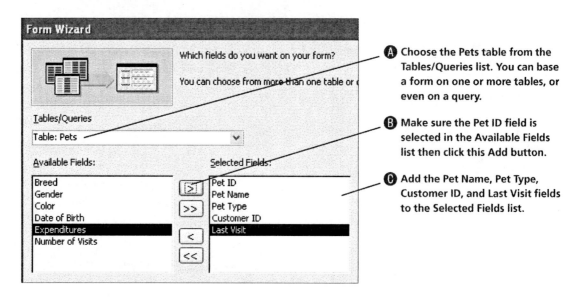

Ⓐ Choose the Pets table from the Tables/Queries list. You can base a form on one or more tables, or even on a query.

Ⓑ Make sure the Pet ID field is selected in the Available Fields list then click this Add button.

Ⓒ Add the Pet Name, Pet Type, Customer ID, and Last Visit fields to the Selected Fields list.

4. Click the Next button to display the next wizard screen.

5. With the Columnar option chosen, click the Next button.

6. Choose Standard as the style then click the Next button.

7. Type the name **Pets Last Visit** as the title and click the Finish button.
   Access will create the form as shown to the right; however, your form may have a slightly different layout. Notice that the form displays the data for Max the Cat and that there are nine records.

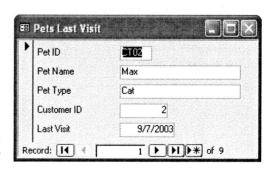

8. Use the record navigation buttons at the bottom of the form to browse through the records in the Pets Last Visit form.

9. Close the form.

Using Reports

Microsoft Office
Specialist
You can create reports to present data in a printed format. You can specify the fields to include in reports and you can format reports using built-in report styles. In Hands-On 3.6, you will create the following report. Notice that the report lists just four fields from the Customers table.

Outstanding Balances

Firstname	Lastname	Phone	Current Balance
Mark	Roth	(510) 234-9090	$235.00
Tony	Simpson	(510) 238-2233	$185.00
Jason	Jones	(415) 312-2312	$48.00
Jacob	Samuels	(404) 367-8002	$250.50

Complexity of Reports

In this lesson, you will use the Report Wizard to create simple reports. However, Access reports can be quite complex. For example, reports can include calculated fields that sum columns of numbers and grouping levels to organize records in logical groups.

AutoReport and the Report Wizard

In the previous Hands-On exercises, you used AutoForm to create forms. AutoForm created a form using all fields from a table and the Form Wizard allowed you to select certain fields to be used on a form. Reports usually require a subset of a table's fields. For example, the report shown in the previous illustration uses just four fields from the Customers table. AutoReport has limited use because it inserts all fields from a table into a report. Fortunately, Access provides a Report Wizard that gives you flexibility when setting up reports. The Report Wizard lets you choose the fields to include in the report. The Report Wizard also lets you specify various formatting options.

QUICK REFERENCE: USING THE REPORT WIZARD

Task	Procedure
Use the Report Wizard to create a report	■ Click the Reports button on the Objects bar in the Database window.
	■ Double-click the Create Report by Using Wizard option. You can also click the New button on the Access Database toolbar then choose Report Wizard from the dialog box.
	■ Choose the desired table or query on which you wish to base the report from the Tables/Queries list and click OK.
	■ Follow the Report Wizard steps to create the desired report.

Previewing and Printing Reports

The Preview button appears on the Access Database toolbar whenever the Reports button is pressed on the Objects bar and a report is chosen. You can open the report in Print Preview mode by clicking the Preview button. The Print Preview window functions the same way with reports as it does with other objects.

FROM THE KEYBOARD
Ctrl+P to display Print dialog box

The Print 🖨 button can be used to print reports directly from the Database window. The Print button also appears on the Print Preview toolbar when a report is chosen. You can print all pages of a report by clicking the Print button. You must use the File→Print command to display the Print dialog box if you want to print a range of pages or set other print options.

Hands-On 3.6   Use the Report Wizard

In this exercise you will create a new report using the Report Wizard.

Create an Outstanding Balances Report

1. Follow these steps to launch the Report Wizard:

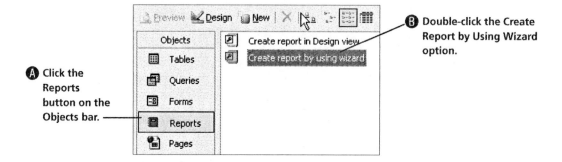

2. Follow these steps to choose the Customers table as the basis for the report and to add the Firstname field to the Selected Fields list:

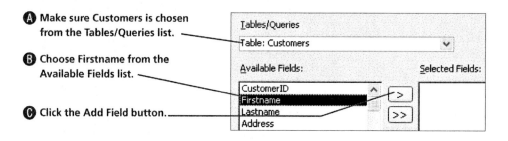

3. Now add the Lastname, Phone, and Current Balance fields. The completed Selected Fields list is shown to the right.

4. Click Next to display the Grouping Levels screen.

5. Click Next to bypass the Grouping Levels screen and display the Sort Order screen.

6. Click Next to bypass the Sort Order screen and display the Layout screen. Make sure the layout options are set as shown in the following illustration.

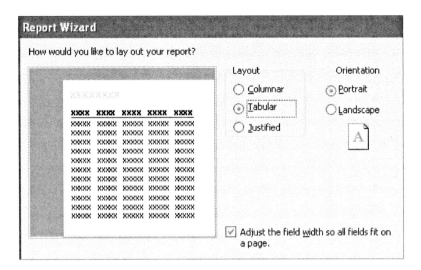

7. Click Next to display the Style screen.

8. Choose Corporate, click Next, and follow these steps to set the final report options:

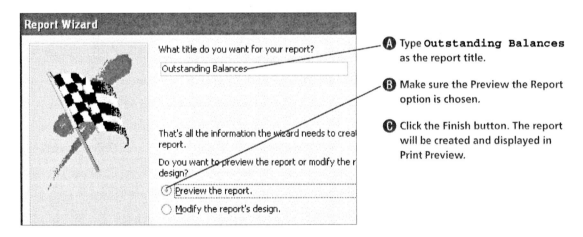

Ⓐ Type **Outstanding Balances** as the report title.

Ⓑ Make sure the Preview the Report option is chosen.

Ⓒ Click the Finish button. The report will be created and displayed in Print Preview.

9. If necessary, maximize the Print Preview window by clicking its Maximize button.

10. Zoom in or out on the report by clicking the mouse pointer anywhere on it.

Outstanding Balances

Firstname	*Lastname*	*Phone*	*Current Balance*
Mark	Roth	(510) 234-9090	$235.00
Tony	Simpson	(510) 238-2233	$185.00
Jason	Jones	(415) 312-2312	$48.00
Jacob	Samuels	(404) 367-8002	$250.50

11. Click the Design view button on the left end of the Print Preview toolbar.
    The report will display in Design view with a report header, page header, detail section, etc. In Design view, you can change the position of objects, add, and remove objects, and change the properties of objects. However, you won't work in Design view at this time.

12. Click the Print Preview button to switch back to Print Preview.

13. Feel free to print the report by clicking the Print button on the Print Preview toolbar.

14. Choose File→Close from the menu bar to close the report.
    The Report will automatically be assigned the name Outstanding Balances, and an Outstanding Balances icon will appear in the Reports section of the database window. As you can see from this example, creating simple reports is quite easy if you use the Report Wizard. You will now continue with the remainder of this exercise, where you will create a report to accompany the Pets table.

Create a Pets Report

15. With the Reports button pressed on the Objects bar, double-click the Create Report by Using Wizard option.

16. Choose the Pets table from the Tables/Queries list.

17. Add the Pet Name, Pet Type, Expenditures, and Number of Visits fields to the Selected Fields list as shown to the right.

Selected Fields:
Pet Name
Pet Type
Expenditures
Number of Visits

18. Click the Finish button to accept all of the remaining default settings. The completed report shown in the following illustration will appear.

Pets

Pet Name	Pet Type	Expenditures	Number of Visits
Wolfy	Dog	$450.00	7
Dillon	Dog	$150.55	3
Bugs	Rabbit	$600.50	4
Max	Cat	$1,450.55	20
Stripes	Cat	$450.00	9
Fetch	Dog	$345.00	3
Tony	Cat	$145.00	6
Ben	Dog	$480.00	3
Spike	Dog	$890.00	12

19. Notice the alignment of the fields within the columns.

Fields have the same left or right alignment in a report as they do in the table on which the report is based.

20. Close the report with the File→Close command.

The Reports section should now have an Outstanding Balance report and a Pets report.

Managing Objects

Occasionally you will have to copy, delete, or rename objects in your database. The ability to copy objects is helpful for making duplicates of the object for a backup or to bring a copy of an object to another database file. Sometimes you may finish up a wizard without realizing you didn't give an object the name you prefer. In that case, the ability to rename an object is extremely helpful.

Copying Objects

You can copy tables, forms, reports, and other types of objects. Objects can be copied and pasted into the same database, to a different database, and to other applications. Copying an object to the same database can be useful if you intend to modify the object. By making a copy, you will have a backup of the object in case the original is damaged. Objects are copied using the Copy and Paste buttons on the Access toolbar.

FROM THE KEYBOARD

Ctrl+C to copy
Ctrl+V to paste

Deleting Objects

Objects can also be deleted from an Access database. However, you must be careful when deleting objects because they will be permanently deleted from the database. Deleting objects can be useful, especially when using wizards and tools like AutoForm. If you make a mistake or are unhappy with the results of an automated process, you can delete the object and start over. You delete an object by choosing the desired object in the database window and issuing the Edit→Delete command. You can also click the Delete button on the Access Database toolbar.

FROM THE KEYBOARD

Delete to delete
selected object

Renaming Objects

Sometimes you will need to rename an object, either because it was given the default name that doesn't adequately describe what the object represents or contains, or it was given an inadequate name. For instance, if you don't give a table a name it will be called Table1. It isn't difficult to rename an object but you need to be careful not to rename objects that other objects are using. If you create a report based on a table and you rename the table, the report will no longer be able to find the data. You rename an object by choosing the object in the database window and choosing Edit→ Rename or by right-clicking on the object and choosing Rename.

FROM THE KEYBOARD

F2 to edit object
name

Hands-On 3.7   **Manage Objects**

In this exercise, you will practice copying, deleting, and renaming objects.

Copy the Report

1. Choose the Pets icon in the Reports section of the database window.

2. Click the Copy 🔲 button on the Access toolbar.

3. Click the Paste 🔲 button on the toolbar and the Paste As box will appear.

4. Type the name **Copy of Pets** in the Paste As box and click OK.
   The Copy of Pets report will appear in the Reports section.

5. Double-click the Copy of Pets report, and it will open.
   Notice that this report is identical to the Pets report.

6. Close the report with the File→Close command.

Delete the Report

7. Make sure the Copy of Pets report is chosen.

8. Click the Delete 🗵 button on the database toolbar.

9. Click Yes to confirm the deletion.
   Keep in mind that you can delete a report (or other object) whenever you want to "get a fresh start." This technique is useful when using wizards and other automated tools. You may need to use this technique in the Skill Builder and Assessment exercises on the following pages. You will create several reports in these exercises that are more complex than the reports you just created. If you make a mistake, remember to delete the report and recreate it with the Report Wizard.

Rename the Report

10. Right-click on the Pets icon in the Reports section of the database window.

11. Click the Rename option, type **Expenditures** to replace the word Pets, and tap the
    Enter key.
    Renaming the report will help you to identify what the report is about just by looking at the title.

12. Close the Pinnacle Pet Care database with the File→Close command.

Concepts Review

True/False Questions

1. Forms can be used to enter data in tables.   TRUE   FALSE

2. The main benefit of forms is that they allow you to view several records simultaneously.   TRUE   FALSE

3. The navigation buttons at the bottom of a form can be used to move between records.   TRUE   FALSE

4. Forms do not display currency symbols ($) and other formatting characters.   TRUE   FALSE

5. AutoForm creates a form for the table selected in the Tables section of the Access window.   TRUE   FALSE

6. The Report Wizard lets you choose the fields you wish to include in a report.   TRUE   FALSE

7. Reports can be printed.   TRUE   FALSE

8. The Report Wizard lets you choose Portrait or Landscape orientations.   TRUE   FALSE

9. Reports can be used to enter data.   TRUE   FALSE

10. An object can be copied and then pasted to a different database.   TRUE   FALSE

Multiple Choice Questions

1. Which of the following statements about forms is true?
   a. Forms can be used to enter records into a table.
   b. Forms can be used to browse the records in a table.
   c. Forms let you focus on one record at a time.
   d. All of the above

2. Which of the following commands can you issue through the navigation buttons on a form?
   a. Add a new record
   b. Delete a record
   c. Change the size of a field
   d. All of the above

3. Which of the following statements about the Report Wizard is true?
   a. The Report Wizard lets you choose Portrait or Landscape orientation.
   b. The Report Wizard lets you choose the fields to include in a report.
   c. The Report Wizard lets you choose a title for the report.
   d. All of the above

4. The Report Wizard is initiated from which section of the database window?
   a. Tables
   b. Reports
   c. Forms
   d. All of the above

Skill Builders

Skill Builder 3.1   Create Forms

In this exercise, you will open the Tropical Getaways database you developed in Lesson 2, Modifying and Maintaining Tables. You will continue to enhance this database as you progress through the Skill Builder exercises in this course.

The Access window should be open from the previous exercise, and all databases should be closed.

Create a Form for the Customers Table

1. Click the Open ![button] button on the Access toolbar, navigate to your file storage location, and open the Tropical Getaways database.

2. Make sure the Tables button is pressed on the Objects bar.

3. Choose the Customers table, click the New Object ![button] drop-down button, and choose AutoForm.
   Access will create the following form. The form uses all of the fields in the Customers table.

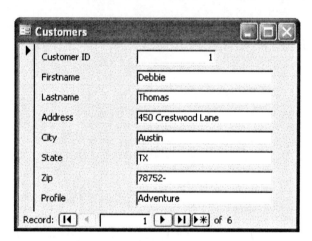

4. Click the New Record ![button] button on the form's navigation bar then add the following records:

Customer ID	Firstname	Lastname	Address	City	State	Zip	Profile
7	Victor	Thomas	2311 Wilmont Street	Danvers	MA	01923	Adventure
8	Lisa	Simms	100 Westside Drive	Batavia	NY	14020	Leisure
9	Ted	Carter	250 Smith Street	Charlton	MA	01507	Family

5. Click the Close ☒ button on the form and choose Yes when Access asks you to save the form.

6. Click OK to accept the proposed name Customers.

Create a Form for the Trips Table

7. Use AutoForm to create a form for the Trips table.

8. Use the form to add the following records to the Trips table:
   Notice the drop-down list in the Category field, which allows you to pick from a list instead of having to type the entry.

Trip ID	Customer ID	Destination	Category	Departure Date	Return Date	Cost
Adv04	1	Swiss Alps	Adventure	10/10/04	11/5/04	$3,500
Adv05	5	Rocky Mountains	Adventure	5/6/04	5/22/04	$2,190
Adv06	5	Baja California	Adventure	8/8/04	8/18/04	$2,900
Lei03	6	Hawaii	Leisure	2/5/04	2/15/04	$4,500
Fam03	7	Hawaii	Family	3/7/04	3/15/04	$5,300

9. Close the form and save it with the proposed name Trips.
   Leave the Tropical Getaways database open. You will continue to use it in the next exercise.

Skill Builder 3.2   Create Forms with the Form Wizard

In this exercise, you will use the Form Wizard to create a new form.

1. Click the Forms button on the Objects bar in the database window.

2. Double-click the Create Form by Using Wizard option.

3. Follow these steps to add the fields from the Customers table:

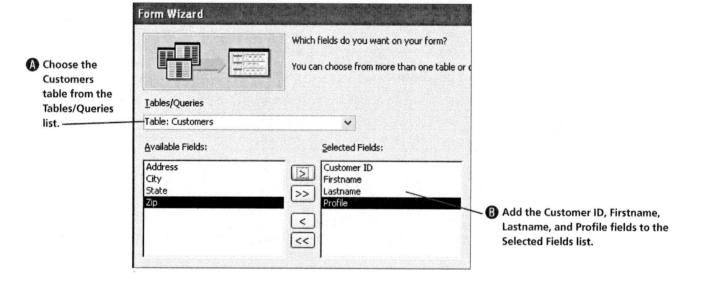

Ⓐ Choose the Customers table from the Tables/Queries list.

Ⓑ Add the Customer ID, Firstname, Lastname, and Profile fields to the Selected Fields list.

4. Click the Next button to display the next wizard screen.

5. With the Columnar option chosen, click the Next button.

6. Choose Standard as the style and click the Next button.

7. Type the name **Customer Profile** as the title then click the Finish button.
Access will create the form shown to the right; however, your form may have a slightly different layout.

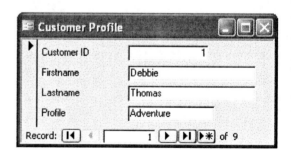

8. Close the form.

Create Reports

In this exercise, you will create reports for the Tropical Getaways database. You will use the sort option in the Report Wizard to sort the records in the reports.

Create a Customer Profiles Report

1. Click the Reports button on the Objects bar.

2. Double-click the Create Report by Using Wizard option.

3. Choose Customers from the Tables/Queries list.

4. Add the Firstname, Lastname, State, and Profile fields to the Selected Fields list.

5. Click the Next button twice to display the Sorting screen.

6. Click the drop-down button on the first sorting box and choose State, as shown to the right.

1	State	⌄	Ascending

   This will group all records with the same state in the report. Notice that you can set additional sort options. For example, imagine that you have a large database and want the records sorted first by state then by zip code within the states. In this situation, you would set the second sort key to zip code.

7. Click the Next button twice to display the Report Style screen.

8. Choose the Soft Gray style and click Next.

9. Type the name **Customer Profiles by State** in the title box of the last screen.

10. Click the Finish button to complete the report.
    Your completed report should match the following illustration. Notice that the State field appears first in the report and the records for each state are grouped. The State field appears first because you sorted on that field.

Customer Profiles by State

State	Firstname	Lastname	Profile
GA	Cheryl	DeMarco	Singles
MA	Ted	Carter	Family
MA	Victor	Thomas	Adventure
NY	Lisa	Simms	Leisure
NY	Wilma	Boyd	Leisure
OR	Rita	Bailey	Family
TX	Alice	Simpson	Family
TX	Ted	Wilkins	Adventure
TX	Debbie	Thomas	Adventure

11. Close the report when you have finished viewing it.
Access will automatically name the report Customer Profiles by State.

Create a Report for the Trips Table

12. Now create the following report for the Trips table. You will need to start the Report Wizard and choose the appropriate fields from the Trips table. Also, sort the report on the Category field, choose the Soft Gray style, and use the report title Trips by Category.

Trips by Category

Category	Destination	Cost
Adventure	Baja California	$2,900.00
Adventure	Rocky Mountains	$2,190.00
Adventure	Swiss Alps	$3,500.00
Adventure	Baja California	$1,750.00
Adventure	Amazon Jungle Trek	$7,765.00
Adventure	Kenyan Safari	$6,600.00
Family	Hawaii	$5,300.00
Family	Hawaii	$3,250.00
Family	Orlando	$3,400.00
Leisure	Hawaii	$4,500.00
Leisure	Swiss Alps	$5,980.00
Leisure	Caribbean Cruise	$2,390.00

13. Close the report when you have finished viewing it.
Your Tropical Getaways database should now have two reports: Customer Profiles by State and Trips by Category.

14. Use the File→Close command to close the database. The Access program window should remain open.

 **Assessments**

Create Forms and Reports

In this exercise, you will open the Classic Cars database you developed in Lesson 2, Modifying and Maintaining Tables. You will continue to enhance this database as you progress through the Assessment exercises in this course.

1. Open the Classic Cars database.

2. Use AutoForm to create the following form for the Collectors table.

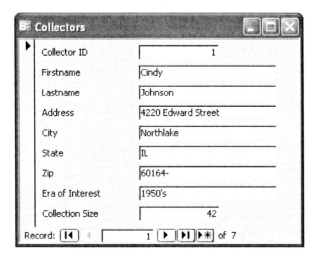

3. Use the form to enter the following new record into the Collectors table:

Collector ID	Firstname	Lastname	Address	City	State	Zip	Era of Interest	Collection Size
8	Jake	Johnson	840 Edgewood Drive	Arcadia	FL	33821	1920s	3

4. Close the form and save it with the proposed name Collectors.

5. Use AutoForm to create the following form for the Cars table.

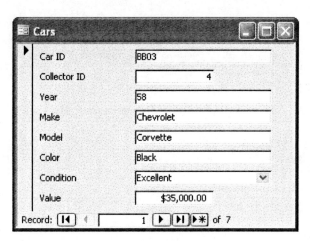

6. Use the form to enter the following new records into the table:

Car ID	Collector ID	Year	Make	Model	Color	Condition	Value
CJ04	1	48	Packard	Custom Eight Sedan	White	Fair	$15,000
JJ01	5	27	Ford	Model A	Black	Mint	$75,000
BB04	4	57	Chevrolet	Corvette	Red	Excellent	$42,000

7. Close the form and save it with the proposed name Cars.

8. Create the following report for the Collectors table. The report sorts the records by the Era of Interest field and it uses the Compact style. Also notice the title is Era of Interest.

Era of Interest

Era of Interest	Firstname	Lastname	Collection Size
1920s	Jake	Johnson	3
1930s	Anthony	Jeffers	3
1940s	Isaac	Williams	6
1950s	Bob	Barker	7
1950s	Cindy	Johnson	42
1960s	Angela	Hall	12
1960s	Tammy	Olson	6
Early 1900s	Ed	Larkson	34

9. Print the report then close it.

10. Create the following report for the Cars table. When adding the fields in the first Report Wizard screen, you will need to add them in the order shown on the report. For example, add the Model field first, the Year field second, the Condition field third, etc. This report is sorted on the Model field and it uses the Compact style.

Models Report

Model	Year	Condition	Color	Value
Camaro	68	Mint	Blue	$27,500.00
Corvette	57	Excellent	Red	$42,000.00
Corvette	58	Excellent	Black	$35,000.00
Corvette	62	Excellent	Blue	$30,000.00
Corvette	58	Mint	Red and white	$65,000.00
Custom Eight Sedan	48	Fair	White	$15,000.00
Model A	27	Mint	Black	$75,000.00
Sedan	41	Fair	Maroon	$4,900.00
Thunderbird	59	Good	Tan	$20,000.00
Tudor	30	Excellent	Black	$35,000.00

11. Print the report then close it.

12. Close the Classic Cars database when you have finished.

Critical Thinking

Critical Thinking 3.1   Create Forms

Linda Holmes has been working with her new database for some time and she has come to realize that working in Datasheet view can be awkward. Linda has asked you to set up a form that can be used for entering data and browsing records. Follow these guidelines to set up the form:

■ Open the Holmestead Realty database you developed in Lesson 2, Modifying and Maintaining Tables. You will continue to develop this database as you progress through the Critical Thinking exercises in this course.

■ Use the AutoForm tool to create a form for the Contacts table.

■ Name the form **Contacts Data Entry**.

■ Use the new form to add the contacts in the following table to the database. If a field is empty in the table then leave it empty on the form as well.

Seller ID	Firstname	Lastname	Spousename	Address	City	ST	Zip	Phone	Contact Type
7	Mark	Thames		76 Haywood Road	Asheville	NC	28801	(828) 252-5676	Primary Residence
8	Cindy	Johnson		24 Maple Drive	Black Mountain	NC	28711	(828) 686-3511	Trustee

It turns out that Susan Jones' name was spelled incorrectly in the Contacts table. She spells her first name Suzanne. She is the spouse of Jeff Jones. In your new form, use the Find feature to locate Jeff Jones' record in the Contacts table and make the correction.

Linda Holmes was so pleased with the form you created that she has asked you to create a form for the Listings table. Follow these guidelines to set up the form:

■ Use the AutoForm tool and name the form **Listings Data Entry**.

■ Use the form to add the following listings to the Listings table:

MLS #	Street #	Address	Price	Listing Date	Expiration Date	Commission Range	Seller ID	Style
52125	76	Haywood Road	$325,000	7/14/04	2/14/05	5%	7	3 Story
52345	625	Brevard Road	$135,000	8/5/04	12/5/05	6%	8	Ranch

You have just been informed that the Woodbridge Lane listing has expired. Use the Listings Data Entry form to remove this listing from the Listings table.

Create Reports

Linda Holmes has promised all of her sellers that she will call them at least once a week. She realizes that to do this she will need a report that displays contact information for her sellers. Follow these guidelines to create the necessary report:

■ Use the Report Wizard to set up the report. The report should extract data from the Contacts table.

■ Display the Firstname, Lastname, Spousename, Contact Type, and Phone fields on the report in the same order listed here.

■ Accept all of the default Report Wizard settings except for the report style: Choose the Casual report style instead.

Name the report **Contact Phone List** and print it when finished.

Linda was caught off guard by the expiration of the Woodbridge listing and she doesn't want this to happen again. Follow these guidelines to create a report that tracks listing expiration dates:

■ Use the Report Wizard to set up the report. The report should extract data from the Listings table.

■ Display the MLS #, Street #, Address, Price, and Expiration Date fields on the report in the same order listed here.

■ Accept all of the default Report Wizard settings except for the sort order and report style. Sort the report in ascending order on the Expiration Date field and choose the Casual report style.

■ Name the report **Expiration Date List** and print it when finished.

■ Save your changes and exit from Access.

LESSON 4

Getting Answers with Queries

In this lesson, you will learn how to set up and use queries. Queries are an essential part of any Access database. They allow you to extract and combine data from tables. You will learn how to specify criteria in queries to extract only the records you desire. You will create calculated fields; work with statistical functions; and sort, group, and print query results.

IN THIS LESSON

Microsoft Office Access 2003 objectives covered in this lesson

Objective Number	Skill Sets and Skills	Concept Page References	Exercise Page References
AC03S-3-4	Format datasheets	109	110
AC03S-3-5	Sort records	97, 99	98–100

Case Study

The staff at Pinnacle Pet Care has used their new database for some time and now they want answers to a variety of questions. For example:

■ What is the current balance of each customer in California?

■ Which customers have a current balance greater than $200?

■ Which customers in California have a current balance greater than $200?

■ What is the average amount of money that customers spend on cats and dogs?

Penny Johnson sets up queries in the Pinnacle Pet Care database to answer these questions. The following illustrations show a query, the Customers table, and the resulting recordset.

Field:	FirstName	LastName	Phone	Current Balance
Table:	Customers	Customers	Customers	Customers
Sort:				Descending
Show:	✓	✓	✓	✓
Criteria:				>200

A query contains fields and criteria used to select records from a table.

Customer ID	Firstname	Lastname	Address	City	State	Zip	Phone	Last Visit	Current Balance
1	Mark	Roth	760 Maple Avenue	Fremont	CA	94538-	(510) 234-9090	7/7/2003	$235.00
2	Tony	Simpson	312 York Lane	Richmond	CA	94804-	(510) 238-2233	9/7/2003	$185.00
3	Jason	Jones	2233 Crystal Street	San Mateo	CA	94403-	(415) 312-2312	7/15/2003	$48.00
4	Jacob	Samuels	2300 North Pratt Str	Atlanta	GA	30309-	(404) 367-8002	10/8/2003	$250.50

FirstName	LastName	Phone	Current Balance
Mark	Roth	(510) 234-9090	$235.00
Jacob	Samuels	(404) 367-8002	$250.50

Access produces a recordset when the query is run.

What Are Queries?

Queries are an essential part of any Access database. Most people use queries to get answers to questions and to extract data from one or more tables. When you run a query, Access creates a temporary table using the fields and criteria you specify in the query. The temporary table is known as a recordset. The recordset is composed of data from one or more tables in your database. A query's recordset can even be used as the basis for forms and reports. Thus, queries give you the ability to produce forms and reports using data from multiple tables.

Working with Select Queries

Select queries are the most common type of query. They let you selectively extract data from one or more tables in a database. When designing select queries, you specify the fields you wish to include in the recordset. You can also specify criteria used to select records from the table(s) in your database. The following illustrations show the Customers table from the Pinnacle Pet Care database and the resulting recordset. Take a few moments to study the illustrations.

Customer ID	Firstname	Lastname	Address	City	State	Zip	Phone	Last Visit	Current Balance
1	Mark	Roth	760 Maple Avenue	Fremont	CA	94538-	(510) 234-9090	7/7/2003	$235.00
2	Tony	Simpson	312 York Lane	Richmond	CA	94804-	(510) 238-2233	9/7/2003	$185.00
3	Jason	Jones	2233 Crystal Street	San Mateo	CA	94403-	(415) 312-2312	7/15/2003	$48.00
4	Jacob	Samuels	2300 North Pratt Str	Atlanta	GA	30309-	(404) 367-8002	10/8/2003	$250.50

FirstName	LastName	Phone	Current Balance
Mark	Roth	(510) 234-9090	$235.00
Jacob	Samuels	(404) 367-8002	$250.50

A query is run that instructs Access to only choose the Firstname, Lastname, Phone, and Current Balance fields from the Customers table for those customers with a Current Balance >$200.

The query produces the recordset shown here. Notice that the recordset only includes the specified fields for customers who have a Current Balance of >$200.

Setting Up Queries

You can use the Query Wizard to assist you in setting up queries, or you can set them up yourself using the Query Design grid. The Design grid gives you complete flexibility in determining the fields, criteria, and other options that you wish to use in the query. The following Quick Reference table describes how to display the Query window and how to add tables to the query. You must add table(s) to the Query window in order to use the desired fields from the table(s) in the query.

QUICK REFERENCE: ADDING TABLES TO THE QUERY WINDOW

Task	Procedure
Add a table to the Query window	■ Open the desired database, and make sure the Queries button is pressed on the Objects bar.
	■ Double-click the Create Query in Design View option.
	■ Choose a table that you want the query to extract data from in the Show Table box and click Add.
	■ Add any other tables from which you wish to extract data.
	■ Click the Close button on the Show Table box.

 Hands-On 4.1   **Set Up a Query**

In this exercise, you will begin setting up a query. You will display the Query window and you will add the Customers table in the Pinnacle Pet Care database to it.

Display the Query window

1. Start Access and open the Pinnacle Pet Care database.

2. Click the Queries button on the Objects bar.

3. Double-click the Create Query in Design View option.
   The Query window will appear and the Show Table dialog box will be displayed. The Show Table dialog box lets you choose the table(s) you wish to use in the query. In this exercise, you will add just the Customers table to the Query window.

4. Choose Customers and click the Add button.
   A Customers field list will appear above the Design grid. The field names in the list are taken from the Customers table. In a moment, you will use the Customers field list to add fields to the query.

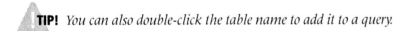

TIP! *You can also double-click the table name to add it to a query.*

5. Click the Close button on the Show Table dialog box.
   You won't be using the other tables in this exercise.

Set Up the Window

6. Make sure both the Access window and the Query window are maximized 🔲 within the Access window.

7. Follow these steps to adjust the size of the Design grid and the Customers field list:

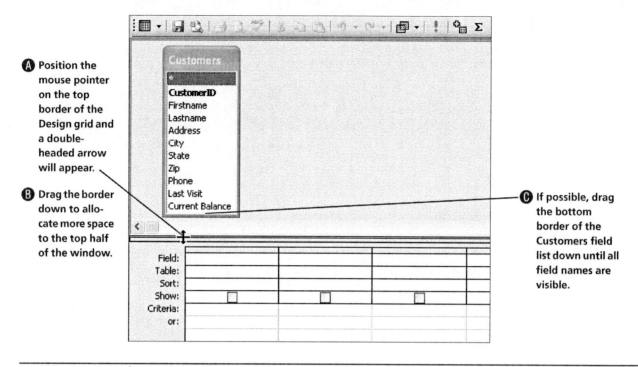

A Position the mouse pointer on the top border of the Design grid and a double-headed arrow will appear.

B Drag the border down to allocate more space to the top half of the window.

C If possible, drag the bottom border of the Customers field list down until all field names are visible.

Working with the Query Design Grid

The Design grid appears when you begin setting up a new query. The Design grid lets you specify the fields to include in the query. You can also use the Design grid to specify criteria and other parameters that affect the query recordset. The following illustration shows the Design grid and the recordset for the sample query shown. You will develop the query shown in the illustration as you progress through the next few exercises.

The Table row indicates the table from which each field is taken. In this example, all fields are taken from the Customers table.

Fields such as Firstname, Lastname, Phone, and Current Balance are added to the columns of the Design grid. These fields will be displayed in the recordset.

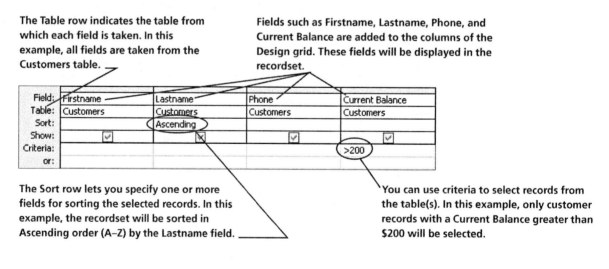

The Sort row lets you specify one or more fields for sorting the selected records. In this example, the recordset will be sorted in Ascending order (A–Z) by the Lastname field.

You can use criteria to select records from the table(s). In this example, only customer records with a Current Balance greater than $200 will be selected.

The recordset includes customer records with a Current Balance greater than $200. Only the fields specified in the query appear in the recordset.

FirstName	LastName	Phone	Current Balance
Mark	Roth	(510) 234-9090	$235.00
Jacob	Samuels	(404) 367-8002	$250.50

Adding Fields to the Design Grid

The first step in defining a query is to add fields to the Design grid. The fields you add to the Design grid will appear in the recordset. Once you have added fields to the Design grid, you can specify sorting options, criteria, and other options that affect the recordset. The following Quick Reference table describes the techniques you can use to add fields to the Design grid.

QUICK REFERENCE: ADDING FIELDS TO THE QUERY DESIGN GRID

Technique	Description
Double-click	You can add a single field to the Design grid by double-clicking the desired field in the field list.
Drop-down list	You can add a single field by clicking in a field cell, clicking the drop-down button that appears, and choosing the desired field from the drop-down menu.
Drag	You can add a single field or multiple fields to the Design grid by dragging them from a field list to the desired cell in the Design grid. You can select multiple fields prior to dragging by pressing and holding the Ctrl key while clicking the desired field names in the field list.
All fields	You can add all fields to the Design grid by double-clicking the asterisk (*) symbol at the top of the desired field list.

 Hands-On 4.2   **Add Fields to the Design Grid**

In this exercise, you will add fields to the Design grid.

1. Follow these steps to add the Firstname field to the Design grid:

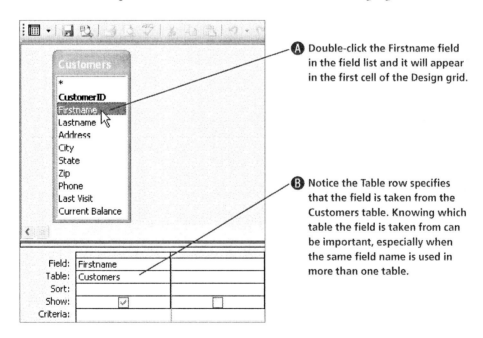

Ⓐ Double-click the Firstname field in the field list and it will appear in the first cell of the Design grid.

Ⓑ Notice the Table row specifies that the field is taken from the Customers table. Knowing which table the field is taken from can be important, especially when the same field name is used in more than one table.

2. Now add the Lastname, Phone, and Current Balance fields to the Design grid by double-clicking them on the field name list. When you have finished adding the filed, the Design grid should match the following illustration.

Field:	FirstName	LastName	Phone	Current Balance
Table:	Customers	Customers	Customers	Customers
Sort:				
Show:	☑	☑	☑	☑
Criteria:				
or:				

Removing Fields from the Design Grid

You can remove fields from the Design grid by clicking in the desired column and choosing Edit→Delete Columns from the menu bar. You may need to remove fields from time to time as you develop queries. Remember to use this technique if you make a mistake and add an incorrect field to the Design grid.

 Hands-On 4.3   Delete a Field

In this exercise, you will practice deleting a field from the Design grid.

1. Click anywhere in the Current Balance column in the Design grid.

2. Choose Edit→Delete Columns from the menu bar and the field will be removed.

3. Follow these steps to reinsert the Current Balance field using the drop-down list technique:

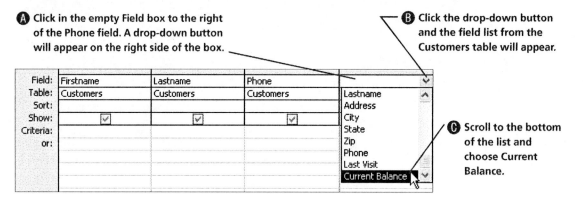

Ⓐ Click in the empty Field box to the right of the Phone field. A drop-down button will appear on the right side of the box.

Ⓑ Click the drop-down button and the field list from the Customers table will appear.

Ⓒ Scroll to the bottom of the list and choose Current Balance.

The Current Balance field should be returned to the grid. As you can see, there are several ways to add fields to the Design grid. Once again, feel free to remove fields from the Design grid whenever you make a mistake or wish to change the order of the fields in the grid.

Running Queries

You can run a query by clicking the Run button on the Access toolbar. When you run a select query, Access selects records and fields from tables in your database and displays the recordset. You can navigate through the recordset or print it if desired. The recordset will always reflect the current data stored in the database.

Editing Data in a Recordset

When you run a select query, the recordset is connected to the underlying table(s) on which the query is based. If you edit data in the recordset, the data in the underlying tables is changed as well. However, most select queries are only used for viewing selective data.

 Hands-On 4.4   **Run the Query**

In this exercise, you will run the query.

1. Click the Run button on the Access toolbar.
   The query will run and the following recordset will appear. Keep in mind that your query is quite basic. It simply displays four fields from each record in the Customers table.

FirstName	LastName	Phone	Current Balance
Mark	Roth	(510) 234-9090	$235.00
Tony	Simpson	(510) 238-2233	$185.00
Jason	Jones	(415) 312-2312	$48.00
Jacob	Samuels	(404) 367-8002	$250.50

2. Now continue with the next topic, in which you will learn how to sort query results.

Sorting Query Results

Microsoft Office Specialist

You can instruct Access to sort the rows in a recordset using one or more fields as sort keys. For example, you may want to view the recordset with the largest current balances displayed first. You sort recordsets by setting the sort box to Ascending or Descending for one or more fields in the Design grid. If you set the sort box for more than one field, the first field is used as the primary sort key, followed by the next field, and so on.

Hands-On 4.5   Sort the Results

In this exercise, you will sort the results of the recordset you created in the last exercise.

1. Notice that the records in the recordset do not appear to be sorted in any particular order.
   Actually, the records are sorted on the Customer ID field, which is the primary key for the Customers table. In the next few steps, you will set the sort key for the Lastname field in the Design grid. When you run the query again the recordset will be sorted by last name with the Jones record first, followed by the Roth record, and so on.

2. Click the Design ![icon] view button on the left end of the Access toolbar.
   The Design grid will reappear. You can always use the Design view button to switch back and forth between the recordset and the Design grid.

3. Follow these steps to set a sort key:

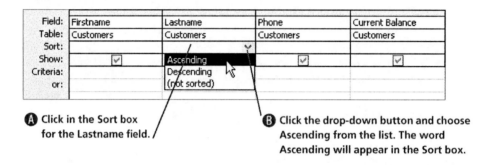

A Click in the Sort box for the Lastname field.

B Click the drop-down button and choose Ascending from the list. The word Ascending will appear in the Sort box.

4. Click the Run ![icon] button and the following recordset will appear.
   Notice that the records are sorted by the Lastname field.

	FirstName	LastName	Phone	Current Balance
	Jason	Jones	(415) 312-2312	$48.00
	Mark	Roth	(510) 234-9090	$235.00
	Jacob	Samuels	(404) 367-8002	$250.50
	Tony	Simpson	(510) 238-2233	$185.00

5. Click the Design ![icon] view button to display the Design grid.

6. Follow these steps to remove the Lastname sort key and to set the sort order to descending based on the Current Balance field:

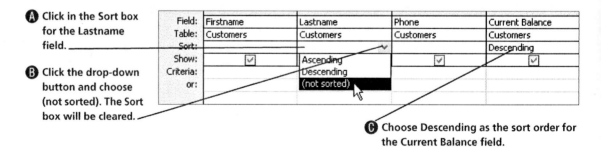

A Click in the Sort box for the Lastname field.

B Click the drop-down button and choose (not sorted). The Sort box will be cleared.

C Choose Descending as the sort order for the Current Balance field.

7. Click the Run [!] button and the following recordset will appear. *Notice that the records with the largest Current Balance are displayed first.*

FirstName	LastName	Phone	Current Balance
Jacob	Samuels	(404) 367-8002	$250.50
Mark	Roth	(510) 234-9090	$235.00
Tony	Simpson	(510) 238-2233	$185.00
Jason	Jones	(415) 312-2312	$48.00

8. Choose File→Close from the menu bar and click the Yes button when Access asks if you want to save the query.

9. Type the name **Sorted Customer Balance** in the Save As box and click OK.

Sorting with Multiple Fields

Microsoft Office Specialist

Access can sort on more than one field at a time. Queries evaluate the sort fields from left to right. If you add more than one sort to a query, Access will run a primary sort on the leftmost field in the Design grid and then run a secondary sort on the next field requested to the right.

Hands-On 4.6   Sort with Multiple Fields

In this exercise, you will sort the Pets table on multiple fields.

1. Double-click the Create Query in Design View option.

2. Choose Pets from the Show Table box and click the Add button.

3. Click the Close button on the Show Table dialog box.

4. Resize the Query Design window to maximize your view of the Design grid and the Pets field list. You used this technique in Hands-On 4.1 with the Customers field list.

5. Add the Pet Name, Pet Type, and Expenditures fields to the Design grid.

6. Follow these steps to sort the Pet Type field in ascending order and the Expenditures field in descending order:

A Click the Sort box for the Pet Type field.

Field:	Pet Name	Pet Type	Expenditures
Table:	Pets	Pets	Pets
Sort:		Ascending	Descending
Show:	✓	Ascending	✓
Criteria:		Descending	
or:		(not sorted)	

B Click the drop-down button and choose Ascending as the sort order.

C Click the Sort box for the Expenditures field then click the drop-down button and choose Descending.

7. Click the Run ![Run button] button and the following recordset will appear.

Notice that the records are sorted first by Pet Type. Within the Pet Type, the records are sorted by Expenditures from largest to smallest amount.

	Pet Name	Pet Type	Expenditures
	Max	Cat	$1,450.55
	Stripes	Cat	$450.00
	Tony	Cat	$145.00
	Spike	Dog	$890.00
	Ben	Dog	$480.00
	Wolfy	Dog	$450.00
	Fetch	Dog	$345.00
	Dillon	Dog	$150.55
	Bugs	Rabbit	$600.50

8. Close the query and click Yes to save. Type **Pet Type Expenditures** in the Save As box.

Using Criteria to Select Records

One of the most important benefits of queries is that you can select specific records by specifying criteria. This gives you the ability to select the precise data you desire from a database. For example, you may want to know how many customers have an outstanding balance greater than $200. Or, perhaps you are interested in viewing only those records where the state is equal to CA. These and other questions are easily answered by specifying criteria in the Query Design grid.

Working with Equality Criteria

You can use equality criteria to choose only those records where a field has a specific value, such as CA. You accomplish this by entering the value you want the field to equal in the Criteria row of the Design grid. The following illustration shows how this is accomplished.

A This is a Criteria row.

Field:	FirstName	LastName	Phone	Current Balance	State
Table:	Customers	Customers	Customers	Customers	Customers
Sort:				Descending	
Show:	☑	☑	☑	☑	☑
Criteria:					CA
or:					

B Entering CA in the State Criteria box instructs Access to select only those records where the state is CA.

C As expected, only records where the state is CA appear in the recordset.

	FirstName	LastName	Phone	Current Balance	State
	Mark	Roth	(510) 234-9090	$235.00	CA
	Tony	Simpson	(510) 238-2233	$185.00	CA
	Jason	Jones	(415) 312-2312	$48.00	CA

Working with Comparison Criteria

You can use the comparison operators > (greater than), < (less than), >= (greater than or equal), <= (less than or equal), and NOT (not equal) when specifying criteria. Access will select only those records matching the criteria. For example, placing the criterion >200 in the Current Balance field instructs Access to select only records where the Current Balance is greater than 200.

The Show Check Box

The Show row in the Design grid contains a check box ☑ for each field. You can prevent a field from displaying in the recordset by removing the check from the Show box. This can be useful in many situations. For example, in the preceding illustration, the State field is used to select only records where the state is equal to CA. The State field must be present in the Design grid in order to specify these criteria. However, you may not want the State field to be displayed in the recordset. You can prevent the State field from being displayed by removing the check from the State field in the Design grid.

 Hands-On 4.7   # Use Criteria

In this exercise, you will experiment with equality and comparison criteria.

1. Double-click the Create Query in Design View option.

2. Choose Customers from the Show Table box and click the Add button.

3. Click the Close button on the Show Table dialog box.

4. Resize the Query Design window to maximize your view of the Design grid and the Pets field list.

5. Add the Firstname, Lastname, Phone, Current Balance, and State fields to the Design grid.

Use an Equality Criterion

6. Follow these steps to set an equality criterion for the State field:

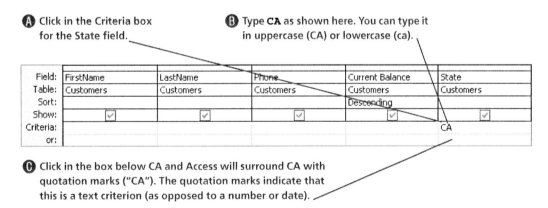

Ⓐ Click in the Criteria box for the State field.

Ⓑ Type **CA** as shown here. You can type it in uppercase (CA) or lowercase (ca).

Field:	FirstName	LastName	Phone	Current Balance	State
Table:	Customers	Customers	Customers	Customers	Customers
Sort:				Descending	
Show:	☑	☑	☑	☑	☑
Criteria:					CA
or:					

Ⓒ Click in the box below CA and Access will surround CA with quotation marks ("CA"). The quotation marks indicate that this is a text criterion (as opposed to a number or date).

7. Click the Run ⚟ button.

The three records with the State field equal to CA should appear in the recordset.

8. Click the Design ⬚ view button to display the Design grid.

Use Comparison Criteria

9. Follow these steps to create a "greater than" comparison criterion for the Current Balance field:

Field:	FirstName	LastName	Phone	Current Balance	State
Table:	Customers	Customers	Customers	Customers	Customers
Sort:					
Show:	☑	☑	☑	☑	☑
Criteria:				>200	

Ⓐ Click in the Criteria box for the Current Balance field and type **>200**.

Ⓑ Click in the Criteria box for the State field and delete the "CA" criterion.

10. Click the Run ⚟ button to produce the following recordset.

Notice that the current balance is greater than $200 for each record.

	FirstName	LastName	Phone	Current Balance	State
	Mark	Roth	(510) 234-9090	$235.00	CA
	Jacob	Samuels	(404) 367-8002	$250.50	GA

11. Click the Design ⬚ view button again to display the Design grid.

12. Change the >200 criterion to **<200** and run the query again.

Only records with current balances less than $200 will appear in the recordset.

Uncheck the Show Box

In the next few steps, you will prevent the State field from appearing in the recordset by removing the check from the Show box.

13. Click the Design ⬚ view button to display the Design grid.

14. Follow these steps to set up the query:

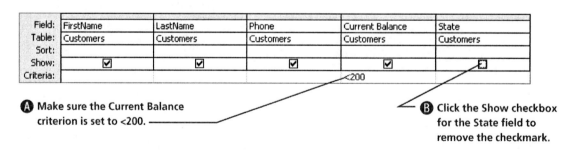

Field:	FirstName	LastName	Phone	Current Balance	State
Table:	Customers	Customers	Customers	Customers	Customers
Sort:					
Show:	☑	☑	☑	☑	☐
Criteria:				<200	

Ⓐ Make sure the Current Balance criterion is set to <200.

Ⓑ Click the Show checkbox for the State field to remove the checkmark.

15. Click the Run ⟨?⟩ button and the State field will be removed from the recordset.

16. Take 10 minutes to experiment with the query you have been using. Try entering various criteria and perhaps adding and removing fields from the Design grid. When you have finished experimenting, continue with the next topic.

Clearing the Design Grid

You can clear all entries from the Design grid with the Edit→Clear Grid command. This command can be used to give you a fresh start when working in the Design grid.

 Hands-On 4.8   **Clear the Grid and Add All Fields**

In this exercise, you will clear the Design grid to get a clean slate. Then you will add all fields from the Customers table into the Design grid.

1. If necessary, click the Design ⟨✎⟩ view button to display the Design grid.

2. Choose Edit→Clear Grid to remove all fields from the grid.

3. Follow these steps to add all fields from the Customers table to the Design grid:

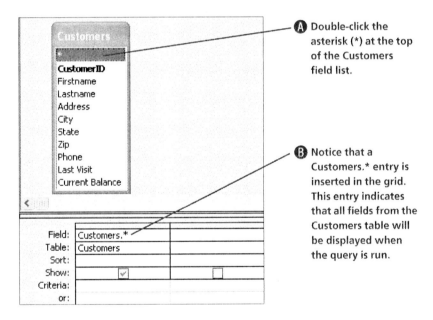

Ⓐ Double-click the asterisk (*) at the top of the Customers field list.

Ⓑ Notice that a Customers.* entry is inserted in the grid. This entry indicates that all fields from the Customers table will be displayed when the query is run.

4. Click the Run ⟨?⟩ button. All records from the Customers table should appear in the recordset.

Use a Criterion to Select the Records

In the next few steps, you will add the Current Balance field to the Design grid and specify a criterion for that field.

5. Click the Design ✏️ view button to display the Design grid.

6. Follow these steps to add the Current Balance field to the grid and to specify a criterion:

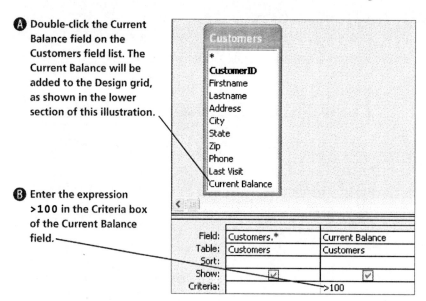

Ⓐ Double-click the Current Balance field on the Customers field list. The Current Balance will be added to the Design grid, as shown in the lower section of this illustration.

Ⓑ Enter the expression **>100** in the Criteria box of the Current Balance field.

7. Run ❗ the query to produce the recordset shown in the following illustration.

Customer ID	Firstname	Lastname	Address	City	State	Zip	Phone	Last Visit	Customers.Curre	Field0
1	Mark	Roth	760 Maple Avenue	Fremont	CA	94538-	(510) 234-9090	7/7/2003	$235.00	$235.00
2	Tony	Simpson	312 York Lane	Richmond	CA	94804-	(510) 238-2233	9/7/2003	$185.00	$185.00
4	Jacob	Samuels	2300 North Pratt Str	Atlanta	GA	30309-	(404) 367-8002	10/8/2003	$250.50	$250.50

Notice that the last two columns of the recordset contain a Customers.Current Balance field and a Field0 field. This unusual nomenclature was used because the Current Balance field was included twice in the Query Design grid. It was included once as part of the Customers.* entry and again as a separate field in the second column. Access cannot display the same field name twice in a table or recordset; therefore, Access changed the names of the column headings in the recordset. You will correct this by removing the check from the Show box in the next few steps.

8. Switch to Design ✏️ view and remove the check from the Show box of the Current Balance field. The Design grid should match the example shown to the right.

Field:	Customers.*	Current Balance
Table:	Customers	Customers
Sort:		
Show:	☑	☐
Criteria:		>100

9. Run the query. Notice that only one Current Balance field is visible.
   The >100 criterion in the Current Balance field selects the appropriate records. However, the field is not displayed in the recordset because the Show box is unchecked.

10. Choose File→Close from the menu bar and click the Yes button to save the query.

11. Type the name **Current Balance** in the Save As box and click OK.

Using Wildcards in Queries

Wildcards are used in queries to find records where a field contains certain values. For example, you may want to display all records where the customer's name begins with the letter J. You can also use wildcards for numeric values. You may want to find the records of all customers who visited the clinic any day in the month of October.

 Hands-On 4.9   Use Wildcards

In this exercise, you will create a wildcard query for the Pet ID criteria.

1. Make sure the queries are displayed in the Database window.

2. Double-click the Create Query in Design View option.

3. Double-click Pets in the Show Table box then click the Close button.

4. Adjust the size of the Design grid and the Pets field list to so you can see the entire content of the field list.

5. Double-click the Pet ID, Pet Name, Pet Type, Color, and Last Visit fields to add those fields to the Design grid.

6. Follow these steps to add a wildcard to the criteria for Pet ID:

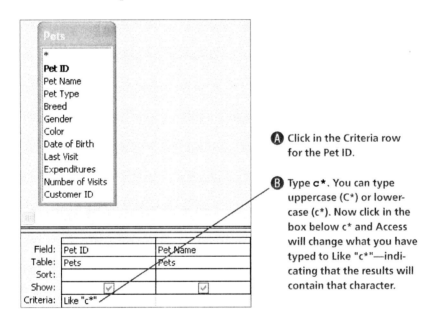

Ⓐ Click in the Criteria row for the Pet ID.

Ⓑ Type **c***. You can type uppercase (C*) or lower-case (c*). Now click in the box below c* and Access will change what you have typed to Like "c*"—indicating that the results will contain that character.

7. Click the Run ⚠️ button to produce the recordset.
   All records shown should have a Pet ID beginning with the letter C.

8. Click the Design ◤ view button to display the Design grid.

9. Click the Criteria box for the Pet ID field and delete the Like "c*" criterion.

10. Click in the Criteria box for Last Visit and type **7/*/2003**.

11. Click the Run ! button to display the following recordset.

	Pet ID	Pet Name	Pet Type	Color	Last Visit
	CT92	Tony	Cat	Brown with black str	7/7/2003
	DG12	Wolfy	Dog	Brown	7/15/2003
	DG13	Dillon	Dog	Black	7/7/2003
	CT16	Stripes	Cat	Black and brown	7/15/2003

12. Choose File→Close from the menu bar and click the Yes button to save the query.

13. Type the name **July Visits** in the Save As box and click OK.

Working with Compound Criteria

Thus far, you have worked with relatively simple queries containing one criterion. However, you will sometimes need to use more than one criterion. Criteria composed of two or more criteria are known as compound criteria. There are two types of compound criteria: AND criteria and OR criteria.

AND Criteria

AND criteria let you select records based on logical AND expressions. In Hands-On 4.10, you will use AND criteria to select records in the Pets table. For example, you will use an AND expression to select all records where the pet type is dog and the number of visits is greater than 5. With AND criteria, Access will only select records when all of the criteria are true.

OR Criteria

OR criteria allow you to select records based on logical OR expressions. For example, you will use an OR expression to select all records where the pet type is dog or the pet type is cat. With OR criteria, Access will select records if any of the criteria are true.

Setting Up Compound Criteria

You set up compound criteria in the Design grid. AND criteria are set up by placing two or more criteria in different fields within the same Criteria row. OR criteria are set up by placing two or more criteria on different rows within the Design grid. The following illustration shows the compound criteria you will set up in Hands-On 4.10.

In this example, the criterion "dog" and >5 are on the same Criteria row. This creates an AND condition. Only records where the Pet Type is dog **and** the Number of Visits > 5 will be chosen.

Field:	Pet Name	Pet Type	Last Visit	Expenditures	Number of Visits
Table:	Pets	Pets	Pets	Pets	Pets
Sort:					
Show:	☑	☑	☑	☑	☑
Criteria:		"dog"			>5

In this example, the criteria are on different rows within the Pet Type field. This creates an OR condition as indicated by the Or heading at the left end of the second Criteria row. All records where the Pet Type is dog **or** the Pet Type is cat will be chosen.

Field:	Pet Name	Pet Type	Last Visit	Expenditures	Number of Visits
Table:	Pets	Pets	Pets	Pets	Pets
Sort:					
Show:	☑	☑	☑	☑	☑
Criteria:		"dog"			
or:		"cat"			

Hands-On 4.10   Use Compound Criteria

In this exercise, you will set up a new query using the Pets table from the Pinnacle Pet Care database. You will use compound criteria to query the database in various ways.

Set Up the Query Window

1. Make sure the queries are displayed in the Database window.

2. Double-click the Create Query in Design View option.

3. Choose Pets from the Show Table box and click the Add button.

4. Click the Close button on the Show Table dialog box.

5. Resize the Query Design window to maximize your view of the Design grid and the Pets field list.

Create an AND Criterion

6. Double-click the Pet Name, Pet Type, Last Visit, Expenditures, and Number of Visits fields on the Pets field list to add those fields to the Design grid.

7. Enter the following criteria into the Pet Type and Number of Visits boxes in the Criteria row:

Field:	Pet Name	Pet Type	Last Visit	Expenditures	Number of Visits
Table:	Pets	Pets	Pets	Pets	Pets
Sort:					
Show:	☑	☑	☑	☑	☑
Criteria:		"dog"			>5

8. Click the Run ! button to produce the following recordset.

	Pet Name	Pet Type	Last Visit	Expenditures	Number of Visits
	Spike	Dog	10/8/2003	$890.00	12
	Wolfy	Dog	7/15/2003	$450.00	7

Notice that each record has Dog as the Pet Type and that the Number of Visits is greater than 5.

Create an OR Criterion

9. Switch to Design view and remove the >5 criterion from the Number of Visits criteria box.

10. Add the **cat** criterion to the row below the dog criterion as shown in the following illustration. It isn't necessary to type the quotation marks, though. Access will add them when you click outside of the field after typing the criterion.

TIP! *When using OR criteria, you can use as many rows as necessary. Each row that you add creates one more condition in the OR expression.*

Field:	Pet Name	Pet Type	Last Visit	Expenditures	Number of Visits
Table:	Pets	Pets	Pets	Pets	Pets
Sort:					
Show:	☑	☑	☑	☑	☑
Criteria:		"dog"			
or:		"cat"			

11. Click the Run ! button to produce the following recordset.

	Pet Name	Pet Type	Last Visit	Expenditures	Number of Visits
	Tony	Cat	7/7/2003	$145.00	6
	Ben	Dog	10/8/2003	$480.00	3
	Spike	Dog	10/8/2003	$890.00	12
	Wolfy	Dog	7/15/2003	$450.00	7
	Dillon	Dog	7/7/2003	$150.55	3
	Max	Cat	9/7/2003	$1,450.55	20
	Stripes	Cat	7/15/2003	$450.00	9
	Fetch	Dog	9/10/2003	$345.00	3

Notice that all records have a Pet Type of Dog or Cat.

Use a Combination of AND and OR Compound Criteria

12. Switch to Design ![icon] view but do not change the "dog" and "cat" criteria.

13. Add the **>5** criteria to the Number of Visits field, as shown in the following illustration.

Field:	Pet Name	Pet Type	Last Visit	Expenditures	Number of Visits
Table:	Pets	Pets	Pets	Pets	Pets
Sort:					
Show:	☑	☑	☑	☑	☑
Criteria:		"dog"			>5
or:		"cat"			>5

These compound criteria will choose all records where the Pet Type is Dog and the Number of Visits is greater than 5 or the Pet Type is Cat and the Number of Visits is greater than 5.

14. Click the Run ![icon] button to produce the following recordset.

Pet Name	Pet Type	Last Visit	Expenditures	Number of Visits
Tony	Cat	7/7/2003	$145.00	6
Spike	Dog	10/8/2003	$890.00	12
Wolfy	Dog	7/15/2003	$450.00	7
Max	Cat	9/7/2003	$1,450.55	20
Stripes	Cat	7/15/2003	$450.00	9

15. Switch to Design view and take 10 minutes to experiment with compound criteria. *Be creative! Query the Pets table for answers to any questions that may come to mind.*

16. When you have finished experimenting, choose File→Close from the menu bar and click the Yes button when Access asks if you want to save the query.

17. Type the name **Compound Criteria** in the Save As box and click OK.

Formatting and Printing Query Results

Microsoft Office Specialist

Although reports are often used to print query results, recordsets can be formatted and printed just like you printed datasheets in Lesson 1, Creating Tables and Entering Data. In Hands-On 4.11 you will format and print the results of a query.

Hands-On 4.11   Format and Print the Query

In this exercise, you will format the Current Balance query then print it.

1. Make sure the Query button is selected in the Objects bar.

2. Double-click the Sorted Customer Balance query to run the query and display the recordset.

3. If necessary open the formatting toolbar by choosing View→Toolbars→Formatting (Datasheet).

4. Follow these steps to format the recordset for printing:

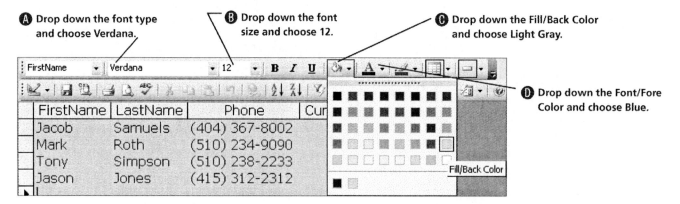

Ⓐ Drop down the font type and choose Verdana.

Ⓑ Drop down the font size and choose 12.

Ⓒ Drop down the Fill/Back Color and choose Light Gray.

Ⓓ Drop down the Font/Fore Color and choose Blue.

5. Position your mouse pointer on the FirstName field, press and hold down the left mouse button, and drag the mouse over all four column headings to select them.

6. Choose Format→Column Width from the menu and click the Best Fit button.

7. Click the Print Preview ⬜ button on the Access toolbar.
The Print Preview window should display the following recordset.

	Sorted Customer Balance		11/17/2003
FirstName	LastName	Phone	Current Balance
Jacob	Samuels	(404) 367-8002	$250.50
Mark	Roth	(510) 234-9090	$235.00
Tony	Simpson	(510) 238-2233	$185.00
Jason	Jones	(415) 312-2312	$48.00

8. Print the query results and close the query.

9. Click the Yes button when Access asks if you want to save the changes.

10. Close the Pinnacle Pet Care database and continue with the end-of-lesson questions and exercises.

Concepts Review

True/False Questions

1. Criteria determine the records selected by a query.　　　　　　　TRUE　FALSE

2. The Query Design grid is where you define a query.　　　　　　　TRUE　FALSE

3. You can add fields to the Design grid by double-clicking the desired fields on the field list(s) above the Design grid.　　　　　　　TRUE　FALSE

4. You can add all fields to the Design grid by double-clicking any field in the field list.　　　　　　　TRUE　FALSE

5. Changing data in the recordset has no impact on the underlying data in the table(s) on which the query is based.　　　　　　　TRUE　FALSE

6. You must type criteria in the same case (uppercase or lowercase) as the data in the tables you are querying or Access will not select the desired records.　　　　　　　TRUE　FALSE

7. If a field has been entered into the Design grid, you cannot prevent the field from appearing in the recordset.　　　　　　　TRUE　FALSE

8. The two types of compound criteria are AND and OR.　　　　　　　TRUE　FALSE

9. You cannot use wildcards for numeric values.　　　　　　　TRUE　FALSE

10. Access can sort on more than one field at a time.　　　　　　　TRUE　FALSE

Multiple Choice Questions

1. Which of the following commands can be used to remove fields from the Design grid?
   a. Field→Remove
   b. Edit→Delete Columns
   c. Edit→Delete Rows
   d. File→Delete Columns

2. Which of the following symbols is used to represent greater than in query criteria?
   a. <
   b. >
   c. <=
   d. >=

3. Which of the following commands is used to clear the Design grid?
   a. File→Clear All
   b. File→Clear Grid
   c. Edit→Clear Grid
   d. The grid cannot be cleared.

4. Which symbol(s) can be used as a Wildcard in query criteria?
   a. !
   b. *
   c. (
   d. &

 **Skill Builders**

Skill Builder 4.1   Use Compound Criteria

In this exercise, you will use compound criteria to query the Customers table in the Tropical Getaways database.

1. Open the Tropical Getaways database and click the Queries button on the Objects bar.

2. Double-click the Create Query in Design view option.

3. Choose Customers in the Show Table box and click the Add button.

4. Click the Close button to close the Show Table dialog box.

5. If necessary, maximize the Query window. Adjust the height of the Design grid and the Customers field list box.

6. Add the Firstname, Lastname, and Profile fields to the Design grid by double-clicking them on the Customers field list.

7. Type the word **adventure** in the Criteria box of the Profile field, as shown here.

Field:	Firstname	Lastname	Profile
Table:	Customers	Customers	Customers
Sort:			
Show:	☑	☑	☑
Criteria:			adventure

8. Run ⚡ the query. Only records with the Adventure profile will be displayed, as shown here.

Firstname	Lastname	Profile
Debbie	Thomas	Adventure
Ted	Wilkins	Adventure
Victor	Thomas	Adventure

9. Switch back to Design 📐 view.

10. Add the State field to the Design grid.

11. Set the criteria for the State field to **TX** and the sort order of the Lastname field to Ascending, as shown in the following figure.

Field:	Firstname	Lastname	Profile	State
Table:	Customers	Customers	Customers	Customers
Sort:		Ascending		
Show:	☑	☑	☑	☑
Criteria:			"adventure"	TX

12. Run the query. Only records where the profile is Adventure and the state is TX will be displayed, as shown in the following figure.

Firstname	Lastname	Profile	State
Debbie	Thomas	Adventure	TX
Ted	Wilkins	Adventure	TX

13. Close the query and save it as **Adventure Profiles**.

Skill Builder 4.2   Use Comparison Criteria

In this exercise, you will use comparison criteria to query the Trips table in the Tropical Getaways database.

1. Double-click the Create Query in Design view option.

2. Choose Trips in the Show Table box and click the Add button.

3. Click the Close button to close the Show Table dialog box.

4. If necessary, maximize the Query window. Adjust the height of the Design grid and the Trips field list box.

5. Add the Destination, Category, and Cost fields to the Design grid by double-clicking on them.

6. Click in the criteria row in the Cost field and type **<3000**, as shown in the following figure.

Field:	Destination	Category	Cost
Table:	Trips	Trips	Trips
Sort:			
Show:	☑	☑	☑
Criteria:			<3000

7. Click the Run ⚡ button. Only records where the cost is below $3,000 will be displayed, as shown here.

Destination	Category	Cost
Caribbean Cruise	Leisure	$2,390.00
Baja California	Adventu	$1,750.00
Rocky Mountains	Adventu	$2,190.00
Baja California	Adventu	$2,900.00

8. Close the query and save it as **Trips Under $3000**.

Skill Builder 4.3   Use Wildcards and Sort Records

In this exercise, you will use wildcards in the criteria and sort records in the Trips table.

1. Double-click the Create Query in Design view option.

2. Choose Trips in the Show Table box and click the Add button.

3. Click the Close button to close the Show Table dialog box.

4. If necessary, maximize the Query window. Adjust the height of the Design grid and the Trips field list box.

5. Add the Trip ID, Destination, Category, and Departure Date fields to the Design grid by double-clicking them on the Trips field list.

6. Type **8/*/2004** in the Criteria box of the Departure date field. When you click in another box, Access will change what you have typed to Like "8/*/2004".

7. Click on the sort row of the Destination field and set the sort order to Ascending, as shown in the following figure.

Field:	Trip ID	Destination	Category	Departure Date
Table:	Trips	Trips	Trips	Trips
Sort:		Ascending		
Show:	☑	☑	☑	☑
Criteria:				Like "8/*/2004"

8. Run 🔲 the query. Only records where the date is in the month of August will be displayed, as shown in the following figure.

Trip ID	Destination	Category	Departure Date
Adv02	Amazon Jungle Trek	Adventu	8/7/2004
Adv06	Baja California	Adventu	8/8/2004
Adv01	Kenyan Safari	Adventu	8/5/2004

9. Close the query and save it as **August Departures**.

10. Close the Tropical Getaways database.

Assessments

Create Queries

In this exercise, you will create a new query to the Classic Cars database.

1. Open the Classic Cars database.

2. Create a new query and add the Collectors table to it.

3. Set up the query to produce the recordset shown in the following illustration. Notice that this query simply chooses the indicated fields and sorts the records in descending order by Collection Size.

Firstname	Lastname	Era of Interest	Collection Size
Cindy	Johnson	1950's	42
Ed	Larkson	Early 1900's	34
Angela	Hall	1960's	12
Bob	Barker	1950's	7
Isaac	Williams	1940's	6
Tammy	Olson	1960's	6
Jake	Johnson	1920's	3
Anthony	Jeffers	1930's	3

4. Run the query and print the recordset. Now close the query and save it as **Collection Sizes**.

5. Create a new query and add the Cars table to it.

6. Set up the query to produce the recordset shown in the following illustration. (You'll run and format the recordset in a moment). Notice that this query only selects records where the model is Corvette and the condition is Excellent. The query also sorts the records by Value, with the largest values appearing first.

7. Run the query, format the recordset by changing the font to Verdana, the font size to 12pt, the text color to Dark Blue, and the background to Light Gray.

8. Autofit the width of all columns to fit the largest entry/heading in the columns.

Make	Model	Year	Color	Condition	Value
Chevrolet	Corvette	57	Red	Excellent	$42,000.00
Chevrolet	Corvette	58	Black	Excellent	$35,000.00
Chevrolet	Corvette	62	Blue	Excellent	$30,000.00

9. Print the recordset. Now close the query and save it as **Excellent Corvettes**.

Assessment 4.2   Create Queries

In this exercise, you will create queries with compound criteria and that are sorted in specific orders.

1. Create a new query and add the Cars table to it.

2. Set up the query to produce the following recordset. Notice that the query selects records where the make is Chevrolet and the Value is under $40,000.

Make	Model	Condition	Value
Chevrolet	Corvette	Excellent	$30,000.00
Chevrolet	Corvette	Excellent	$35,000.00
Chevrolet	Camaro	Mint	$27,500.00

3. Run the query and print the recordset. Now close the query and save it as **Chevrolets Under $40000**.

4. Create a new query and add the Cars table to the Query Design grid.

5. Set up the query to produce the following recordset. Notice that this query only selects records where the year begins with a 5 and is sorted by Make in Alphabetical order.

Car ID	Year	Make	Model
BB04	57	Chevrolet	Corvette
BB03	58	Chevrolet	Corvette
CJ01	58	Chevrolet	Corvette
CJ22	59	Ford	Thunderbird

6. Run the query and print the recordset. Now close the query and save it as **50s Cars**.

7. Close the Classic Cars database when you have finished then exit from Access.

Critical Thinking

Create Select Queries

Linda Holmes has created an add-on service for investor contacts only. She has asked you to create a select query that chooses only the records from the Contacts table in which the contact type is Investor. Open the Holmestead Realty database and follow these guidelines to create a select query:

- The recordset should display only the Firstname, Lastname, Spousename, Phone, and Contact Type fields from the Contacts table.

- Only contacts with a contact type of Investor should appear in the recordset.

- Save the query as **Investors**.

Linda has published a brochure that she sends only to contacts who have a contact type of Primary Resident or Trustee. Follow these guidelines to set up a select query:

- The recordset should display only the Firstname, Lastname, Address, City, State, Zip, and Contact Type fields from the Contacts table.

- Only contacts with a contact type of Primary Residence or Trustee should appear in the recordset.

- Save the query as **Non-Investors**.

Create Queries

Linda has a customer who would like to purchase a duplex under $200,000. She has asked you to create a query that shows only those records.

- The recordset should display only the MLS#, Street#, Address, Price, and Style fields.

- Only listings with the style of duplex and a price under $200,000 should appear in the recordset.

- Save the query as **Duplexes Under $200000**.

Linda would like to increase the advertising on the listings that will expire in the next month. She would like you to create a query that lists the listings that will expire in the month of January.

- The recordset should display only the MLS#, Seller ID, and Expiration Date.

- Only listings that have a date that begins with 01 should appear in the recordset.

- Save the query as **Listings Expiring in January**.

- Save the changes to Holmestead Realty database, close it, and exit from Access.

Unit 2

Forms and Queries

The lessons in this unit cover more advanced topics for designing queries and forms. After completing this unit, you will be able to create complex queries with calculated fields, statistical functions, and pop-up boxes. You will also be able to create complex and impressive forms that include subforms, calculated fields, and totals. Also discussed in this unit are techniques to enhance your forms with color and images, and controls to navigate through fields more efficiently.

Lesson 5: Creating Advanced Queries

Lesson 6: Customizing Forms and Using Advanced Controls

Lesson 7: Working with Subforms and Calculated Controls

LESSON 5

Creating Advanced Queries

In this lesson, you will set up and use advanced queries. You will often have more than one table in a database. Relationships are set up to tie tables together whenever possible. Often you will need to extract data from more than one table and tie the information. For instance, in the Pinnacle Pet Care database, you have a Customers table and a Pets table. These tables are related in that the customers have pets and the pets belong to the customers. The common field in both tables is Customer ID.

Using the Customer ID, you can run a query that shows the pet information and the owner's address or phone number. In this lesson, you will learn how to set up a variety of queries that select data from multiple tables. You will create calculated fields, work with statistical functions, and sort and group query results. You will also set up parameter queries that prompt users to enter a criteria range and action queries that modify tables. Any of these queries can be used as the basis for reports.

Microsoft Office Access 2003 objectives covered in this lesson

Objective Number	Skill Sets and Skills	Concept Page References	Exercise Page References
AC03S-1-5	Create and modify one-to-many relationships	122	123–124, 145–146
AC03S-1-6	Enforce referential integrity	123	125
AC03S-1-7	Create and modify queries	137–138	134–135, 137–139, 155–157
AC03S-1-10	Create reports		151–152
AC03S-3-1	Create and modify calculated fields and aggregate functions	127–128, 131	128–129, 131–132, 147–149, 153

Additional learning resources are available at labpub.com/learn/access03/

Case Study

The office staff at Pinnacle Pet Care is excited about the information they can retrieve with queries. They have asked Al Smith to include more queries. They would like to see:

- Total expenditures for each pet

- Average amount spent on cats and dogs

They would also like to be able to run reports showing pets overdue for visits so the office staff can contact the owners.

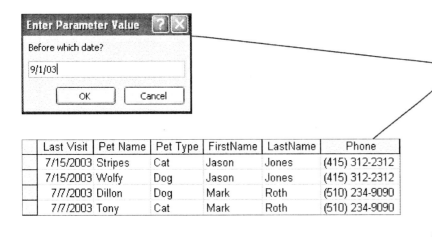

A parameter query creates a pop-up box that requires you to enter a criterion. This one asks for a date. This date is placed in the criteria of the query as <9/1/03. The query runs and produces this recordset. This recordset is used as the dataset for this report.

Last Visit	Pet Name	Pet Type	FirstName	LastName	Phone
7/15/2003	Stripes	Cat	Jason	Jones	(415) 312-2312
7/15/2003	Wolfy	Dog	Jason	Jones	(415) 312-2312
7/7/2003	Dillon	Dog	Mark	Roth	(510) 234-9090
7/7/2003	Tony	Cat	Mark	Roth	(510) 234-9090

Overdue for Visit

Last Visit	Pet Name	Pet Type	FirstName	LastName	Phone
7/7/2003	Dillon	Dog	Mark	Roth	(510) 234-9090
7/7/2003	Tony	Cat	Mark	Roth	(510) 234-9090
7/15/2003	Stripes	Cat	Jason	Jones	(415) 312-2312
7/15/2003	Wolfy	Dog	Jason	Jones	(415) 312-2312

Working with Relationships

Microsoft Office Specialist In a properly designed Access database, different types of data are stored in separate tables. For example, all customer data is stored in a Customers table and all pet data is stored in the Pets table. Storing data in separate tables is essential if you want to create a clean and flexible database system. However, it is also important to have a mechanism that allows you to "bring the data back together." For example, suppose you need to create a report that displays data from both the Customers and Pets tables. To accomplish this, you must create a relationship between the tables. Relationships determine how the records in one table are related to the records in another table. For example, each pet in the Pinnacle Pet Care database is owned by or related to a customer in the Customers table.

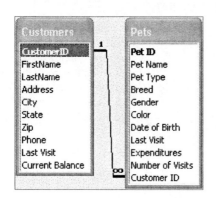

The relationship between the Customers and Pets tables is established through the Customer ID field, which appears in both tables. Each customer can have many pets. Thus, a one-to-many relationship will be established between the tables.

Establishing Table Relationships

You create relationships between tables by matching key fields in the tables. The key fields are typically the primary key in one table and a foreign key in the other table. The key fields typically have the same name, and they must have the same data type. For example, the relationship used in the preceding illustration matches the Customer ID field in the Customers table with the Customer ID field in the Pets table. The Customer ID field determines the relationship between the two tables. The primary purpose of the relationship is to synchronize the records. For example, imagine you create a report that lists each pet in the database along with the pet owner. The relationship between the Customer ID fields in both tables will ensure that the proper customer is displayed for each pet.

One-to-Many Relationships

A one-to-many relationship is common. When you define a relationship, the one-to-many is the default type. It exists between two tables when one record in a primary table relates to many records in the secondary table. For instance, one customer can have many pets but each pet can only have one customer related to it.

Many-to-Many Relationships

A many-to-many relationship exists when more than two tables are involved. The relationship is defined between a primary table, a secondary table, and a junction table. The junction table contains fields that are the primary keys in the primary and secondary tables. For instance, we have three tables: a Customers table, a Pets table, and a Visits table. Any one customer can have many pets and can have many visits to the clinic.

Enforcing Referential Integrity

When you create a relationship, Access gives you the option of enforcing referential integrity between the tables. Referential integrity prevents you from using a value in the foreign key of one table unless the same value exists as a primary key in the other table. For example, in the Pinnacle Pet Care database, referential integrity will allow you to enter a Customer ID in the Pets table only if that Customer ID is used in the Customers table. In other words, referential integrity ensures that every pet is associated with a customer. Referential integrity also prevents you from deleting a customer record from the Customers table if a record in the Pets table uses that Customer ID.

QUICK REFERENCE: ESTABLISHING RELATIONSHIPS

Task	Procedure
Establish a relationship between tables	■ Open the desired database and click the Relationships button or choose Tools→Relationships from the menu bar.
	■ Use the Show Table box to add the tables between which you wish to establish the relationship.
	■ Close the Show Table box.
	■ Drag the field that will be used to establish the relationship from the primary table to the field to which it will be linked in the secondary table.
	■ If desired, use the Join button to change the join, or relationship, type.
	■ If desired, use the Enforce Referential Integrity box to enforce referential integrity.
	■ Click the Create button to create the relationship.
	■ Close the Relationships window.

 Hands-On 5.1

Establish a Relationship and Enforce Referential Integrity

In this exercise, you will establish a relationship between the Customers and Pets tables in the Pinnacle Pet Care database.

1. Start Access and open the Pinnacle Pet Care database.

2. Click the Relationships button on the Access toolbar.
   The Relationships window will open and the Show Table box will appear.

3. Choose the Customers table and click the Add button.
   The Customers table will be added to the Relationships window.

4. Now add the Pets table to the Relationships window and close the Show Table box.

5. Follow these steps to adjust the size of the Customers and Pets field lists:

A Position the
mouse pointer
on the bottom
edge of the
Customers
field list and a
double-headed
arrow will
appear.

B Drag the
bottom edge
of the list
down until all
fields are
visible.

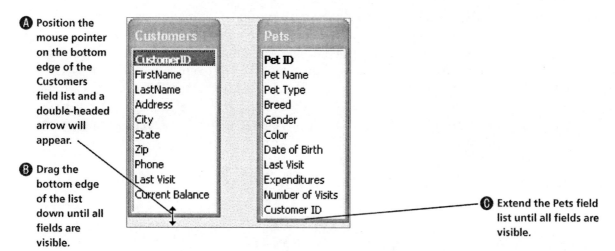

C Extend the Pets field
list until all fields are
visible.

6. Follow these steps to establish a relationship between the Customer ID fields:

A Position the mouse pointer on the
Customer ID field in the Customers
table and press and hold down the
left mouse button.

B Drag the mouse pointer until it is
over the Customer ID field in the
Pets table and a rectangular icon will
appear, as shown here.

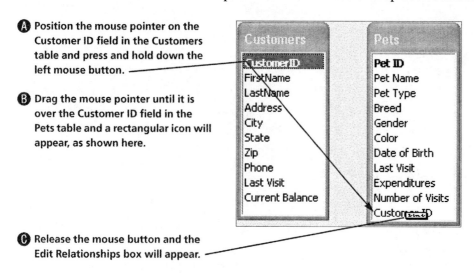

C Release the mouse button and the
Edit Relationships box will appear.

The Edit Relationships box lets you choose the desired relationship type. The default relationship type is one-to-many.

!TIP! *If you have any trouble establishing a relationship, go back to your table design and make sure the fields you are using have the same data type.*

7. Follow these steps to enforce referential integrity and to examine the options in the Edit Relationships box:

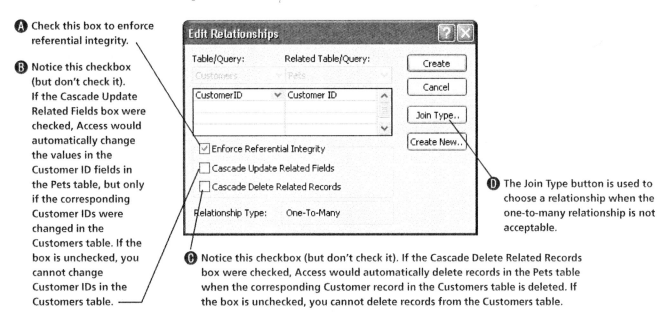

A Check this box to enforce referential integrity.

B Notice this checkbox (but don't check it). If the Cascade Update Related Fields box were checked, Access would automatically change the values in the Customer ID fields in the Pets table, but only if the corresponding Customer IDs were changed in the Customers table. If the box is unchecked, you cannot change Customer IDs in the Customers table.

D The Join Type button is used to choose a relationship when the one-to-many relationship is not acceptable.

C Notice this checkbox (but don't check it). If the Cascade Delete Related Records box were checked, Access would automatically delete records in the Pets table when the corresponding Customer record in the Customers table is deleted. If the box is unchecked, you cannot delete records from the Customers table.

8. Click the Create button to complete the relationship.
   A join line will connect the Customer ID fields in the tables.

9. Follow these steps to understand the relationship:

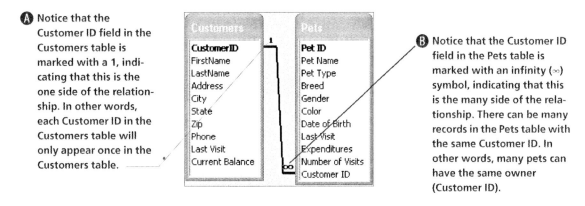

A Notice that the Customer ID field in the Customers table is marked with a 1, indicating that this is the one side of the relationship. In other words, each Customer ID in the Customers table will only appear once in the Customers table.

B Notice that the Customer ID field in the Pets table is marked with an infinity (∞) symbol, indicating that this is the many side of the relationship. There can be many records in the Pets table with the same Customer ID. In other words, many pets can have the same owner (Customer ID).

The relationship is now established and can be used to help you develop queries, forms, and reports.

10. Leave the Relationships window open and continue with the next topic.

Modifying Relationships

 You can add tables and set relationships at any time, but they are most easily added after a relationship has been established. A table is added to the relationship window by clicking the Show Table button on the toolbar then double-clicking on the table you would like to add. Once the table is added, relationships can be established between it and the other tables in the relationship window.

Hands-On 5.2   Add Tables and Relationships

In this exercise, you will add a table and establish additional relationships between the Visits table and the Pets table.

1. Click the Show Table button.

2. Add the Visits table and close the Show Table box.
   If you accidentally add a table twice, click the title bar of the extra table and press the Delete *key on the keyboard.*

3. Drag the bottom edge of the field list down until all fields are visible.

4. Position the mouse pointer over the Pet ID field on the Pets list.

5. Press the left mouse button and drag until the Pet ID field is over the Pet ID field in the Visits list.
   The Relationships window will open.

6. Check the Enforce Referential Integrity box.

7. Click the Create button to complete the relationship.
   Your relationship window should match the following illustration.

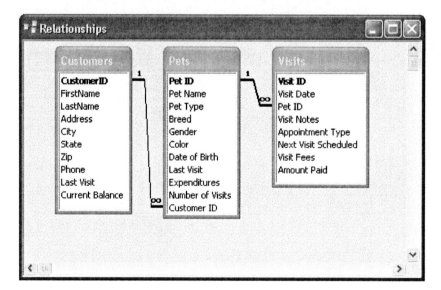

Printing Relationships

The File→Print Relationships command is available whenever the Relationships window is open. When you choose this command, Access prepares a report that displays the same relationships that are displayed in the Relationships window. You can then print the relationships by clicking the Print button on the Access toolbar.

 Hands-On 5.3 **Print Relationships**

In this exercise, you will print the relationship you created in Hands-On 5.2. The Relationships window should still be displayed.

1. Choose File→Print Relationships from the menu bar.
    Access will require a few moments to prepare the report.

2. If desired, click the Print button on the toolbar to print the report.

3. Close the report window without saving the report.

4. Close the Relationships window and click Yes if Access asks you to save the changes.

Working with Advanced Queries

Microsoft Office Specialist

So far, you have worked with simple queries. Now we will look at Access' other, more complex queries. Calculated fields, statistical functions, parameter queries, crosstab queries, and action queries are among the more advanced query tools available.

Calculated Fields

Access lets you create calculated fields within queries. Calculated fields perform calculations using values from other fields within the query or from fields in the underlying table(s). For example, in Hands-On 5.4, you will set up a new query based on the Pets table. The Pets table contains an Expenditures field that represents the total expenditures for a particular pet. The Pets table also contains a Number of Visits field that represents the total number of visits by the pet. You will create a calculated field within the query named Expenditures Per Visit, which will be calculated as the Expenditures divided by the Number of Visits. The following illustration shows the Design grid with the Pet Name and Pet Type fields and the Expenditures Per Visit calculated field.

Field:	Pet Name	Pet Type	Expenditures Per Vis
Table:	Pets	Pets	
Sort:			
Show:	☑	☑	☑
Criteria:			

Expenditures Per Visit is a calculated field. It is too wide to be completely visible in the cell. The complete content of the cell is Expenditures Per Visit: [Expenditures]/[Number of Visits].

The following illustration outlines the syntax that must be used with calculated fields.

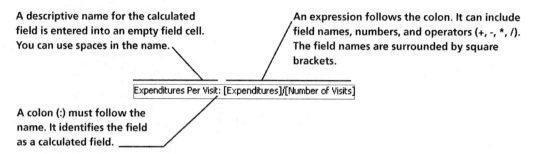

A descriptive name for the calculated field is entered into an empty field cell. You can use spaces in the name.

An expression follows the colon. It can include field names, numbers, and operators (+, -, *, /). The field names are surrounded by square brackets.

Expenditures Per Visit: [Expenditures]/[Number of Visits]

A colon (:) must follow the name. It identifies the field as a calculated field.

The Zoom Box

Calculated field expressions can be quite long and complex. For this reason, you may not be able to see the entire expression as you enter it in a cell. Fortunately, Access provides a Zoom command that displays a Zoom box. When you enter the desired expression into the Zoom box, you can see the entire expression as it is entered. In Hands-On 5.4, you will use the Zoom box to enter an expression. You display the Zoom box by right-clicking the cell where the expression will be entered and choosing Zoom from the pop-up menu.

 Hands-On 5.4 **Create a Calculated Field**

In this exercise, you will set up a query with a calculated field.

1. Click the Queries button on the Objects bar.

2. Create a new query in Design view and add the Pets table to it.

3. Close the Show Tables dialog box.

4. Add the Pet Name and Pet Type fields to the Design grid.

5. Follow these steps to display the Zoom box:

Ⓐ Click in the empty field cell to the right of Pet Type.

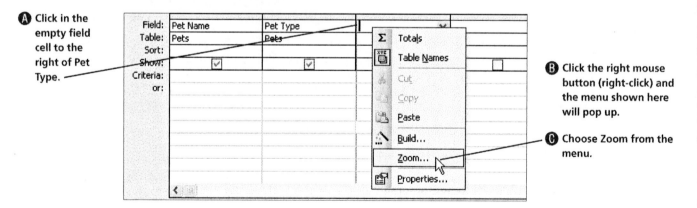

Ⓑ Click the right mouse button (right-click) and the menu shown here will pop up.

Ⓒ Choose Zoom from the menu.

6. Enter the calculated field expression shown in the following illustration into the Zoom box.

Make sure you enter the expression exactly as shown. In particular, make sure you use a colon (:) and not a semicolon (;), correctly spell the field names, use the correct open and closed brackets [ ], and use the forward slash (/) to represent division. Access is lenient when it comes to spaces, so you can omit the spaces that come after the colon and before and after the forward slash if you desire. Access is not lenient when it comes to the spelling of field names. They must be spelled exactly as they appear in the field name—including spaces.

7. Click OK to insert the expression in the field.

8. Make sure the syntax is correct as shown in the preceding illustration. If necessary, you can edit the expression within the cell or redisplay the Zoom dialog box and make any necessary changes.

9. Click the Run ⏺ button to produce the recordset shown to the right.

The numbers shown in the Expenditures Per Visit field represent the average expenditure for each pet on each visit. Notice the excessive number of decimal places that are displayed in the calculated field. In Hands-On 5.5, you will reduce the number of displayed decimal places by changing one of the properties of the Expenditures Per Visit field.

Pet Name	Pet Type	Expenditures P
Max	Cat	72.5275
Stripes	Cat	50
Tony	Cat	24.1666666667
Wolfy	Dog	64.2857142857
Dillon	Dog	50.1833333333
Fetch	Dog	115
Ben	Dog	160
Spike	Dog	74.1666666667
Bugs	Rabbit	150.125

10. Switch to Design 📐 view and continue with the next topic.

Modifying Query Properties

The Properties 🔲 button on the Access toolbar displays the Properties dialog box. You use this dialog box to change the properties of any Access object, including fields within queries. Properties can affect the appearance and format of objects. For example, in Hands-On 5.5, you will set the Format property of the Expenditures Per Visit calculated field to Currency. The Currency format will reduce the number of displayed decimal places in the recordset.

 **Hands-On 5.5   Set the Format Property**

In this exercise, you will format the results of the calculation to show as currency. The Query Design grid should be displayed from the previous exercise.

1. Click in the Expenditures Per Visit box then click the Properties [⬜] button on the toolbar.
   The Field Properties dialog box will appear.

2. Follow these steps to set the format of this field to Currency:

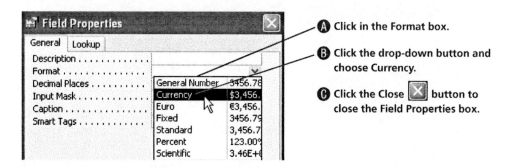

Ⓐ Click in the Format box.

Ⓑ Click the drop-down button and choose Currency.

Ⓒ Click the Close [⬜] button to close the Field Properties box.

When the query is run, the Currency format will display a dollar sign and two decimal places in the Expenditures Per Visit field.

3. Click the Run [!] button.
   The numbers in the Expenditures Per Visit field should now be formatted with the Currency format. Note the dollar sign and two decimal places.

4. Switch to Design [⬜] view.

Insert a Criterion

5. Click in the Criteria box for the Pet Type field and type **dog**.

Field:	Pet Name	Pet Type	Expenditures Per Vis
Table:	Pets	Pets	
Sort:			
Show:	☑	☑	☑
Criteria:		dog ◄	

6. Click the Run [!] button.
   Pet Name, Pet Type, and Expenditures Per Visit will be displayed for records where the Pet Type is Dog. As you can see, Access allows you to combine criteria, calculated fields, and other parameters within a query.

7. Choose File→Close to close the query and save it as **Expenditures Per Visit**.

Statistical Functions

Access provides built-in statistical functions for calculating statistical information within a query. The built-in statistical functions include Sum (summation), Avg (average), Min (minimum), Max (maximum), Count, Var (variance), First, and Last. Adding statistical functions is simple and can enhance your queries. For example, you can use the Avg function to compute the average expenditures on pets, or you can use the Count function to track the number of dogs that attend the Pinnacle Pet Care clinic.

The Total Row

To use the statistical functions, you must first click the Totals button to display a Total row in the Query Design grid. Once the Total row is displayed, you can choose statistical function(s) for the desired field(s) in the query. Queries that use statistical functions will sometimes have just one or two fields.

Statistical functions are entered in the
Total row of the Query Design grid.

 Hands-On 5.6   **Use Statistical Functions**

In this exercise, you will use a statistical function to show the average of pet expenditures.

1. Set up a new query in Design view and add the Pets table to it.

2. Close the Show Tables dialog box.

3. Add the Expenditures field to the Design grid.

4. Click the Totals Σ button on the toolbar and a Total row will appear below the Table row.
   The Total row lets you choose statistical functions and set grouping for fields. You will learn about grouping in the Using Grouping with Statistical Functions section on page 133.

5. Follow these steps to choose the Avg function for the Expenditures field:
   When you run the query, Access will determine the average expenditure for all pets. Access will display a single cell in the recordset containing the result of the average calculation.

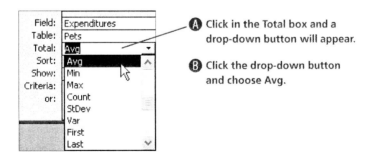

Ⓐ Click in the Total box and a drop-down button will appear.

Ⓑ Click the drop-down button and choose Avg.

6. Click the Run ▣ button.
   The result should be $551.29. In other words, each pet has been responsible for an average of $551.29 in revenue.

7. Switch to Design ▣ view and click in the Total box that currently contains the Avg function.

8. Click the drop-down button, scroll to the top of the list, and choose Sum.

9. Run ▣ the query again. This time the result should be $4,961.60.
   This number represents the summation of the expenditures for all pets.

10. Switch to Design ▣ view and continue with the next topic.

Using Criteria with Statistical Functions

You can combine criteria with statistical functions to refine your statistical calculations. For example, imagine you want to determine the total expenditures for dogs at Pinnacle Pet Care. The answer can be found by summing the expenditures of all records where the Pet Type is dog. The following illustration shows how this is expressed in the Design grid.

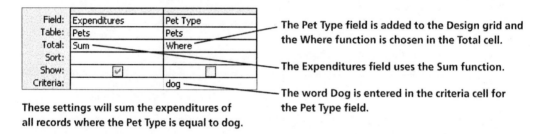

Field:	Expenditures	Pet Type
Table:	Pets	Pets
Total:	Sum	Where
Sort:		
Show:	☑	☐
Criteria:		dog

The Pet Type field is added to the Design grid and the Where function is chosen in the Total cell.

The Expenditures field uses the Sum function.

The word Dog is entered in the criteria cell for the Pet Type field.

These settings will sum the expenditures of all records where the Pet Type is equal to dog.

 Hands-On 5.7   Use Criteria with Statistical Functions

In this exercise, you will use a statistical function to show the average expenditures of just the dogs.

1. Double-click the Pet Type field on the Pets field list to add it to the Design grid.

2. Follow these steps to specify criteria for the Pet Type field:

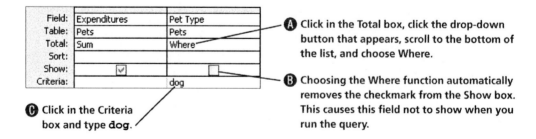

Field:	Expenditures	Pet Type
Table:	Pets	Pets
Total:	Sum	Where
Sort:		
Show:	☑	☐
Criteria:		dog

Ⓐ Click in the Total box, click the drop-down button that appears, scroll to the bottom of the list, and choose Where.

Ⓑ Choosing the Where function automatically removes the checkmark from the Show box. This causes this field not to show when you run the query.

Ⓒ Click in the Criteria box and type **dog**.

3. Run the query. The result should be $2,315.55.
   This number represents the total expenditures on dogs.

4. Switch back to Design view and continue with the next topic.

Using Grouping with Statistical Functions

The Total row in the Design grid has a Group By option that can be used in conjunction with statistical functions. If you choose Group By for a field and run the query, Access will group all records that have the same value in the Group By field. For example, if the Pet Type field is set to Group By, all records with Cat as the Pet Type will be in one group. Likewise, all records with a Pet Type of Dog will be in another group. If you are also performing a statistical calculation, it will be performed on each group. For example, if you use the Sum function to calculate the expenditures for the groups just mentioned, the total expenditures for cats will be calculated, as will the total expenditures for dogs.

Hands-On 5.8 **Use the Group By Setting**

In this exercise, you will group the averages of pet expenditures by pet type.

1. Follow these steps to set grouping for the Pet Type field:

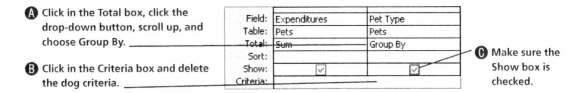

Ⓐ Click in the Total box, click the drop-down button, scroll up, and choose Group By.

Ⓑ Click in the Criteria box and delete the dog criteria.

Field:	Expenditures	Pet Type
Table:	Pets	Pets
Total:	Sum	Group By
Sort:		
Show:	☑	☑
Criteria:		

Ⓒ Make sure the Show box is checked.

2. Run the query to produce the following recordset.

SumOfExpendit	Pet Type
$2,045.55	Cat
$2,315.55	Dog
$600.50	Rabbit

The recordset displays the total expenditures for each pet type.

3. Save the query as **Expenditures by Pet Type** then close it.

Basing a Query on Multiple Tables

You can use a query to select data from multiple tables. However, it is important that a relationship be established between the tables so the records remain synchronized. You can establish temporary relationships within the query window. However, these temporary relationships can only be used within the query. The best to way to create relationships is in the Relationships window. You used the Relationships window to create a relationship between the Customers and Pets tables in Hands-On 5.1. Relationships established within the Relationships window are then used in forms, queries, reports, and other objects dependent on the relationship.

Al Smith wants a report that lists pets and the corresponding customer information based on the last visit date of the pet. This way, his staff can contact customers if the pet has not visited the clinic recently. In this exercise, you will create a query that selects the appropriate data from the Pets and Customers tables. In Hands-On 5.11, you will use the query as the basis for a report.

The Pinnacle Pet Care database should still be open.

1. Click the Queries button on the Objects bar.

2. Double-click the Create Query in Design View option.
   The Design grid will appear and the Show Table box will be displayed.

3. Add both the Customers and Pets tables to the query window and close the Show Table box.

4. Maximize 🔲 the query window.

5. Follow these steps to size the window objects and to examine the relationship:

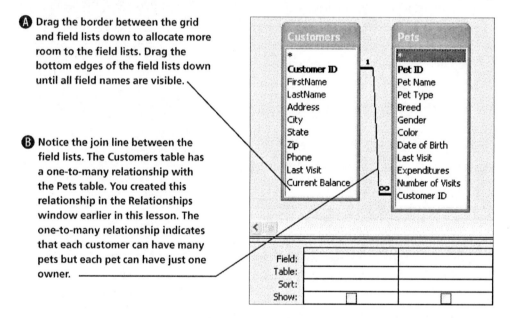

Ⓐ Drag the border between the grid and field lists down to allocate more room to the field lists. Drag the bottom edges of the field lists down until all field names are visible.

Ⓑ Notice the join line between the field lists. The Customers table has a one-to-many relationship with the Pets table. You created this relationship in the Relationships window earlier in this lesson. The one-to-many relationship indicates that each customer can have many pets but each pet can have just one owner.

6. Double-click the Last Visit field on the Pets field list (not the Customers field list) to add that field to the Design grid.

7. Now add the Pet Name and Pet Type fields from the Pets field list to the Design grid.

8. Add the Firstname, Lastname, and Phone fields from the Customers field list to the Design grid. The Design grid should contain the field names shown here.

Field:	Last Visit	Pet Name	Pet Type	FirstName	LastName	Phone
Table:	Pets	Pets	Pets	Customers	Customers	Customers
Sort:						
Show:	☑	☑	☑	☑	☑	☑
Criteria:						
or:						

9. Set the Sort key for the Last Visit field to Descending.
When you run the query, the pet with the longest absence will appear first.

Last Visit	Pet Name	Pet Type	FirstName	LastName	Phone
10/8/2003	Spike	Dog	Jacob	Samuels	(404) 367-8002
10/8/2003	Ben	Dog	Jacob	Samuels	(404) 367-8002
9/10/2003	Fetch	Dog	Jason	Jones	(415) 312-2312
9/7/2003	Bugs	Rabbit	Tony	Simpson	(510) 238-2233
9/7/2003	Max	Cat	Tony	Simpson	(510) 238-2233
7/15/2003	Wolfy	Dog	Jason	Jones	(415) 312-2312
7/15/2003	Stripes	Cat	Jason	Jones	(415) 312-2312
7/7/2003	Dillon	Dog	Mark	Roth	(510) 234-9090
7/7/2003	Tony	Cat	Mark	Roth	(510) 234-9090

10. Click the Run 🔘 button to produce the query results shown to the right.
Notice that the query selects every record in the Pets table and displays the corresponding customer information. The relationship ensures that the correct customer information is associated with each pet.

11. Click the Design 🔘 view button on the Access toolbar.
In Hands-On 5.10, you will add a pop-up box to the query. The pop-up box will prompt you to enter a date.

Parameter Queries

A parameter query displays a pop-up dialog box that prompts the user for the criteria each time it is run. You can design a parameter query to prompt for one value, or for several. For example, if you design it to prompt for two dates, Access will retrieve all data with values between those two dates. Parameter queries are useful when a query is run often but uses slightly different criteria each time. You can build a form or report on a parameter query so the user will have to provide the criteria to produce the desired recordset.

In Hands-On 5.10, you will add a criterion to the Last Visit field in the query you just created. The criterion will display a pop-up box prompting you to enter a date. The only records that will be selected when you run the query are those with a Last Visit date prior to the date you specify. This technique is quite useful because the pop-up box is also displayed when reports that are based on the query are run.

Syntax for Parameter Query Criteria

The following illustration shows the criterion that you will enter into the Last Visit field and the pop-up box that will appear. Take a few moments to study the criterion syntax.

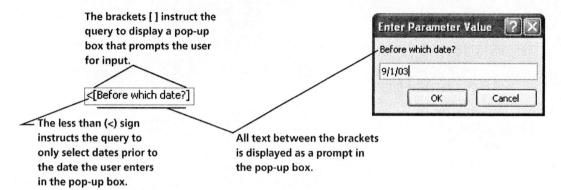

The brackets [ ] instruct the query to display a pop-up box that prompts the user for input.

<[Before which date?]

The less than (<) sign instructs the query to only select dates prior to the date the user enters in the pop-up box.

All text between the brackets is displayed as a prompt in the pop-up box.

 Hands-On 5.10   **Create a Pop-Up Box in a Parameter Query**

In this exercise, you will add a criterion to the Last Visit field in that will display a pop-up box prompting you to enter a date. The Query Design grid should still be displayed.

1. Click in the Criteria box for the Last Visit field and enter the criteria shown here. Begin with a less than (<) sign and enclose the text in square [] brackets.

Field:	Last Visit	Pet Name	Pet Type
Table:	Pets	Pets	Pets
Sort:	Descending		
Show:	✓	✓	✓
Criteria:	<[Before which date?]		
or:			

2. Run ⚡ the query and the pop up box will appear.

3. Type **9/1/03** in the box and click OK.

   The recordset shown to the right should appear. Notice that only pets whose last visit was prior to 9/1/03 were selected.

Last Visit	Pet Name	Pet Type	FirstName	LastName	Phone
7/15/2003	Stripes	Cat	Jason	Jones	(415) 312-2312
7/15/2003	Wolfy	Dog	Jason	Jones	(415) 312-2312
7/7/2003	Dillon	Dog	Mark	Roth	(510) 234-9090
7/7/2003	Tony	Cat	Mark	Roth	(510) 234-9090

4. Choose File→Close to close the query window.

5. Click Yes when Access asks if you want to save the query.

6. Enter the name **Overdue for Visit** in the Save As box and click OK.

Query Wizards

The 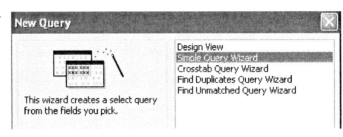 button on the Access Database toolbar displays the New Query box. The New Query box provides access to four different query wizards. The query wizards can be used as an alternative to Query Design view to set up new queries. The following table describes the various query wizards.

Query Wizards

Wizard Type	Description
Simple Query Wizard	This wizard is used to set up simple, select queries. It is usually easiest to use Query Design view to set up select queries.
Crosstab Query Wizard	This wizard creates crosstab queries used to display data in a spreadsheet-like format, with one type of data presented down the left side and the other presented across the top of the datasheet.
Find Duplicates Query Wizard	This wizard is used to locate records with duplicate field values in a table or query.
Find Unmatched Query Wizard	This wizard locates records in one table that have no related records in another table.

 Hands-On 5.11   **Use the Simple Query Wizard**

In this exercise, you will set up a simple query using the Simple Query Wizard.

1. Make sure the Queries button is chosen on the Objects bar then click the New button on the Access Database toolbar.

2. Choose Simple Query Wizard and click OK.
The select query you will create will list customer names, telephone numbers, and last visit dates.

3. Choose the Customers table from the Tables/Queries list.

4. Choose the Firstname field and click the Add Field > button to add it to the Selected Fields list.

5. Now add the Lastname, Phone, and Last Visit fields to the Selected Fields list.

6. Click the Next button to display the second and final wizard screen.

7. Type **Last Visit Date** as the query name and click the Finish button.
The recordset will be displayed. As you can see, it would be just as easy to set up simple queries in Query Design view. However, you may want to use the wizard to help set up queries and modify them in Design view.

8. Close the query.

Crosstab Queries

Microsoft Office
Specialist
A crosstab query groups, summarizes, and arranges a recordset to make it more easily visible and with less data repetition. A crosstab query uses both row headings and column headings, displaying data in a spreadsheet format and making it easier to read and analyze. Crosstab queries calculate a Sum, Average, Count, or other type of statistic for data grouped by at least two categories. A crosstab query uses at least three fields: one as the column heading, one as the row heading, and one on which to run the statistical function. In Hands-On 5.12, you will use Pet types as the row heading and Breeds as the column heading. The statistical function will be run on Expenditures so you will get an average of the expenditures for each pet type as well as the averages of expenditures for each breed.

Pet types are listed as row headings.

Breeds are the column headings.

Pet Type	Total Of Expend	Chow	German Shephe	Jack	Mutt	Terrier	Tortoise shell	Unknown
Cat	$681.85						$450.00	$797.78
Dog	$463.11	$890.00	$397.50		$150.55	$480.00		
Rabbit	$600.50			$600.50				

The total column displays an average of expenditures for the Pet Type. We will choose the average function when we set up the query. The spreadsheet also shows averages of expenditures for each breed.

 Hands-On 5.12   Use the Query Wizard to Create a Crosstab Query

In this exercise you will set up a crosstab query based on the Pets table. This query will show the averages of expenditures by pet type.

1. Make sure the Queries button is chosen on the Objects bar then click the [New] button on the Access Database toolbar.

2. Choose Crosstab Query Wizard and click OK.

3. Make sure the Tables option button is selected then click Table:Pets on which to base your crosstab query and click Next.

4. Choose the Pet type field, click the Add Field [>] button to add Pet Type to the Selected Fields list, and click Next
    This will be our row heading.

5. Now choose the Breed field and click Next.
    This will be our column heading.

6. Follow these steps to choose the function of this crosstab query:

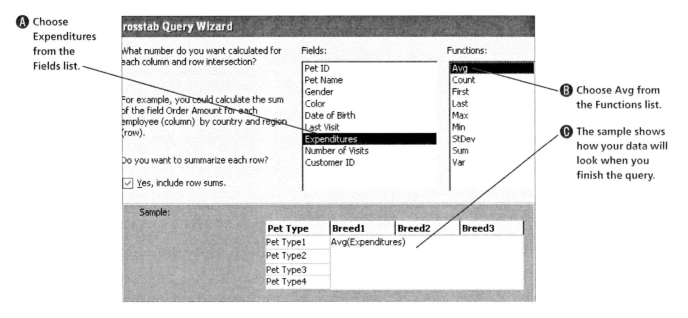

A Choose Expenditures from the Fields list.

B Choose Avg from the Functions list.

C The sample shows how your data will look when you finish the query.

7. Click the Next button to display the final wizard screen.

8. Click Finish to accept Pets_Crosstab as the query name.

9. Follow these steps to examine the recordset:

A Notice that the second column calculates an average of the expenditures for each Pet Type (Cat, Dog, Rabbit).

	Pet Type	Total Of Expend	Chow	German Shephe	Jack	Mutt	Terrier	Tortoise shell	Unknown
	Cat	$681.85						$450.00	$797.78
	Dog	$463.11	$890.00	$397.50		$150.55	$480.00		
▶	Rabbit	$600.50			$600.50				

B Notice that the remaining columns display the average expenditures for each Breed.

With a regular query you could produce a recordset that shows the average for each Breed or an average for each Pet Type, but not both at the same time. A crosstab query will allow you to see both of those averages at the same time.

10. Close the query, saving if necessary.

Action Queries

An action query usually makes changes to one or more tables. Action queries can create a new table or change an existing table by adding data to it, deleting data from it, or updating it. Because an action query is so powerful—and actually changes table data—you should consider backing up your data before running one. You can back up your tables by making copies of the ones you will be using in the query, or you can back up the entire database. The four types of action queries are:

- Delete—Deletes a group of records from one or more tables
- Update—Makes changes to records in one or more tables
- Append—Adds records to the end of one or more tables
- Make Table—Creates a new table from the records in one or more tables

To begin an action query, create a new query, or open an existing query in Design view and choose the Query Type button on the Query Design toolbar. You can use the Query Design grid to specify how you would like the data to be modified.

QUICK REFERENCE: USING ACTION QUERIES

Task	Procedure
Use an action query	■ Create a new query or open the desired query in Design view.
	■ Click the Query Type button on the Query Design toolbar.
	■ Choose one of the four action queries.
	■ Set the criteria in the Design grid.
	■ Click the Datasheet view button if you want to view your results before running the query.
	■ Click the Run button on the Query Design toolbar.
	■ Accept or reject the message in the alert box. Rejecting the message cancels the action.

 Hands-On 5.13   **Create a Make-Table Action Query**

In this exercise, you will use the July Visits query to make a new table that will contain the records for pets that haven't been to the clinic since September 30th, 2003.

1. Make sure the Queries button is chosen on the Objects bar.

2. Choose the July Visits query and click the Design ![design icon] view button.
   This query uses the Pets table.

3. Click the Query Type 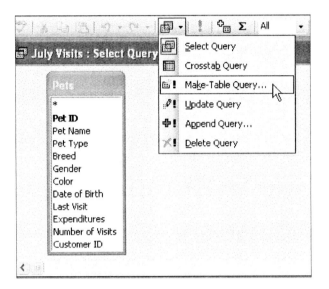 button and choose Make-Table Query, as shown here.

4. Type **Archived Pet Visits** in the Table Name box and click OK.
This will create a new table to hold the records that match the criteria you will enter next.

5. Click in the criteria box for Last Visit, remove the criteria, and type **<9/30/03**.

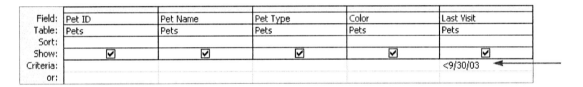

6. Click the Datasheet ⬜ view button to view your results.

7. Click the Design ⬛ view button to go back to the Design grid.

8. Click the Run ⚡ button to run the make-table query. You will see the following alert box.

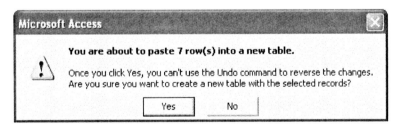

This query will copy the records that fit the criteria, adding them to the new Archived Pet Visits table. This alert box lets you know how many records will be copied.

9. Click the Yes button on the alert box to accept the action. Close the query without saving the changes.

10. Click the Tables button on the Objects bar and notice the new Archived Pet Visits table just created.

11. Double-click the Archived Pet Visits table and notice that the records all have Last Visit dates before 9/30/2003.

12. Close the Archived Pet Visits table and double-click the Pets table.
   The make-table query copies the records that match the criteria from the Pets table and adds them to the new Archived Pet Visits table.

13. Close the Pets table.

Basing Reports on Queries

You can use a query as the basis for a report. This can be useful if you want the report to display data from multiple tables, or if you want the report to display only certain records from the tables. You can use the Report Wizard to create a report based on a query. The first screen in the Report Wizard lets you choose a table or query as the basis for the report.

 Hands-On 5.14 Create a Report Based on a Query

In this exercise, you will create a report based on a query.

1. Click the Reports button on the Objects bar in the database window.

2. Double-click the Create Report by Using Wizard option.

3. Follow these steps to choose the desired query and fields for the report:

Ⓐ Choose Query: Overdue for Visit from the Tables/Queries list.

Ⓑ Click the Add All Fields button to choose all fields.

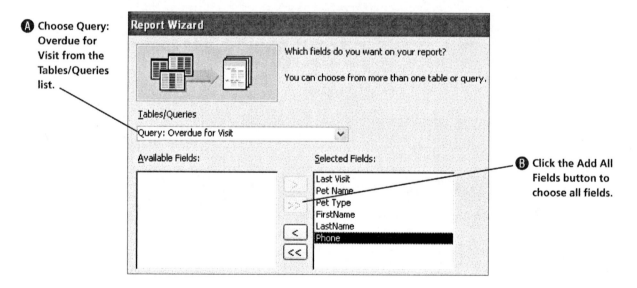

4. Click the Next button.

5. Make sure the By Pets option is chosen in the second wizard screen and click Next.
   The By Pets option will base the report on the records in the Pets table. The corresponding customer information will be displayed with the pet information.

6. Click Next two more times and the Layout and Orientation options will appear.

7. Make sure the layout is set to Tabular and set the orientation to Landscape.
   Landscape orientation will set the report horizontally on the page.

8. Click Next and choose the Corporate report style.

9. Click Next and type **Overdue for Visit** as the report name in the last wizard screen.

10. Click the Finish button.
    Access will display the pop-up box prompting you to enter a date. The pop-up box appears because the report is based on the Overdue for Visit query, which contains the criterion that generates the parameter query.

11. Enter the date **9/1/03** and click OK.
    The following report should be generated.

Overdue for Visit

Last Visit	Pet Name	Pet Type	FirstName	LastName	Phone
7/15/2003	Stripes	Cat	Jason	Jones	(415) 312-2312
7/15/2003	Wolfy	Dog	Jason	Jones	(415) 312-2312
7/7/2003	Tony	Cat	Mark	Roth	(510) 234-9090
7/7/2003	Dillon	Dog	Mark	Roth	(510) 234-9090

12. Close the report then close the Pinnacle Pet Care database.

Concepts Review

True/False Questions

1. Access lets you enforce referential integrity when creating relationships. TRUE FALSE

2. The Zoom box is used to print recordsets. TRUE FALSE

3. The outcome of an action query can easily be undone. TRUE FALSE

4. Built-in statistical functions include Sum and Avg. TRUE FALSE

5. The primary purpose of the relationship is to relate a field from one table to a field TRUE FALSE
   of the same data type in another table.

6. Once you define a relationship, you cannot change it. TRUE FALSE

7. A parameter query is useful when the criteria are slightly different each time the TRUE FALSE
   query is run.

8. To find the largest value in a recordset, you use the Count function. TRUE FALSE

9. Queries can select data from multiple tables. TRUE FALSE

10. Pop-up boxes that prompt the user for input are created by placing criteria in the TRUE FALSE
    Query Design grid.

Multiple Choice Questions

1. Which of the following buttons is used to display the Relationships window?
   a.
   b.
   c.
   d.

2. Which pair of symbols should surround the desired phrase you want displayed in a pop-up dialog box of a parameter query?
   a. ( )
   b. [ ]
   c. < >
   d. { }

3. Which symbol(s) must be placed after the field name when creating a calculated field?
   a. :
   b. ;
   c. ( )
   d. [ ]

4. An update query _____.
   a. deletes a group of records
   b. makes a new table
   c. makes changes to a group of records
   d. moves records from one table to another

Skill Builders

Establish Relationships

In this exercise, you will establish a relationship between tables in the Tropical Getaways database.

1. Open the Tropical Getaways database.

2. Click the Relationships ⬚ button on the Access toolbar.

3. Choose Customers in the Show Table box and click the Add button.
   The Customers table will be added to the Relationships window.

4. Add the Trips table and the Custom Packages table to the Relationships window then close the Show Table box.

5. If necessary, drag the bottom edges of the Customers and Trips field lists down until all field names are visible.

6. Follow these steps to establish a relationship between the Customer ID fields:

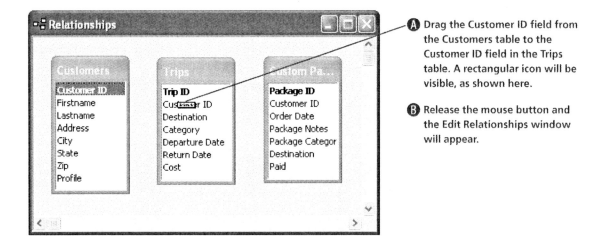

Ⓐ Drag the Customer ID field from the Customers table to the Customer ID field in the Trips table. A rectangular icon will be visible, as shown here.

Ⓑ Release the mouse button and the Edit Relationships window will appear.

7. Follow these steps to enforce referential integrity:

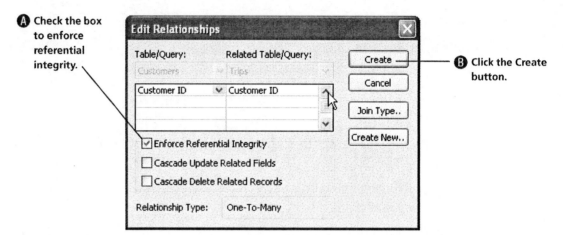

A Check the box to enforce referential integrity.

B Click the Create button.

Referential integrity will require that every record in the Trips table has a corresponding Customer ID in the Customers table.

8. Follow these steps to establish a relationship between the Custom Packages table and the Customers table:

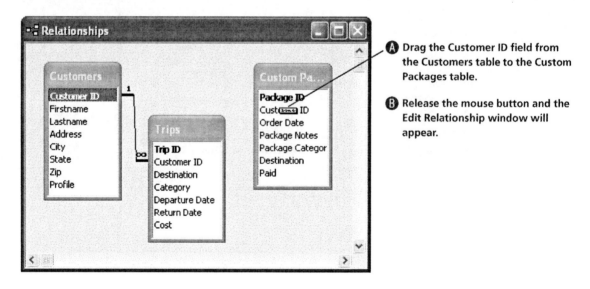

A Drag the Customer ID field from the Customers table to the Custom Packages table.

B Release the mouse button and the Edit Relationship window will appear.

9. Check the Enforce Referential Integrity box in the Edit Relationships window, and then click OK.

10. Click the Close [X] button at the top-right corner of the Relationships window.

11. Click Yes when Access asks if you want to save the changes to the relationship.
The relationship is now established and can be used to help you develop queries, forms, and reports.

Nest Calculated Fields

In this exercise, you will use calculated fields in the Tropical Getaways database.

1. Set up a new query in Design view and add the Trips table to it.

2. Close the Show Tables dialog box.

3. Add the Destination, Category, and Cost fields to the Design grid.

4. Set the Sort box for the Category field to Ascending.

5. Follow these steps to display the Zoom box for a new calculated field:

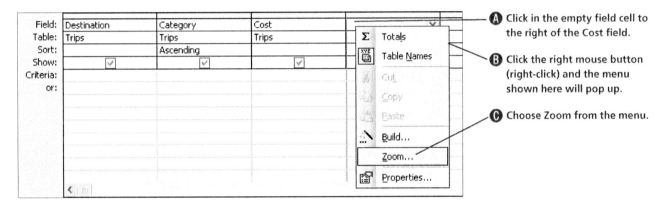

Ⓐ Click in the empty field cell to the right of the Cost field.

Ⓑ Click the right mouse button (right-click) and the menu shown here will pop up.

Ⓒ Choose Zoom from the menu.

6. Enter the following expression into the Zoom box. Make sure you type the expression exactly as shown, including the colon after the word Duration.

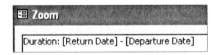

When you run the query, this expression will calculate the duration of each trip. You can perform calculations using dates in Access and Excel.

7. Click OK. Check your new calculated field for errors and correct any errors you find.

8. Run the query to produce the following recordset.

Destination	Category	Cost	Duration
Baja California	Adventu	$2,900.00	10
Rocky Mountains	Adventu	$2,190.00	16
Swiss Alps	Adventu	$3,500.00	26
Baja California	Adventu	$1,750.00	5
Amazon Jungle Trek	Adventu	$7,765.00	38
Kenyan Safari	Adventu	$6,600.00	30
Hawaii	Family	$5,300.00	8
Hawaii	Family	$3,250.00	5
Orlando	Family	$3,400.00	6
Hawaii	Leisure	$4,500.00	10
Swiss Alps	Leisure	$5,980.00	18
Caribbean Cruise	Leisure	$2,390.00	9

In the next few steps, you will add another field that calculates the average daily cost of each trip. The average daily cost will be calculated as the Cost divided by Duration. This new calculated field will use the Duration calculated field. Access allows you to nest calculated fields in this manner.

9. Switch to Design view.

10. Right-click in the empty cell to the right of the Duration cell and choose Zoom from the pop-up menu.

11. Enter the following expression into the Zoom box:

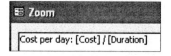

Cost per day: [Cost] / [Duration]

12. Click OK to insert the Cost Per Day calculated field into the cell.

13. Run the query to produce the following recordset.

Destination	Category	Cost	Duration	Cost per day
Baja California	Adventu	$2,900.00	10	290
Rocky Mountains	Adventu	$2,190.00	16	136.875
Swiss Alps	Adventu	$3,500.00	26	134.615384615
Baja California	Adventu	$1,750.00	5	350
Amazon Jungle Trek	Adventu	$7,765.00	38	204.342105263
Kenyan Safari	Adventu	$6,600.00	30	220
Hawaii	Family	$5,300.00	8	662.5
Hawaii	Family	$3,250.00	5	650
Orlando	Family	$3,400.00	6	566.666666667
Hawaii	Leisure	$4,500.00	10	450
Swiss Alps	Leisure	$5,980.00	18	332.222222222
Caribbean Cruise	Leisure	$2,390.00	9	265.555555556

Notice that the Cost Per Day numbers are not formatted with the Currency format. You will correct this in the next few steps.

14. Switch to Design view.

15. Right-click on the Cost Per Day field and choose Properties from the pop-up menu.

16. Click in the Format box, click the drop-down button, and choose Currency.

17. Close ☒ the Properties box.

18. Run the query. The Cost Per Day numbers should be formatted as Currency with two decimal places.

19. Close the query, and save it as **Cost Per Day**.

Skill Builder 5.3   Create a Query

In this exercise, you will set up a new query in the Tropical Getaways database. The query will select data from both the Customers and Trips tables.

1. Click the Queries button on the Objects bar in the database window.

2. Double-click the Create Query in Design view option.

3. Add both the Customers and Trips tables to the query window then close the Show Table box.

4. Maximize ▣ the Query window and adjust the size of the window objects until all field names in the Customers and Trips field lists are visible.

5. Add the Firstname and Lastname fields from the Customers field list to the Design grid.

6. Add the Destination, Category, Departure Date, Return Date, and Cost fields from the Trips field list to the grid.
   At this point, the Design grid should contain the fields shown here.

Field:	Firstname	Lastname	Destination	Category	Departure Date	Return Date	Cost
Table:	Customers	Customers	Trips	Trips	Trips	Trips	Trips
Sort:							
Show:	☑	☑	☑	☑	☑	☑	☑
Criteria:							

7. Click the Run ▣ button and the following query results should appear.

Firstname	Lastname	Destination	Category	Departure Date	Return Date	Cost
Debbie	Thomas	Kenyan Safari	Adventu	8/5/2004	9/4/2004	$6,600.00
Debbie	Thomas	Amazon Jungle Trek	Adventu	8/7/2004	9/14/2004	$7,765.00
Debbie	Thomas	Baja California	Adventu	4/17/2004	4/22/2004	$1,750.00
Debbie	Thomas	Swiss Alps	Adventu	10/10/2004	11/5/2004	$3,500.00
Wilma	Boyd	Caribbean Cruise	Leisure	9/19/2004	9/28/2004	$2,390.00
Wilma	Boyd	Swiss Alps	Leisure	5/5/2004	5/23/2004	$5,980.00
Alice	Simpson	Orlando	Family	3/4/2004	3/10/2004	$3,400.00
Alice	Simpson	Hawaii	Family	7/15/2004	7/20/2004	$3,250.00
Rita	Bailey	Rocky Mountains	Adventu	5/6/2004	5/22/2004	$2,190.00
Rita	Bailey	Baja California	Adventu	8/8/2004	8/18/2004	$2,900.00
Cheryl	DeMarco	Hawaii	Leisure	2/5/2004	2/15/2004	$4,500.00
Victor	Thomas	Hawaii	Family	3/7/2004	3/15/2004	$5,300.00

Notice that the query selects every record in the Trips table and displays the corresponding customer information.

8. Click the Design ▣ view button to return to Design view.
In the next step, you will enter a criterion in the Category criteria box. The criterion will display a pop-up box that prompts the user to enter a category. The query will only select trips with the same category type entered in the pop-up box.

9. Type the criterion **[Enter a Category]** into the Category criteria box.

Field:	Firstname	Lastname	Destination	Category
Table:	Customers	Customers	Trips	Trips
Sort:				
Show:	☑	☑	☑	☑
Criteria:				[Enter a Category]
or:				

When you run the query, the square brackets surrounding the Enter a Category phrase will instruct Access to display a pop-up box. Access will only select records where the Category is the same as the category you enter in the box. What you enter in the pop-up box must be spelled exactly as the data in the table or your recordset will be blank. If this happens, close and run the query again, making sure your spelling is correct.

10. Run ▣ the query and the pop-up box will appear.

11. Type **Adventure** in the box and click OK.
The following query results will appear. Notice that only trips with a Category of Adventure have been selected.

	Firstname	Lastname	Destination	Category	Departure Date	Return Date	Cost
	Debbie	Thomas	Kenyan Safari	Adventure	8/5/2004	9/4/2004	$6,600.00
	Debbie	Thomas	Amazon Jungle Trek	Adventure	8/7/2004	9/14/2004	$7,765.00
	Debbie	Thomas	Baja California	Adventure	4/17/2004	4/22/2004	$1,750.00
	Debbie	Thomas	Swiss Alps	Adventure	10/10/2004	11/5/2004	$3,500.00
	Rita	Bailey	Rocky Mountains	Adventure	5/6/2004	5/22/2004	$2,190.00
	Rita	Bailey	Baja California	Adventure	8/8/2004	8/18/2004	$2,900.00

12. Choose File→Close from the menu bar to close the query window.

13. Click Yes when Access asks if you want to save the query.

14. Type the name **Trips-Specific Category** in the Save As box and click OK.
    In Skill Builder 5.4, you will use the query as the basis for a report.

Skill Builder 5.4   **Create a Report Based on a Query**

In this exercise, you will make a copy of the Trips-Specific Category query. You will modify the new query and create a new report based on the query.

1. Click the Queries button on the Objects bar in the database window.

2. Choose the Trips–Specific Category query and click the Copy 📋 button on the Access toolbar.

3. Click the Paste 📋 button and the Paste As box will appear.

4. Type the name **Trips–Cost Greater Than** and click OK.

5. Choose the Trips–Cost Greater Than query and click the ✓ Design button.

6. Select [Enter a Category] in the Category criteria box and tap the Delete key to remove it.

7. Enter the criterion **>[Cost Greater Than]** in the Criteria box of the Cost field, as shown here.

Field:	Firstname	Lastname	Destination	Category	Departure Date	Return Date	Cost
Table:	Customers	Customers	Trips	Trips	Trips	Trips	Trips
Sort:							
Show:	✓	✓	✓	✓	✓	✓	✓
Criteria:							>[Cost Greater Than]
or:							

When the query is run, this criterion will display a pop-up box that prompts you to enter a cost. Only records where the cost is greater than what you enter will be selected.

8. Run [!] the query and the pop-up box will appear.

9. Type **4000** in the box and click OK.
   The following query results will appear. Notice that only trips with a cost greater than 4000 have been selected.

Firstname	Lastname	Destination	Category	Departure Date	Return Date	Cost
Debbie	Thomas	Kenyan Safari	Adventure	8/5/2004	9/4/2004	$6,600.00
Debbie	Thomas	Amazon Jungle Trek	Adventure	8/7/2004	9/14/2004	$7,765.00
Wilma	Boyd	Swiss Alps	Leisure	5/5/2004	5/23/2004	$5,980.00
Cheryl	DeMarco	Hawaii	Leisure	2/5/2004	2/15/2004	$4,500.00
Victor	Thomas	Hawaii	Family	3/7/2004	3/15/2004	$5,300.00

10. Choose File→Close from the menu bar and choose Yes to save the query changes.

11. Now use the Report Wizard and Choose the Trips–Cost Greater Than query.
    Use the fields shown in the illustration under step 16.

12. Choose the By Trips option when Access asks how you want to view the data in the second wizard screen.

13. Make sure the layout is set to Tabular and set the orientation to Landscape.

14. Click Next and choose the Soft Gray report style.

15. Click Next and enter the title **Trips by Cost**.

16. Click the Finish button.
    The following example shows the report when a cost of 4,000 is entered in the pop-up box.

Trips by Cost

Firstname	Lastname	Destination	Category	arture Date	tetum Date	Cost
Debbie	Thomas	Kenyan Safari	Adventure	8/5/2004	9/4/2004	$6,600.00
Debbie	Thomas	Amazon Jungle Trek	Adventure	8/7/2004	9/14/2004	$7,765.00
Wilma	Boyd	Swiss Alps	Leisure	5/5/2004	5/23/2004	$5,980.00
Cheryl	DeMarco	Hawaii	Leisure	2/5/2004	2/15/2004	$4,500.00
Victor	Thomas	Hawaii	Family	3/7/2004	3/15/2004	$5,300.00

17. Close the report when you have finished and save any changes.

Skill Builder 5.5   Use Statistical Functions

In this exercise, you will create a query to perform statistical calculations in the Tropical Getaways database.

1. Create a new query that uses the Trips table.

2. Add the Cost field to the Design grid.

3. Display the Total row by clicking the Totals Σ button on the toolbar.

4. Choose the Avg function in the Total box, as shown here.

Field:	Cost
Table:	Trips
Total:	Avg
Sort:	
Show:	☑
Criteria:	

5. Run the query. The average cost of a trip should be calculated as $4,127.08.

6. Switch to Design view.

7. Add the Category field to the Design grid.
   The Total box will automatically be set to Group By. When you run the query, the Avg function in the Cost field will calculate the average cost for each Category of Trip.

Field:	Cost	Category
Table:	Trips	Trips
Total:	Avg	Group By
Sort:		
Show:	☑	☑
Criteria:		

8. Run the query to produce the following recordset.

	AvgOfCost	Category
	$4,117.50	Adventu
	$3,983.33	Family
▶	$4,290.00	Leisure

9. Close the query and save it as **Cost by Category**.

Skill Builder 5.6   Create an Update Query

In this exercise, you will create an action query that increases the cost of the trips by 10%.

1. Click the Queries button on the Objects bar in the database window.

2. Double-click the Create Query in Design view option.

3. Add the Trips table to the query window and close the Show Table box.

4. Close the Show Table box and add the Cost field.

5. Click the Query Type [icon] ▾ button and choose Update Query.

6. Follow these steps to add 10% to the cost of the trips:

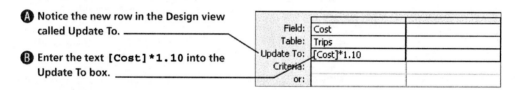

Ⓐ Notice the new row in the Design view called Update To. ─────

Ⓑ Enter the text [Cost]*1.10 into the Update To box. ─────

Field:	Cost	
Table:	Trips	
Update To:	[Cost]*1.10	
Criteria:		
or:		

This will increase the cost by 10%.

7. Run the query and you will see the following alert box.

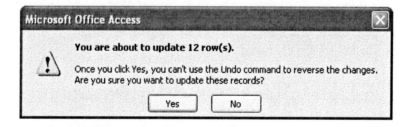

Microsoft Office Access

⚠ **You are about to update 12 row(s).**

Once you click Yes, you can't use the Undo command to reverse the changes. Are you sure you want to update these records?

[Yes]   [No]

If you click Yes, you will update 12 records in the Trips table, increasing of the cost by 10%.

8. Click Yes to accept the action.

9. Click Datasheet view to see the changes in the trip costs.

Cost
$7,260.00
$8,541.50
$1,925.00
$3,850.00
$2,409.00
$3,190.00
$3,740.00
$3,575.00
$5,830.00
$2,629.00
$6,578.00
$4,950.00

This action changes the Costs in the Trips table.

10. Close the query without saving it.
You rarely save an update query. This is mainly because each time someone double-clicks the query to open it, the query will run and update the records.

Skill Builder 5.7   Create a Crosstab Query

In this exercise, you will create a crosstab query based on the Cost Per Day query to show the average cost per day for each Category of Trip as well as the average cost per day for each destination.

1. Make sure the Queries button is chosen on the Objects bar and click the [New] button.

2. Choose the Crosstab Query Wizard and click OK.

3. Make sure the Queries option button is selected, choose the Cost Per Day query, and click Next.

4. Add the Destination field to be the row heading and click Next.

5. Make sure you have the Category field as the column heading and click Next.

6. Click the Cost Per Day field and the Avg function. Your Query Wizard screen should match the following illustration.

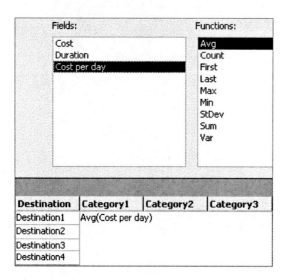

7. Click the Next button then click Finish to accept Cost per day_Crosstab as the query name. Study the following illustration to understand the query:

Destination	Total Of Cost pe	Adventure	Family	Leisure
Amazon Jungle Trek	224.776315789	224.776315789		
Baja California	352	352		
Caribbean Cruise	292.111111111			292.111111111
Hawaii	646.25		721.875	495
Kenyan Safari	242	242		
Orlando	623.333333333		623.333333333	
Rocky Mountains	150.5625	150.5625		
Swiss Alps	256.760683761	148.076923077		365.444444444

The query shows the average cost per day for each destination.

It also shows the average cost per day for each category.

8. Click the Design view button to format these numbers.
You will change the format of the numbers to currency.

9. Right-click the Cost Per Day field and choose Properties.

10. Choose Currency from the Format box.

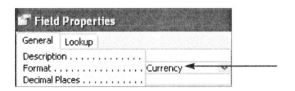

11. Format the Total Of Cost Per Day: Cost Per Day field to Currency.

12. Switch to Datasheet view to see the results.

Destination	Total Of Cost pe	Adventure	Family	Leisure
▶ Amazon Jungle Trek	$224.78	$224.78		
Baja California	$352.00	$352.00		
Caribbean Cruise	$292.11			$292.11
Hawaii	$646.25		$721.88	$495.00
Kenyan Safari	$242.00	$242.00		
Orlando	$623.33		$623.33	
Rocky Mountains	$150.56	$150.56		
Swiss Alps	$256.76	$148.08		$365.44

13. Save and close the query.

14. Close the Tropical Getaways database.

Assessments

Assessment 5.1   Create a Parameter Query and Report

In this exercise, you will create a parameter query and a report based on that query to show specific models of cars in the Classic Cars database.

1. Open the Classic Cars database.

2. Create a one-to-many relationship between the Collector ID fields in the Collectors and Cars tables, as shown to the right. Enforce referential integrity then close and save the relationship.

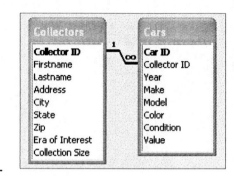

3. Create a parameter query that extracts data from the Cars and Collectors tables. The query should display a pop-up box that requests the user to enter a model. Once a model is entered, the query should only select records containing the model the user enters. The pop-up box should display the phrase **Enter a Model**. The following example assumes that the model name Corvette has been entered into the pop-up box. Assign the name **Specific Model** to the query.

	Year	Make	Model	Color	Condition	Value	Firstname	Lastname
	58	Chevrolet	Corvette	Red and white	Mint	$65,000.00	Cindy	Johnson
	62	Chevrolet	Corvette	Blue	Excellent	$30,000.00	Tammy	Olson
	58	Chevrolet	Corvette	Black	Excellent	$35,000.00	Bob	Barker
	57	Chevrolet	Corvette	Red	Excellent	$42,000.00	Bob	Barker

4. Create a report based on the Specific Model query and that produces the results shown in the following illustration. The report should display the data in Landscape mode. Use the Compact report style. Assign the name **Specific Model** to the report.

Specific Model

Year	Make	Model	Color	Condition	Value	Firstname	Lastname
58	Chevrolet	Corvette	Red and white	Mint	$65,000.00	Cindy	Johnson
62	Chevrolet	Corvette	Blue	Excellent	$30,000.00	Tammy	Olson
58	Chevrolet	Corvette	Black	Excellent	$35,000.00	Bob	Barker
57	Chevrolet	Corvette	Red	Excellent	$42,000.00	Bob	Barker

5. Save and close all objects when you have finished.

Use Statistical Functions

In this exercise, you will create a query that finds the average value of the models of cars in this table.

1. Create a new query and add the Cars table to the query.

2. Set up the query to produce the following recordset. Notice that the Model field and the Value field have been added and the average value of each model group has been calculated. The query groups the records on the Model field then calculates the average on the Value field. The query also sorts the records by Value, with the largest values appearing first.

Model	AvgOfValue
Model A	$75,000.00
Corvette	$43,000.00
Tudor	$35,000.00
Camaro	$27,500.00
Thunderbird	$20,000.00
Custom Eigh	$15,000.00
▶ Sedan	$4,900.00

3. Run the query then close and save it as **Average Value of Model Groups**.

Create an Action Query

The staff of Classic Cars has decided to add a five dollar charge to all entrance fees to cover mailings and other costs. In this exercise, you will create an update query that adds the five dollars to the existing entrance fees.

1. Create a new query using the Events table.

2. Add the Entrance Fee field to the Design grid.

3. Create an Update query, as shown here.

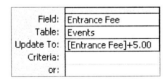

Field:	Entrance Fee
Table:	Events
Update To:	[Entrance Fee]+5.00
Criteria:	
or:	

4. Run the query, choosing Yes in the Alert box.

5. Switch to Datasheet view to see the results.

	Entrance Fee
	$55.00
	$30.00
	$15.00

The entrance fee was increased by five dollars in each record. This updates the Events table with these new values.

6. Close the query without saving it.

7. Close the Classic Cars database when you have finished then exit from Access.

Critical Thinking

Critical Thinking 5.1   Use Calculated Fields in Queries

It is important to Linda Holmes to know how much potential commission she can earn for each of her listings. Open the Holmestead Realty database and follow these guidelines to set up a query that calculates the commission for each listing:

- Use the Listings table as the basis for the query.

- Include the Seller ID, MLS #, Street #, Address, Price, and Commission Rate fields in the query. All of these fields should appear in the recordset in the same order shown here except for the Commission Rate field. Do not include the Commission Rate field in the recordset (but do include it in the query).

- Create a calculated field named **Commission** that multiplies Price by Commission Rate.

- Format the Commission calculated field with the Currency format.

- Sort the recordset in ascending order based on the Seller ID field.

- Save the completed query as **Commission**.

Critical Thinking 5.2   Use Statistical Functions in Queries

The broker in charge at Holmestead Realty wants to know the average price of all Linda's listings. Follow these guidelines to set up the query:

- Create a select query that calculates the average price of Linda's listings.

- Add a criterion that calculates the average price for Ranch style houses only.

- Save the query as **Average Price-Ranch**.

Linda's broker would also like to see the total dollar value of listings grouped by commission rate. Follow these guidelines to set up the query:

- The recordset should display a sum of the Price field.

- The commission rates should be grouped and displayed in the recordset next to the sums.

- Save your completed query as **Sum by Commission Rate**.

Critical Thinking 5.3   Create a Parameter Query

Each month, Linda would like to contact sellers who have listings that will expire that month. Follow these guidelines to set up a select query that extracts data from both the Listings and Contacts tables:

- Use the following fields in the query. The Listings table fields should appear first, followed by the Contacts table fields. All fields should follow the order shown in the table.

Listings Table	Contacts Table
Street #	FirstName
Address	LastName
Expiration Date	SpouseName
	Phone

- Enter the expression **Between [Enter First Date] and [Enter Second Date]** in the criteria box of the Expiration Date field. When the query is run, this expression will display a pop-up box that allows users to enter a date range. Any listings with an expiration date within the range you specify will appear in the recordset.

- Save the query as **Expires this Month**.

- Check the expiration dates in the Listings table then run the query using a date range that will display one or more expiration dates.

- Close Access when you are finished.

LESSON 6

Customizing Forms and Using Advanced Controls

Forms are an important part of any Access database because they are the primary objects through which users interact with a database. The Forms Wizard can be used to set up forms that display data from more than one table. In addition, Access's Form Design view allows you to customize forms to meet your needs. Access provides a variety of form controls to assist users with data entry. These controls include Yes/No checkboxes, combo boxes, and memo boxes. In this lesson, you will customize a form by adding new controls and enhancing the appearance of the form.

Microsoft Office Access 2003 objectives covered in this lesson

Objective Number	Skill Sets and Skills	Concept Page References	Exercise Page References
AC03S-1-8	Create forms		202–203
AC03S-1-9	Add and modify form controls and properties	184, 186, 188	185, 188–190
AC03S-3-2	Modify form layout	177–180	177–178, 181–184, 206–209

Additional learning resources are available at labpub.com/learn/access03/

Case Study

Al Smith wants a form to track pet visits to Pinnacle Pet Care. The form needs to display data from two tables—the Pets table and Visits table. Al wants the form to be easy to use and designed to prevent data entry errors. In this lesson, you will set up the form that Al requests. The form will contain new types of controls, including checkboxes, combo boxes, and a memo field. You will create a header with formatted text and a picture to enhance the appearance of the form. The form you will create is shown in the following illustration. It also defines several of the controls you will set up.

Combo boxes
let you enter
data by
choosing
options from
drop-down
lists.

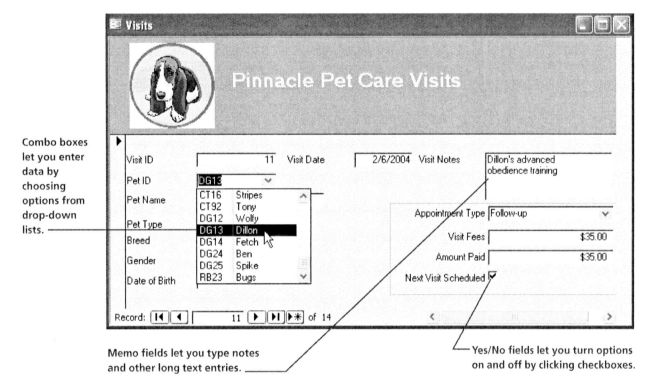

Memo fields let you type notes
and other long text entries.

Yes/No fields let you turn options
on and off by clicking checkboxes.

Customizing Forms in Design View

The Design view button appears on the left end of the Access toolbar when a form is open in Forms view. You must switch to Design view to modify forms. Forms and other database objects can contain controls. For example, look at the Pets form in Design view. You should be able to see text boxes for the Pet Name, Pet Type, and other fields. Notice the descriptive labels to the left of the text boxes. All of these objects are types of controls. In Design view, you can add, delete, move, and modify controls. This gives you the ability to customize forms and other database objects.

Designing Forms

In the first few exercises in this lesson, you will use a wizard to create a form. The first form will include the Pets table and the Customers table. You can use fields from multiple tables in a form, provided that a relationship has been established between the tables. In Lesson 5, Creating Advanced Queries, you established the relationship. The relationship keeps the tables synchronized so the form always displays the appropriate records.

Hands-On 6.1 Create a Form Using Fields from Two Tables

In this exercise, you will create a form that combines fields from both the Pets table and the Customers table.

1. Start Access and open the Pinnacle Pet Care database.

2. Click the Forms button on the Objects bar.

3. Double-click the Create Form by Using Wizard option.
   In the next few steps, you will choose the fields that will be displayed on the form. It is important that you choose the fields in the order specified because it determines the order in which the fields are placed on the form. Doing this will make it easy for you to modify the form later in this lesson.

4. Follow these steps to add fields from the Pets table:

A Choose the Pets table from the Tables/Queries list. You can base a form on one or more tables, or even on a query.

B Click the Add All Fields button to move all fields to the Selected Fields list.

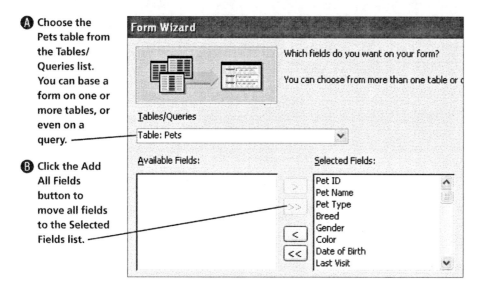

5. Follow these steps to add three fields from the Customers table:

Ⓐ Choose the Customers table from the Tables/Queries list.

Ⓑ Add the FirstName, LastName, and Phone fields to the Selected Fields list by choosing them one at a time and clicking the Add Field button. The fields will appear at the bottom of the Selected Fields list.

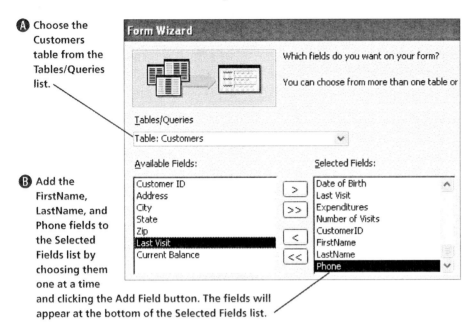

6. Click the Next button to display the next wizard screen.

7. Make sure the View Your Data option is set to By Pets.
The By Pets option instructs Access to base the form on the Pets table. The customer data for a particular pet is then displayed on the form with the pet data.

8. Click the Next button.

9. Make sure the Columnar option is chosen in the next screen and click Next.

10. Choose Standard as the style and click Next.

11. Type the name **New Pets** as the title and click the Finish button.
Access will create the form shown to the right; however, your form may have a slightly different layout. The relationship between the Customer ID fields in the Pets and Customers tables will ensure that Access displays the appropriate customer for each pet.

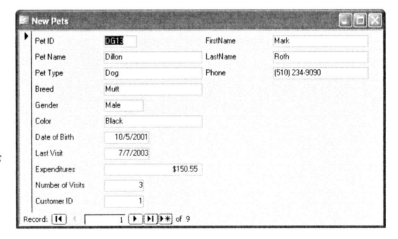

12. Leave the form open.

Inserting Hyperlinks

FROM THE KEYBOARD

Ctrl+K to display Insert Hyperlink box

Hyperlinks can be used to open forms and reports, to navigate to Web pages, and to prepare email messages for delivery. When you click a hyperlink, Access opens the form, report, or Web page to which the hyperlink points. You must switch to Design view to insert hyperlinks. Once in Design view, choose Insert→Hyperlink or click the Insert Hyperlink button on the Access toolbar. The following illustration describes the options available in the Insert Hyperlink box.

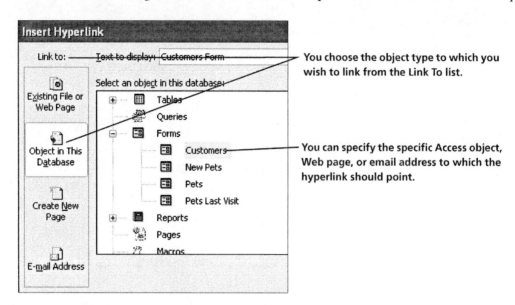

 Hands-On 6.2   Insert a Hyperlink

In this exercise, you will switch to Design view and insert a hyperlink in the New Pets form. The hyperlink will be used to open the Customers form. This will allow you to open the Customers form directly from the New Pets form. The New Pets form should still be open.

1. Click the Design ✎ view button on the left end of the Access toolbar.
   Access will display the form in Design view, and a variety of dialog boxes and/or toolbars may appear.

2. Click the Insert Hyperlink 🔗 button on the Access toolbar.

3. Follow these steps to choose the Customers form as the desired hyperlink destination:

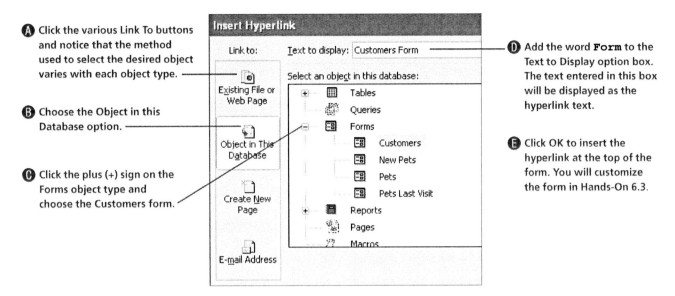

A Click the various Link To buttons and notice that the method used to select the desired object varies with each object type.

B Choose the Object in this Database option.

C Click the plus (+) sign on the Forms object type and choose the Customers form.

D Add the word **Form** to the Text to Display option box. The text entered in this box will be displayed as the hyperlink text.

E Click OK to insert the hyperlink at the top of the form. You will customize the form in Hands-On 6.3.

Move the Hyperlink

4. Follow these steps to explore the Design view window and adjust the size of the window:

A Notice the Form Header and Detail bars at the top and the Form Footer bar at the bottom of the window. A form is divided into these three sections. You can place controls in any of them. In this lesson, you will only work with the Detail section.

B Notice that this hyperlink is selected. A selected control has sizing handles on its edges. You can move and size a control once it is selected.

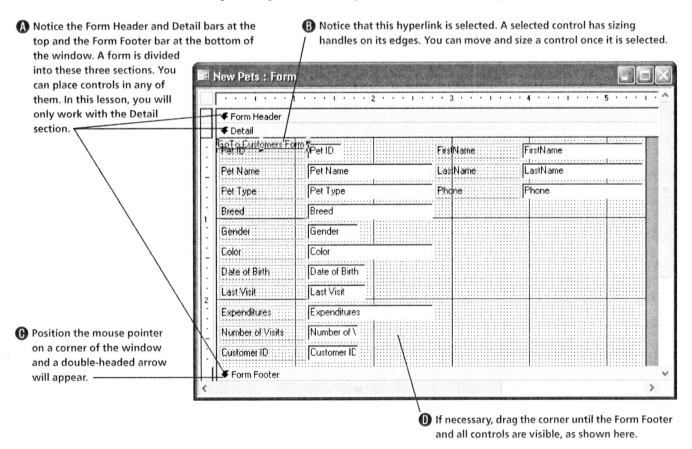

C Position the mouse pointer on a corner of the window and a double-headed arrow will appear.

D If necessary, drag the corner until the Form Footer and all controls are visible, as shown here.

5. Follow these steps to practice selecting controls:

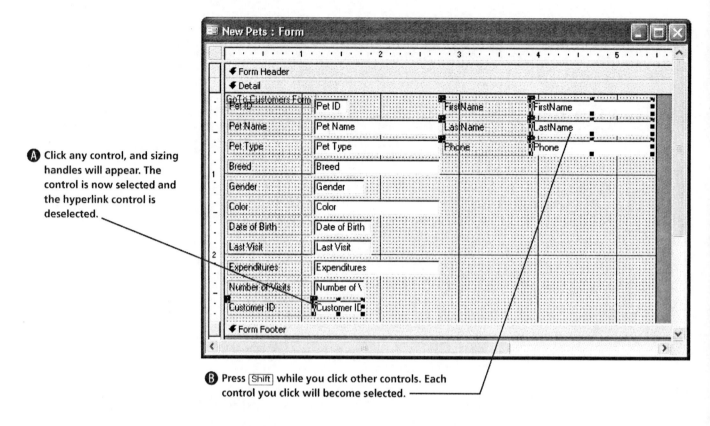

A Click any control, and sizing handles will appear. The control is now selected and the hyperlink control is deselected.

B Press `Shift` while you click other controls. Each control you click will become selected.

6. Follow these steps to select and move the hyperlink control:

A Release the `Shift` key and click the hyperlink control.

B Position the mouse pointer on the bottom edge of the control, and a hand icon will appear.

C Drag the hyperlink to below the Phone control.

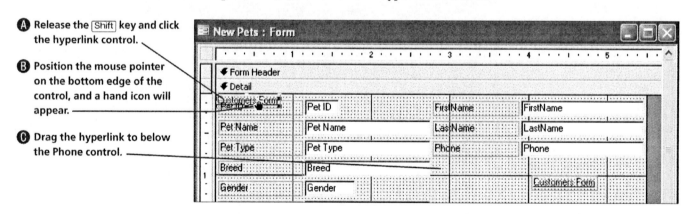

Modify the Hyperlink Text

In the next few steps, you will modify the hyperlink text. The hyperlink will continue to point to the Customers form but it will have a more descriptive name.

7. Follow these steps to modify the hyperlink text:

Ⓐ Make sure the hyperlink is selected then click anywhere on the hyperlink text. The flashing insertion point will be positioned on the hyperlink text.

Ⓑ Use the left arrow ← key to position the insertion point at the beginning of the word Customers.

Ⓒ Type **Go To**, tap the Spacebar, and click anywhere outside the hyperlink to complete the editing process.

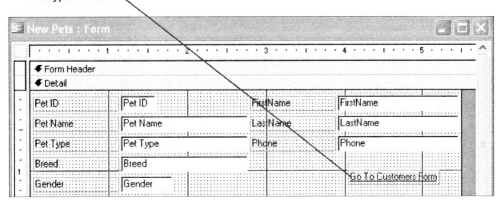

8. Your completed form should match the following example. If necessary, move the other controls on the form until your form has this layout.

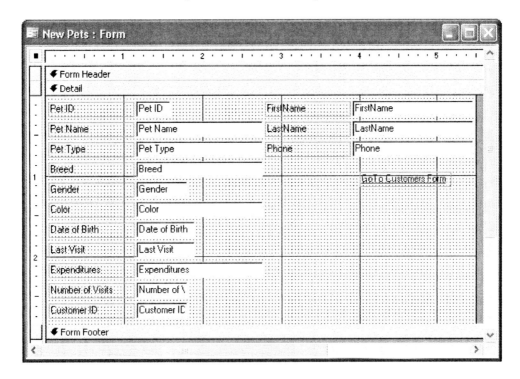

Use the Hyperlink

9. Click the Forms ⊞ view button on the left end of the Access toolbar.
You must be in Forms view to use a form.

10. Follow these steps to use the hyperlink:

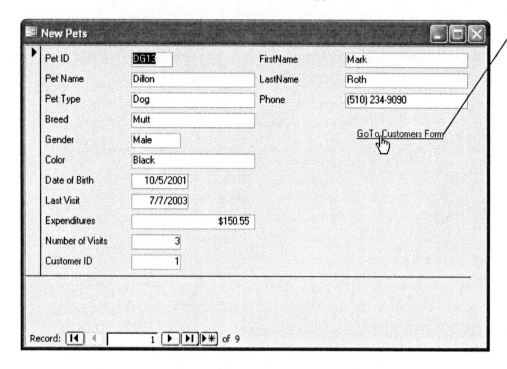

A Position the mouse pointer on the hyperlink, and it will have a pointing finger shape. The mouse pointer always has this shape when it is positioned on a hyperlink.

B Click the hyperlink, and the Customers form will appear. Notice that the New Pets form remains open.

C Feel free to browse through the records in the Customers form. Since both forms are open, you can easily move between them by clicking on the desired form.

Insert a Hyperlink in the Customers Form

11. Make sure the Customers form is active.
You can determine that a form is active because the title bar at the top of the form will have a blue color.

12. Click the Design ✎ view button on the left end of the Access toolbar.

13. Click the Insert Hyperlink 🔗 button.

14. Choose New Pets from the list of forms and click OK.

15. Follow these steps to change the dimensions of the form and to move the hyperlink:

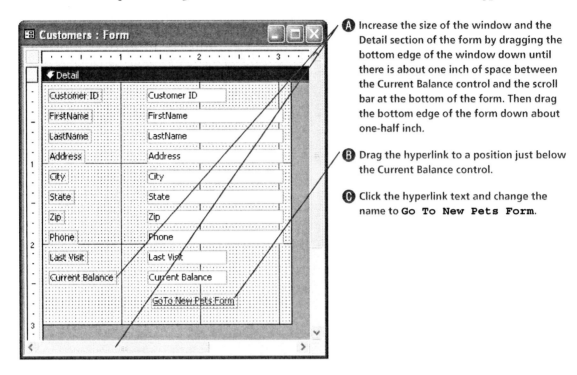

A Increase the size of the window and the Detail section of the form by dragging the bottom edge of the window down until there is about one inch of space between the Current Balance control and the scroll bar at the bottom of the form. Then drag the bottom edge of the form down about one-half inch.

B Drag the hyperlink to a position just below the Current Balance control.

C Click the hyperlink text and change the name to `Go To New Pets Form`.

Use the Hyperlink

16. Click the Forms ▦ view button on the left end of the Access toolbar.

17. Click the Go To New Pets Form hyperlink.
The New Pets form was already open, so it will simply move in front of the Customers form. If the form had been closed, the hyperlink would have opened it.

18. Notice that the hyperlink in the New Pets form now has a different color.
This is because the hyperlink has been used. Hyperlinks change color once they have been clicked.

19. Now continue with the next topic, in which you will learn how to restrict data entry in controls.

Restricting Data Entry in Forms

The New Pets form contains controls that display data from fields in the Pets and Customers tables. This form will be used to enter and edit data in the Pets table. However, the customer information is displayed on the form for informational purposes only. In other words, you won't use this form to edit the customer name and telephone number. The customer data will be entered and edited using the Customers form. For this reason, you will prevent data entry from occurring in the customer information controls on the New Pets form. You will accomplish this by setting the Enabled property for the customer controls.

The Enabled and Locked Properties

The Properties button on the Access toolbar displays the Properties box. The Data tab in the Properties box can be used to set the Enabled and Locked properties. The Enabled and Locked properties are described in the following table.

Property	Description
Enabled	The Enabled property determines whether or not a control can have the focus. Having the focus allows you to position the insertion point in the control. If the Enabled property is set to No, the control appears dimmed on the form and you cannot position the insertion point in the control.
Locked	The Locked property determines whether or not data entry can occur in a control. If the Locked property is set to No, data cannot be entered in the control.

Hands-On 6.3   Restrict Data Entry in Form Controls

In this exercise, you will format the properties of the customer information fields so users cannot enter data or edit these fields.

1. In the New Pets form, click the Design view button.

2. Follow these steps to select the customer information controls:

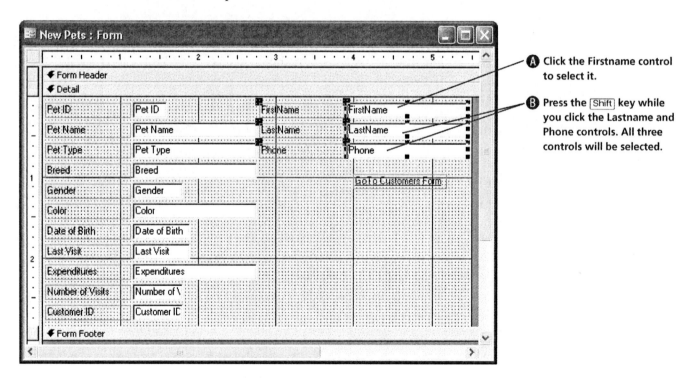

3. If necessary, click the Properties button on the Access toolbar to display the Properties box. The Properties button will be highlighted when the box is displayed.

4. Follow these steps to set the Enabled property to No for the three controls:

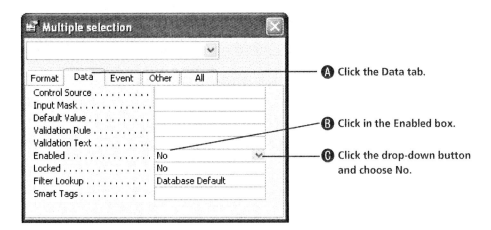

A Click the Data tab.

B Click in the Enabled box.

C Click the drop-down button and choose No.

5. Close the Properties box.
   Notice that the customer information controls now appear dimmed on the form.

6. Click the Forms ⊞ view button on the left end of the toolbar.

7. Try clicking the dimmed customer information controls and notice that the insertion point cannot be positioned in them.
   Setting the Enabled property to No prevents the controls from receiving the focus.

8. Browse through the records on the New Pets form, and the correct customer information will continue to be displayed for each pet.

9. Close both the New Pets and Customers forms by clicking the Close ⊠ buttons at the top-right corner of the forms. Choose Yes for both forms when Access asks if you want to save the changes.
   The Access database window should be displayed.

Designing the Visits Form

The second form you will create will be one that tracks pet visits to the Pinnacle Pet Care clinic. This form will include fields from both the Pets and Visits tables. In Lesson 5, Creating Advanced Queries, you set up a one-to-many relationship between these two tables. Each pet will be allowed to have many visits to the clinic but each visit will be associated with just one pet.

 Hands-On 6.4   **Set Up the Visits Form**

In this exercise, you will create the Visits form using the wizard.

1. Click the Forms button on the Objects bar.

2. Double-click the Create Form by Using Wizard option.
   In the next few steps, you will choose the fields that will be displayed on the form. It is important that you choose the fields in the order specified. This will make it easy for you to modify the form later.

3. Follow these steps to add the fields from the Visits table:

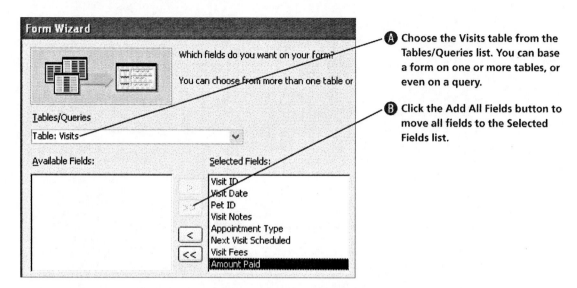

A Choose the Visits table from the Tables/Queries list. You can base a form on one or more tables, or even on a query.

B Click the Add All Fields button to move all fields to the Selected Fields list.

4. Follow these steps to add five fields from the Pets table:

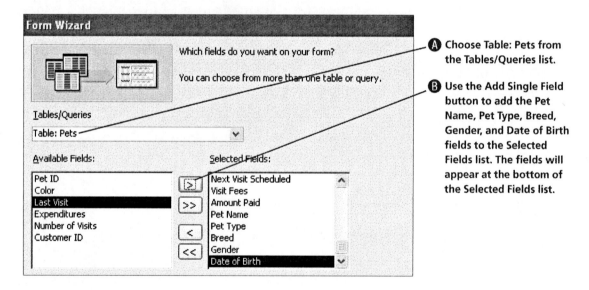

A Choose Table: Pets from the Tables/Queries list.

B Use the Add Single Field button to add the Pet Name, Pet Type, Breed, Gender, and Date of Birth fields to the Selected Fields list. The fields will appear at the bottom of the Selected Fields list.

5. Click the Next button to display the next wizard screen.

6. Make sure the View Your Data option is set to By Visits and click Next.
The By Visits option instructs Access to base the form on the Visits table. The pet data for a particular pet is then displayed on the form along with the visit data.

7. Make sure the Columnar option is chosen in the next screen and click Next.

8. Choose Standard as the style and click Next.

9. Choose the Modify the Form's Design option in the last wizard screen and click the Finish button.

Access will create the form and display it in Design view as shown in the following illustration; however, your form may have a different layout. Notice that the form contains a checkbox for the Next Visit Scheduled field. If you create a form with the Form Wizard, Access creates a checkbox for fields that have a Yes/No data type. A Yes/No field in the underlying table is set to Yes when a box is checked and No when the box is unchecked. Also notice the large field for Visit Notes. Access creates a large block for fields that have a Memo data type. This way, you can type large amounts of text in the field. You will make extensive modifications to the Visits form as you progress through this lesson.

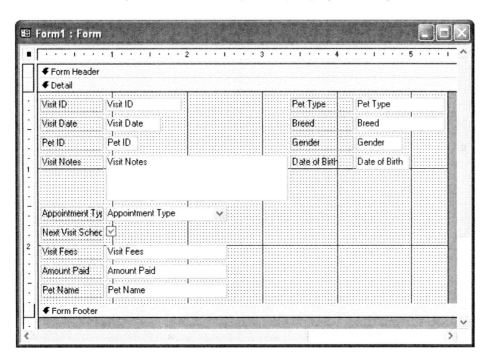

Working with Form Sections

Microsoft Office
Specialist

A form is composed of a header, a detail section, and a footer. Typically, controls that display data are positioned in the detail section of a form. The displayed data in the detail section changes as different records are displayed in the form. The header and footer sections typically contain labels, pictures, command buttons, and other objects that do not display data. This way, the header and footer remain the same regardless of the data displayed on the form. When you first create a form, the header area is not exposed. To expose the header area, you simply drag the Detail bar down slightly while working in Design view. Once the header is exposed, you can insert objects in it. The footer area is already exposed when a form is first created.

 Hands-On 6.5   Expose the Header and Expand the Detail Section

In this exercise, you will expose the header area of a form. The Visits form should already be displayed in Design view.

1. Click the Maximize button at the top-right corner of the Visits form window.
   Maximizing the window will give you more room to work.

2. Follow these steps to expose the header area:

Ⓐ Position the mouse pointer on the top edge of the Detail bar so a double-headed arrow appears. ———

Ⓑ Drag the Detail bar down until the header area is approximately one inch high.

Ⓒ Drag the Form Footer bar down until it nearly touches the bottom of the window. This will expand the Detail area. Expanding the Detail area will give you more room to rearrange controls.

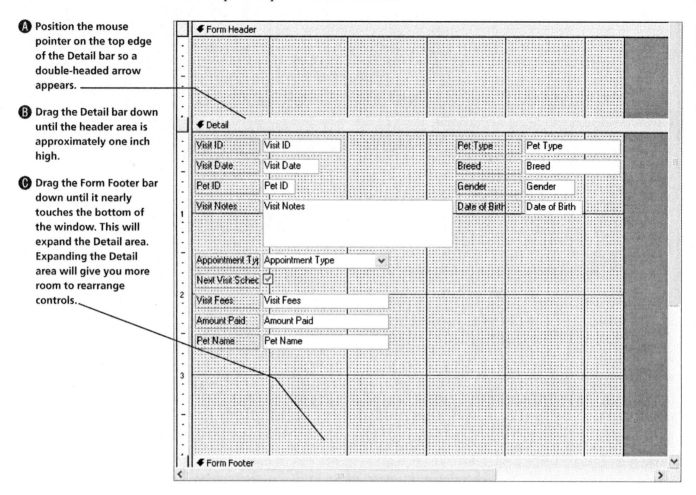

3. Take a moment to examine the form.

Notice that the form window has a light gray area and a dark gray area. The light area automatically expands when controls and other objects are positioned over the dark area. The appearance of the window is a bit deceiving. Both the light and dark areas appear in the same light gray color when the form is displayed in Forms view.

Working with Controls

Microsoft Office Specialist Controls are objects that display data, initiate events, or enhance the appearance of a form or report. Controls can be categorized as either bound or unbound. Bound controls are linked to a field in an underlying table. Bound controls are most often used for entering and editing data. For example, all controls with a white background on the Visits form are bound to fields in either the Visits or Pets tables. Unbound controls, on the other hand, have no data source in the underlying table. Examples of unbound controls include labels, pictures, lines, and rectangles.

Selecting Controls

In Hands-On 6.6, you will move controls by selecting and dragging them to the desired location. You select a control by clicking anywhere on it. You can also select a group of controls by pressing and holding the [Shift] key while clicking the desired controls, by dragging a selection box around every control to be selected, or by clicking in the horizontal or vertical ruler to select all controls in the selection line.

QUICK REFERENCE: SELECTING CONTROLS

Task	Procedure
Select a control with click [Shift]+click	Click on one control then press and hold the [Shift] key and click each of the other controls.
Select a control with the selection box	Place the mouse at the top-left edge of desired controls, press the left mouse button, and drag a box around the controls you would like to select.
Select a control by clicking on the ruler	Click in either the vertical or horizontal ruler to select all controls in line with that point on the ruler.
Select a control by dragging through the ruler	Click and drag to the right on the horizontal ruler or drag down on the vertical ruler to select all controls within that area of the ruler.

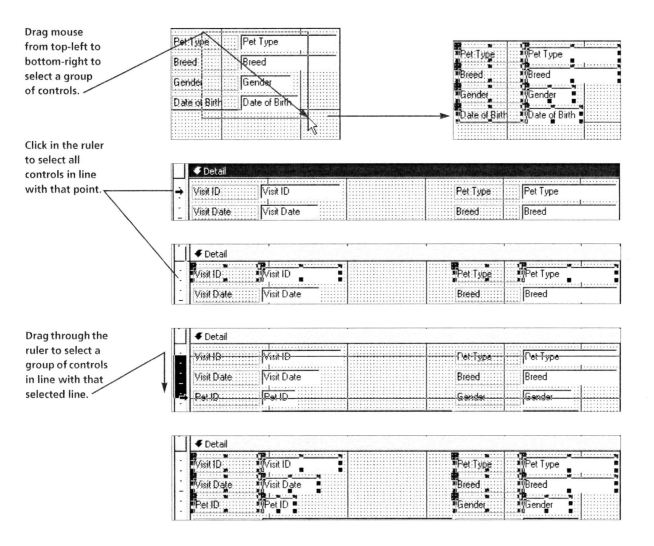

Drag mouse from top-left to bottom-right to select a group of controls.

Click in the ruler to select all controls in line with that point.

Drag through the ruler to select a group of controls in line with that selected line.

Moving Controls

You move a control or group of selected controls by pointing to an edge of a control and, when you see the open hand, dragging it to the desired location. You can also move selected controls with the keyboard by tapping the arrow keys. You can nudge the selected controls in smaller movements by pressing Ctrl while tapping the arrow keys on the keyboard.

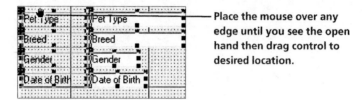

Place the mouse over any edge until you see the open hand then drag control to desired location.

The Grid

The Form Design view window displays a grid of lines and dots. The grid is used to align objects and thus helps you lay out a form in an organized manner. However, you may want to turn off the grid because it clutters the view. You turn the grid on and off with the View→Grid command.

Aligning Controls

You can use certain design techniques to improve the appearance of forms. One important technique is to align controls and other objects in vertical columns or horizontal rows. Your forms will have a clean and organized appearance if the controls are aligned. Access lets you align selected controls with the Format→Align command. You can align selected controls on the left, right, top, and bottom.

Adjusting the Size of Controls

The forms in the Pinnacle Pet Care database contain a variety of controls. You can adjust the width of any control by selecting the control and dragging the sizing handles. The size of the control only affects the appearance of the control on the form. The underlying fields in a table are not affected when controls are resized.

In this exercise, you will use several methods to move controls to different locations on the form.

1. Follow these steps to reposition the Pet Type, Breed, Gender, and Date of Birth controls:

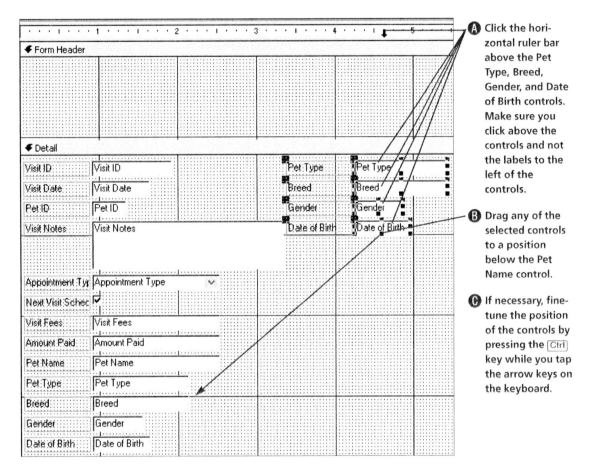

Ⓐ Click the horizontal ruler bar above the Pet Type, Breed, Gender, and Date of Birth controls. Make sure you click above the controls and not the labels to the left of the controls.

Ⓑ Drag any of the selected controls to a position below the Pet Name control.

Ⓒ If necessary, fine-tune the position of the controls by pressing the Ctrl key while you tap the arrow keys on the keyboard.

2. Follow these steps to adjust the size of the Visit Notes control:

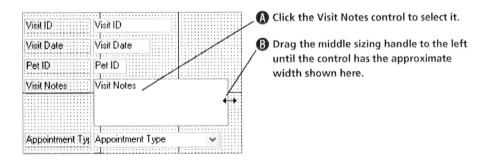

Ⓐ Click the Visit Notes control to select it.

Ⓑ Drag the middle sizing handle to the left until the control has the approximate width shown here.

3. Follow these steps to reposition the Visit Date and Visit Notes controls and to select the controls:

After you move the Visit Notes you may want to adjust the right edge of your form to make a bit more room.

Ⓐ Drag the Visit Date control to the right of the Visit ID control, as shown here. The Visit Date label will move with the control.

Ⓑ Now drag the Visit Notes control to the right of the Visit Date control.

Ⓒ Select the Visit ID, Visit Date, and Visit Notes controls by clicking the ruler bar to the left of the controls.

Ⓓ Choose Format→Align→Top to align the controls vertically.

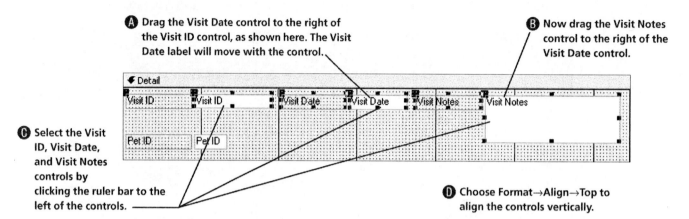

Access will move two of the controls up so they are aligned with the highest of the three selected controls. Access will move only the selected controls.

4. Follow these steps to reposition the Appointment Type and delete the Next Visit Scheduled controls:

Ⓐ Click the Appointment Type control and drag the control below the Visit Notes control. If necessary, use the Ctrl+arrow keys technique to fine-tune the position of the controls.

Ⓑ Click the Next Visit Scheduled control and tap the Delete key.

5. Follow these steps to move the Pet ID control up:

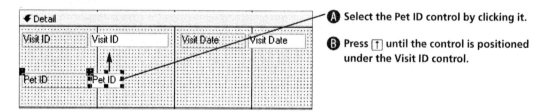

Ⓐ Select the Pet ID control by clicking it.

Ⓑ Press ↑ until the control is positioned under the Visit ID control.

6. Drag through the vertical ruler bar to select the Visit Fees and Amount Paid controls.

7. Use the ⬆ and the ➡ keys to move the controls up and to the right until they are positioned just below the Appointment Type control, as shown here. Use the Ctrl+➡ keystroke combination if necessary.

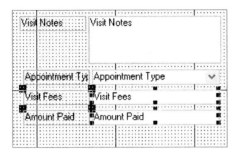

8. Use one of your selection techniques to select the Pet Name, Pet Type, Breed, Gender, and Date of Birth controls.

9. Use Ctrl+⬆ to move the controls up until they are positioned just below the Pet ID control, as shown here.

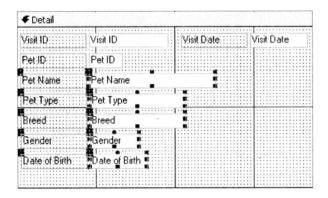

Resize a Label

10. Follow these steps to move and resize the Appointment Type label box:

A Click the Appointment Type label to select it.

B Place your mouse over the sizing handle at the top-left edge of the label. Your pointer will turn into a pointing finger.

C Press and drag the label to the left. When you drag with the open hand you will move both the label and the control boxes.

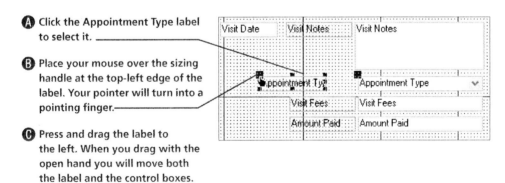

11. Follow these steps to enlarge the label:

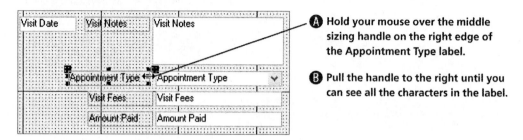

A Hold your mouse over the middle sizing handle on the right edge of the Appointment Type label.

B Pull the handle to the right until you can see all the characters in the label.

12. Now choose Edit→Select All to select all objects on the form.

13. Tap ⌗Ctrl⌗+⌗↓⌗ 15 times to move all of the objects down slightly.
Your completed form should closely match the following example.

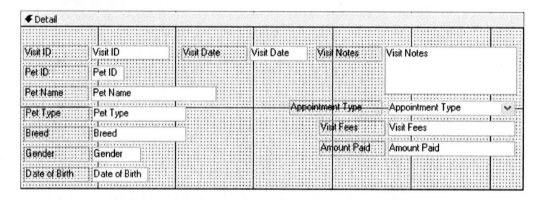

14. Save 🖫 the changes to your form but leave it open.

Adding Fields to Forms

Even if you added your fields earlier when you used the wizard to create the form, you can still add additional fields if you need them. There are two ways to add fields to forms: add a text box and assign it to a field in the properties box or open the list of fields associated with the open form and drag the desired field to the form. In Hands-On 6.7 you will add an additional field to the Visits form using the drag method.

QR

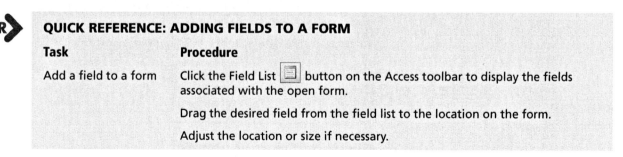

QUICK REFERENCE: ADDING FIELDS TO A FORM

Task	Procedure
Add a field to a form	Click the Field List 🖾 button on the Access toolbar to display the fields associated with the open form.
	Drag the desired field from the field list to the location on the form.
	Adjust the location or size if necessary.

Hands-On 6.7   Add Additional Fields to the Form

In this exercise, you will use the drag method of placing new fields on a form.

1. Click the Field List button on the Access toolbar to display the list of fields in the tables that are associated with this form.

2. Follow these steps to add the Next Visit Scheduled field:

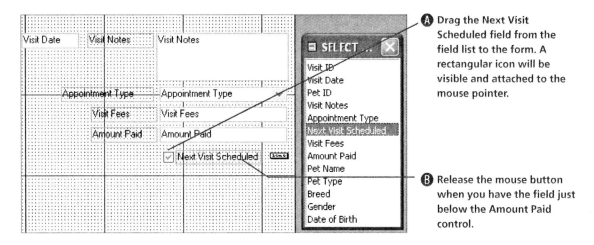

Ⓐ Drag the Next Visit Scheduled field from the field list to the form. A rectangular icon will be visible and attached to the mouse pointer.

Ⓑ Release the mouse button when you have the field just below the Amount Paid control.

3. Move the label over to the left side of the checkbox by dragging the control box on the label with the finger pointer.

4. Line up the controls. You may also have to enlarge the label so you can see all the characters in the label.

5. Your control should match the following example.

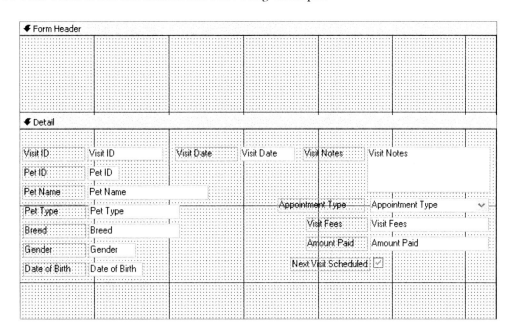

6. Save the changes to your form but leave it open.

The Toolbox

Microsoft Office
Specialist
You use the toolbox in Form Design view to add new controls to a form. Access usually provides wizards and other guidance when you attempt to add controls to a form. You can display or hide the toolbox with the View→Toolbox command. The toolbox is shown in the following illustration with descriptions of several frequently used buttons. You will use these buttons to add controls to the Visits form. The toolbox may also be visible on your screen in Form Design view.

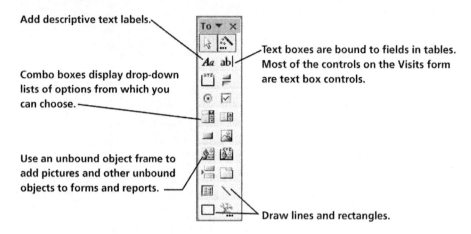

Add descriptive text labels.

Text boxes are bound to fields in tables. Most of the controls on the Visits form are text box controls.

Combo boxes display drop-down lists of options from which you can choose.

Use an unbound object frame to add pictures and other unbound objects to forms and reports.

Draw lines and rectangles.

Adding Pictures to Forms

The Image tool lets you position images in forms. Access displays the Insert Picture dialog box when you click in a form after clicking the Image button. The Insert Picture dialog box lets you choose the file you wish to insert. To size a picture once inserted, you display the Properties box for the picture and set the Size Mode setting to Zoom. You can adjust the size of the picture without distorting it once the Size Mode setting is set to Zoom.

 Hands-On 6.8   **Insert a Picture**

In this exercise, you will insert a picture into the header of a form.

1. If necessary, choose View→Toolbox to display the toolbox.
   The toolbox will be displayed as a floating palette or a toolbar.

2. Click anywhere in the header area to highlight the Form Header bar.

3. Click the Image button on the toolbox.

4. Click in the top-left corner of the header area to specify the picture location.

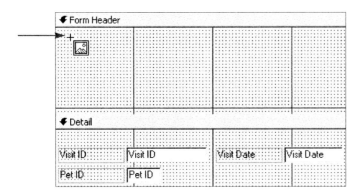

Access will display the Insert Picture dialog box.

5. Navigate to your file storage location, select the Pet file, and click OK.
Notice that the inserted picture is quite large. In the next few steps, you will correct this by changing the Size Mode property setting.

6. Make sure the picture is selected and has sizing handles around it.

7. If necessary, click the Properties 🛅 button on the Access toolbar to display the Image Properties box.

8. If necessary, click the Format tab in the Properties box and set the Size Mode option (the third option in the box) to Zoom.

9. Reduce the size of the picture by dragging a corner-sizing handle until it is approximately one inch high by one inch wide.

10. Follow these steps to reposition the picture and reduce the height of the header area:

A If necessary, drag the picture to the top-left corner of the header area.

B Drag the top edge of the Detail bar up until the header has the height shown here.

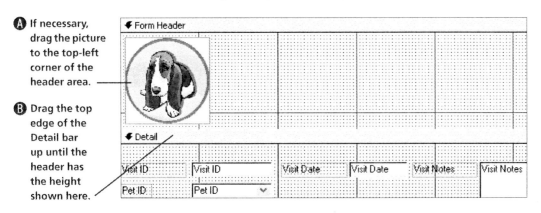

Adding Labels to Forms

Microsoft Office
Specialist

 You can use the Label button on the toolbox to easily add descriptive text labels to forms. Text labels can be placed in headers, footers, and detail sections. Text labels are not bound to fields in tables. They simply allow you to place text anywhere on a form. You insert labels by clicking the Label button, clicking at the desired location in the form, and typing the label text.

Formatting Labels and Other Controls

You can format labels and other controls using formatting buttons on the Access toolbar or by setting format properties in the Format tab of the Properties box. You can specify the font, font size, color, and other properties. The formats you apply affect all text in a label.

Hands-On 6.9   Insert and Format a Label

In this exercise, you will add and format a label in the header area.

Insert the Label

1. Click the Label button on the toolbox.

2. Follow these steps to insert the label:

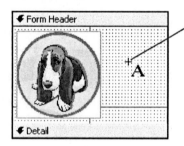

Ⓐ Click just to the right of the picture, as shown here. A thin box with the flashing insertion point will appear.

Ⓑ Type **Pinnacle Pet Care Visits**.

3. Click anywhere outside the label.

Format the Label

4. Click anywhere on the label and it will become selected (sizing handles will surround it). *If you have trouble selecting the label, click outside of it and try again.*

5. Use the Formatting toolbar to set the font size to 18 and to apply Bold **B** formatting. *The text will be too large for the box and will be hidden from view.*

6. Follow these steps to adjust the label box size:

Ⓐ Drag the corner sizing handle until all the text is visible.

Ⓑ If necessary, use Ctrl+arrow key(s) to adjust the position of the box as shown here.

7. With the label still selected, follow these steps to change the text color:

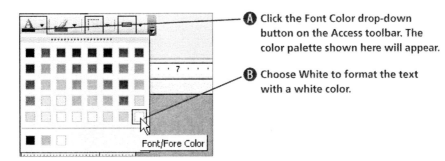

Ⓐ Click the Font Color drop-down button on the Access toolbar. The color palette shown here will appear.

Ⓑ Choose White to format the text with a white color.

> **TIP!** *Double-click any of the sizing handles to AutoFit the label box to the text.*

Format the Header Background

8. Click the Form Header bar and it will become selected as shown here.

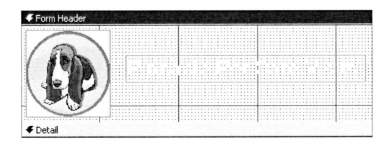

Any changes made to the background color will only impact the selected section.

9. Follow these steps to change the background color:

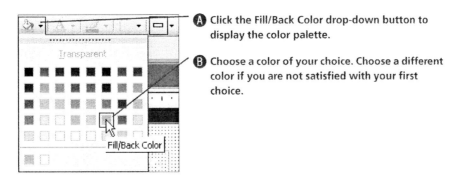

Ⓐ Click the Fill/Back Color drop-down button to display the color palette.

Ⓑ Choose a color of your choice. Choose a different color if you are not satisfied with your first choice.

10. Click the Forms 📇 view button on the left end of the Formatting toolbar.
Your form should match the following example. Notice that the form is maximized and thus occupies the entire window. You will continue to enhance and develop the form while it is maximized. Maximizing the form gives you a larger working area and makes it easier to rearrange objects and modify the layout.

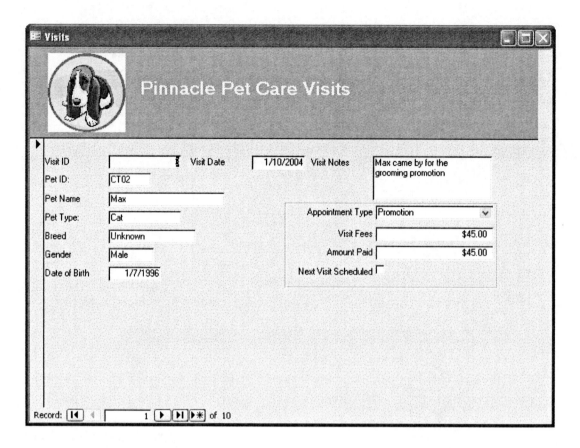

11. Click the Design view button.

12. Save your changes.

Using Controls to Ensure Data Integrity

Keeping data reliable is one of the biggest challenges facing database designers. Thus far, you have learned that Access uses referential integrity to help ensure data integrity. Access provides a variety of other features that also help ensure data integrity. In particular, Access provides various types of controls that are specifically designed to restrict data entry in fields.

Combo Boxes

Perhaps the most useful type of control for restricting data entry is the combo box. A combo box is bound to a table field and contains a drop-down button. A list of values is displayed when a user clicks the drop-down button. Only values on the drop-down list can be chosen and entered into the bound field. Thus, a combo box ensures data integrity by forcing users to only choose data from the combo box drop-down list. The following illustration shows one of the combo boxes you will add to the Visits form.

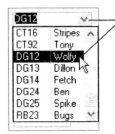

A list of values displays when you click the drop-down button on a combo box. A value is entered into a field in the underlying table when you choose a row from the list. In this combo box, the Pet ID in the first column is entered into the Pet ID field in the Visits table.

Lookup Tables and Other Combo Box Data Sources

The list of values that a combo box displays can come from either of two sources. You can specify the values for the list when you create a combo box; however, this approach is restrictive since the list is only available in that combo box, and adding and deleting values to/from the list is cumbersome. A better approach is to create a lookup table as the data source for the combo box. A lookup table typically contains just one field. The values in that field are used as the data source for the combo box. The following illustrations show a combo box and the associated lookup table that you will create in the Pinnacle Pet Care database.

 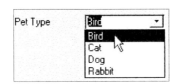

The values from the Pet Type lookup table are displayed on the combo box list when the drop-down button is clicked.

Setting Up Combo Boxes

The Combo Box button on the toolbox initiates the Combo Box Wizard. The Combo Box Wizard guides you through the process of setting up combo boxes. The wizard prompts you to specify the field to which the combo box will be bound (the field in which data are stored), the number of columns to display in the combo box, and the lookup table or other data source for the combo box list. The wizard is initiated when you click in the form after clicking the Combo Box button.

Hands-On 6.10   Replace the Pet ID Control with a Combo Box

In this exercise, you will remove the Pet ID control from the Visits form. You will replace the control with a combo box. The combo box will be bound to the Pet ID field in the Visits table. The Pet ID field in the Pets table will be used as the data source for the combo box. This way, you will choose Pet IDs from the Pets table where the Pet ID is the primary key. The Pet ID you choose will be entered into the Visits table. This will ensure that each Pet ID in the Visits table has a matching Pet ID in the Pets table.

Create the Combo Box

1. Follow these steps to delete the Pet ID control from the form:

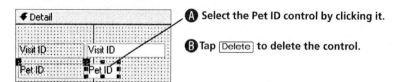

Ⓐ Select the Pet ID control by clicking it.

Ⓑ Tap ⌈Delete⌋ to delete the control.

2. Click the Combo Box ▦ button on the toolbox.

3. Click just below the Visit ID control to specify the combo box position on the form.

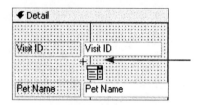

The first wizard screen will ask where the combo box will get its values. Your combo box will get its values from the Pet ID and Pet Name fields in the Pets table.

4. Make sure the I Want the Combo Box to Look Up the Values in a Table or Query option is chosen and click Next.
The next screen will ask which table or query should provide the values for the combo box.

5. Choose the Pets table and click Next.
The next screen will ask which fields you want included in the combo box.

6. Use the Add Field ⌈ > ⌋ button to add the Pet ID and Pet Name fields to the Selected Fields list.
When the drop-down button is clicked on the combo box, the data in these fields will be displayed as columns in the combo box.

7. Click Next twice and follow these steps to display the Pet ID column and to adjust the column widths:

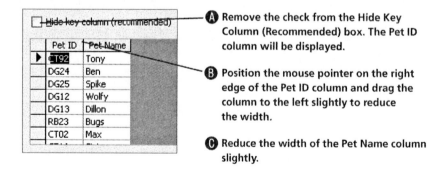

Ⓐ Remove the check from the Hide Key Column (Recommended) box. The Pet ID column will be displayed.

Ⓑ Position the mouse pointer on the right edge of the Pet ID column and drag the column to the left slightly to reduce the width.

Ⓒ Reduce the width of the Pet Name column slightly.

8. Click Next and the wizard will ask you to choose a field that uniquely identifies the row.
   In the next step, you will choose the Pet ID field. This will instruct the wizard to choose the Pet ID field from the Pets table when you enter data into the database and choose a row from the combo box. Notice that you can specify either the Pet ID field or the Pet Name field. The wizard requires you to choose one field because data from only one of the fields will be stored in the Pet ID field of the Visits table. In this combo box, the Pet Name field is used just for display purposes to help the user choose the correct Pet ID.

9. Choose Pet ID and click Next.

10. Follow these steps to instruct the wizard to store the value chosen from the combo box in the Pet ID field of the Visits table:

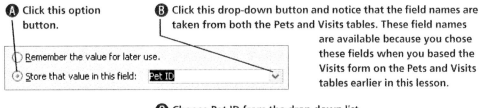

These settings will create a combo box that displays a list of Pet IDs and Pet Names for each pet in the Pets table. When you choose a pet from the combo box, Access will take the Pet ID from the Pets table and enter it into the Pet ID field in the Visits table. Thus, each record in the Visits table will have a Pet ID that also exists in the Pets table. The one-to-many relationship you created earlier will ensure that the Visits form always displays the proper pet information for each visit.

11. Click Next to display the final wizard screen.

12. If necessary, type the name **Pet ID** in the label box and click the Finish button.
    You will adjust the position and alignment of the combo box in a moment.

Use the Combo Box to Enter Data

13. Click the Forms 🔳 view button on the Access toolbar.

14. Click the Add a New Record ▶ button on the Navigation bar at the bottom of the form.

15. Tap the [Tab] key and the insertion point will move from the Visit ID field to the Visit Date field.

16. Follow these steps to enter data into the form:

A Type the visit date shown here then tap the Tab key to move to the Visit Notes memo field.

B Type the text shown here into the Visit Notes memo field. A scroll box on the memo control will allow you to scroll up or down if necessary.

C Click the drop-down button on the Pet ID combo box and choose Dillon. Access will display all information for Dillon in the Pet Name, Pet Type, Breed, Gender, and Date of Birth fields. The relationship between the Pet ID fields in the Pets and Visits tables allows Access to synchronize the tables on the form. In other words, all information for Dillon will appear on the form whenever the Visit ID 11 record is displayed.

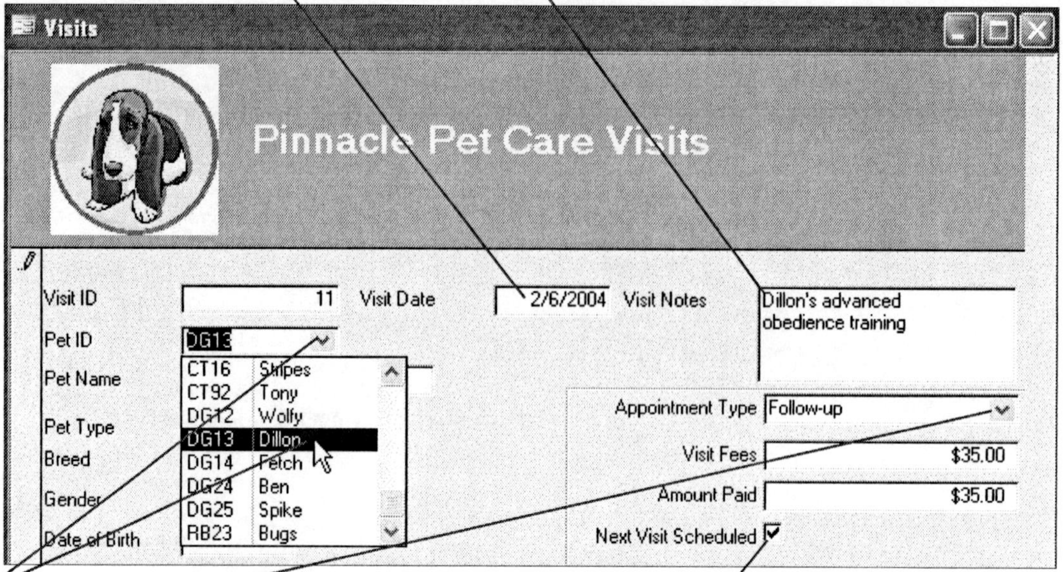

Visits

Pinnacle Pet Care Visits

Visit ID   11   Visit Date   2/6/2004   Visit Notes   Dillon's advanced obedience training

Pet ID   DG13

Pet Name

CT16	Stripes
CT92	Tony
DG12	Wolfy
DG13	Dillon
DG14	Fetch
DG24	Ben
DG25	Spike
RB23	Bugs

Pet Type

Breed

Gender

Date of Birth

Appointment Type   Follow-up

Visit Fees $35.00

Amount Paid $35.00

Next Visit Scheduled ☑

D Click in the Appointment Type field and choose Follow-Up from the drop-down list. Using Tab to change fields, type **35** in the Visit Fee and Amount Paid fields.

E Click the Next Visit Scheduled box and a check will appear. This field is now set to Yes in the underlying Visits table.

17. Take a moment to examine the following illustration. It describes the relationships between the tables, fields, controls, and the Visits form.

The Visit ID, the primary key field in the Visits table, controls the form. Each visit has a unique Visit ID assigned by the AutoNumber data type of the Visit ID field.

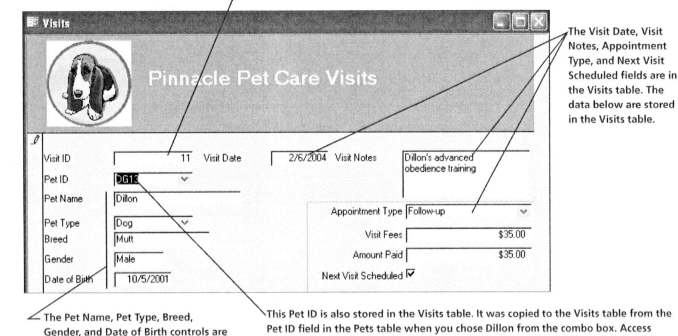

The Visit Date, Visit Notes, Appointment Type, and Next Visit Scheduled fields are in the Visits table. The data below are stored in the Visits table.

The Pet Name, Pet Type, Breed, Gender, and Date of Birth controls are displaying data from the Pets table.

This Pet ID is also stored in the Visits table. It was copied to the Visits table from the Pet ID field in the Pets table when you chose Dillon from the combo box. Access displays Dillon's information from the Pets table because there is a relationship between the Pet ID fields in the two tables. The relationship ensures that Dillon's information will always be displayed along with the Visit information for Visit ID 11.

Using Lookup Tables with Combo Boxes

Lookup tables can be used as data sources for combo boxes. Lookup tables are like any other Access table, though they usually contain just one or two fields. Lookup tables are beneficial because you can easily add and remove data to and from them. Combo boxes always reflect the most recent changes made in the lookup tables. The Combo Box Wizard gives you the option of using a lookup table as a data source.

Hands-On 6.11   Use a Lookup Table with a Combo Box

In this exercise, you will create a lookup table and add a combo box to the Visits form

Create the Lookup Table

1. Close the Visits form and save any changes that have been made.

2. Click the Tables button on the Objects bar in the Access database window.

3. Double-click the Create Table in Design View option.

4. Add a field named **Pet Type** to the table.

5. Leave the Data Type set to Text but change the Field Size to **30**, as shown to the right.

6. Click on the phrase Pet Type then click the Primary Key button to make Pet Type a primary key.

7. Click the Datasheet view button on the Access toolbar, choose Yes, and save the table as **Pet Type**.

8. Enter the four records shown to the right into the table.

9. Close the table.

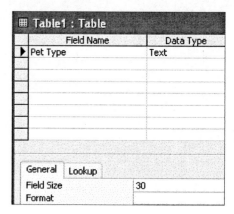

Create the Combo Box

10. Click the Forms button on the Objects bar in the database window.

11. Choose the Visits form and click the ☑ Design button.

12. Click the Pet Type control and tap the Delete key to remove the control and the label to the left of the control.

13. Click the Combo Box button on the toolbox.

14. Click just above the Breed control to specify the position of the combo box.

15. Click the Next button on the first wizard screen.

16. Choose Pet Type from the list of tables and click Next.

17. Add the Pet Type field to the Selected Fields list and click Next twice.

18. Adjust the column width to fit the Pet Type heading and click Next.

19. Choose Pet Type from the Store that Value in this Field box and click Next.

20. If necessary, type the name **Pet Type** in the final wizard screen and click Finish. *Access will create the Pet Type combo box.*

Adjust the Size and Position of Labels

21. Press the [Shift] key while you click the Visit ID, Pet ID, Pet Name, Pet Type, Breed, Gender, and Date of Birth labels.

Make sure you click the labels and not the controls to the right of the labels. The labels will become selected, as shown here.

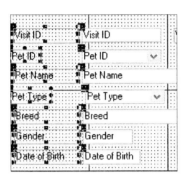

22. Choose Format→Align→Left from the menu bar.
Access will align the labels with the leftmost of the seven labels.

23. Click the Appointment Type label.

24. Press [Shift] and click the Visit Fees, Amount Paid, Next Visit Scheduled labels.

25. Choose Format→Align→Right to align those labels.

26. Align any other labels as necessary and make any other adjustments to your form so it matches the following example.

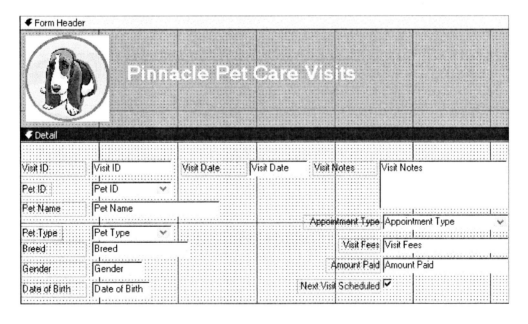

27. Save the changes to the form.

Enter Data

28. Click the Forms ▦ view button.

29. Click the New Record ▶⁑ button on the navigation bar at the bottom of the form.

30. Enter three new visit records using the following data:
You will need to type data in some fields or choose the desired data from combo boxes. The Tab *key will not take you from one field to the next because you blended multiple tables into this form. Notice that there are no instructions for entering the Pet Name, Pet Type, Breed, Gender, and Date of Birth data. This data will simply be reflected from the Pets table when you choose the indicated Pet IDs. Also, you should check the Next Visit Scheduled box to set that field to Yes and leave the box unchecked to set that field to No. Finally, you don't need to enter the Visit IDs since the Visit IDs auto number data type will automatically number the records as you enter data in the other fields.*

Visit ID	Pet ID	Visit Date	Appointment Visit Notes	Appointment Type	Next Visit Scheduled	Visit Fee	Amt Paid
12	CT16	2/15/04	Stripes came by for the grooming promotion.	Promotion	No	45	45
13	DG14	2/17/04	Fetch is here for yearly shots.	Scheduled	No	135	135
14	CT02	2/21/04	Max in for yearly shots.	Scheduled	Yes	165	50

31. Leave the Visits form open and continue with the next topic.

Adding Lines, Rectangles, and Color

The Line ╲ and Rectangle ▢ buttons on the toolbox and the Line/Border Color ◿ button on the Formatting toolbar can be used to enhance the appearance of forms.

 Hands-On 6.12   Add a Line, Rectangle, and Finishing Touches

In this exercise, you will add the finishing touches to the Visits form.

Add a Line and Rectangle

1. Click the Design ◿ view button.

2. Turn off the gridlines by choosing View→Grid.
You can see the rectangles and lines better with the gridlines off.

3. Click the Rectangle ▢ tool on the toolbox.

4. Follow these steps to draw a rectangle and a line:

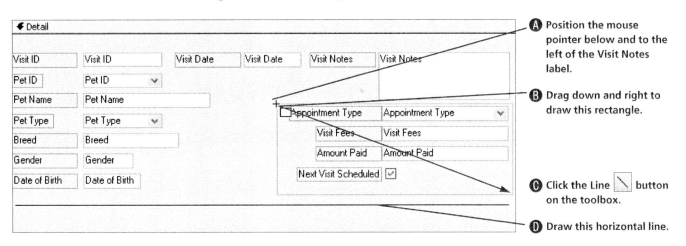

TIP! *Holding down the [Shift] key while dragging a line will keep it straight.*

5. Feel free to change the color of the line or rectangle with the Line/Border Color 🖌️ button on the formatting toolbar. You must select the line or rectangle before using the button.

Add Finishing Touches

6. Follow these steps to right-align the Visit Date, Visit Notes, Appointment Type, Visit Fees, and Amount Paid labels:
Right-aligning the label will position it closer to the control.

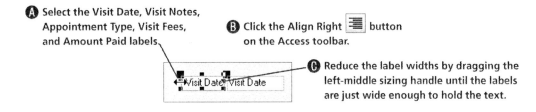

7. If necessary, continue to adjust the positions and size of your labels until they are nicely aligned.

8. Turn the gridlines back on by choosing View→Grid.

9. Switch to Forms 🖼️ view to view your completed form.
Your form should resemble the following example.

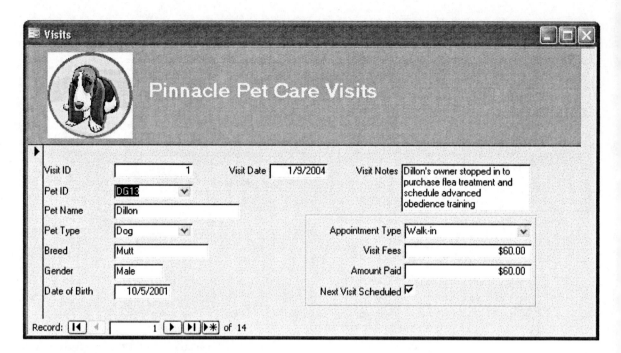

10. Close the form when you have finished and save the changes.

11. Close the Pinnacle Pet Care database.

Concepts Review

True/False Questions

1. A control can be sized by the dragging sizing handles on the edges of the control. TRUE FALSE

2. If the form header isn't visible, it can be exposed by dragging down the Form Header bar. TRUE FALSE

3. Bound controls are linked to fields in underlying tables. TRUE FALSE

4. Pictures can be inserted using the Image ☒ button on the toolbox. TRUE FALSE

5. Lookup tables must contain at least three fields. TRUE FALSE

6. Controls can be used to help ensure data integrity. TRUE FALSE

7. Combo boxes always use lookup tables as their data sources. TRUE FALSE

8. The Rectangle Wizard is used to draw rectangles. TRUE FALSE

9. Lookup tables can be used as data sources for combo boxes. TRUE FALSE

10. You use the toolbox in Form Design view to add new controls to a form. TRUE FALSE

Multiple Choice Questions

1. Which of the following buttons is used to insert hyperlinks?
   a. ☒
   b. ☒
   c. ☒
   d. ☒

2. Which of the following commands is used to align controls?
   a. Format→Align
   b. Edit→Align
   c. Click the Align button on the toolbox.
   d. Controls cannot be aligned.

3. Which of the following sections is a part of a form?
   a. Header
   b. Detail
   c. Footer
   d. All of the above

4. Which of the following buttons initiates the Combo Box Wizard?
   a. ☒
   b. ☒
   c. ☒
   d. ☒

Skill Builders

Skill Builder 6.1   Create a Form with the Form Wizard

In this exercise, you will use the Form Wizard to create a new form. The form will use fields from both the Customers and Trips tables.

1. Open the Tropical Getaways database.

2. Click the Forms button on the Objects bar in the database window.

3. Double-click the Create Form by Using Wizard option.

4. Follow these steps to add the fields from the Trips table:

A Choose the Trips table from the Tables/ Queries list.

B Click the Add All Fields button to move all fields to the Selected Fields list.

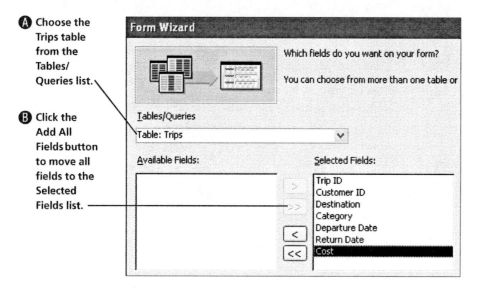

5. Follow these steps to add five fields from the Customers table:

A Choose Tables: Customers from the Tables/ Queries list.

B Use the Add Field button to add the Firstname, Lastname, Profile, City, and State fields one field at a time.

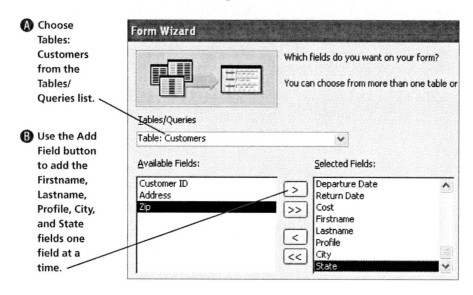

6. Click the Next button to display the next wizard screen.

7. Make sure the options are set to By Trips and click the Next button.

8. Make sure the Columnar option is chosen and click the Next button.

9. Choose Standard as the style and click the Next button.

10. Type the name **New Trips** as the title and click the Finish button.

11. Leave the form open because you will use it in the next exercise.

Skill Builder 6.2   Insert Hyperlinks

In this exercise, you will insert hyperlinks in the New Trips and Customers forms. You will also modify the Forms in Design view.

1. Click the Design ![icon] view button on the Access toolbar.

2. Click the Insert Hyperlink ![icon] button.

3. Make sure the Objects in this Database button is chosen on the left side of the dialog box.

4. Choose Customers from the Forms list and click OK to insert the hyperlink at the top of the form.

5. Follow these guidelines to modify the appearance of the form:

   ■ If necessary, increase the size of the form until it is large enough for the control arrangement shown in the following illustration. You can accomplish this by dragging a corner-sizing handle.

   ■ Rearrange the controls and the hyperlink until your form matches the example. Keep in mind that you can select multiple controls by pressing the [Shift] key while clicking the desired controls. Notice that all of the controls currently reside on a light gray area of the form. If you move controls out of the light gray area, this area will automatically expand to accommodate the new positions of the controls.

   ■ Modify the hyperlink text by clicking the hyperlink and typing the text shown.

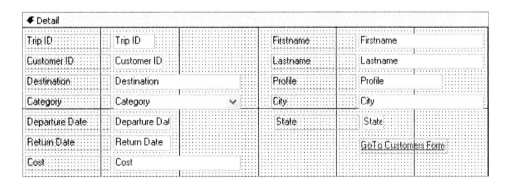

6. Click the Forms 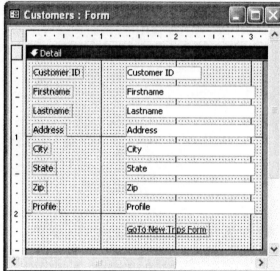 view button on the left end of the Access toolbar.

7. Click the hyperlink to open the Customers form.

8. Click the Design view button.

9. Insert a hyperlink in the Customers form that opens the New Trips form when clicked. Adjust the size of the form and the position of the hyperlink, then change the hyperlink text to match the example shown to the right.

10. Click the Forms view button then click the hyperlink.
    The New Trips form should become active.

11. Switch to Design view.

12. Select the Firstname, Lastname, Profile, City, and State controls by pressing the [Shift] key while clicking each.

13. If necessary, click the Properties button on the Access toolbar to display the Properties dialog box.

14. Click the Data tab.

15. Set the Enabled property to No and the Locked property to Yes.

16. Click the Forms view button on the toolbar.
    The Firstname, Lastname, Profile, City, and State controls will appear to be active. However, you will not be able to click in the controls because of the Enabled and Locked settings.

17. Feel free to browse through the records on the New Trips form and modify the form if desired.

18. Close both the New Trips and Customers forms and save any changes.
    The Database window should be displayed. You will continue to modify the database in the following exercises.

Set Up a Form

In this exercise, you will use the Form Wizard to set up a form that displays fields from both the Customers and Custom Packages tables.

1. Click the Forms button on the Objects bar.

2. Double-click the Create Form by Using Wizard option.

3. Add all fields from the Custom Packages table to the Selected Fields list as shown to the right.

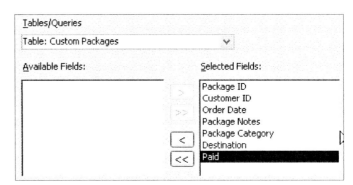

4. Add the Firstname, Lastname, Address, City, State, Zip, and Profile fields from the Customers table. The fields will appear at the bottom of the Selected Fields list.

5. Click the Next button to display the next wizard screen.

6. Make sure the options are set to By Custom Packages.

7. Click the Next button.

8. Make sure the Columnar option is chosen and click the Next button.

9. Choose Standard as the style and click the Next button.
   Access should propose the name Custom Packages in the title box.

10. Choose Modify the Form's Design in the last wizard screen then click the Finish button.

Skill Builder 6.4 Customize the Appearance of a Form

In this exercise, you will finish up the form by customizing its appearance.

1. Maximize ▣ the Custom Packages form window.

2. Position the mouse pointer on the top edge of the Form Footer bar then drag the bar down to enlarge the working area.

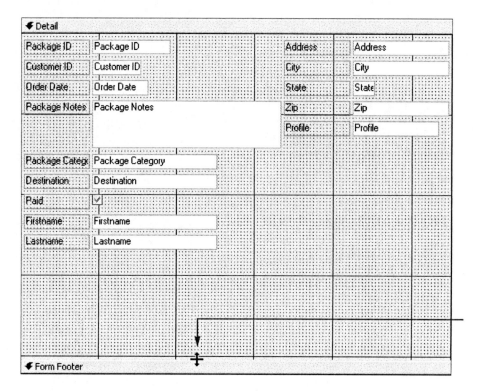

3. Follow these guidelines to reorganize the form as shown in the following illustration:
   - ▪ Reduce the width of the Package Notes control.
   - ▪ Rearrange the controls.
   - ▪ Right-align the text in the Order Date label.
   - ▪ Widen the Package Category label until all text is visible.
   - ▪ Use the Format→Align→Left command to align the Package Notes, Package Category, Destination, and Paid labels.
   - ▪ Drag the Form Footer bar up until it is about one inch below the controls.

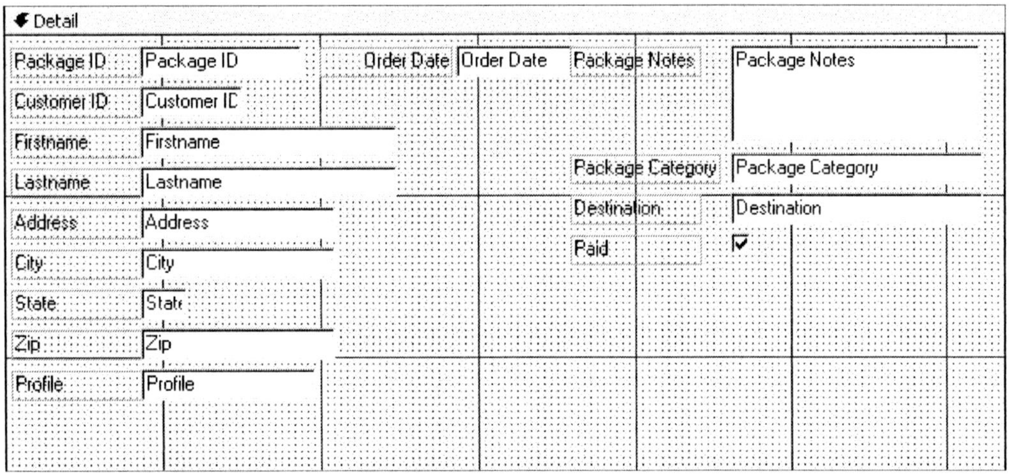

4. Save the changes to the form.

Skill Builder 6.5 Set Up a Form Header

In this exercise, you will set up the header to put a graphic on the form.

1. If necessary, click View→Form Header/Footer to display the form header.
2. Position the mouse pointer on the top edge of the Detail bar then drag the bar down as shown here.

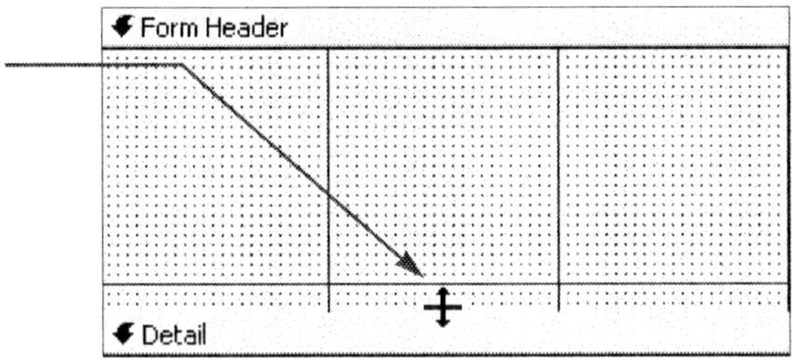

3. Click anywhere in the header area, and the header section bar will become highlighted.
4. Click the Image button on the toolbox.

5. Specify the picture placement by clicking in the top-left corner of the header area as shown here.

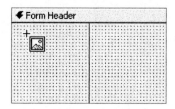

The Insert Picture dialog box will appear.

6. Navigate to your file storage location, select the Parrot file, and click OK.

7. Make sure the picture is selected (has sizing handles surrounding it).

8. If necessary, click the Properties ⌧ button on the Access toolbar to display the Properties box.

9. If necessary, click the Format tab in the Properties box and set the Size Mode option to Zoom.

10. Adjust the size of the picture so it fits within the header area.

11. If necessary, reposition the picture and reduce the height of the header area until the picture is located in the top-left corner, as shown to the right.

12. Click the Label 𝐴𝛼 button on the toolbox.

13. Click just to the right of the picture to place the label at that location.

14. Type **Tropical Getaways - Custom Packages** in the label box.

15. Click anywhere outside of the label then click the label to select it.

16. Use the Formatting toolbar to set the font size to 14 and click the Bold **B** button.

17. Increase the size of the label so the text is visible.

18. Feel free to use the Font Color **A** button on the Formatting toolbar to add color to the label.

19. Feel free to use the Fill/Back Color ⌧ button to change the color of the header section.

20. Click the Forms ⌧ view button to view the completed form.

21. Click the Restore ⌧ button at the top-right corner of the form.

22. Adjust the size of the form by dragging the edges of the form window until your form has the approximate dimensions shown here.

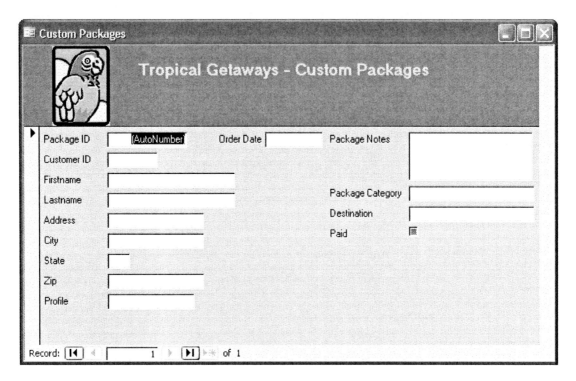

23. Click the Design ![icon] view button to return to Design view.

24. Click the Save ![icon] button.

Set Up a Combo Box

In this exercise, you will replace the Customer ID field with a combo box.

1. Click the Customer ID control and tap the [Delete] key to remove the Customer ID control from the form.

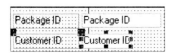

2. Click the Combo Box ![icon] button on the toolbox.

3. Click just below the Package ID control to specify the position of the combo box.
   The first wizard screen will ask where the combo box will get its values. Your combo box will get its values from the Customer ID, Firstname, and Lastname fields in the Customers table.

4. Make sure the I Want the Combo Box to Look up the Values in a Table or Query option is chosen and click Next.
   The next screen will ask which table or query should provide the values for the combo box.

5. Choose the Customers table and click Next.
   The next screen will ask which fields you want included in the combo box.

6. Use the Add Field > button to add the Customer ID, Firstname, and Lastname fields to the Selected Fields list.
   When the drop-down button is clicked on the combo box, the data in these fields will appear as columns in the combo box.

7. Click Next twice, remove the check from the Hide Key Column (Recommended) box, and resize the columns.
   The Customer ID column will appear along with the Firstname and Lastname columns.

8. Click Next and the wizard will ask you to choose a field that uniquely identifies the row.

9. Choose Customer ID and click Next.

10. Choose the Store Value in This Field option and choose Customer ID from the drop-down list.
    These settings will store the Customer ID chosen from the combo box in the Customer ID field of the Custom Packages table. The Customer ID chosen in the combo box will be taken from the Customers table. Thus, choosing a Customer ID will copy the Customer ID from the Customers table to the Custom Packages table.

11. Click Next and the final wizard screen will appear.

12. If necessary, type **Customer ID** in the label box, then click the Finish button.

13. Adjust the position of the label and combo box control until your combo box is aligned as shown to the right.

14. Save the changes to your form.

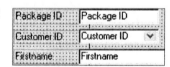

Skill Builder 6.7   Use Lookup Tables

In this exercise, you will create a lookup table. In Skill Builder 6.8 you will use the lookup table as a data source for a combo box.

1. Close the Custom Packages form.

2. Click the Tables button on the Object bar in the Access database window.

3. Double-click the Create Table in Design View option.

4. Set up a single field named **Destination**. Leave the Data Type set to Text and the field set to 50.

5. Make the Destination field a primary key.

6. Switch to Datasheet ⊞ view and save the table as **Destinations**.

7. Add the records shown to the right to the table.

8. Close the table when finished.

Destination
Amazon Jungle
Baja California
Caribbean Cruise
Hawaii
Kenyan Safari
Orlando
Rocky Mountains
Swiss Alps

Set Up a Combo Box

In this exercise, you will create a new combo box on the Custom Packages form. The lookup tables you created in Skill Builder 6.7 will be used as data sources.

Set Up Combo Boxes

1. Open the Custom Packages form in Design view.

2. Delete the Destination control and its associated label.

3. Follow these guidelines to set up the combo box to replace the Destination control. The combo box should be positioned below the Package Category control.

   ■ Use the Combo Box Wizard.

   ■ The combo box should look up values in the Destinations lookup table and store the values in the Destination field of the Custom Packages table.

   ■ Assign the name **Destination** to the combo box.

   ■ Adjust the width of the label after the box is created so the name is completely visible.

   ■ Your combo box should display the following list when the drop-down button is clicked.

4. Adjust the position of the combo boxes and other controls so the form matches the following example when in Forms view.

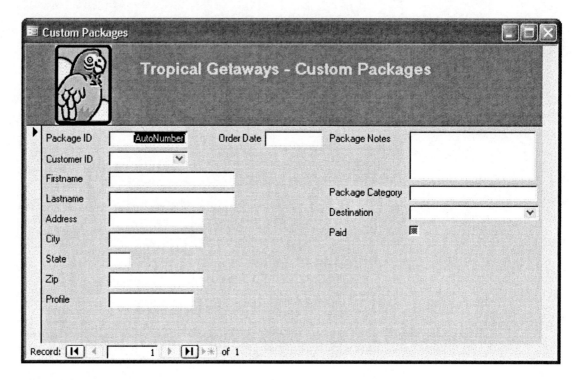

5. Save the changes to your form.

Enter Data

In this exercise, you will enter data using the Custom Packages form.

1. If necessary, display the Custom Packages form in Forms 🖽 view.

2. Enter 10 records using the following data:
   You will need to type data in some fields or choose the desired data from combo boxes. Notice that there are no instructions for entering the Firstname, Lastname, Address, City, State, Zip, and Profile data. This data will be reflected from the Customers table when you choose the indicated Customer IDs. Also, you should check the Paid box to set that field to Yes and leave the box unchecked to set that field to No. You won't need to enter the Package IDs because that field has an auto number data type.

Package ID	Customer ID	Order Date	Package Notes	Package Category	Destination	Paid
1	4	7/8/04	Need to secure non-smoking rooms prior to departure.	Family	Orlando	Yes
2	1	9/9/04	Debbie needs special meals	Adventure	Baja California	No
3	5	9/10/04		Adventure	Rocky Mountains	No
4	6	10/8/04		Leisure	Caribbean Cruise	Yes
5	2	10/8/04	Need to book Wilma's room in the same section as Lisa Simms.	Leisure	Caribbean Cruise	Yes
6	4	12/11/04		Family	Hawaii	Yes
7	3	12/20/04		Adventure	Kenyan Safari	No
8	6	1/5/05	Request vegetarian meals.	Leisure	Hawaii	No
9	1	1/7/05		Adventure	Swiss Alps	Yes
10	5	1/10/05		Adventure	Baja California	Yes

3. When you have finished, carefully check all of your data to make sure it is accurate.

4. Close and save the database.

Assessments

Assessment 6.1   Customize the Events Form

In this exercise, you will create and enhance a form for Events.

1. Open the Classic Cars database.

2. Create a one-to-many relationship between the Collector ID fields in the Collectors and Events tables as shown to the right. Enforce referential integrity and activate cascade updating of related fields and cascade deleting of related records.

   If you have trouble establishing this relationship, remember that the two fields must have the same data type. If necessary, go back and change the data type of the Collector ID in the Events table to Number.

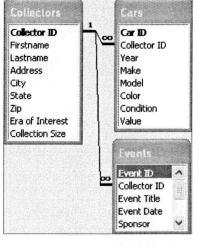

3. Create the lookup table shown to the right. The table should have just one field named Sponsor, and it should be a primary key. Set the data type of the Sponsor field to Text and leave the size set to 50. Switch to Datasheet view and save the table with the name **Sponsors**. Enter the records shown to the right into your new lookup table.

Sponsor
American Collector's Association
Arizona Auto Enthusiast
California Auto Collectors
Classic Automobiles Magazine
Classic Cars
Classic Cars - Bay Chapter
Paramount Auto Parts

4. Follow these guidelines to create the completed form shown in the following illustration:

   ■ Use the Form Wizard to set up the form using fields from both the Collectors and Events tables. Take all fields from the Events table. Take the Firstname and Lastname fields from the Collectors table. Name the form **Events**.

   ■ Create and format the form header as shown. Use the Antique Car picture from your file storage location. Format the header background with the color of your choice. Format the Classic Cars - Scheduled Events label by increasing the size of the text and adding color to the label.

   ■ Use Design view to arrange the controls as shown. You will also need to adjust the size of several controls.

   ■ Delete the Collector ID control that the wizard sets up and create a Collector ID combo box to display the drop-down list shown to the right. The Collector ID, Firstname, and Lastname fields from the Collectors table should be used as the data source for the combo box. When a row is chosen from the combo box, the

Collector ID			Event Da
	1	Cindy	Johnson
Firstname	2	Tammy	Olson
	3	Ed	Larkson
Lastname	4	Bob	Barker
	5	Isaac	Williams
	6	Angela	Hall
	7	Anthony	Jeffers
	8	Jake	Johnson
Notes			

Collector ID should be copied from the Collectors table to the Collector ID field in the Events table. This field identifies a Collector as the person who is coordinating the event. The Firstname and Lastname fields on the form should simply be reflected from the Collectors table.

- Set up the Sponsor combo box to display the drop-down list shown to the right. The Sponsors lookup table should be used as the data source for the combo box. When a row is chosen from the combo box, a sponsor should be copied from the Sponsors lookup table to the Sponsor field in the Events table. This field identifies the sponsor that is supporting the event.

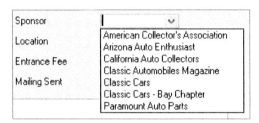

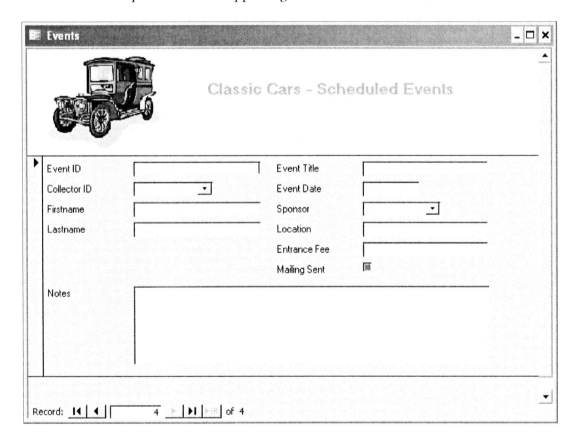

5. Enter three records using the following data:

You will need to type data in some fields or choose the desired data from combo boxes. Notice that there are no instructions for entering the Firstname and Lastname data. These data will be reflected from the Collectors table when you choose the indicated Collector ID. Also, you should check the Mailing Sent box to set that field to Yes and leave the box unchecked to set that field to No.

Event ID	Collector ID	Event Title	Event Date	Sponsor	Location	Entrance Fee	Mailing Sent	Notes
4	1	Chicago Classic Auto Show	4/8/04	Classic Automobiles Magazine	Chicago	$45	No	The location is being decided.
5	5	Early American Auto Show	6/14/04	American Collector's Association	Detroit	$15	No	
6	2	Classic Corvette Show	7/11/04	California Auto Collectors	Sacramento	$35	No	The date is tentative.

6. When you have finished, carefully check all of your data to make sure they are accurate.

7. Close and save the Classic Cars database when you have finished.

Critical Thinking

Create Advanced Forms

In Lesson 5, Creating Advanced Queries, you set up a table in the Holmestead Realty database for Linda Holmes' Feels Like Home service. Now Linda needs to modify the Holmestead Realty database to keep track of houses that receive the Feels Like Home service and the specific type of service they receive. Open the Holmestead Realty database and follow these guidelines to set up a table and form to meet these needs:

■ Establish a relationship between the primary key field in the Listings table and the field with the same name in the Feels Like Home table. This should be a one-to-many relationship with enforced referential integrity.

■ Add a field to the Feels Like Home table called **Vacant** in which the data type is Yes/No.

■ Create a form using the Form Wizard. Add all fields from the Feels Like Home table to the new form. Add the Street #, Address, Expiration Date, and Vacant fields from the Listings table.

■ Accept all of the default Form Wizard settings.

■ Save your new form as **Feels Like Home Data Entry**.

Format Form Controls

Follow these guidelines to enhance the appearance of the Feels Like Home Data Entry form. Use your creativity and have a little fun. There are no correct or incorrect solutions to this exercise.

■ Consider adding a descriptive label and a picture to the header section.

■ Align, size, and rearrange controls to improve the organization of the form. Use rectangles and lines to separate groups of controls.

■ Format the form using background colors and font sizes/colors.

Ensure Data Integrity

Linda employs her nephew to complete data entry work for Holmestead Realty. He is a good worker but he sometimes makes errors. Linda decides to add a combo box to the Feels Like Home Data Entry form to help reduce data entry errors. Follow these guidelines to add a combo box to the form:

■ Replace the MLS # control with a combo box.

■ Show the Street # and Address in the combo box. Do not hide the key column.

■ Store the value in the MLS # field.

■ Name this combo box **MLS #**.

Critical Thinking 6.4   Data Entry

Use the Feels Like Home Data Entry form to enter the following data into the database. Only enter data into the fields shown here. The other form controls will simply reflect data from the Listings table.

Service ID	Plan	Special Instructions	Invoice	MLS #	Vacant
5	Winter	Wrap pipes under deck	Y	52236	Y
6	Check-up	Make sure doors are locked	N	52511	Y
7	Summer	Do not mow back yard	N	52425	Y
8	Set-up	Pick up key from owner	N	52912	N

LESSON 7

Working with Subforms and Calculated Controls

Access databases are often used for entering order information. In a typical order entry database, order information is stored in an orders table, while order details are stored in an order details table. Order data may include the customer's name, address, telephone number, credit card number, etc. The order details table includes the individual transaction items, such as the products ordered, price, quantity, etc. Subforms are useful in order entry systems for displaying order details on a main order form.

Access also lets you use calculated controls on forms to calculate order totals, sales tax, freight charges, and other calculations. In this lesson, you will use Access's Subform Wizard to easily set up an order entry system.

Microsoft Office Access 2003 objectives covered in this lesson

Objective Number	Skill Sets and Skills	Concept Page References	Exercise Page References
AC03S-1-9	Add and modify form controls and properties	232–236, 240	236–244

Case Study

Al Smith has decided to integrate order entry into his Access database system. He realizes that Access is a powerful database system that can automate his order-taking process. Al decides that the best place to display order information is on the Visits form in the Pinnacle Pet Care database. He adds a Visit Details subform to the Visits form to record service and product information and to calculate subtotals, totals, and sales tax.

Study the following form. In Hands-On 7.1 you will begin to set up the Visits Details subform displayed here.

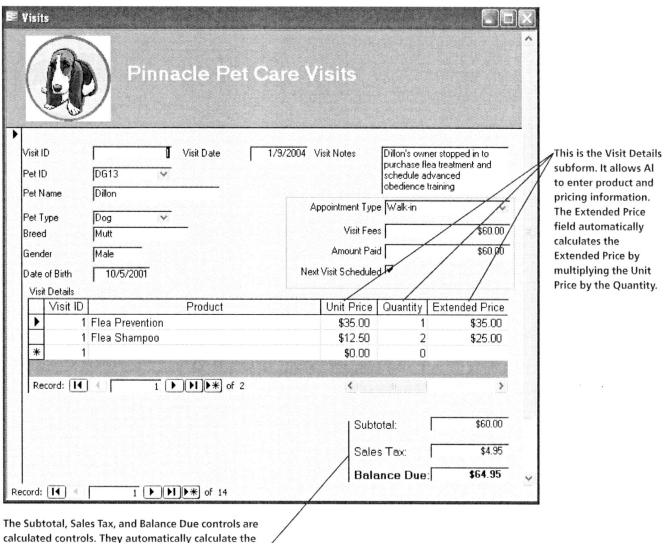

This is the Visit Details subform. It allows Al to enter product and pricing information. The Extended Price field automatically calculates the Extended Price by multiplying the Unit Price by the Quantity.

The Subtotal, Sales Tax, and Balance Due controls are calculated controls. They automatically calculate the Subtotal, Sales Tax, and Balance Due for each order.

Understanding Subforms

A subform is a form within a form. Subforms are often used to display detailed order information, especially when the order information comes from a combination of tables. For example, in this lesson you will create a subform within the Visits form.

The Visits form is called the main form.

This subform is based on the Visit Details query. It will display the products purchased during the visit.

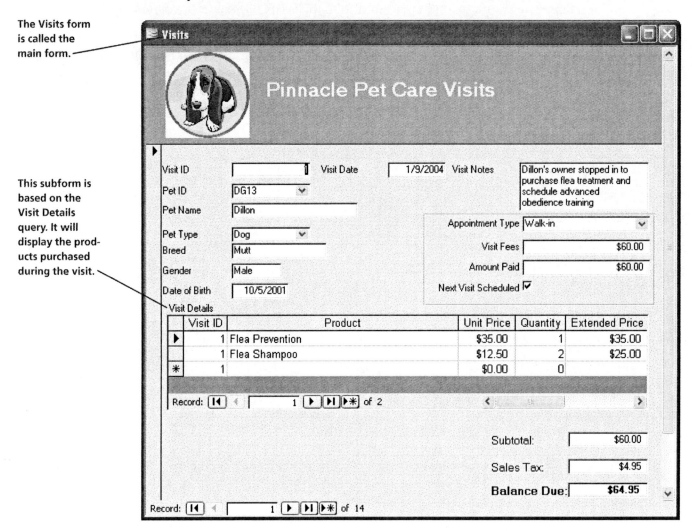

 Hands-On 7.1 **Set Up the Visit Details Table**

In this exercise, you will set up a table to record visit details in the Pinnacle Pet Care database. The visit detail records will be displayed in the subform.

1. Start Access and open the Pinnacle Pet Care database.

2. Click the Tables button on the Objects bar.

3. Double-click the Create Table in Design View option.

4. Follow these steps to set up the Visit Details table:

Ⓐ Type these field names and choose the data types shown for each. Make sure you spell the field names correctly.

Field Name	Data Type
Visit ID	Number
Product	Text
Unit Price	Currency
Quantity	Number

Ⓑ Leave the field size for the Product field set to 50. Set the number of decimal places for the Unit Price field to 2.

5. Do not set a primary key for this table.
   You will learn why a primary key is unnecessary (and undesirable) in this particular table as you work through this lesson.

6. Close the table and click Yes when Access asks if you want to save the table.

7. Type the name **Visit Details** in the Save As box and click OK.
   Access will display a warning box indicating that a primary key has not been defined.

8. Click No to save the table without defining a primary key.
   Once again, you will learn why a primary key is unnecessary as you work through this lesson.

Basing Subforms on Queries

Subforms can be based on tables or queries. When you run a query, Access displays the query results in a recordset. If you change data in the recordset, the data in the underlying table(s) that the query is based on may change as well. Access has a rather complex set of rules that determine when a query can be used to update underlying tables. Basically, if a query is based on a single table, the data in the underlying table are updateable. In other words, if you change data in the query recordset, the data in the underlying table are changed as well. This is also true of a form based on a query. If a form is based on a query and you enter or change data in the form, the data in the underlying table that the query is based on are updated as well. This allows you to use queries as the basis for subforms.

Another benefit of using queries as the basis for subforms is that queries can contain calculated fields. Calculated fields are often used to determine extended prices and for other types of calculations on order entry forms.

Hands-On 7.2 **Set Up the Visit Details Query**

In this exercise, you will set up a query based on the Visit Details table. The query will contain a calculated field named Extended Price. The Extended Price field will multiply the Unit Price of each item by the Quantity ordered.

1. Click the Queries button on the Objects bar.

2. Double-click the Create Query in Design View option.

3. Choose Visit Details in the Show Table box and click the Add button.

4. Close the Show Table box.

5. Add all fields to the Design grid by double-clicking them on the Visit Details field list.

6. Follow these steps to display the Zoom dialog box:

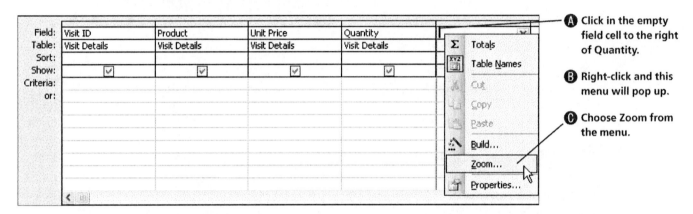

In the next few steps, you will enter a calculated field into the Zoom dialog box.

7. Enter the following expression into the Zoom box. Make sure to enter the expression exactly as shown. In particular, make sure you use a colon (:) and not a semicolon (;), correctly spell the field names, and use the correct open and closed brackets [ ] as shown.

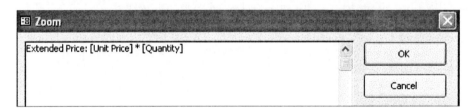

8. Click OK to insert the expression into the field.
   When you create the subform in Hands-On 7.3, this expression will calculate the extended price for each row in the subform.

9. Make sure the syntax of your expression is correct. If necessary, edit the expression within the cell or redisplay the Zoom dialog box and make any necessary changes.

Field:	Visit ID	Product	Unit Price	Quantity	Extended Price: [Ur
Table:	Visit Details	Visit Details	Visit Details	Visit Details	
Sort:					
Show:	☑	☑	☑	☑	☑
Criteria:					

10. Close the query and save it as **Query - Visit Details**.
   You cannot give the query the name Visit Details because the Visit Details table already has that name. In Access, you cannot give a table and a query the same name.

11. Continue with the next topic, in which you will learn how to create subforms.

The Subform Wizard

The Subform Wizard is initiated by clicking the Subform 🔲 button on the toolbox while working in Form Design view. The Subform Wizard makes it easy to set up subforms within an existing main form. The Subform Wizard automatically synchronizes the subform with the main form, provided that you have set up the underlying table and/or query properly. Synchronization ensures that the appropriate records are displayed in the subform for each record in the main form.

Synchronizing a Main Form and a Subform

The Subform Wizard automatically synchronizes a main form and a subform, provided that a relationship has been established between the tables or queries on which the forms are based. Synchronization also occurs automatically if the subform and main form have a field with the same name defined as a primary key in the main form. The matching field name technique will be used to synchronize the Visit Details subform with the Visits form in the Pinnacle Pet Care database.

 Hands-On 7.3   **Set Up the Subform**

In this exercise, you will add a subform to the bottom of the Visits form.

1. Click the Forms button on the Objects bar.

2. Choose the Visits form and click the 🖉 Design button.
   A subform is set up while the main form is open in Design view.

3. If necessary, click the Maximize 🔲 button to maximize the form.

4. If necessary, use the View→Toolbox command to display the toolbox.

5. Follow these steps to make room for the subform and to specify the subform location:
The first screen will ask if you would like to build a new subform using an existing table or query.

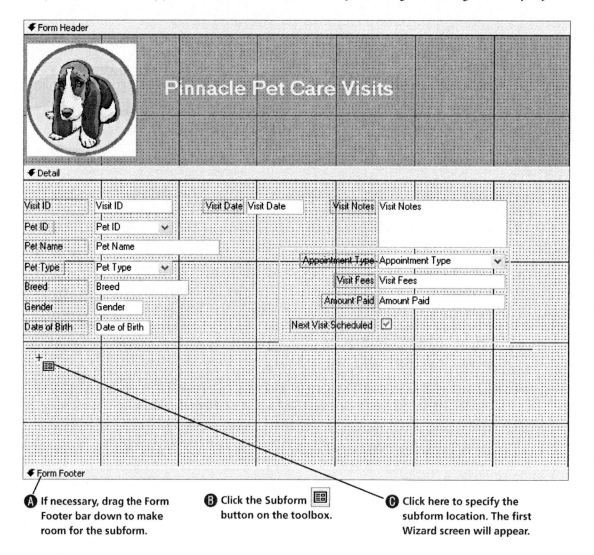

Ⓐ If necessary, drag the Form Footer bar down to make room for the subform.

Ⓑ Click the Subform button on the toolbox.

Ⓒ Click here to specify the subform location. The first Wizard screen will appear.

6. Click the Next button to choose the Use Existing Tables and Queries option.

7. Follow these steps to choose options in the second Wizard screen:

Ⓐ Choose Query - Visit Details from the Tables/Queries list. You will need to scroll to the bottom of the list.

Ⓑ Click the Add All Fields button to move all fields to the Selected Fields list.

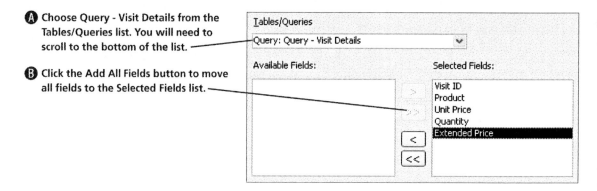

8. Click the Next button.

9. Leave the option in the third wizard screen set to Choose from a List.
   The wizard will automatically create a link between the Visit ID fields in the two tables when this option is chosen. This link will keep the main form and subform synchronized.

10. Click the Next button.

11. Type **Visit Details** in the last wizard screen and click the Finish button.

12. Maximize 🔲 the Visits form window again, and a placeholder box for the subform will appear.
    A subform appears as a large placeholder box when the main form is displayed in Design view.

13. Click the Form 🔲 view button on the Access toolbar.

14. Examine the following illustration to understand the relationship between the main form and subform:

Ⓐ Notice that Access automatically inserts the same number in the Visit ID field of the subform and the main form. As you enter data in the subform, Access will automatically assign the Visit ID currently displayed in the main form to the subform records. This keeps the main form record synchronized with the subform records.

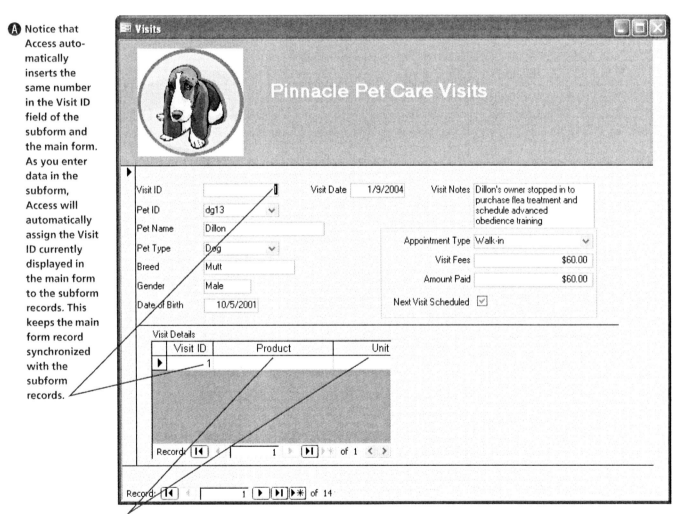

Ⓑ Notice that the subform displays the fields from the underlying Query - Visit Details query (although they are not all visible at this point), on which the subform is based. When you enter data in these fields, the data will be stored in the underlying Visit Details table, on which the query is based. However, data will not be stored in the Extended Price field (not visible) because it is a calculated field. In fact, the Extended Price field does not even exist in the Visit Details table. The Extended Price will simply be calculated by the query

15. Make sure the flashing insertion point is positioned in the Visit ID field at the top of the form.

16. Click the Sort Ascending ![A↓] button on the toolbar.
    This will ensure that the records in the main form are sorted on the Visit ID field. The Dillon the Dog record should be displayed because it has Visit ID 1.

17. Click the Design ![icon] view button on the Access toolbar to return to Design view.
    In Hands-On 7.4, you will adjust the size of the subform placeholder box in Design view. The subform will then display all five columns from the Visit Details query.

Adjusting the Size of a Subform

You can change the overall size of a subform within a main form by displaying the main form in Design view, clicking the box, and dragging the sizing handles. You can also specify a precise size for the subform by clicking the subform to select it then setting the Width and Height properties in the Properties dialog box.

Adjusting Subform Column Widths

To adjust the individual column widths of a subform, you must first open the subform in Form view. The column widths can then be adjusted by dragging the column headings or by clicking the column headings and using the Format→Column Width command to specify precise widths. You can also double-click the border between two column headings to AutoFit a column.

Hands-On 7.4   **Adjust the Size of the Subform**

In this exercise, you will adjust the size of the subform by dragging the sizing handles.

Adjust the Overall Size of the Subform

1. Follow these steps to adjust the size of the subform placeholder box:

Ⓐ If necessary, click the edge of the subform box to select it. Notice the sizing handles.

Ⓑ Drag a corner-sizing handle until the subform has the approximate size shown here. You can also drag the bottom or side sizing handles as necessary.

Breed	Breed			Visit Fees	Visit Fees
Gender	Gender			Amount Paid	Amount Paid
Date of Birth	Date of Birth		Next Visit Scheduled	☑	

Visit Details

⬥ Form Header
⬥ Detail

Visit ID	Visit ID
Service/Product	Service/Product
Unit Price	Unit Price

⬥ Form Footer

Ⓒ If necessary, use Ctrl+arrow key to position the subform box as shown here.

2. Click the Form [⊞] view button and the subform should have the same dimensions in Form view that it had in Design view.
   At this point, the subform column widths may not fill the subform. You will widen the columns in the following steps.

3. Close the Visits form and save the changes.

Adjust Subform Column Widths

4. If necessary, click the Forms button on the Objects bar in the database window.
   Notice the Visit Details form. The Subform Wizard created the Visit Details form.

5. Double-click the Visit Details form to open it in Form view.

6. Follow these steps to adjust the subform column widths:
   This will adjust the column widths to fill the space on the subform, provided you used the correct field names in the Visit Details table.

Ⓐ Double-click the border between the Visit ID and Product column headings to AutoFit the Visit ID column.

Ⓑ Click the Product column heading, choose Format→Column Width, and set the width to **47**.

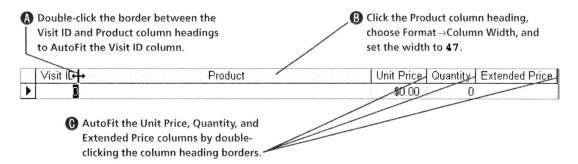

Visit ID	Product	Unit Price	Quantity	Extended Price
▶		$0.00	0	

Ⓒ AutoFit the Unit Price, Quantity, and Extended Price columns by double-clicking the column heading borders.

7. Close the Visit Details subform, and Access should automatically save the changes.

8. Double-click the Visits form to open it in Form view. Your completed main form and subform should closely match the following example.

If necessary, make adjustments to the subform column widths and/or the overall size of the subform. To adjust the subform column widths, open the Visit Details subform in Form view. To adjust the overall subform size, display the Visits form in Design view.

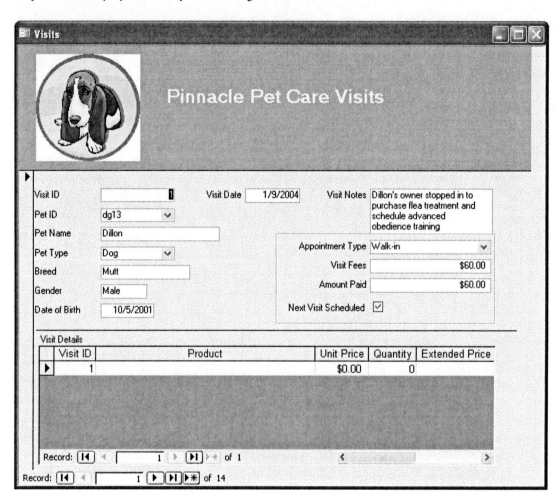

Entering Data into Subforms

You can enter data into a subform just as you enter data into a main form. If the subform is set up properly, Access will automatically keep the main form and subform synchronized by entering the appropriate record identifiers into the subform records. For example, Access will automatically enter the appropriate Visit ID in the Visit ID field of your subform records.

 Hands-On 7.5   **Enter Data and Navigate through Records**

In this exercise, you will add records to the subform.

1. Follow these steps to enter two records into the subform:

Ⓐ Click the Product box in the subform and type **Flea Prevention**.

Ⓑ Tap the [Tab] key and type **35** in the Unit Price field.

Ⓒ Tap [Tab] and type **1** in the Quantity field. Access will automatically apply the Currency format to the Unit Price.

Ⓓ Click in the Product field for the second record, and Access will calculate the Extended Price for the first record. The Extended Price is automatically calculated by the query on which the subform is based.

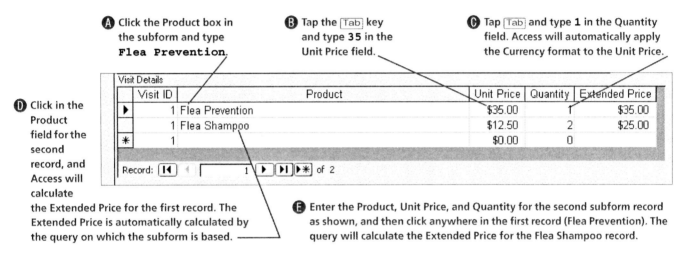

Ⓔ Enter the Product, Unit Price, and Quantity for the second subform record as shown, and then click anywhere in the first record (Flea Prevention). The query will calculate the Extended Price for the Flea Shampoo record.

2. Follow these steps to understand the relationship between the record navigation bars on the forms, and to navigate to another Visit record:

Ⓐ This navigation bar moves you through the subform records. However, your subform contains only two records for the current record on the main form, so this navigation bar has little use. It becomes useful when you have many subform records for the current record in the main form.

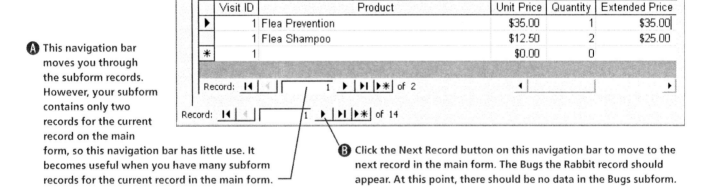

Ⓑ Click the Next Record button on this navigation bar to move to the next record in the main form. The Bugs the Rabbit record should appear. At this point, there should be no data in the Bugs subform.

3. Enter the following Visit Details data in the subform for Bugs the Rabbit:

	Visit ID	Product	Unit Price	Quantity	Extended Price
▶	2	Grooming Tools	$45.00	1	$45.00
	2	Pet Shampoo	$8.50	3	$25.50
*	2		$0.00	0	

Record: I◀ ◀ | 1 | ▶ ▶I ▶* of 2   ◀   ▶

4. Click the Next Record ▶ button on the record navigation bar of the Visits form (not the Visit Details subform).
The Max the Cat record should appear.

5. Enter the following Visit Details data in the subform for Max the Cat:

	Visit ID	Product	Unit Price	Quantity	Extended Price
▶	3	Leather Collar	$23.89	1	$23.89
	3	Deluxe Chain	$16.50	1	$16.50
*	3		$0.00	0	

Record: I◀ ◀ | 1 | ▶ ▶I ▶* of 2   ◀   ▶

6. Close the Visits form and, if necessary, save any changes.

Using Calculated Controls in Forms

Microsoft Office Specialist

Subforms are often used in order entry systems to enter and display order detail records. The order detail records usually contain pricing information and other numeric data. For example, the Visit Details subform records product order information. Main forms often require subtotal, sales tax, freight, and balance due controls. Calculated controls can be placed on main forms to perform these and other calculations. Main form controls can also be used to display the results of calculated controls on subforms. Take a moment to review the following illustration. You will add the Subtotal, Sales Tax, and Balance Due controls to the Visits form in the following exercises.

232 UNIT 2 Forms and Queries   Lesson 7: Working with Subforms and Calculated Controls

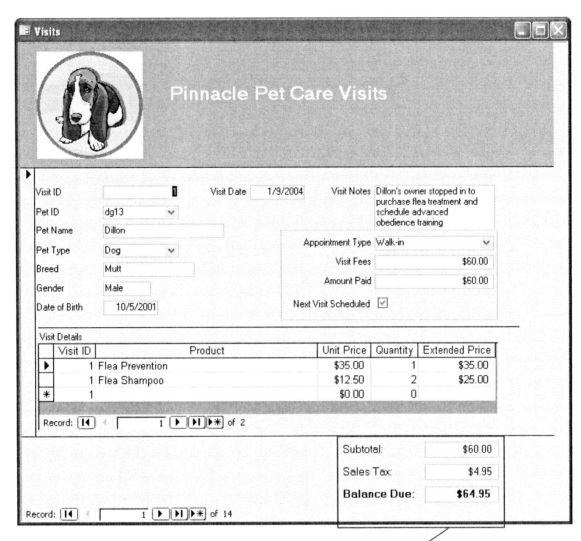

The subtotal is calculated in the Visit Details subform and displayed in the Subtotal control on the Visits main form. The Sales Tax and Balance Due calculations are performed within calculated controls on the main form.

Calculating Subtotals in Subforms

You can subtotal the detail records in subforms by placing a text box control in the footer section of the subform. The text box control contains a mathematical Sum function which adds the detail rows. The main form contains another text box control that simply reflects the subtotal calculated in the subform footer. The following illustration shows a subform calculated control that sums the detail records in the subform.

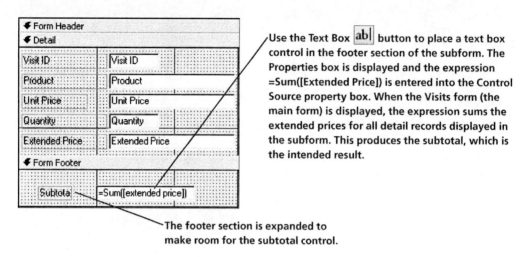

Use the Text Box [ab] button to place a text box control in the footer section of the subform. The Properties box is displayed and the expression =Sum([Extended Price]) is entered into the Control Source property box. When the Visits form (the main form) is displayed, the expression sums the extended prices for all detail records displayed in the subform. This produces the subtotal, which is the intended result.

The footer section is expanded to make room for the subtotal control.

Using Expressions in Text Box Controls

Earlier in this lesson, you created a calculated field within a query. You used the expression Extended Price: [Unit Price]*[Quantity] to calculate the extended price. Expressions can also be used within text box controls on forms and reports to perform calculations. For example, the expression =Sum([Extended Price]) is used within a subform to calculate subtotals. The following illustrations discuss the process and syntax required to create calculated controls on a form.

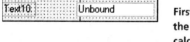

First, the Text Box [ab] button is used to add a text box control to the form. The control must be placed in the footer section if you are calculating a subtotal in a subform.

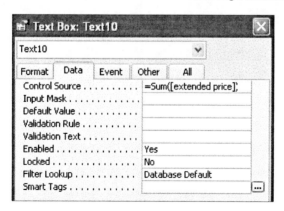

Next, while the control is selected, an expression is entered into the Control Source field of the Properties box. Here, the expression calculates the sum of the extended prices.

Finally, the control displays the expression entered into the Control Source box. In this example, the Text10 label has also been changed to Subtotal.

Expression Syntax

You must use proper syntax when creating expressions. Otherwise, Access will either reject the expression or perform an incorrect calculation. Expression syntax is discussed in the following illustrations. You will use all four of these expressions when you add calculated controls to the Visits and Visit Details forms.

- Example 1—The expression =Sum([Extended Price]) will calculate the sum of the extended prices in the Visit Details subform. This expression will be placed in a text box control in the footer section of the subform.

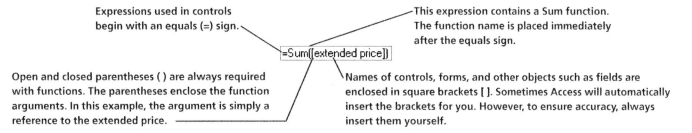

Expressions used in controls begin with an equals (=) sign.

This expression contains a Sum function. The function name is placed immediately after the equals sign.

=Sum([extended price])

Open and closed parentheses ( ) are always required with functions. The parentheses enclose the function arguments. In this example, the argument is simply a reference to the extended price.

Names of controls, forms, and other objects such as fields are enclosed in square brackets [ ]. Sometimes Access will automatically insert the brackets for you. However, to ensure accuracy, always insert them yourself.

The following illustration shows the Subtotal, Sales Tax, and Balance Due controls you will add to the Visits form. The illustration also shows the expressions you will assign to the controls. A detailed discussion of each expression follows the illustration.

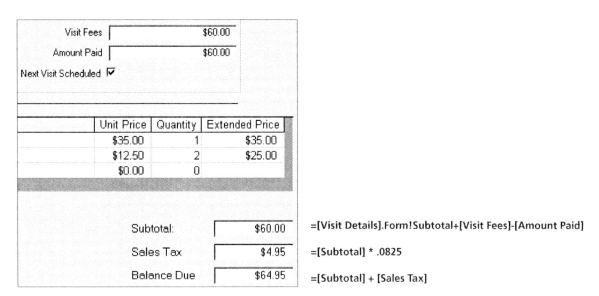

Visit Fees	$60.00
Amount Paid	$60.00
Next Visit Scheduled	✔

	Unit Price	Quantity	Extended Price
	$35.00	1	$35.00
	$12.50	2	$25.00
	$0.00	0	

Subtotal:	$60.00	=[Visit Details].Form!Subtotal+[Visit Fees]-[Amount Paid]
Sales Tax	$4.95	=[Subtotal] * .0825
Balance Due	$64.95	=[Subtotal] + [Sales Tax]

- Example 2—The expression=[Visit Details].[Form]![Subtotal]+[Visit Fees]-[Amount Paid]] gets the subtotal from the Visit Details subform, adds the Visit Fee from the main form, then subtracts the Amount Paid (also from the main form). Visit Detail is the name of the form that holds the subtotal. We don't need to add the form where Visit Fees and Amount paid are found because they are on the same form as this expression.

The period (.) is called a dot operator. It is used to separate the name of the object [Visit Details] from the object type [Form]. You must use this syntax when referring to a control outside the current object.

The exclamation point (!) is called a bang operator. It separates the object type [Form] from the control [Subtotal].

Notice that all elements are enclosed in square brackets.

=[Visit Details].[Form]![Subtotal]+[Visit Fees]-[Amount Paid]

This expression says: go to the Visit Details form, get the subtotal, then add the Visit Fees and subtract the Amount Paid from this form.

- Example 3—The expression =[Subtotal] * .0825 calculates the sales tax by multiplying the subtotal by .0825 (8.25%). Notice that the control name Subtotal is surrounded by square brackets. Also, notice that the asterisk (*) is used to represent multiplication. Finally, spaces are used before and after the asterisk. Access is quite forgiving when it comes to blank spaces, so spaces are optional in this expression.

- Example 4—The expression =[Subtotal]+[Sales Tax] calculates the Balance Due as the Subtotal plus Sales Tax. Once again, square brackets surround the control names and spaces are optional before and after the plus (+) sign.

 Hands-On 7.6 Insert Expressions in the Visit Details Subform

In this exercise, you will place a subtotal calculation in the subform and a subtotal, sales tax, and balance due calculation on the Visits form.

Display the Footer Area

1. If necessary, click the Forms button on the Objects bar.

2. Choose the Visit Details subform and click the ⌨ Design button.

3. If necessary, maximize 🔲 the window.

Set Up the Calculated Control

4. Click the Text Box abl button on the toolbox.

5. Click in the footer area below the Extended Price control to specify the text box position. The text box will be inserted and the word Unbound will appear in the box.
Unbound means the control is not linked to a field in an underlying table and no expression has been assigned to it. The position of this text box is not critical as long as it is in the footer area. This box will simply perform the calculation.

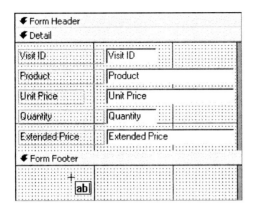

In the next few steps, you will assign the =Sum([Extended Price]) expression to the control. You will also assign the name Subtotal to the control.

6. If necessary, use the Properties [⊞] button to display the Properties box.

7. Click the Data tab and enter the expression **=Sum([Extended Price])** in the Control Source box.

8. Follow these steps to assign a name to the control:

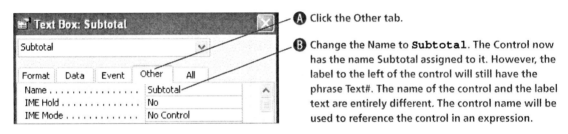

Ⓐ Click the Other tab.

Ⓑ Change the Name to **Subtotal**. The Control now has the name Subtotal assigned to it. However, the label to the left of the control will still have the phrase Text#. The name of the control and the label text are entirely different. The control name will be used to reference the control in an expression.

9. Click the label to the left of the control twice and change the label text to **Subtotal**. *The completed Visit Details form should match the following example.*

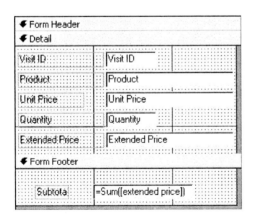

10. Close the Visit Details form and save the changes.

Place a Subtotal Control on the Visits Form

11. Open the Visits form in Design view.

12. If necessary, maximize the form.

13. Follow these steps to prepare the form for the Subtotal, Sales Tax, and Balance Due controls:

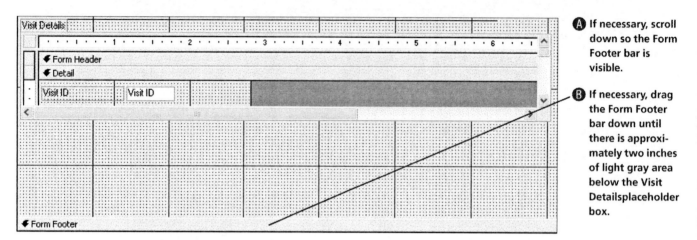

A If necessary, scroll down so the Form Footer bar is visible.

B If necessary, drag the Form Footer bar down until there is approximately two inches of light gray area below the Visit Detailsplaceholder box.

At this point, you may find that your form is too large to fit on the screen. You can address this issue in one of two ways. First, you can ignore the problem and use the vertical scroll bar to move up and down through the form in both Design and Form views. Or, you can rearrange the controls so the form requires less vertical space. You can also decrease the height of the Visit Details placeholder box. However, if you do this, you won't be able to see as many detail rows when you view the Visits form in Form view.

14. Click the Text Box abl button on the toolbox.

15. Click just below the subform placeholder box to specify the text box position.

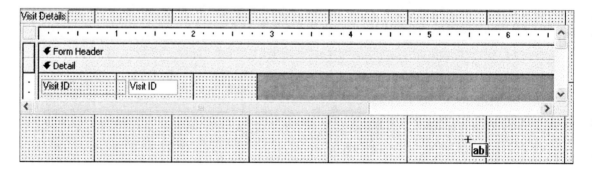

16. If necessary, display the Properties box and click the Data tab.

17. Enter the expression `=[Visit Details].[Form]![Subtotal]+[Visit Fees]-[Amount Paid]` in the Control Source box. Make sure you include the open and closed brackets [ ], the period, and the exclamation mark as shown.

18. Click the Other tab and type **Subtotal** in the Name box.

19. Click the label to the left of the control on the form twice and change the label text to **Subtotal**.

The completed control should match the following example. Don't be concerned with the position of the control or the label. You will adjust the positions later.

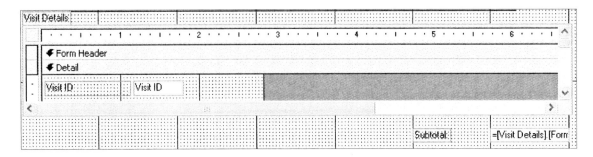

20. Click the Form ⊞ view button on the toolbar.

Access should calculate the subtotal for the current record. In Hands-On 7.7, you will format the Subtotal and other calculated controls so the numbers are displayed in Currency format.

21. Feel free to browse through the records on the Visits form using the navigation bar at the bottom of the form.

Access will calculate the subtotal each time you go to a new record. However, at this point, only three records on the main form should have detail records. You will complete the data entry later.

Place Sales Tax and Balance Due Controls on the Visits Form

22. Switch to Design ⊿ view.

23. Use these guidelines to add the Sales Tax and Balance Due controls to the form as shown in the following illustration:

■ Use the Text Box abl button to add the controls to the form.

■ Set the Control Source property for the Sales Tax control to **=[Subtotal]*.0825**. Change the name of the Sales Tax control to **Sales Tax**. You can accomplish this in the Other tab of the Properties dialog box. Change the label in front of the control to **Sales Tax**.

■ Set the Control Source property for the Balance Due control to **=[Subtotal]+[Sales Tax]**. Change the name of the Balance Due control to **Balance Due**. You can accomplish this in the Other tab of the Properties dialog box. Change the label in front of the control to **Balance Due**.

■ Don't be concerned with the alignment and position of the controls. You will change the alignment and position in Hands-On 7.7.

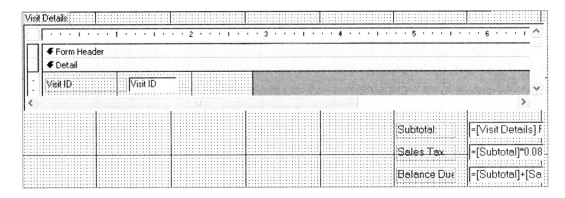

24. Click the Form view button on the toolbar.

Access should calculate the Subtotal, Sales Tax, and Balance Due for the current record. However, the numbers may have a large number of decimals and be aligned on the left side of the boxes.

25. Feel free to browse through the records on the Visits form using the navigation bar at the bottom of the form.

Access will calculate the Subtotal, Sales Tax, and Balance Due for each record.

26. Switch back to Design view.

Modifying Control Properties

Microsoft Office
SpecialistThe Format tab in the Properties box gives you complete control over the formatting of controls. For example, the Format tab lets you adjust the size of controls and the format of numbers. You will use the Properties box to format the numbers in the Subtotal, Sales Tax, and Balance Due controls. You will also change the size of the controls, the font used in the controls, and the position of the controls on the form.

Changing the Tab Order

The tab order is the order in which fields are encountered when the [Tab] key is used to navigate through the fields on a form. When fields are added or controls are moved, the tab order may not be in the most logical sequence. If you open the Visits form and tap [Tab] you will notice that you don't flow through the form in the order that makes the most sense. You want to design a form so users require minimal keystrokes to enter data. The tab order can be modified from Design view by choosing View→Tab Order. You can then rearrange the order by dragging the items as necessary. You will adjust the tab order in Hands-On 7.7.

Hands-On 7.7   Format and Position Controls

In this exercise, you will format the expressions, arrange the controls, and set the tab order on the Visits form.

Set Number Properties

1. Click the Subtotal control then press [Shift] while you click the Sales Tax and Balance Due controls.

Make sure you click the controls and not the labels to the left of the controls.

2. Follow these steps to format the controls with the Currency format:

Ⓐ Click the Format tab in the Properties box.

Ⓑ Click in the Format box, click the drop-down button, scroll through the list, and choose Currency.

Ⓒ Click in the Decimal Places box and set the number of decimals to **2**.

Multiple selection
Format   Data   Event   Other   All
Format . . . . Currency
Decimal Places 2
Visible . . . . Yes

Set Text Format Properties

3. Now press ⌈Shift⌉ while you click each label to the left of the selected controls.
All three labels and all three controls should be selected.

4. Scroll through the list of properties on the Format tab and set the Font Size property to **10**.
You can set all text formats using either the buttons on the toolbar or the Properties box. Notice that the font size increased but that the height and width of the controls and labels remained the same. In the next step, you will increase the height of all selected objects by setting the Height property in the Properties box.

5. Scroll up through the Format properties until you locate the Height property.

6. Change the Height property setting to **.2** and tap ⌈Enter⌉.
The height of all six selected objects will increase.

7. Click in an empty part of the form to deselect the controls.

8. Use the ⌈Shift⌉ key technique to select only the Subtotal, Sales Tax, and Balance Due labels to the left of the controls.

9. Click in the Width box (within the Properties box), set the width to **1**, and tap ⌈Enter⌉.

10. Select all three labels and use the Format→Align→Left command to align the labels on the left.

11. Use the ⌈Shift⌉ key technique to select only the Subtotal, Sales Tax, and Balance Due controls (not the labels to the left of the controls).

12. Use the Format→Align→Left command to align the controls on the left.

13. Use the ⌈Ctrl⌉+arrow keystroke combinations to adjust the position of the controls as shown in the following illustration.
You may need to deselect the controls and move them one at a time to achieve the intended results. Notice that the right edges of the controls are aligned with the right edge of the subform.

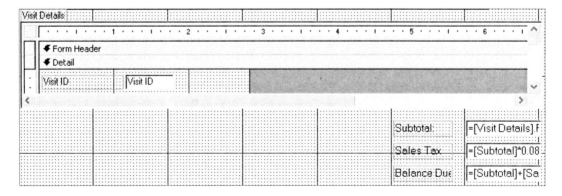

14. Use the ⟨Shift⟩ key technique to select only the Balance Due label and the Balance Due control.

15. Set the Font Weight format property to Bold (you may need to scroll down).

16. Click in the Fore Color format property box and click the Ellipses ⟨...⟩ button that appears in the box.
    Access will display a color palette.

17. Choose a dark blue color and click OK.
    A number will be displayed in the Font Color property. The number represents the color you chose.

Rename Controls

18. Click the Pet ID control then click the Other tab in the Properties box.

19. Enter the name **Pet ID** in the Name box.

20. Click the Pet Type control and enter the name **Pet Type** in the Name box.

Change the Tab Order

21. Choose View→Tab Order from the menu bar.

22. Follow these steps to change the tab order:

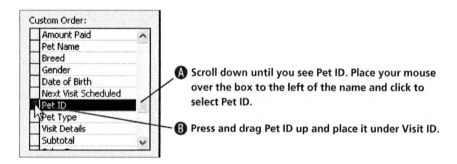

Ⓐ Scroll down until you see Pet ID. Place your mouse over the box to the left of the name and click to select Pet ID.

Ⓑ Press and drag Pet ID up and place it under Visit ID.

23. Move Next Visit Scheduled so it is under Amount Paid.
    Your tab order box should match this one.

24. Click OK and save your form.

Examine the Completed Form and Enter Data

25. Click the Form 📼 view button on the toolbar to view the completed form.
Your form should closely match the following example.

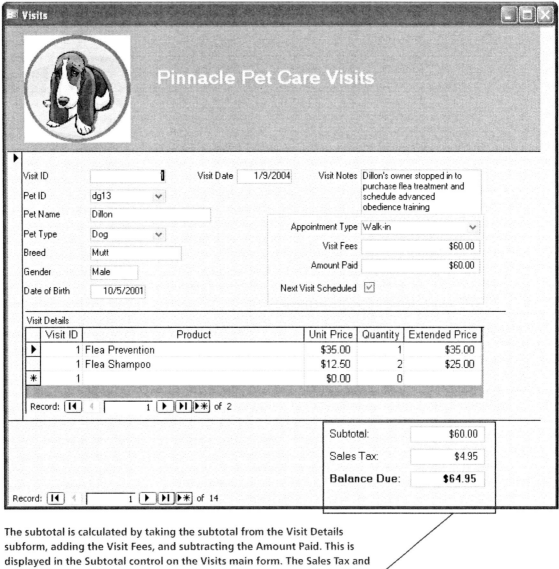

The subtotal is calculated by taking the subtotal from the Visit Details
subform, adding the Visit Fees, and subtracting the Amount Paid. This is
displayed in the Subtotal control on the Visits main form. The Sales Tax and
Balance Due calculations are performed within calculated controls on the
main form.

26. Test your tab order by tapping the ⌷Tab⌷ key several times.
*Your tab should move from Visit ID field to Pet ID field to Visit Date field and so on, according to the
order you set in the Tab Order dialog box.*

27. Use the navigation bar at the bottom of the Visits form to navigate to the record with Visit
ID 4 (the Stripes the Cat record).

28. Enter the following data into the Stripes the Cat record:

As you enter the data, Access will automatically calculate the Subtotal, Sales Tax, and Balance Due.

Visit Details					
	Visit ID	Product	Unit Price	Quantity	Extended Price
	4	Grooming kit	$35.00	1	$35.00
	4	Pet Shampoo	$12.50	2	$25.00
▶	4		$0.00	0	

Record: 3 of 3

Subtotal:	$118.00
Sales Tax	$9.74
Balance Due	**$127.74**

29. Enter the following data into the subform for Visit IDs 5–7.

Visit ID	Product	Unit Price	Quantity
5	Premium Dog Food	15.00	1
	Antibiotics	50.00	1
6	Deluxe Pet Toy	6.00	1
	Pet Shampoo	8.50	3
7	Flea Prevention	55.00	1
	Flea Shampoo	12.50	5

30. If necessary, make any adjustments to your form so it matches the preceding illustration.

31. Close the form when you have finished and save the changes.

32. Close the Pinnacle Pet Care database and continue with the end-of-lesson questions and exercises.

Concepts Review

True/False Questions

1. A subform is a form within a form. TRUE FALSE

2. Subforms are not based on tables or queries. TRUE FALSE

3. Synchronization between a main form and a subform occurs automatically when a relationship has been established between the forms. TRUE FALSE

4. Calculated controls cannot be used in subforms. TRUE FALSE

5. A subtotal is calculated in a subform by placing a calculated control in the subform footer. TRUE FALSE

6. Calculated control expressions are placed in the Control Source box of the Properties box. TRUE FALSE

7. Expressions can contain functions such as Sum. TRUE FALSE

8. The Data tab in the Properties box is used to set formatting options for controls. TRUE FALSE

9. You can enter data into a subform just as you enter data into a main form. TRUE FALSE

10. You cannot change the tab order on your forms. TRUE FALSE

Multiple Choice Questions

1. Which of the following buttons initiates the Subform Wizard?
   a. [...]
   b. [▦]
   c. [▦]
   d. [!]

2. Which of the following symbols is used to enclose function arguments in expressions?
   a. { }
   b. ( )
   c. [ ]
   d. < >

3. Which of the following symbols is used to enclose the names of controls, forms, and other objects?
   a. { }
   b. ( )
   c. [ ]
   d. < >

4. Which of the following symbols is used to separate the object type from the control?
   a. =
   b. -
   c. .
   d. !

Skill Builders

Skill Builder 7.1   Set Up a Package Details Table

In this exercise, you will set up a new table in the Tropical Getaways database. The table will be used to record package details for the Custom Packages program.

1. Open the Tropical Getaways database.

2. Click the Tables button on the Objects bar.

3. Double-click the Create Table in Design View option.

4. Follow these steps to set up the Package Details table:

   Ⓐ Type the field names shown here and choose the data types shown for each field name. Be sure to spell the field names correctly.

Field Name	Data Type
Package ID	Number
Item	Text
Unit Price	Currency
Quantity	Number

   Ⓑ Leave the field size for the Item field set to **50**. Set the number of decimals for the Unit Price field to **2**.

5. Do not set a primary key for this table.

6. Close the table and choose Yes when Access asks if you want to save the table.

7. Type the name **Package Details** in the Save As box and click OK.
   Access will display a warning box indicating that a primary key has not been defined.

8. Choose No to save the table without defining a primary key.

Set Up a Query with a Calculated Field

In this exercise, you will create a query based on the Package Details table. The query will contain an Extended Price field.

1. Click the Queries button on the Objects bar.

2. Double-click the Create Query in Design View option.

3. Choose Package Details in the Show Table box and click the Add button.

4. Close the Show Table box.

5. Add all fields to the design grid by double-clicking them on the Package Details field list.

6. Click in the empty field to the right of the Quantity field.

7. Click the right mouse button and choose Zoom from the pop-up menu.

8. Enter the expression **Extended Price:[Unit Price]*[Quantity]** and click OK. *Your completed query should match the following example.*

Field:	Package ID	Item	Unit Price	Quantity	Extended Price: [ur
Table:	Package Details	Package Details	Package Details	Package Details	
Sort:					
Show:	✓	✓	✓	✓	✓

9. Close the query and save it as **Query - Package Details**.

Skill Builder 7.3   **Insert a Subform**

In this exercise, you will use the Subform Wizard to insert a subform in the Custom Packages form, which you created in Lesson 6, Customizing Forms and Using Advanced Controls. You will base the subform on the Query - Package Details query.

Insert the Subform

1. Click the Forms button on the Objects bar.

2. Choose the Custom Packages form and click the 🖊️ Design button.

3. If necessary, click the Maximize 🔲 button to maximize the form.

4. Follow these steps to make room for the subform and to specify the subform location:

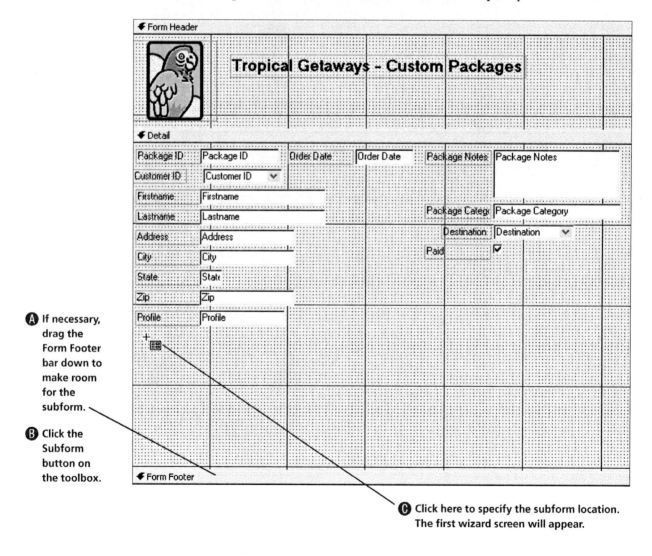

A If necessary, drag the Form Footer bar down to make room for the subform.

B Click the Subform button on the toolbox.

C Click here to specify the subform location. The first wizard screen will appear.

5. Click the Next button to choose the Use Existing Tables and Queries option in the first wizard screen.

6. Choose the Query - Package Details query in the second wizard screen and add all fields to the Selected Fields list.

7. Click the Next button.

8. Leave the option in the third wizard screen set to Choose from a List and click Next.

9. Type the name **Package Details** in the last wizard screen and click the Finish button.

10. Maximize the Visits form window again, and a placeholder box for the subform will appear.

Adjust the Overall Subform Size

11. Make sure the subform is selected and, if necessary, click the Properties button to display the Properties box.

12. If necessary, click the Format tab on the Properties box.

13. Set the Width property to **6.6"** and the Height property to **1.15"**.

14. Close the Custom Packages form and save the changes.

Adjust Subform Column Widths

15. If necessary, click the Forms button on the Objects bar in the database window.
    Notice the Package Details form created by the Subform Wizard.

16. Double-click the Package Details form to open it in Form view.

17. AutoFit the widths of the Package ID, Unit Price, Quantity, and Extended Price columns by double-clicking the right edge of their column headings.

18. Select the Item column by clicking the column heading.

19. Choose Format→Column Width and set the width to **50**.

20. Close the Package Details subform, and Access should automatically save the changes.

21. Double-click the Custom Packages form to open it in Form view. Your completed main form and subform should closely match the following example.

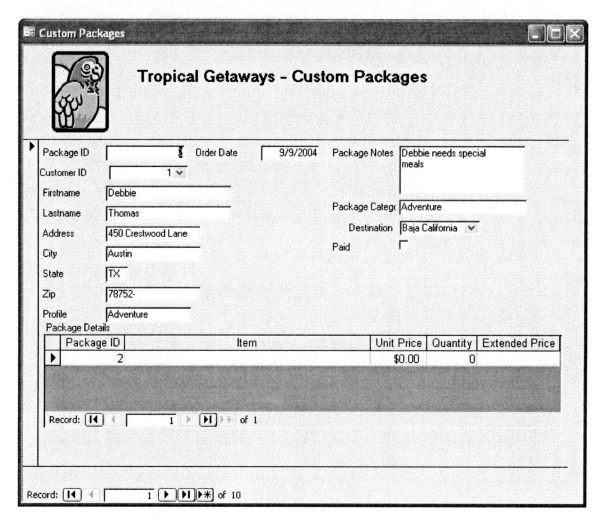

If necessary, make adjustments to the subform column widths and/or the overall size of the subform. To adjust the subform column widths, open the Package Details subform in Form view. To adjust the overall subform size, display the Custom Packages form in Design view.

22. Close the Custom Packages form when you have finished.

Insert a Calculated Control

In this exercise, you will create a Subtotal control in the Package Details form.

1. Open the Package Details form in Design view.

2. Maximize ▣ the form window.

3. Click the Text Box button on the toolbox.

4. Click below the Form Footer bar under the Extended Price control. The dark area of the footer will become light gray behind the text box control.

5. Make sure the text box control is selected and, if necessary, display the Properties box.

6. Click the Data tab in the Properties box and enter the expression **=Sum([Extended Price])** in the Control Source property. Be sure to use the open and closed parentheses ( ) and open and closed brackets [ ].

7. Click the Other tab and enter the name **Subtotal** in the Name box.

8. Click the label on the form to the left of the Subtotal control twice, and change the label text to **Subtotal**.

9. Close the Package Details form and save the changes.

Add Calculated Controls

In this exercise, you will add Subtotal, Sales Tax, and Total controls to the Custom Packages form.

1. Open the Custom Packages form in Design view and maximize ▣ the form.

2. Use these guidelines to add the Subtotal, Sales Tax, and Total controls to the form, as shown in the following example:

   ■ If necessary, drag the Form Footer bar down to make room for the controls below the subform.

   ■ Use the Text Box ⌗ab⌗ button to add three controls to the form.

   ■ Set the Control Source property for the Subtotal control to the expression **=[Package Details].[Form]![Subtotal]**. Change the name of the Subtotal control to **Subtotal**. You can accomplish this in the Other tab of the Properties box. Change the label in front of the control to **Subtotal**.

   ■ Set the Control Source property for the Sales Tax control to **=[Subtotal]*.075**. This expression assumes the sales tax rate is 7.5%. Change the name of the Sales Tax control to **Sales Tax**. Change the label in front of the control to **Sales Tax**.

■ Set the Control Source property for the Total control to **=[Subtotal]+[Sales Tax]**. Change the name of the Total control to **Total**. Change the label in front of the control to **Total**.

■ Don't be concerned with the layout of the controls. In a moment, you will format the controls and modify their positions.

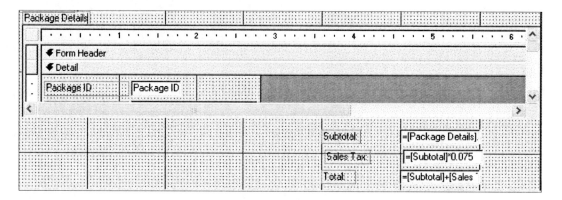

3. Use the ⟦Shift⟧ key technique to select all three controls and labels.

4. Click the Format tab in the Properties box.

5. Set the Font Size property to **10**.

6. Set the Height property to **.2**.

7. Click on a blank area of the form to deselect the controls.

8. Select only the three labels to the left of the controls.

9. Set the Width property to **.8**.

10. Use the Format→Align→Left command to align the selected labels.

11. Select only the Subtotal, Sales Tax, and Total controls.

12. Set the Format property to Currency and the Decimal Places property to **2**.

13. Use the Format→Align→Left command to align the selected controls.

14. Click on a blank area of the form to deselect the controls.

15. Select only the Total control and the Total label.

16. Use the Bold **B** button on the Formatting toolbar to apply bold formatting.
    You can apply text formats using buttons on the Formatting toolbar or properties in the Properties box.

17. Use the Font Color **A** button on the Formatting toolbar to apply the color of your choice to the Total Label and the Total Control.

18. Use the [Ctrl]+arrow keys technique to position the controls under the Visit Details subform as shown in the following illustration.

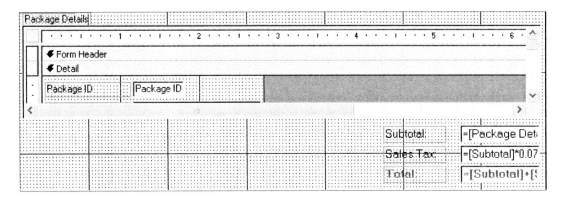

19. Switch to Form 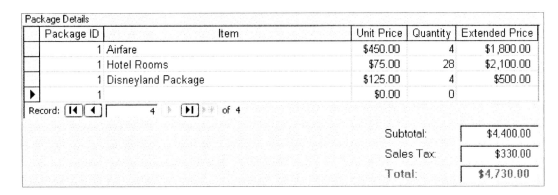 view.

Skill Builder 7.6   Enter Data in the Subform

In this exercise, you will change the tab order and enter data into the Custom Packages form.

1. Make sure the flashing insertion point is positioned in the Package ID field at the top of the Custom Packages main form.

2. Click the Sort Ascending ![button] button on the Access toolbar.
   The records in the main form should now be sorted by Package ID. The Alice Simpson record should appear first because it has Package ID 1.

3. Enter the following three items into the Package Details subform:

Package Details

Package ID	Item	Unit Price	Quantity	Extended Price
1	Airfare	$450.00	4	$1,800.00
1	Hotel Rooms	$75.00	28	$2,100.00
1	Disneyland Package	$125.00	4	$500.00
1		$0.00	0	

Record: |◄ | ◄ | 4 | ► | ►| | ►* | of 4

Subtotal:	$4,400.00
Sales Tax:	$330.00
Total:	$4,730.00

The Extended Price, Subtotal, Sales Tax, and Total should automatically be calculated as shown. If your controls do not calculate correctly, switch to Design view and modify the calculated control expressions.

Rename Controls and Change the Tab Order

4. Switch to Design view.

5. Change the name of the Customer ID and the Destination controls in the Properties box by choosing the control, then clicking the Other tab and entering **Customer ID** for the Customer ID control and **Destination** for the Destination control.

6. Change the Tab Order, as shown in the following illustration.

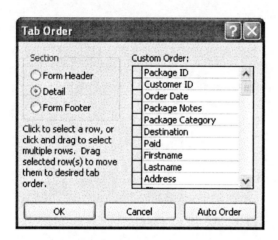

7. Switch to Form view and enter the following data into the subform for Package IDs 2–10:

Package ID	Item	Price Unit	Quantity
2	Airfare	$375.00	1
	Deep sea fishing package	$500.00	1
	Snorkeling package	$450.00	1
3	Airfare	$175.00	1
	Rental car	$25.00	4
	Climbing package	$350.00	1
4	Airfare	$485.00	1
	All inclusive cruise package	$2,790.00	1
5	Airfare	$485.00	1
	All inclusive cruise package	$2,790.00	1
6	Airfare	$525.00	4
	Hotel rooms	$145.00	24
	Rental car	$28.50	7
7	Airfare	$1,890.00	2
	All inclusive safari package	$3,450.00	2
8	Airfare	$300.00	1
	Hotel room	$85.00	6
	Touring package	$235.00	1
9	Airfare	$1,560.00	1
	Climbing package	$2,750.00	1
10	Airfare	$375.00	1
	Deep sea fishing package	$500.00	1
	Snorkeling package	$450.00	1

8. Close the Custom Packages form when you have finished and save any changes.

9. Close the Tropical Getaways database.

 **Assessments**

Assessment 7.1   Add a Subform

In this exercise, you will add a subform, based on a query, to the Events form.

1. Open the Classic Cars database.

2. Use these guidelines to set up a new table with the structure shown in the following illustration:
   - Use the field names and data types shown.
   - Leave the field length of the Item field set to 50.
   - Set the number of decimal places for the Daily Cost field to **2**.
   - Do not set a primary key.
   - Close the table and save it as **Event Details**.

Field Name	Data Type
Event ID	Number
Item	Text
Daily Cost	Currency
Number of Days	Number

3. Use these guidelines to set up a query with the structure shown in the following illustration:
   - Add all fields from the Event Details table to the query.
   - Create the calculated field named Total shown below. Enter the expression **Total:[Daily Cost]*[Number of Days]** to calculate the Total.
   - Close the query and save it as **Query - Event Details**.

Field:	Event ID	Item	Daily Cost	Number of Days	Total: [Daily Cost]*
Table:	Event Details	Event Details	Event Details	Event Details	
Sort:					
Show:	☑	☑	☑	☑	☑
Criteria:					

4. Use the Subform Wizard and the following guidelines to insert a subform in the Events form:

- Use the Query - Event Details query as the basis for the subform. Add all fields from the query to the subform.

- Let the wizard automatically synchronize the Events form with the Subform by choosing the Choose From a List option in the third wizard screen.

- Assign the name **Event Details** to the subform.

- Adjust the size of the subform placeholder box and the column widths of the subform so it closely matches the following example.

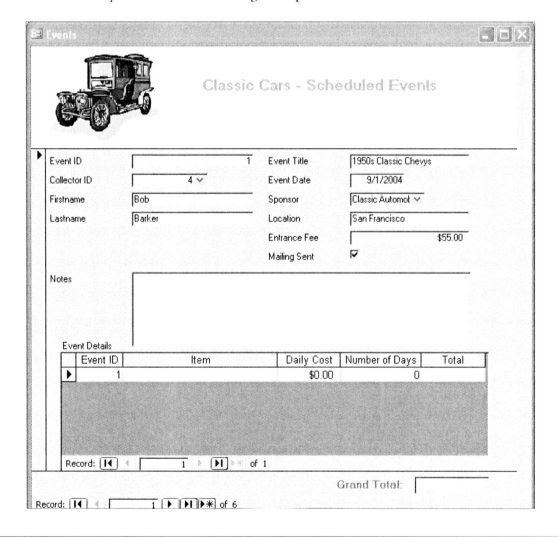

Assessment 7.2   Add a Calculated Control

In this exercise, you will modify the controls on the form.

1. Use these guidelines to add a calculated control to the footer section of the Event Details subform, as shown in the following example. This control is similar to the Subtotal controls you created in the Hands-On and Skill Builder exercises in this lesson.

   - Use the expression shown to sum the Total fields in the query.
   - Assign the name **Grand Total** (in the Properties box) to the control.
   - Change the label text in front of the control to **Grand Total**.

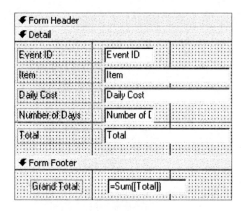

2. Open the Events form and sort the records in the Events form by Event ID.
   The Bob Barker record should be visible, because it has Event ID 1.

3. Use these guidelines to add a Grand Total control to the Events form, as shown in the following illustration:

   - Use an expression that references the Grand Total control in the Event Details subform. The Grand Total from the subform should be reflected in the new control on the Events form.
   - Assign the name **Grand Total** to the new control.
   - Change the label text in front of the control to **Grand Total**.
   - Change the font size of the control and the label in front of the control to **10**.
   - Increase the height of the control and the label to **.2"**.
   - Increase the width of the label so all text is visible in the label.
   - Apply bold formatting and a color to both the control and the label.
   - Set the Format property of just the control to Currency and set the Decimal Places property to **2**.
   - Change the name on the Collector ID and Sponsor controls.

- Set the tab order to a logical progression.
- The following form shows three records in the Event Details subform. Add these records to the subform in your database. Your Grand Total should be calculated as shown.

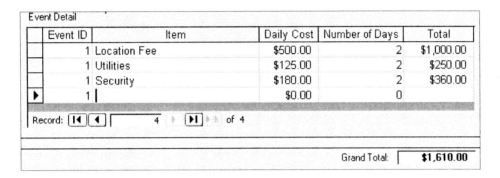

4. Enter the following data into the subform for Event IDs 2–6:

Event ID	Item	Daily Cost	Number of Days
2	Location fee	$850.00	4
	Set-up fees	$3,000.00	1
	Utilities	$350.00	4
3	Location fee	$3,500.00	2
	Set-up fees	$3,400.00	1
	Utilities	$235.00	2
4	Location fee	$5,600.00	3
	Set-up fees	$8,500.00	1
	Security	$400.00	3
5	Location fee	$8,500.00	2
	Set-up fees	$6,500.00	1
	Utilities	$650.00	2
6	Location fee	$1,200.00	1
	Utilities	$235.00	1

5. Close the Events form when you have finished and save any changes.

6. Close the Classic Cars database.

Critical Thinking

Critical Thinking 7.1   Create Subforms

Linda finds that managing the Feels Like Home service for Holmestead Realty is just too much work. So, she decides to subcontract the service to the Hearthfire Enterprises company. Linda negotiates an agreement with Hearthfire in which she is charged a fee for each type of service performed. In addition, Hearthfire bills Linda for their mileage expenses to and from each house they service. Linda asks you to add a subform to the Feels Like Home Data Entry form that calculates and displays these charges. Open the Holmestead Realty database and follow these guidelines to set up the subform:

- Create a new table named **Feels Like Home Detail**.

- Use the field names, data types, and field properties listed in the following table.

- Leave all other field properties set to their default values.

Feels Like Home Detail Table

Field Name	Data Type	Field Properties
Service ID	Number	There is no primary key for this table
Service	Text	
Date of Service	Date/Time	Short Date
Price	Currency	
Cost	Currency	
Mileage	Number	

In this table, the Cost field represents the fee Hearthfire charges Linda for each service. The Price field represents the amount Linda bills the property owner for the service. The Mileage field contains the number of miles Hearthfire travels to a particular property. Now you will create a select query that extracts all data from the Feels Like Home Detail table and calculates the total cost of Hearthfire's services for each property. The total cost will be calculated by an Extended Cost field. Follow these guidelines to set up the query:

- Include all fields from the Feels Like Home Detail table in the select query.

- Create a calculated field named Extended Cost using the following expression. Notice that the mileage cost is $0.345 per mile in the expression.

    Extended Cost:(([Mileage]*0.345)+[Cost])

- Format the Extended Cost field as Currency.

- Save the query as **Extended Cost**.

Follow these guidelines to insert a subform at the bottom of the Feels Like Home Data
Entry form:

- Position the subform just below the fields at the bottom of the Feels Like Home Data Entry form.

- Use the Extended Cost query as the basis of the subform and add all fields to the subform.

- Accept all of the default Subform Wizard settings.

- Name the subform **Plan Details**.

Follow these guidelines to enter data using the new subform:

- Open the Feels Like Home Data Entry form and sort the records on the Service ID field.

- Adjust the size of the subform and the column widths for ease of viewing and uniformity.

- Enter the following data:

Service ID	Service	Date of Service	Price	Cost	Mileage
1	Clean House	2/1/04	$50	$25	25
2	Clean House	6/5/04	$50	$25	15
3	Check Home and Basement	5/1/04	$15	$10	25
3	Check Home and Basement	7/1/04	$15	$10	25
3	Check Home and Basement	9/1/04	$15	$10	25
4	Clean House	10/5/04	$50	$25	6
4	Remove Construction Debris	10/5/04	$20	$15	0
5	Wrap Pipes under Deck	10/15/04	$20	$10	8
5	Winterize Home	10/15/04	$20	$15	0

Critical Thinking 7.2   Create Calculated Controls on Forms

Now that Linda has the extended cost of each house serviced, she wants to calculate the profit for each Service ID. Linda asks you to add calculated controls to the Feels Like Home Data Entry form to calculate the profit. Follow these guidelines to set up the calculated controls:

- Add a text box to the footer section of the Plan Details subform that calculates the total price. Name the control **Invoice Seller** and change the text box label to **Invoice Seller**.

- Create another text box in the footer section of the Plan Details subform that calculates the total Extended Cost. Name the control **Total Cost** and change the text box label to **Total Cost**.

- Save the changes to the subform and close it.

- Create a text box in the footer section of the Feels Like Home Data Entry form that displays the Invoice Seller amount from the Plan Details subform. Name the control **Invoice Seller** and change the text box label to **Invoice Seller**.

- Create another text box in the footer section of the Feels Like Home Data Entry form that displays the Total Cost amount from the Plan Details subform. Name the control **Total Cost** and change the text box label to **Total Cost**.

- Create a third text box in the footer section of the Feels Like Home Data Entry form that calculates the difference between the Invoice Seller amount and the Total Cost. Name the control **Difference** and change the text box label to **Difference**.

- Format each of these controls using the Currency property. Also, apply text formats to these controls to make them match the formatting of other controls on the form.

- Enter the following data into the Plan Details subform:

Service ID	Service	Date of Service	Price	Cost	Mileage
6	Check Home and Basement	11/5/03	$15	$10	6
7	Mow Yard	7/5/03	$20	$15	15
7	Mow Yard	8/5/03	$20	$15	15
8	Clean House	10/6/03	$50	$25	20

Unit 3

Customization and Integration

This unit begins with techniques to import data from other applications into Access. You will customize reports by adding charts and use calculated fields to get subtotals and totals. You will create a switchboard that functions like a menu to help users navigate to the desired form or report. You will learn how to create macros to automate processes and initiate events, such as opening and closing forms or reports. You will learn how to create a mail merge between Access and Word. To finish off the unit, you will learn the techniques necessary to maintain and secure your databases.

Lesson 8: Importing Data and Customizing Reports

Lesson 9: Using Switchboards, Macros, and Command Buttons

Lesson 10: Integrating Access with Word, Excel, and the Web

LESSON 8

Importing Data and Customizing Reports

The database needs of many organizations evolve over time, requiring more and more sophisticated database systems. These organizations often begin by storing data in Excel worksheets, Word data source files, or older databases such as Dbase. As their needs become more sophisticated, an organization will often need to use data stored in these formats within an Access database. Fortunately, Access lets you import data from these—and other—data sources. In this lesson, you will import an Excel worksheet, sort the records in the imported worksheet, and apply input masks to facilitate the entry of phone numbers and other data. In addition, you will learn how to customize reports to suit your needs. You will add calculated controls to reports, work with report sections and groups, and enhance the appearance of reports.

Microsoft Office Access 2003 objectives covered in this lesson

Objective Number	Skill Sets and Skills	Concept Page References	Exercise Page References
AC03S-1-11	Add and modify report control properties	277–279	279–283, 288–289
AC03S-2-3	Import data to Access	268	269–272
AC03S-3-3	Modify report layout and page setup	276–279	281–283
AC03S-3-5	Sort records	272	272

Additional learning resources are available at labpub.com/learn/access03/

Case Study

The staff at Pinnacle Pet Care has been storing employee information in an Excel worksheet. Al Smith has been so pleased with Pinnacle's Access database system that he wants to bring all data at Pinnacle Pet Care into Access. Al also wants his staff to enter data, so he decides to apply input masks to two fields in the new employee table. The input masks allow the staff to easily enter telephone numbers and zip codes. Al also needs a report that summarizes all visit information, including the services and products purchased. He wants the report to provide a total for each visit, a grand total, and an average for all visits made to the clinic. To accomplish this, Al must create a custom report that uses calculated controls to perform the desired calculations.

Firstname	Lastname	Title	Address	City	State	Zip	Telephone
Reggie	Williams	Veterinarian	1200 Palmer Cc	El Sobrante	CA	94803-2323	(510) 223-4545
Samantha	Torres	Trainer	2450 Wilson La	El Sobrante	CA	94804-	(510) 222-3222
Carl	Adamson	Receptionist	2100 Valley Vie	El Sobrante	CA	98408-	(510) 222-4343

Visit ID	Product	Unit Price	Quantity	Extended Price
1	Flea Shampoo	$12.50	2	$25.00
1	Flea Prevention	$35.00	1	$35.00
			Visit Total	$60.00

The Visit Details report uses calculated controls to calculate totals for each visit, a grand total, and an average for all visits.

Importing Data

Microsoft Office Specialist Access can import data from other databases, text files, spreadsheets, and HTML documents. The database formats supported include dBASE, Paradox, and SQL. The supported spreadsheet formats include Lotus 1-2-3 and Excel. Data can be imported to a new table or appended to an existing table.

Initiating an Import

The File→Get External Data command is used to initiate the import process. This command also gives you the option of linking to an external file. Linking can be useful if you want to maintain the data outside of Access but use it from within Access. Once you initiate the File→Get External Data Command, Access displays an Import box. The Import box lets you choose the location and type of file you wish to import. Access then initiates wizards or displays dialog boxes to guide you through the import process.

Importing Structured Data

Perhaps the most common type of import is when structured data such as an Excel worksheet is imported into Access as a new table. Excel and Access both store data in a table structure; this facilitates the import of Excel worksheets into Access. In addition, the Import Spreadsheet Wizard guides you step-by-step through the process of importing a worksheet.

Preparing to Import a Worksheet

The first row in your worksheet contains column headings. The Import Spreadsheet Wizard uses those headings as the field names in the new Access table. In addition, the wizard assigns data types to the fields in the Access table, depending on the formats used in the worksheet. For example, a column of names will be assigned a text data type while a column of numbers formatted as Currency in Excel will be assigned the Currency format in Access. The wizard examines the first few rows in the worksheet to determine which data types to assign to the fields. You can include rows at the top of the worksheet with "dummy" data and the formats you desire to trick the wizard into assigning a desired data type.

In this exercise, you will import a worksheet containing employee data into the Pinnacle Pet Care database.

Examine the Worksheet

1. Start Excel and open Pinnacle Employee Data from your file storage location.

	A	B	C	D	E	F	G	H	I	J
1	Prefix	Firstname	Lastname	Title	Address	City	State	Zip	Telephone	Status
2	Dr.	Al	Smith	President	2300 Wilson Lane	Walnut Creek	CA	94432	9252345463	Partner
3	Dr.	Mary	Boyd	Chief Veterinarian	4350 Birch Lane	Pleasant Hill	CA	94523	9259456578	Salaried
4	Mr.	Alex	Larkson	Boarding Manager	2100 Maple Street	Berkeley	CA	94720	5106673232	Salaried
5	Ms.	Cindy	Marshall	Training Manager	3450 Pierce Avenue	Berkeley	CA	94721	5106478909	Salaried
6	Dr.	David	Sylvester	Veterinarian	1800 Lexington Avenue	El Cerrito	CA	94834	5102378990	Salaried
7	Dr.	Nancy	Carlin	Veterinarian	2345 Vermont Court	Oakland	CA	92345	5105532323	Salaried
8	Ms.	Cathy	Bollinger	Grooming Specialist	9089 Oakland Avenue	Berkeley	CA	94720	5106458756	Hourly
9	Mr.	Anthony	Robinson	Receptionist	3210 Washington Street	Oakland	CA	92345	5105543456	Hourly
10	Ms.	Wendy	Allison	Trainer	2345 San Pablo Avenue	Richmond	CA	94834	5102284567	Hourly
11	Ms.	Kimberly	Watson	Trainer	2134 Addison Lane	Richmond	CA	94823	5102123456	Hourly
12	Mrs.	Maria	Vasquez	Accountant	2390 Crestview Drive	Berkeley	CA	94724	5106545656	Salaried
13	Mrs.	Theresa	Chin	Office Manager	3456 Ridge Court	Pleasant Hill	CA	94523	9259443456	Partner
14	Mr.	Carlos	Martinez	Partner	3456 Forest Lane	Bandon	OR	97411	5413474567	Partner
15	Mr.	Richard	Sample	Partner	4567 Carlton Avenue	Albuquerque	NM	87103	5057689090	Salaried

2. Notice that the first row of the worksheet contains headings.
   The Import Spreadsheet Wizard will use these headings as the field names in the Access table.

3. Notice that all fields contain text except for the Zip and Telephone fields.
   The Import Wizard will assign the Text data type to all text fields and the Number data type to the numeric fields. The Address field contains a mixture of numbers and text, so it will be assigned the Text data type.

4. Close the Pinnacle Employee Data worksheet and exit Excel.

Initiate the Import Wizard

5. Start Access and open the Pinnacle Pet Care database.

6. Choose File→Get External Data→Import from the menu bar.
   The Import box will appear.

7. Choose Microsoft Excel from the Files of Type list as the bottom of the dialog box.

8. Choose the location where your Pinnacle Employee Data file is stored from the Look In list at the top of the dialog box.

9. Choose the Pinnacle Employee Data workbook and click the Import button.
   The first Import Spreadsheet Wizard screen will appear.

Use the Import Spreadsheet Wizard

10. Click the Next button on the first wizard screen to choose the Show Worksheets option.
The wizard lets you import entire worksheets or named ranges within worksheets.

11. Check the First Row Contains Column Headings option in the second wizard screen.
The wizard will display the first worksheet row with a gray background. These headings will become the field names in the table.

12. Click Next to display the third wizard screen.

13. Click Next again to instruct the wizard to store the data in a new table.
The Existing Table option lets you append the data to the end of an existing table.

14. Follow these steps to examine the Field Options screen (don't change any of the options):

Ⓐ Notice that the current field name and its data type are displayed here. You can enter a different field name if desired; however, you can't change the data type from within the wizard.

Ⓑ This option lets you index fields. Indexing helps Access search large databases efficiently.

Ⓒ You can choose to not import a field by checking this box.

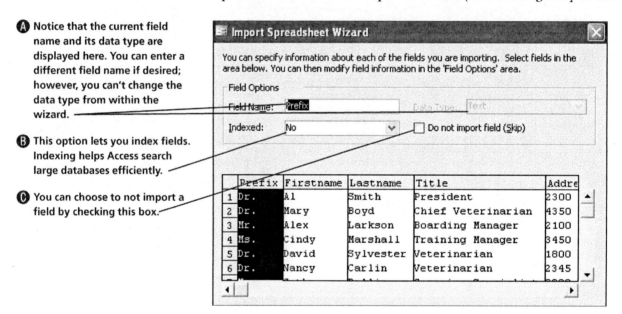

15. Click Next without changing any of the field options to display the next wizard screen.
The wizard will propose a primary key field named ID. This primary key will use an AutoNumber data type.

16. Click Next to accept the proposed primary key.

17. Type the name **Employees** in the last wizard screen and click the Finish button.

18. Click OK on the message box that appears to complete the import.

Examine the Imported Table

19. Double-click the Employees table in the Tables section of the database window to open it in Datasheet view.
All 14 records from the Excel worksheet should be present.

20. Click the Design ✎ view button on the left end of the toolbar.

21. Change the name of the ID field to **Employee ID**.

22. Take a moment to examine the other fields and their data types.

23. Click in the Zip field and change the data type from Number to Text.

24. Change the data type of the Telephone field from Number to Text.

Apply the Zip Code Input Mask

25. Click in the Zip field then click in the Input Mask box in the Field Properties section in the lower part of the window.
The Build button will appear on the right side of the Input Mask box.

26. Click the Build ⟨…⟩ button, and Access will prompt you to save the table.

27. Click the Yes button to save the table.

28. Choose the Zip Code format in the first wizard screen and click the Next button.
The second wizard screen will display a sample and allow you to change the placeholder character.

29. Click Next to accept the defaults and display the next screen.
The next screen will give you the option of saving the data with or without the symbol characters in the mask. Storing the symbol characters with the data can be useful if you want to export the characters along with the data to Excel or another program. For our purposes, however, we will not save the characters with the data.

30. Make sure the Without the Symbols option is chosen and click Next.

31. Click the Finish button to complete the input mask.
Access will display the input mask characters 00000/-9999;;_ in the Input Mask box. In a moment, you will view the formatted data.

Apply the Telephone Input Mask

32. Click in the Telephone field then click in the Input Mask box.

33. Click the Build ⟨…⟩ button and choose Yes to save the table.

34. Make sure the Phone Number mask is chosen in the first wizard screen and click Next.

35. Click Next on the second wizard screen to accept the proposed mask format.

36. Make sure the Without the Symbols option is chosen in the third wizard screen and click Next.

37. Click the Finish button to complete the input mask.
Access will display the input mask characters !(999) 000-0000;;_ in the Input Mask box.

Enter Data with Masks

38. Click the Datasheet ⟨⟩ view button on the Access toolbar and choose Yes to save the table.

39. Scroll to the right until the Zip and Telephone fields are visible.
Notice that the input masks have formatted the previously unformatted data.

40. Enter the following data into a new record at the bottom of the datasheet

Employee ID	Prefix	First-name	Last-name	Title	Address	City	State
15	Dr.	Reggie	Williams	Veterinarian	1200 Palmer Court	El Sobrante	CA

Access will automatically assign the Employee ID. You will enter the zip, telephone, and status data in the next few steps.

41. Click in the Zip field, type **948032323**, and tap the ⌈Tab⌉ key.
Notice that the input mask assists you with the data entry by positioning the hyphen between the first five and last four digits.

42. Type **5102234545** in the phone field and tap the ⌈Tab⌉ key.
As you can see, the phone input mask is quite useful for entering telephone numbers.

43. Type **Salaried** in the Status field.

44. Leave the Employees table open and continue with the next topic.

Sorting Records

Microsoft Office Specialist

The Sort Ascending ![icon] and Sort Descending ![icon] buttons on the Access toolbar let you sort records in datasheets and forms. By default, Access sorts records based on the primary key field. If a table does not have a primary key, Access sequences the records in the order in which they were entered. You can use the Sort Ascending and Sort Descending buttons to change the sort order. Simply click in the desired datasheet column or form field and click the desired button to sort the records. When you close a table that has been sorted, Access will ask if you want to save the changes. If you save the changes, the records will appear in the new sort order the next time the table is opened in Datasheet view. Access automatically saves the new sort order when a sorted form is closed.

 Hands-On 8.2   Sort Records in Datasheet View

In this exercise, you will sort the records in the Employees table using the sort buttons on the toolbar.

1. Make sure the Employees table is displayed in Datasheet view.

2. Notice that the records are sorted based on the Employee ID field.
The Employee ID is the primary key field, so Access uses that field as the default sort key.

3. Click in any cell in the Lastname column then click the Sort Ascending ![icon] button.
The records should now be sorted on the Lastname field.

4. Click in the Zip column then click the Sort Descending ![icon] button.
The records should be sorted in descending order based on the Zip field.

5. Click in the Employee ID column then click the Sort Ascending ![icon] button.

6. Close the table and save the changes.

The Lookup Wizard

As you learned in Lesson 2, Modifying and Maintaining Tables, the Lookup Wizard is initiated in Table Design view by clicking in the Data Type box of the desired field and choosing Lookup Wizard from the Data Type list. In Hands-On 8.3 you will create a lookup table to enter the values that will be in the drop-down list then use the table in the Lookup Wizard.

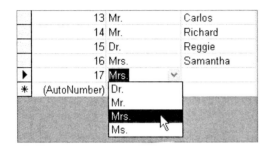

In this example, the Lookup Wizard was used to set up a lookup field within the Prefix field in the Employees table. In Datasheet view, a drop-down button appears and a list of acceptable prefixes is displayed. The lookup field receives its values from a Prefix lookup table.

 Hands-On 8.3   **Use Lookup Lists**

In this exercise, you will set up lookup fields for the Prefix and Status fields in the Employees table. The lookup fields will receive their values from Prefix and Status lookup tables, which you will create.

Set up Lookup Tables

1. Double-click the Create Table in Design View option in the Tables section of the database window.

2. Type the name **Prefix** in the first Field Name box and change the field size to **4** in the Field Properties section at the bottom of the dialog box.

3. Click in the Prefix field name box then click the Primary Key 🔑 button on the Access toolbar.

4. Save the table with the name **Prefix**.

5. Click the Datasheet 📄 view button on the left end of the Access toolbar.

6. Enter into the table the four records shown to the right:

7. Close the table when you have finished.
   You just set up a Prefix lookup table. The values from this table will be displayed on the Prefix lookup in a moment.

Prefix
Mr.
Mrs.
Ms.
Dr.

8. Follow these guidelines to set up another lookup table:
   - Create a new table with a single field named **Status**.
   - Set the field size of the Status field to **10**.
   - Make the Status field a primary key.
   - Save the table with the name **Status**.
   - Enter into the table the data shown to the right then close the table.

Status
Hourly
Partner
Salaried

Use the Lookup Wizard to Create a Prefix Lookup Field

9. Open the Employees table in Design view.

10. Follow these steps to initiate the Lookup Wizard:

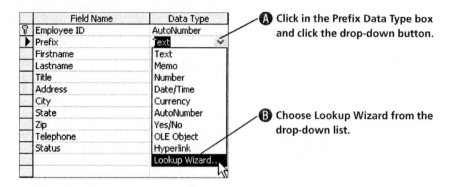

The first wizard screen will ask where the lookup column will get its values. Your lookup column will get its values from the Prefix field in the Prefix table.

11. Make sure the I Want the Lookup Column to Look Up the Values in a Table or Query option is chosen and click Next.
   The next screen will ask which table or query should provide the values for the lookup column.

12. Choose the Prefix table and click Next.
   The next screen will ask which fields you want included in the lookup column.

13. Use the Add Field > button to add the Prefix field to the Selected Fields list.

14. Click Next then click Next again to bypass the screen that asks you to adjust the column width.

15. Make sure the name **Prefix** is entered in the label box of the final wizard screen then click the Finish button.

16. Choose Yes when Access asks if you want to save the table.

Use the Lookup Wizard to Create a Status Lookup Column

17. Click in the Data Type box for the Status field and choose Lookup Wizard from the drop-down list.

18. Make sure the I Want the Lookup Column to Look Up the Values in a Table or Query option is chosen in the first wizard screen and click Next.

19. Choose the Status table in the second wizard screen and click Next.

20. Use the Add Field > button to add the Status field to the Selected Fields list in the third screen and click Next.

21. Click Next twice to bypass the sort order and column width screens.

22. Make sure the name **Status** is entered in the label box of the final wizard screen then click the Finish button.

23. Choose Yes when Access asks if you want to save the table.

Use the Lookup Columns to Enter Data

24. Click the Datasheet ▦ view button on the left end of the Access toolbar.

25. Follow these steps to begin entering data:

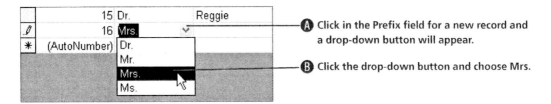

Ⓐ Click in the Prefix field for a new record and a drop-down button will appear.

Ⓑ Click the drop-down button and choose Mrs.

26. Complete the current record and add another record using the following data. Use the drop-down lists in the Prefix and Status columns to enter these data items.

	Employee ID	Prefix	Firstname	Lastname	Title	Address	City	State	Zip	Telephone	Status
	16	Mrs.	Samantha	Torres	Trainer	2450 Wilson Lane	El Sobrante	CA	94804-	(510) 222-3222	Salaried
	17	Mr.	Carl	Adamson	Reception	2100 Valley View	El Sobrante	CA	94804-	(510) 222-4343	Hourly

27. Save ▦ the Employees table then close it.

Subdatasheets

Subdatasheets allow you to display records related to records in an open table from within the open table. The following illustration shows the Pets table with a subdatasheet displayed. The subdatasheet displays related records from the Visits table.

A minus (-) sign appears when a subdatasheet is expanded.
Clicking the minus sign collapses the subdatasheet.

	Pet ID	Pet Name	Pet Type	Breed	Gender	Color	Date of Birth	Last Visit	Expenditures	Number of Visits	CustomerID
+	CT02	Max	Cat	Unknown	Male	White	1/7/1996	9/7/2003	$1,450.55	20	2
▶ −	CT16	Stripes	Cat	Tortoise shell	Male	Black and brown	10/8/2000	7/15/2003	$450.00	9	3

	Visit ID	Visit Date	Visit Notes	Appointment Ty	Next Visit Sche	Visit Fees	Amount Paid
▶	5	1/11/2004	Stripes was suffering from a virus	Walk-in	☑	$78.00	$20.00
	6	1/12/2004	Stripes viral infection seems to have been cure	Follow-up	☐	$20.00	$20.00
	12	2/15/2004	Stripes came by for the grooming promotion	Promotion	☐	$45.00	$45.00
*	(AutoNumber)				☐	$0.00	$0.00

	Pet ID	Pet Name	Pet Type	Breed	Gender	Color	Date of Birth	Last Visit	Expenditures	Number of Visits	CustomerID
+	CT92	Tony	Cat	Unknown	Male	Brown with black str	4/3/1999	7/7/2003	$145.00	6	1
+	DG12	Wolfy	Dog	German Shepherd	Male	Brown	6/6/1998	7/15/2003	$450.00	7	3
+	DG13	Dillon	Dog	Mutt	Male	Black	10/5/2001	7/7/2003	$150.55	3	1
+	DG14	Fetch	Dog	German Shepherd	Male	Black and brown	8/12/1999	9/10/2003	$345.00	3	3
+	DG24	Ben	Dog	Terrier	Male	Black	6/1/2002	10/8/2003	$480.00	3	4

When a one-to-many relationship has been established between two tables, plus (+) signs appear next to records in the table on the one side of the relationship. When you click a plus sign, the related records on the many side of the relationship are expanded and displayed in a subdatasheet. This example shows the visits for Stripes the Cat.

Hands-On 8.4 **Use Subdatasheets**

In this exercise, you will explore the subdatasheet in the Pets table.

1. Double-click the Pets table in the Tables section of the database window.
   Notice the plus sign next to each record. The plus signs indicate that the table has a relationship with another table. In this case, it is a one-to-many relationship established between the Pet ID fields in the Pets and Visits tables. The relationship establishes that each pet can have many visits but each visit can be associated with just one pet. Clicking a plus sign will display all visit records for that pet.

2. Click any plus sign to view the subdatasheet.
   You can enter data into the subdatasheet and it will be stored in the Visits table.

3. Click the minus sign to collapse the subdatasheet.

4. Feel free to expand and collapse other subdatasheets as desired.

5. Close the Pets table when you have finished.

Customizing Reports

Report Design view is used to customize reports. You can set up a report from scratch using Report Design view, or you can use the Report Wizard to set up a report, and then modify it in Design view. The second approach is often the most efficient, as the wizard can set up basic report structures.

 Hands-On 8.5 **Use the Report Wizard to Create a Report**

In this exercise, you will use the Report Wizard to set up a visit details report. In the next few topics, you will use Report Design view to customize the report.

1. Click the Reports button on the Objects bar in the database window.

2. Double-click the Create Report by Using Wizard option.

3. Choose the Query - Visit Details query from the Tables/Queries list in the first wizard screen.

4. Add all fields to the Selected Fields list and click the Next button.

5. Click Next again to bypass the Grouping screen.
   In Hands-On 8.6 you will use Report Design view to establish grouping levels.

6. Click Next two more times to accept the default wizard options.

7. Choose the Corporate style in the next wizard screen and click Next.

8. Type the report name **Visit Details Report** in the final wizard screen then click Finish.
   Access will display a preview of the report.

9. Take a moment to examine the report.

Notice that the report displays the visit details for each visit. The report is based on the Query - Visit Details query. This query displays the Visit ID, Product, Unit Price, and Quantity fields and calculates the extended price.

10. Click the Design ![button] view button on the left end of the Access toolbar.

Access will display the report in Report Design view. You will use Report Design view to customize the report.

Report Sections

Reports include various sections. For example, the report you just displayed in Design view has Report Header, Page Header, Detail, Page Footer, and Report Footer sections. Each section is used for a particular purpose, as described in the following table. The table also describes the Group Header and Group Footer sections, which you will add to the report in a moment.

Report Section	Purpose
Report Header	The Report Header prints at the top of the first page only. This section typically contains just the report title.
Page Header	The Page Header prints at the top of every page. This section typically contains descriptive headings for the fields displayed in the Detail section. In your report, the Visit ID, Service/Product, Unit Price, Quantity, and Extended Price labels in the Page Header section will print at the top of every page.
Detail	The Detail section typically contains text box controls that display data from the table or query on which the report is based. Your report has Visit ID, Service/Product, Unit Price, Quantity, and Extended Price controls in the Detail section. When the report is displayed in Print Preview, the Query - Visit Details query (on which the report is based) is run and the records are displayed in the Detail section of the report. The report will use as many pages as necessary to display all records generated by the query.
Page Footer	The Page Footer prints at the bottom of every page. The Page Footer typically contains page numbers, the date and/or time, and other elements.
Report Footer	The Report Footer prints below the last detail record on the last report page. It may not be used or it may only contain calculated controls that produce totals of all detail records on the report.
Group Header	Reports can group records on one or more fields. For example, in your report you will group the records on the Visit ID field. This way, all of the detail records for a particular visit will be grouped. The Group Header section can be used to print a descriptive heading for each group.
Group Footer	The Group Footer section is typically used to calculate totals for each group of records. For example, you will insert a calculated control in the Group Footer section to calculate a total for each group of visit detail records. This will produce a total for each Visit ID.

Report Groups

The Sorting and Grouping button on the Report Design view toolbar displays the Sorting and Grouping box. This box is used to establish report groups. You can group records on one or more fields. The Sorting and Grouping box lets you display a group header and footer. As noted in the preceding table, the group header displays descriptive headings for groups, while the group footer typically contains calculated controls. The calculated controls in the footer are typically used to sum one or more fields in each group. The following illustration describes the Sorting and Grouping box.

The Sorting and Grouping box lets you choose one or more fields from the table or query on which the report is based. —

The Group Properties for the current field are displayed here. You can set the Group Header and/or Group Footer properties to Yes to display a group header and/or footer in the report. —

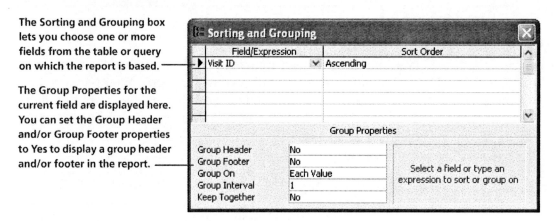

Hands-On 8.6 Establish a Group

In this exercise, you will create a group footer. The Visit Details report should be displayed in Design view.

1. If necessary, click the Sorting and Grouping button on the Access toolbar or choose View→Sorting and Grouping to display the Sorting and Grouping box.

2. Click in the first Field/Expression box, click the drop-down button, and choose Visit ID.

3. Click in the Group Footer box near the bottom of the dialog box and set the Group Footer property to Yes.
   A Visit ID Footer section will be added to the report. You will work with this section in Hands-On 8.7. You won't display a Group Header section for this report.

4. Close the Sorting and Grouping box.

Using Controls in Reports

Microsoft Office Specialist

You can use the Toolbox in Report Design view to add controls to reports. Controls can be placed in any report section. You can format controls using the Properties box or with formatting buttons on the Access toolbar.

The Text Box button is used to add calculated controls to report sections. Calculated controls in reports use the same rules and syntax as calculated controls in forms. Calculated controls added to a group footer section perform calculations on the records in that group. Calculated controls added to the Report Footer section calculate grand totals for the report. These concepts are discussed in the following illustration.

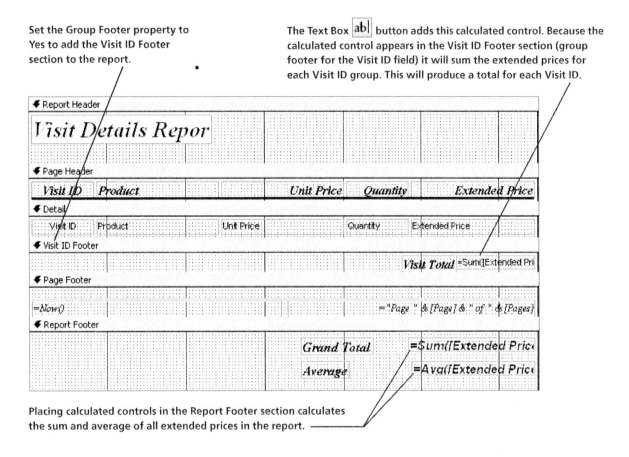

Set the Group Footer property to Yes to add the Visit ID Footer section to the report.

The Text Box button adds this calculated control. Because the calculated control appears in the Visit ID Footer section (group footer for the Visit ID field) it will sum the extended prices for each Visit ID group. This will produce a total for each Visit ID.

Placing calculated controls in the Report Footer section calculates the sum and average of all extended prices in the report.

Hands-On 8.7   Customize the Report

In this exercise, you will add calculated controls to the bottom of a report.

Add a Calculated Control to the Group Footer

1. If necessary, click the Properties button on the Access toolbar to display the Properties box.

2. Click the Text Box button on the toolbox.

3. Follow these steps to add a calculated control to the Visit ID Footer section:

Ⓐ Click in the Visit ID Footer section to position the Text Box control.

Ⓑ Click the Data tab on the Properties box and type `=Sum([Extended Price])` in the Control Source box. Be sure to enter the expression exactly as shown.

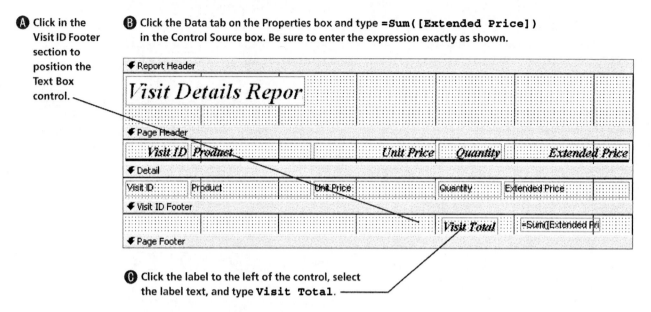

Ⓒ Click the label to the left of the control, select the label text, and type `Visit Total`.

4. Click the View 🔲 button on the left end of the Access toolbar to display the report. *The calculated control should calculate a total for each group.*

5. Follow these steps to examine the report:

Ⓐ This report header prints only at the top of the report.

Ⓑ The page header prints at the top of every page.

Ⓒ The records are grouped on the Visit ID field.

Ⓓ The Visit ID Footer calculates the total for each group. At this point, the calculated control does not use the Currency format nor are the totals aligned with the Extended Price controls.

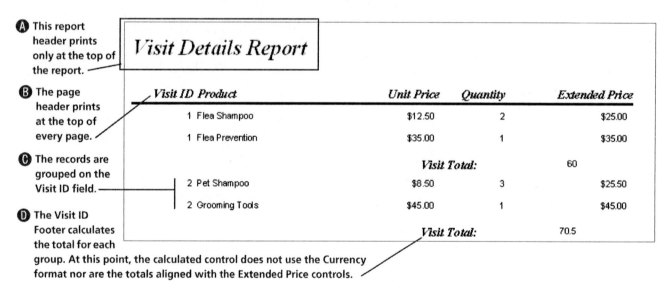

Format the Controls

6. Click the Design 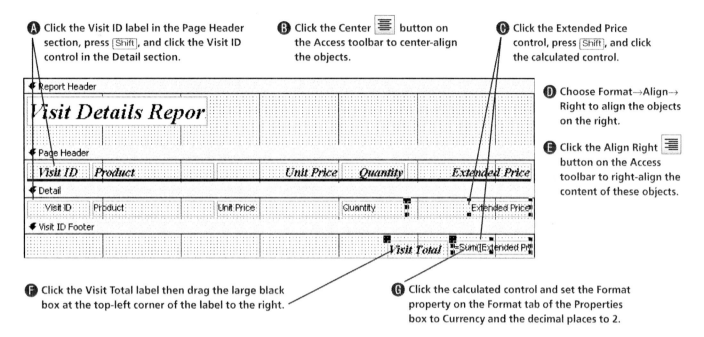 view button on the left end of the Access toolbar to switch back to Report Design view.

7. Follow these steps to align the controls and to set the format property of the calculated control:

Ⓐ Click the Visit ID label in the Page Header section, press Shift, and click the Visit ID control in the Detail section.

Ⓑ Click the Center ≡ button on the Access toolbar to center-align the objects.

Ⓒ Click the Extended Price control, press Shift, and click the calculated control.

Ⓓ Choose Format→Align→ Right to align the objects on the right.

Ⓔ Click the Align Right ≡ button on the Access toolbar to right-align the content of these objects.

Report Header

Visit Details Repor

Page Header

Visit ID   Product   Unit Price   Quantity   Extended Price

Detail

Visit ID   Product   Unit Price   Quantity   Extended Price

Visit ID Footer

                                                      Visit Total =Sum([Extended Pri]

Ⓕ Click the Visit Total label then drag the large black box at the top-left corner of the label to the right.

Ⓖ Click the calculated control and set the Format property on the Format tab of the Properties box to Currency and the decimal places to 2.

8. Click the View 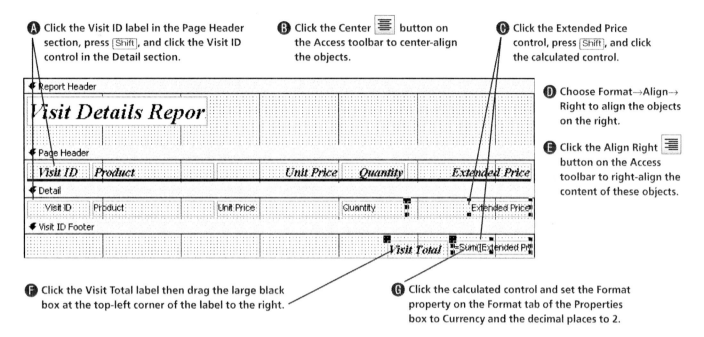 button to display the report.
The Visit Totals should now have a Currency format and be right-aligned with the visit detail records.

9. Click the Design view button to switch back to Report Design view.

10. Enlarge your Report Footer area by dragging the divider down.

Add Calculated Controls in the Report Footer

11. Click the Text Box 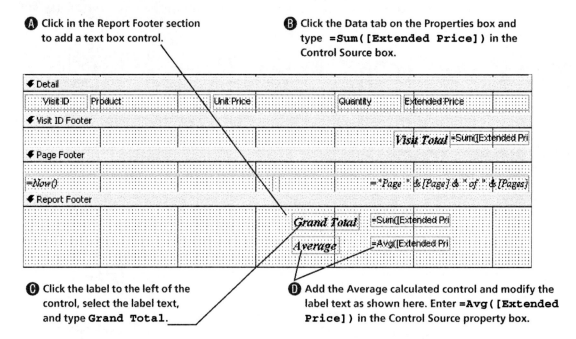 button on the toolbox.

12. Follow these steps to add calculated controls to the Report Footer section:

Ⓐ Click in the Report Footer section to add a text box control.

Ⓑ Click the Data tab on the Properties box and type **=Sum([Extended Price])** in the Control Source box.

Ⓒ Click the label to the left of the control, select the label text, and type **Grand Total.**

Ⓓ Add the Average calculated control and modify the label text as shown here. Enter **=Avg([Extended Price])** in the Control Source property box.

At this point, you won't be able to see the entire expressions within the text box controls.

13. Click the View button to display the report.
You should see a grand total and average calculation displayed below the last Visit ID total. In the next few steps, you will format the controls.

14. Click the Design view button.

Format the Grand Total and Average Labels

15. Click the Grand Total label, press [Shift], and click the Average label to select both labels.

16. Use the Font Size button on the Access toolbar to set the font size to 12.

17. Click on an empty part of the report to deselect the labels.

18. Click the Grand Total label and widen the label slightly by dragging the right middle sizing handle. Make the label just wide enough so the label text is completely visible.

19. Now widen the Average label slightly so it is completely visible.

Format the Calculated Controls

20. Click the Grand Total calculated control, press [Shift], and click the Average calculated control to select both controls.

21. Use the Font Size button on the Access toolbar to set the font size to 11.

22. Click the Bold **B** and Italic *I* buttons on the Access toolbar.

23. Use the Font Color **A** button on the Access toolbar to apply a font color of your choice.

24. Click the Format tab in the Properties box, click in the Format box, and set the Format property to Currency.

Your controls will be too narrow to completely display the expressions within the controls. This is OK because the control only needs to be wide enough to display the calculated numbers when the report is previewed or printed.

25. Follow these steps to align the controls and labels:

Ⓐ Select the calculated controls and the control in the Page Footer section then use the Format→Align→ Right command to align the controls.

Ⓑ Move the Grand Total and Average labels close to the calculated controls and align them as shown.

✦ Visit ID Footer				
			Visit Total	=Sum([Extended Pri
✦ Page Footer				
=Now()				="Page " & [Page] & " of " & [Pages]
✦ Report Footer				
			Grand Total	=Sum([Extended Pric
			Average	=Avg([Extended Pric

Ⓒ Arrange the controls until they match this example. Keep in mind that your calculated controls will be too narrow to completely display the expressions.

26. Click the View button to display the report.

The Grand Total and Average labels and controls should now be properly formatted and aligned.

27. Choose File→Page Setup. Change the left and right margins to .75.

If you like, click the Page tab and change the layout from Portrait to Landscape.

28. Feel free to make additional adjustments to your report.

You will need to switch to Design view to make any changes.

29. When you have finished, close the report and save the changes.

Adding a Chart to a Report

You can use the Chart Wizard to add a chart to your report. Charts can be useful as a visual representation of your data. Charts can be based on a table or a query and can be placed at the end of the report to represent all of the data combined or at the end of each record to represent the data from one record at a time. To add a chart, choose Insert→Chart from the menu bar. This opens the Chart Wizard, which allows you to make choices about where to get the data and what kind of chart you want. In Hands-On 8.8 you will add a chart to the Expenditures report.

Hands-On 8.8   Add a Chart to a Report

In this exercise, you will open the Expenditures report and add a chart that will visually represent the data from the Pet Type Expenditures query.

1. Click the Reports button on the Objects bar.

2. Open the Expenditures report in Design view.

3. If necessary, maximize 🔲 your window.

4. Choose Insert→Chart from the menu bar.
   This will provide you with the icon tool to place the chart where you want it to go and activate the Chart Wizard.

5. Click in the area shown in the following illustration to specify the chart location.

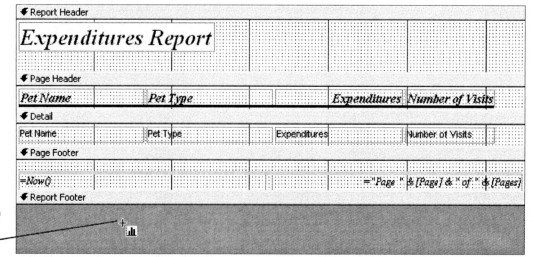

Ⓐ This will auto-matically begin the Chart Wizard.

Placing the chart here will keep it at the bottom of the report no matter how many pages the report contains.

6. Choose Queries and locate the Query: Pet Type Expenditures.

7. Click the Next button.

8. Add the Pet Type and the Expenditures fields and click the Next button.
   This chart will be a summary of the expenditures of each pet type.

9. Click Next to choose the Column chart.

10. Click the Next button to choose the layout.
    In some cases you will have to change the layout. In this case, the current layout will produce the desired results.

11. Follow these steps to change the linked fields:

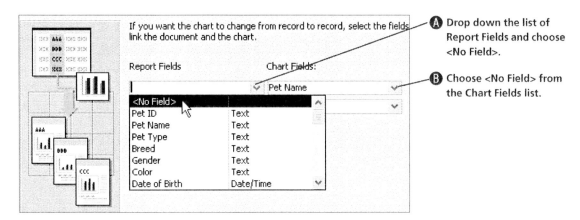

Since we are placing this chart at the end of the report, we want it to show all the data for all the records in one chart. In some cases you might want to place a chart after the results of each record. In this case, you should link the field in the chart to the field in the record so that the chart will change to represent each record.

12. Click Next.

13. Choose No, Don't Display a Legend and click Finish to accept the name Pet Type Expenditures for your chart.
    Your chart will look like it has incorrect data. Until you choose the View option for your report, your chart will resemble the following illustration.

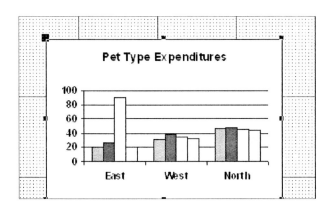

14. If necessary click the Properties ⊞ button on the Access toolbar to display the Properties box.
Your chart should still be selected.

15. Click the Format tab and set the Height to 3" and the Width to 4".

16. Move the chart to the center of the Report Footer area.

17. Click the View ⊞ button to display the report.

18. Feel free to make any adjustments to your report.
You will need to switch to Design view to make changes.

19. When you are finished, close the report, save the changes, and close the database.

Concepts Review

True/False Questions

1. Imported data can be placed in a new table or appended to an existing table. TRUE FALSE
2. The Report Header prints at the top of every report page. TRUE FALSE
3. The Group Footer is typically used to calculate totals for each group of records. TRUE FALSE
4. Records can be sorted while working in Table Datasheet view. TRUE FALSE
5. The Lookup Wizard is used to create drop-down lists in forms. TRUE FALSE
6. Subdatasheets are used primarily for running queries from Table Datasheet view. TRUE FALSE
7. Reports can have a maximum of three sections. TRUE FALSE
8. The primary purpose of groups is to sort records in a report. TRUE FALSE
9. Reports created with the Report Wizard cannot be altered. TRUE FALSE
10. Charts can be placed at the end of the report or at the end of each record. TRUE FALSE

Multiple Choice Questions

1. Which command initiates the Import Wizard?
   a. File→Import Data
   b. File→Get External Data
   c. Insert→File→External
   d. Insert→External Data

2. From which view is the Lookup Wizard initiated?
   a. Table Datasheet view
   b. Table Design view
   c. Form view
   d. Form Design view

3. What happens when you click a plus sign to the left of the first field when a table is in Datasheet view?
   a. A query is run.
   b. The table is displayed in Design view.
   c. A new record is added to the end of the table.
   d. A subdatasheet is displayed.

4. Where is the Page Header printed on reports?
   a. At the top of every page
   b. At the top of the first page only
   c. At the bottom of the report
   d. Next to the Page Footer

Skill Builders

Skill Builder 8.1   Use the Report Wizard

In this exercise, you will use the Report Wizard to set up a report. In the next two Skill Builders, you will customize the report.

1. Open the Tropical Getaways database and click the Reports button on the Objects bar.

2. Double-click the Create Report by Using Wizard option.

3. Choose the Query - Package Details query in the first wizard screen, add all fields to the Selected Fields list, and click the Next button.

4. Click Next three times to bypass the next three screens.

5. Choose the Soft Gray report style in the next screen and click Next.

6. Enter the report name **Package Details Report** in the last wizard screen and click the Finish button.
   The report will display all of the package details records, along with the extended prices. The extended prices are calculated in the Query - Package Details query.

7. Click the Design view 🖺 button.

Skill Builder 8.2   Add Calculated Controls to the Report

In this exercise, you will add calculated controls to the report.

Set Up a Group

1. Click the Sorting and Grouping 🔢 button to display the Sorting and Grouping box.

2. Choose Package ID in the Field/Expression box to create a Package ID group.

3. Set the Group Footer property for the Package ID field to Yes and close the Sorting and Grouping box.
   A Package ID Footer section should appear on the report.

Add a Subtotal Control

4. Click the Text Box 📄 button on the toolbox.

5. Click in the Package ID Footer section to position the control.

6. Set the Control Source property on the Data tab of the Properties box to **=Sum([Extended Price])**.
   Be sure to enter the expression exactly as shown.

7. Click the Other tab in the Properties box and set the Name property to **Subtotal**.
   You will reference this name in the Sales Tax and Total controls.

8. Change the label text to the left of the control to **Subtotal**.

Add Sales Tax and Total Controls

9. Follow these steps to add a Sales Tax control:

A Drag the Page Footer bar down to increase the height of the Package ID Footer section. Make sure there is enough room for two additional controls below the Subtotal control.

B Click the Text Box [ab] button then click below the Subtotal control to position the new control.

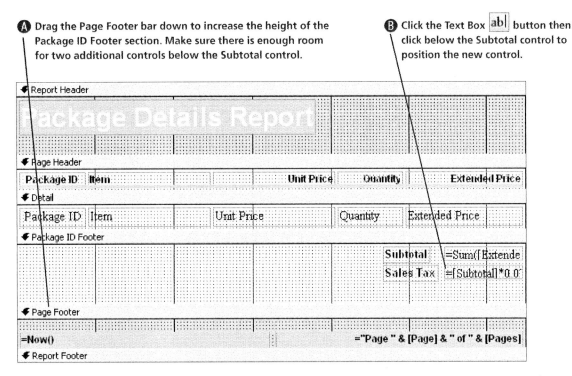

C Set the Control Source property on the Data tab to =[Subtotal]*0.075, set the Name property on the Other tab to **Sales Tax**, and change the label text to **Sales Tax**.

10. Add another text box control below the Sales Tax control.

11. Set the Control Source property of the new control to =[Subtotal]+[Sales Tax].

12. Set the Name property of the new control to **Total**.

13. Change the label text to the left of the control to **Total**.

14. Click the View button on the left end of the toolbar to view the report.
The Subtotal, Sales Tax, and Total controls should display calculations for each group of Packaged IDs. The calculations for Package ID 1 should be Subtotal=4400, Sales Tax=330, and Total=4730.

15. Click the Design view button to switch to Design view.

16. If your controls did not calculate correctly, check the expressions and the names in the Name property. Correct any mistakes. Continue to debug your report until the controls calculate correctly.

17. Save the changes to the report.

Skill Builder 8.3 Format the Report

In this exercise, you will format the controls on a report.

1. Select all three calculated controls and set the Format property on the Format tab of the Properties box to Currency.

2. Set the Decimal Places property to **2**.

3. Right-align the controls with the Extended Price control in the Detail section.

4. Move the Subtotal, Sales Tax, and Total labels closer to the controls and left-align the labels.

5. Apply Bold formatting to the Total control.

6. Center ▤ the Package ID label and control in the Page Header and Detail sections.

7. Click the View 🔍 button. Your report should closely match the following example, which shows only the first Package ID records.

Package ID	Item	Unit Price	Quantity	Extended Price
1	Hotel Rooms	$75.00	28	$2,100.00
1	Disneyland Package	$125.00	4	$500.00
1	Airfare	$450.00	4	$1,800.00
			Subtotal	$4,400.00
			Sales Tax	$330.00
			Total	**$4.730.00**

Package Details Report

8. If necessary, maximize 🔲 the report and use the record navigation bar to view the various pages. Your report should have two or three pages.

9. Save the changes when you have finished and close the report.

Add a Chart to a Report

In this exercise, you will open the Trips by Category report and add a chart.

1. Open the Trips by Category report in Design view.

2. If necessary, maximize the report window.

3. Choose Insert→Chart from the menu bar.

4. Click in the Report footer to set the location for the chart and activate the Chart Wizard.

5. Choose the Trips table and click the Next button.

6. Add the Destination and Cost fields to the Fields for Chart list.

7. Click Next twice to accept the column chart type.

8. Click Next to accept the layout.

9. Change the Report Fields and the Chart Fields to <No Field> and click Next.

10. Leave the title of the chart as Trips, choose No, Don't Display a Legend, and click the Finish button.
    The chart will be displayed at the bottom of the Report in the Report Footer.

11. Move and enlarge the chart.
    You can go back and forth between Print Preview and Design until you are satisfied with the placement.

Format the Chart Area

The Category Axis labels are too large. Changing the font size will allow all of the labels to show.

12. If necessary, switch to Design view.

13. Double-click on the chart.
This will open a datasheet with the chart detail.

14. Follow these steps to change the font size of the Category Axis:

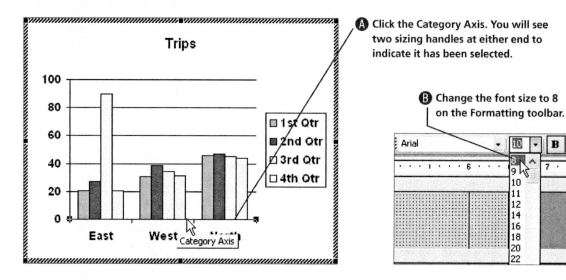

A Click the Category Axis. You will see two sizing handles at either end to indicate it has been selected.

B Change the font size to 8 on the Formatting toolbar.

15. Click in the Report Footer to deselect the chart area then switch to Print Preview to view the changes.
If necessary, switch to Design view and adjust the size of the font or the chart until the Destinations are visible.

16. Save and close the report and the Tropical Getaways database.

 # Assessments

Assessment 8.1   Customize a Report

In this exercise, you will create a report and add grouping levels and calculated controls.

1. Open the Classic Cars database.

2. Use the Report Wizard and these guidelines to set up a new report:
   - Use the Query - Event Details query as the basis for the report.
   - Use all fields from the query in the report.
   - Do not use the Report Wizard to set up grouping levels or sorting.
   - Bypass the fourth wizard screen and choose the Compact report style in the fifth screen.
   - Assign the name **Event Details Report** to the report in the last wizard screen.

3. Follow these guidelines to modify the report in Design view:
   - Establish a grouping level for the Event ID field.
   - Display a group footer for the Event ID group.
   - Add a calculated control to the Event ID Footer section that sums the detail records in each group.
   - Change the label text to the left of the calculated control to **Event Total**.

4. Follow these guidelines to format the report:
   - Format the calculated control with a Currency format with two decimals.
   - Right-align the calculated control with the Total control in the Detail section.
   - Apply bold formatting to the calculated control.
   - Move the Event Total label close to the calculated control.
   - Center-align the Event ID label in the Page Header section and the Event ID control in the Detail section.

5. Your completed report should closely match the following example.

Event Details Report

Event ID	Item	Daily Cost	Number of Days	Total
1	Utilities	$125.00	2	$250.00
1	Security	$180.00	2	$360.00
1	Location fee	$500.00	2	$1,000.00
			Event Total	$1,610.00
2	Location fee	$850.00	4	$3,400.00
2	Set up fees	$3,000.00	1	$3,000.00
2	Utilities	$350.00	4	$1,400.00
			Event Total	$7,800.00

6. Follow these guidelines to add a calculated control that finds the total of all detail records on the report:

   - The control should appear at the end of the report.
   - Format the control with the Currency format with two decimals.
   - Change the label text to the left of the calculated control to **Grand Total**.
   - Apply any text formats you desire.

7. Save the changes and close the report.

8. Close the Classic Cars database.

■

Critical Thinking

Import an Excel Worksheet

Linda's Feels Like Home service has been quite successful. She decides to market her service to homeowners advertising homes for sale in local newspapers. Her nephew has been gathering listing information from local newspapers and entering it into an Excel spreadsheet. Linda asks you to import this information into the Holmestead Realty database. Open the Holmestead Realty database and follow these guidelines to import the data:

■ Use the Import Spreadsheet Wizard to import the Prospects worksheet into the Holmestead Realty database as a new table named **Prospects**. The field names in the new table should match the headings in the Excel worksheet.

■ Choose the Phone Number field as the primary key.

■ Sort the records in the Prospects table in descending order by Sales Price.

■ Examine the data types of the first four fields in the following table to verify that they match the Prospects table. Then, change the field properties of the Date of Ad field as shown in the table.

Field Name	Data Type	Field Properties
Phone Number	Text	Primary Key
Sales Price	Currency	
Ad	Memo	
Media	Text	
Date of Ad	Date/Time	Short Date: Apply the Short Date input mask

Critical Thinking 8.2   Create a Lookup List

Linda's nephew gathers his prospect data from three local newspapers: the *Citizen Times*, the *IWANNA*, and the *Mountain Express*. To help ensure accurate data entry, Linda asks you to create a lookup list in the Prospect table. Follow these guidelines to create the lookup list:

■ Create a new table named **Media Lookup** which contains a single field named Media. Make the Media field a primary key.

■ Enter the following data into the lookup table:

Media Type
Citizen Times
IWANNA
Mountain Express

■ Make the Media field in the Prospects table a lookup field using the Media Lookup table as the data source.

■ Enter the following records into the Prospects table using the Media lookup list to enter the Media data:

Phone Number	Sales Price	Ad	Media	Date of Ad
277-7355	$356,000	Upscale Contemporary Home, 5BR/2.5BA, $356,000 277-7355	Mountain Express	10/4/04
686-2040	$50,000	Cute Duplex 2/1 in need of a little TLC. $50K, 686-2040	IWANNA	10/2/04

Create a Custom Report

Linda asks you to create an invoice report that allows her to compare the invoices sent by Hearthfire Enterprises to the data in her Access database. Follow these guidelines to set up a query that will be used as the basis for the custom report:

- Copy the Extended Cost query and paste it as the **Hearthfire Invoice** query.

- Remove the Price field.

- Add the Feels Like Home table to the Query Design grid.

- Add the Invoice field from the Feels Like Home table to the query. Set a criterion of No for the Invoice field but do not show the Invoice field in the recordset.

Follow these guidelines to set up the custom report:

- Use the Report Wizard to set up a new report using the Hearthfire Invoice query as the basis for the report. Choose all fields from the query and accept all default options offered by the wizard. Name the report **Hearthfire Invoice**.

- Use the Sorting and Grouping feature in Report Design view to group on the Service ID field. This will create a Service ID group footer section.

- Add a calculated control to the Service ID group footer section that calculates the total Extended Cost for each Service ID number. Name this control **Total Per Service Call** and change the control label text to **Total Per Service Call**.

- Feel free to format the calculated control and other report controls to enhance their appearance. For example, consider adjusting the positions, alignment, font sizes, and font formats (such as bold).

- Add a calculated control to the Report Footer section that calculates the sum of the Extended Costs. Name this control **Total Due** and change the control label text to **Total Due**.

- Add a calculated control to the Report Footer section which calculates the average of the Extended Costs. Name this control **Average** and change the control label text to **Average**.

- Feel free to format the calculated controls in the Report Footer section by adjusting the positions, alignment, font sizes, and font formats (such as bold). Also, apply the Currency format to the Total Due and Average controls.

LESSON 9

Using Switchboards, Macros, and Command Buttons

Making databases user friendly is one of the main goals of database designers. User friendliness begins with an easy-to-use switchboard form that provides quick access to the most frequently used database objects. In this lesson, you will set up a switchboard form that provides one-click access to forms and reports. The switchboard will also automatically open when the database is started.

Macros are little programs that automate processes. Access lets you create many macros. Macros can be assigned to command buttons so that an event (such as clicking) automatically opens a form, report, query, or even multiple objects. In this lesson, you will use macros to simplify data entry, open forms, and navigate to records.

Microsoft Office Access 2003 objectives covered in this lesson

Objective Number	Skill Sets and Skills	Exercise Page References
AC03S-1-9	Add and modify form controls and properties	300, 306–309, 317, 323

Additional learning resources are available at labpub.com/learn/access03/

Case Study

Al Smith realizes that the staff at Pinnacle Pet Care is constantly changing. New employees are hired and current employees occasionally leave. In addition, Al frequently needs to employ temporary personnel. For this reason, he wants to make the database as easy to use as possible. Al sets up a switchboard form that provides easy access to common forms and reports. In addition, he simplifies data entry by creating macros. He sets up the database so that when a user clicks a date field, the current date is automatically entered in the field. The switchboard form that Al sets up is shown in the following illustration.

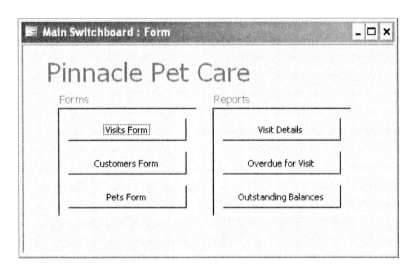

Working with Switchboards

Database systems are often used by data entry personnel with little computer experience. For this reason, database designers must make databases easy to use. For example, many databases have a main switchboard that functions as a launch pad to various parts of the database. Switchboards are forms often used as opening menus. They usually contain command buttons that initiate events. You can easily create a switchboard by setting up a form and adding command buttons to it. Most switchboards also contain text boxes, rectangles, and other objects to enhance their appearance.

 Hands-On 9.1   Create a Switchboard

In this exercise, you will set up a switchboard in the Pinnacle Pet Care database.

1. Start Access and open the Pinnacle Pet Care database.

2. Click the Forms button on the Objects bar then double-click the Create Form in Design View option.
   Access will set up a new form in the Design view window. This form is not attached to an underlying table or query so it is ideal for a switchboard. Switchboards contain command buttons, hyperlinks, and other unbound objects not dependent on an underlying table or query.

3. Follow these steps to begin setting up the form:

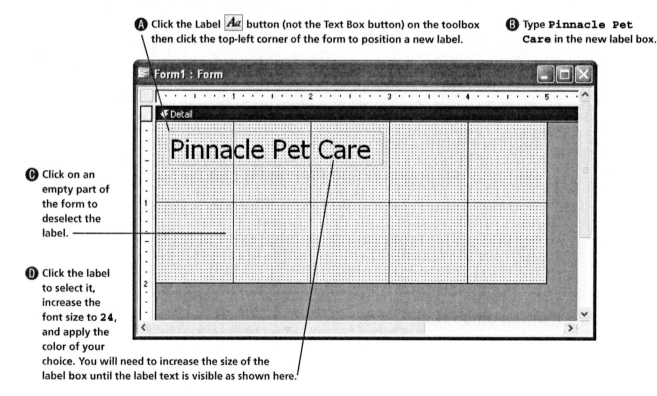

Ⓐ Click the Label 𝐴𝑎 button (not the Text Box button) on the toolbox then click the top-left corner of the form to position a new label.

Ⓑ Type **Pinnacle Pet Care** in the new label box.

Ⓒ Click on an empty part of the form to deselect the label.

Ⓓ Click the label to select it, increase the font size to **24**, and apply the color of your choice. You will need to increase the size of the label box until the label text is visible as shown here.

4. Save 🖫 the form as **Main Switchboard** then close it.
   You will continue to modify the form as you progress through this lesson.

Working with Macros

Macros are automated procedures that contain one or more Access command. They are used to automate database activities and routine tasks.

Attaching Macros and Specifying Events

Database objects—such as forms, reports, and command buttons—have a variety of events associated with them. For example, events occur when buttons are clicked and when forms and reports are opened and closed. In Access, you can attach macros to forms, reports, command buttons, and other objects. Furthermore, you can specify the event(s) that must occur to initiate the macro. For example, you can instruct Access to run a particular macro when a command button is clicked.

The Macro Window

The [New] button appears on the toolbar in the Macros section of the database window. This button displays an empty Macro window from which you can choose the commands or actions you wish to include in your macro. You can also specify arguments for each action. The following illustration shows the macro you will create in Hands-On 9.2. The macro will open the Visits form and display a new record in it. In Hands-On 9.4, you will attach this macro to a command button on the Main Switchboard. The command button will run the macro when it is clicked.

Macro actions are entered into the Action column. This macro has two actions. Actions are executed sequentially when the macro is run.

The Action Arguments section lets you specify arguments for each action. The arguments shown here are for the Open-Form action, which is selected in the Action column. Notice that the argument specifies Visits as the Form Name. This instructs the macro to open the Visits form when the OpenForm action is executed.

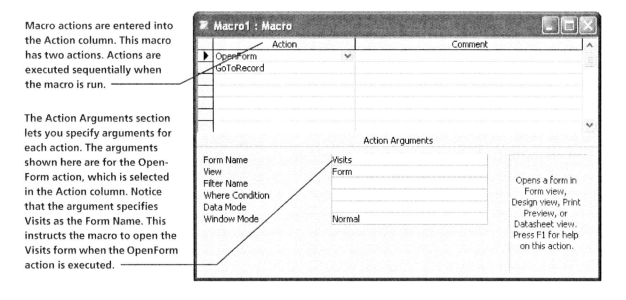

 Hands-On 9.2   **Create a Macro for the Visits Form**

In this exercise, you will create a macro that opens to a new record in the Visits form.

1. Click the Macros button on the Objects bar in the database window.

2. Click the [New] button to display the Macro window.

3. Follow these steps to choose the Open Form action and to specify the argument:

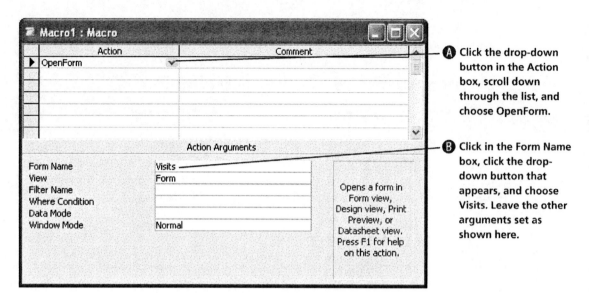

A Click the drop-down button in the Action box, scroll down through the list, and choose OpenForm.

B Click in the Form Name box, click the drop-down button that appears, and choose Visits. Leave the other arguments set as shown here.

4. Follow these steps to choose the GoToRecord action and specify the argument:

A Click in the second Action box and choose GoToRecord.

B Click in the Record box and choose New. This argument will display a new record after the form is opened.

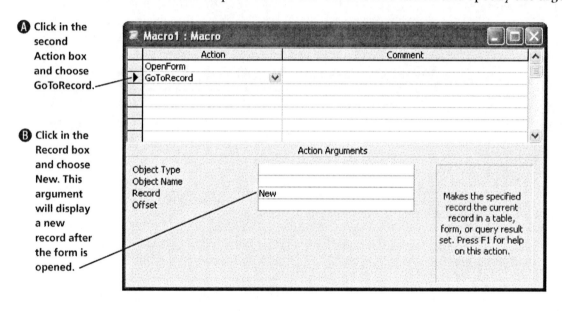

OpenForm and GoToRecord are the only actions that your macro will have. In the next few steps, you will save and close the Macro box. Macros are saved with a descriptive name like any other object.

5. Click the Close ⊠ button at the top-right corner of the macro window.

6. Click Yes when Access asks if you want to save the macro.

7. Type the name **Open Visits Form** in the Save As box and click OK.
The Open Visits Form macro will appear in the database window.

Testing and Editing Macros

You should run a macro after creating it to make sure it functions properly. You run a macro by choosing it in the Macros section of the database window and clicking the Run button. You can also edit a macro by choosing it in the Macros section and clicking the Design button. Access also has a macro debugging mode known as Single Step mode. Single Step mode executes a macro one step at a time so you can determine where any problems occur.

 Hands-On 9.3   **Test the Macro**

In this exercise, you will test the macro you created.

1. Make sure the Open Visits Form macro is chosen then click the Run button.
   The Visits form should open. The GoToRecord command instructed Access to display a new empty record.

2. Close the Visits form without entering any data.

3. If your macro did not perform as expected, choose it in the database window, click the Design button, and follow the instructions in Hands-On 9.2 until the macro is correct. You can rerun the macro after it has been edited.

Working with Command Buttons

The Command ◢ button on the Form Design toolbox initiates the Command Button Wizard, which guides you through the process of creating command buttons. You can use command buttons to open forms and reports, run macros, and perform other tasks. Command buttons are usually placed on switchboards or in the header or footer sections of forms.

 Hands-On 9.4   **Set Command Buttons and Macros**

In this exercise, you will create several macros and command buttons.

Create the Visits Form Command Button

1. Click the Forms button on the Objects bar in the database window.

2. Choose the Main Switchboard form and click the ◢ Design button.

3. If necessary, use the View→Toolbox command to display the toolbox.

4. Click the Command Button ◢ on the toolbox.

5. Click below the Pinnacle Pet Care label to make the first wizard screen appear.

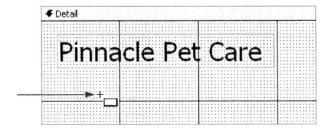

6. Follow these steps to explore the Category and Action options and choose the Run Macro action:

Ⓐ Click the various categories and notice the available actions in the right column. You can assign any of these actions to a command button.

Ⓑ Choose the Miscellaneous category and the Run Macro action.

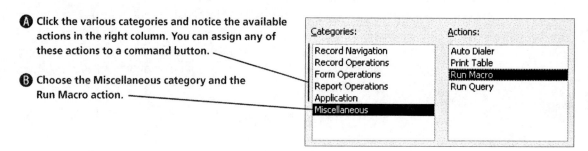

7. Click the Next button.
The wizard will display a list of macros that have been created in the database. At this point, the Open Visits Form macro will be the only macro listed.

8. Click the Next button to choose the Open Visits Form macro.
The third wizard screen gives you the option of displaying a picture/icon on the button or using descriptive text on the button.

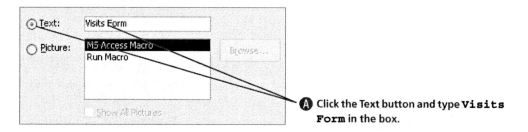

Ⓐ Click the Text button and type **Visits Form** in the box.

The phrase Visits Form will appear on the command button when the button is created.

9. Click Next, type the name **Visits Form** in the last wizard screen, and click the Finish button.
The button should appear below the Pinnacle Pet Care label.

10. Click the Form view 🔲 button on the Access toolbar. Your switchboard should be similar to the following example.

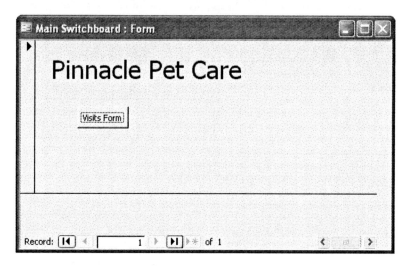

11. Click the Visits Form button and notice the new record.
    Clicking the Visits Form button runs the Open Visits Form macro. The macro opens the Visits form and displays the new record.

12. Close the Visits form.

13. Close the Main Switchboard form and save the changes.

Create a Macro to Open the Customers Form

14. Click the Macros button on the Objects bar.

15. Click the ⟦New⟧ button.

16. Set up the OpenForm and GoToRecord actions as shown in the following illustration. Make sure you set the Form Name argument to Customers for the OpenForm action. Also, change the Record argument for the GoToRecord action to New.

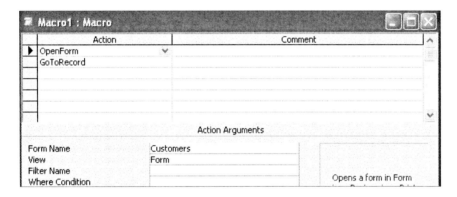

17. Close the macro when you have finished and give it the name **Open Customers Form**.

18. Test the macro by choosing it in the Macros window and clicking ⟦ Run⟧.

19. Close the Customers form without entering data.

Create a Macro to Open the Pets Form

20. Set up another new macro, as shown in the following illustration. Make sure you set the Form Name argument to Pets for the OpenForm action. Also, change the Record argument for the GoToRecord action to New.

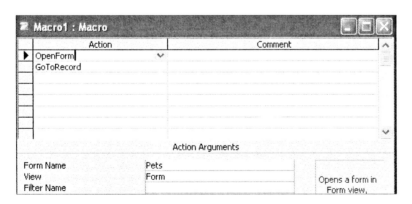

21. When you have finished, close the macro and save it as **Open Pets Form**.

22. Test the macro to make sure it functions correctly.

Assign the New Macros to Command Buttons

23. Click the Forms button on the Objects bar and open the Main Switchboard in Design view.

24. Click the Command Button ▨ on the toolbox and click below the Visits Form button to position the new button on the Main Switchboard form.

25. Choose the Miscellaneous category in the first screen and choose the Run Macro action.

26. Click Next and choose Open Customers Form in the second wizard screen.

27. Click Next, choose the Text option, and type **Customers Form** in the third wizard screen.

28. Click Next, type **Customers Form** in the last screen, and click the Finish button.
    In the next step, you will place another command button on the Main Switchboard form. If you need more room on the Main Switchboard, drag its bottom and/or right edge to increase the size.

29. Create another command button that runs the Open Pets Form macro. Use the phrase **Pets Form** on the face of the button as shown in the illustration under step 34. Assign the name **Pets Form** to the button in the last wizard screen.

30. Switch to Form ▨ view to review the Main Switchboard form.
    Your switchboard should have three command buttons. Don't be concerned if your buttons are not aligned. You will align the buttons and enhance the appearance of the form in a moment.

31. Test your new command buttons by clicking them.
    The Customers form and Pets form should open when the buttons are clicked.

32. Close the Customers and Pets forms.

Create Command Buttons to Open Reports

In the next few steps, you will create three new command buttons. The command buttons will display reports in Print Preview mode. You will use the Command Button Wizard's built-in actions for previewing reports. These built-in actions eliminate the need for macros to perform certain actions, such as previewing reports.

33. Make sure the Main Switchboard form is active and switch to Design ▨ view.

34. Use the Command Button Wizard ▨ button and these guidelines to add the three command buttons shown in the following illustration to the switchboard:

    - Position the command buttons as shown. You will need to choose the Report Operations category and the Preview Report action in the first wizard screen.

    - Assign the Visit Details Report, Overdue for Visit, and Outstanding Balances reports to the buttons as shown. Also, assign any name you desire to the buttons in the last wizard screen.

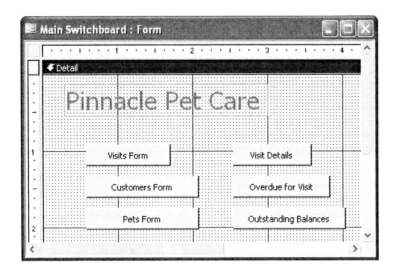

35. When you have finished, switch to Form view and test the buttons.

The buttons should display the indicated reports. The Overdue for Visit report will require you to enter a date in a pop-up box. Use the date 9/1/03. This report requests you to enter a date because it is based upon a query with a parameter criterion.

Removing Objects from Switchboard Forms

Switchboard forms are used as launch pads for opening forms, reports, and other objects. For this reason, the controls on switchboards are typically limited to command buttons and controls that enhance the appearance of the switchboard. Scroll bars, record navigation bars, the record selection bar, and dividing lines are unnecessary on switchboards and are often removed. You can remove any of these objects by first selecting the form in Design view with the Edit→Select Form command. Then, you can remove objects by setting properties on the Format tab of the Properties box as described in the following Quick Reference table.

QR⟩ QUICK REFERENCE: REMOVING OBJECTS FROM SWITCHBOARD FORMS

Task	Procedure
Remove a scroll bar	Set the Scroll Bars property to Neither
Remove a record navigation bar	Set the Navigation Buttons property to No
Remove a record selection bar	Set the Record Selectors property to No
Remove dividing lines	Set the Dividing Lines property to No

Hands-On 9.5   Remove Objects from the Switchboard

In this exercise, you will remove the scroll bars, navigation bar, record selector bar, and dividing lines from the switchboard. You will also add rectangles and labels and enhance the appearance of the switchboard.

1. Click the Design ![icon] view button.

2. Click the box at the upper-left corner of the form to select it. Double-clicking will select the whole form and open the Properties box.

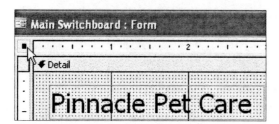

3. Click the Format tab in the Properties box.

4. Set the Scroll Bars property to Neither, the Record Selectors property to No, the Navigation Buttons property to No, and the Dividing Lines property to No.

5. Switch to Form ![icon] view, and the objects should be removed from the form.

6. Switch back to Design ![icon] view.

7. Follow these steps to select multiple items on the form at once:

A With your mouse, drag a box around the items to be selected, starting at the top-left corner and dragging to the bottom-right corner.

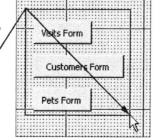

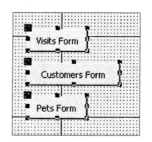

B This will select the items you draw the box around all at once.

8. Follow these guidelines to enhance the appearance of the form so it matches the following illustration:

   ■ In the Format tab of the Properties box, set the width of the buttons to 1.5".
   ■ Use the Format→Align commands to align the buttons as shown.
   ■ Move the buttons down as shown.
   ■ Use the Rectangle ![icon] tool to add rectangles to the form as shown. While the rectangle is still selected, go to the Format Tab on the Properties box and change the Special Effect to Sunken.

- Use the Label 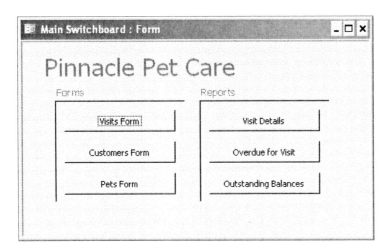 button to add the Forms and Reports labels. Increase the size of the text to 10 and use the same color you used for the Pinnacle Pet Care label.
- Adjust the size of the form until it has the approximate dimensions shown, reducing the light gray area on the form and the overall size of the form in Design view.

9. Switch to Form ▦ view and your form should match the preceding illustration.

10. Close the Main Switchboard form when you have finished and save the changes.

Creating Startup Options for Databases

Access lets you create startup options that specify a form to open whenever a database is started. A main switchboard form is usually specified as the startup form. This way, the switchboard automatically appears when the database is opened. For the user, the switchboard, forms, and reports are the only objects they will see and use. The switchboard can serve as a main menu. You display the Startup options dialog box from the main database window with the Tools→Startup command.

In this exercise, you will set up the switchboard to open automatically when this Access file is opened.

1. Choose Tools→Startup from the menu bar.

2. Follow these steps to specify the Main Switchboard as the startup form:

Ⓐ Choose Main Switchboard from this drop-down list. This instructs Access to display the Main Switchboard form when this database is started.

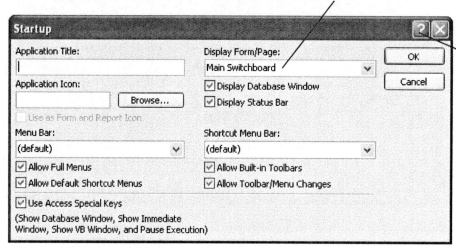

Ⓑ Take a moment to check out the other options (but do not change them). You can get information on an option by clicking this Help button then clicking the option.

3. Click OK to set the Display Form option.

4. Close the Pinnacle Pet Care database.

5. Now open the Pinnacle Pet Care database, and the Main Switchboard form will appear. *The Main Switchboard will appear whenever this database is started.*

6. Close the Switchboard.

The SetValue Action

The SetValue Action is a frequently used action in macros. The SetValue action can be used to copy data from a field in one table or form to a field in another table or form. This action can also be used to set the value of a date field to the current date. This is accomplished by setting the value of the date field to Now( ). Now( ) is a built-in Access function that assigns the current date to a field.

The Expression Builder

The Build ⟦...⟧ button appears in many property and argument boxes. In many cases, the Build button displays the Expression Builder box. The Expression Builder lets you create expressions to use in macros, forms, and other objects. You build expressions by navigating through a series of folders that represent the objects you wish to reference in the expression. You will use the Expression Builder in Hands-On 9.7 to set up the SetValue action in a macro.

Events

Events can be used to initiate macros. For example, in Hands-On 9.7, you will set the On Click event for the Visit Date control in the Visits form. Whenever the Visit Date control is clicked, the event will initiate a macro that contains a SetValue action. The SetValue action will set the value to the current date using the Now( ) function. This process will allow you to enter the current date by simply clicking the control.

 Hands-On 9.7   **Create a Macro and Specify an Event**

In this exercise, you will create a macro that enters today's date into the Visit Date field.

1. Click the Macros button on the Objects bar then click the ⟨New⟩ button.

2. Follow these steps to choose the Set Value action and initiate the Expression Builder:

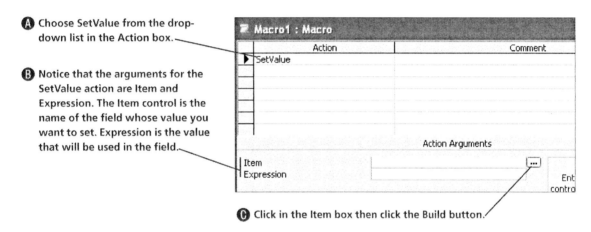

A Choose SetValue from the drop-down list in the Action box.

B Notice that the arguments for the SetValue action are Item and Expression. The Item control is the name of the field whose value you want to set. Expression is the value that will be used in the field.

C Click in the Item box then click the Build button.

3. Follow these steps to build an expression that will specify the Visit Date control on the Visits form:

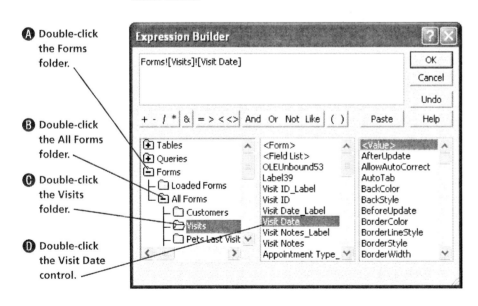

A Double-click the Forms folder.

B Double-click the All Forms folder.

C Double-click the Visits folder.

D Double-click the Visit Date control.

Notice that the expression Forms![Visits]![Visit Date] appears at the top of the Expression Builder. Keep in mind that this exercise is not designed to make you an expert on using the Expression Builder. The purpose of this exercise is to introduce you to the capabilities of the Expression Builder. A complete discussion of the Expression Builder (and expressions, for that matter) is beyond the scope of this course.

4. Click OK and the expression should appear in the Item box.

5. Click in the Expression box and type the expression **Now()**. You could have used the Expression Builder to build this expression but the expression is relatively simple, so it is easier just to type it. Now() is the expression for the current date. At this point, your dialog box should match this example.

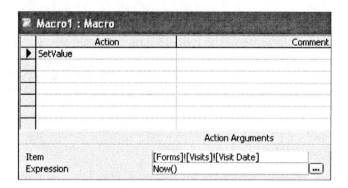

6. Click the Close [X] button on the Macro window.

7. Click the Yes button and save the macro as **Set Visit Date**.

Attach the Macro to the Visit Date Control

8. Open the Visits form in Design view.

9. Click the Visit Date control near the top of the form to select it.

10. Make sure the Properties box is displayed then follow these steps to attach the Set Visit Date macro to the On Click event:

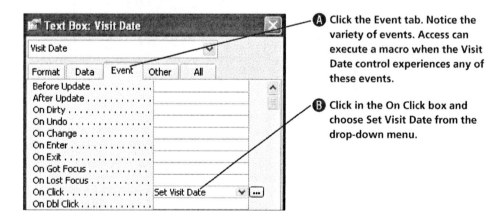

Ⓐ Click the Event tab. Notice the variety of events. Access can execute a macro when the Visit Date control experiences any of these events.

Ⓑ Click in the On Click box and choose Set Visit Date from the drop-down menu.

This event setting will run the Set Visit Date macro whenever the Visit Date control is clicked on the Visits form. The macro will then set the date to the current date.

11. Close the Visits form and save the changes.

Conditional Expressions in Macros

The macros we have used so far are designed to execute when the user takes action (clicks a command button). Macros can be written to execute automatically when a certain condition is met. A conditional expression is evaluated as either true or false. You can design a macro to evaluate the entry in a field. If it is true, the macro action will execute; if it is false, nothing will happen. For example, imagine you want to write a macro that executes when the customer's payment leaves a balance due. The macro can alert the user to ask the customer to make arrangements to pay the balance. A true condition would be that there is a balance due after payment is made. The expression to evaluate the balance due in this example is shown in the following illustration.

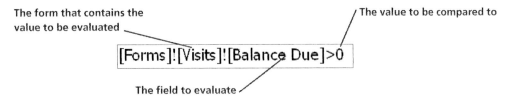

The form that contains the value to be evaluated

The value to be compared to

[Forms]![Visits]![Balance Due]>0

The field to evaluate

Conditional Formatting

If you want to monitor a value in a control on a form or report, you can apply conditional formatting to the control to make it stand out. For example, you can set conditional formatting so that if the balance due is greater than zero the background of the field will be yellow. You can change the color of the text or make it bold, italic, or underlined when it meets or doesn't meet criteria you specify.

You can use the Field Has Focus to make any selected field a different color.

You can change the default formatting for a field if the criteria are not met.

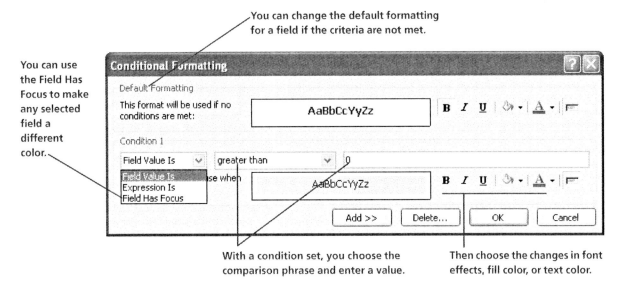

With a condition set, you choose the comparison phrase and enter a value.

Then choose the changes in font effects, fill color, or text color.

Hands-On 9.8 **Create a Conditional Macro**

In this exercise, you will set up a macro to run if the balance due is more than zero. The macro will remind the user to ask the customer to make arrangements to pay the balance due. You will also add conditional formatting so the balance field will change color if the balance is more than zero.

1. Click the Macros button on the Objects bar in the database window.

2. Click the New button to display the Macro window.

3. Click the Conditions button to open the conditions box.

4. Follow these steps to create the macro:

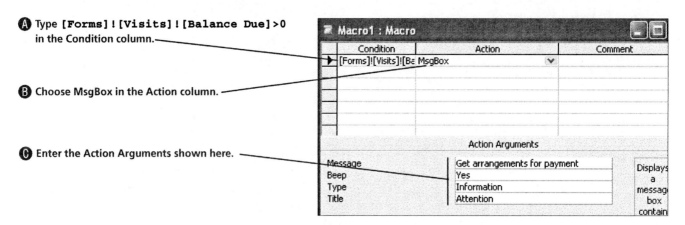

Ⓐ Type [Forms]![Visits]![Balance Due]>0 in the Condition column.

Ⓑ Choose MsgBox in the Action column.

Ⓒ Enter the Action Arguments shown here.

5. Close the macro and save it as **Make Arrangements**.

Assign the Macro to the Form

6. Open the Visits form in Design View.

7. Select the Amount Paid control.

8. Make sure the Properties box is displayed then follow these steps to enter the Make Arrangements macro in the After Update Event:

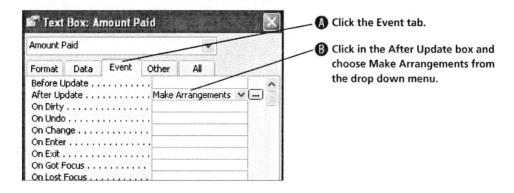

Ⓐ Click the Event tab.

Ⓑ Click in the After Update box and choose Make Arrangements from the drop down menu.

This will cause the Make Arrangements macro to run after the value in Amount Paid is updated (changed).

Set the Conditional Formatting

9. Select the Balance Due control.

10. Choose Format from the menu bar then choose Conditional Formatting.

11. Follow these steps to set the conditional formatting:

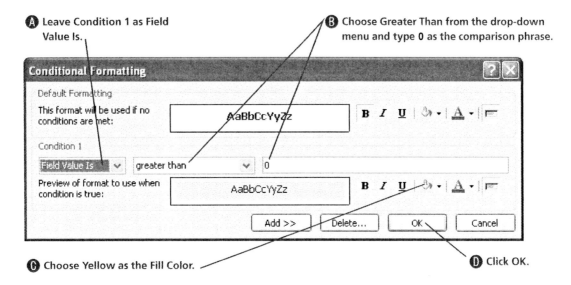

Ⓐ Leave Condition 1 as Field Value Is.

Ⓑ Choose Greater Than from the drop-down menu and type **0** as the comparison phrase.

Ⓒ Choose Yellow as the Fill Color.

Ⓓ Click OK.

This will change the background color of the field to yellow if the customer has a balance due.

12. Close and save the Visits form.

13. Open the Main Switchboard form.

Use the Macro to Enter Data into a New Record

14. Click the Visits Form button on the Main Switchboard.
The Visits form will open and a new record will be displayed.

15. Click the Visit Date control, and Access will set the date to the current date.

16. Choose Pet ID DG24 from the Pet ID drop-down list.
Access will display all of the pet information for Ben the Dog.

17. Enter data into the remaining fields as shown in the following illustration. Your Visit Date should be set to the current date (not the date shown).

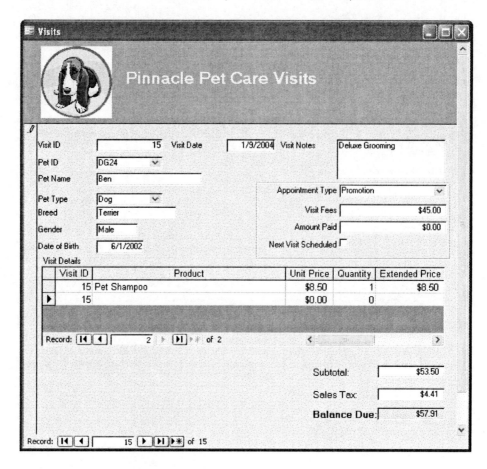

Notice that the background of the Balance Due field is yellow because it contains a value greater than zero.

18. Close the Visits form and the switchboard when you have finished.

Set Command Buttons on Forms

In Hands-On 9.4, you set command buttons on the Main Switchboard to go to other forms. Often the forms are set up not to show the close button or the navigational buttons. Therefore, your forms must have command buttons to navigate to another record, close the form, or return to the Main Switchboard.

Add a Command Button to the Visits Form

In this exercise, you will place a command button on the Visits form that will close the form and return the user to the Main Switchboard.

Create a Macro to Return to Main Switchboard
This macro will also save and close the Visits form.

1. Click the Macros button on the Objects bar.

2. Click the ⌐New button.

3. Set up the OpenForm actions as shown in the following illustration. Make sure you set the Form Name argument to Main Switchboard.

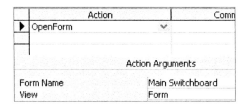

4. Set up the CloseForm actions as shown in the illustration to the right. Make sure to set the Object Name argument to Visits and the Save argument to Yes.

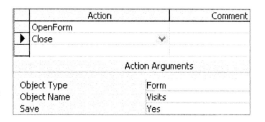

5. Close the macro when you have finished and give it the name **Back to Main Switchboard**.

Assign the Macro to a Command Button

6. Click the Forms button on the Objects bar then open the Visits form in Design view.

7. Click the Command ⌐ button then position the new button on the Visits form to the left of the totals.
   This will open the Command Button Wizard.

8. On the first screen, choose the Miscellaneous category on the left and the Run Macro action on the right.

9. Click Next and choose Back to Main Switchboard.

10. Click Next, choose the Text option, and type **Return**.

11. Click Next, type **Return to Switchboard**, and click Finish.

12. Switch to Form view and test your new command button.
    Clicking your new button will take you back to the Main Switchboard.

13. Close the Pinnacle Pet Care database and continue with the end-of-lesson questions and exercises.

Concepts Review

True/False Questions

1. Switchboard forms must be based on a table or query.   TRUE   FALSE

2. Macros are limited to just one action per macro.   TRUE   FALSE

3. Events can be used to initiate macros.   TRUE   FALSE

4. Macros are created in the Macros window.   TRUE   FALSE

5. Command buttons can only be used to initiate macros.   TRUE   FALSE

6. Scroll bars cannot be removed from switchboard forms.   TRUE   FALSE

7. Dividing lines can be removed from forms by setting the Dividing Lines property   TRUE   FALSE
   to No.

8. The SetValue action can be used to set the values of controls on forms.   TRUE   FALSE

9. Conditional formatting means that if a condition is met, some change in the   TRUE   FALSE
   format will be generated

10. Once you have placed an item on the Switchboard, you cannot remove it.   TRUE   FALSE

Multiple Choice Questions

1. What macro action is used to open a form?
   a. DisplayForm
   b. OpenForm
   c. GoToForm
   d. None of the above

2. What macro action is used to go to a specific record?
   a. GoToRecord
   b. GoToNext
   c. GoToNew
   d. None of the above

3. Which of the following commands is used to display the Startup options box?
   a. Tools→Startup
   b. Edit→Startup
   c. Format→Startup
   d. None of the above

4. Which of the following commands is used to select an entire form?
   a. Format→Form→Select
   b. File→Select Form
   c. Edit→Select Form
   d. None of the above

Skill Builders

Skill Builder 9.1   Create a Switchboard

In this exercise, you will create a switchboard for the Tropical Getaways database.

1. Open the Tropical Getaways database.

2. Click the Forms button on the Objects bar and double-click the Create Form in Design View option.

3. Add a label with the text **Tropical Getaways** at the top-left corner of the form.

4. Increase the size of the label text to 18, apply the color of your choice, and increase the size of the label box so all text is visible.

5. Use the Edit→Select Form command to select the entire form.

6. If necessary, display the Properties box and click the Format tab.

7. Set the Scroll Bars property to Neither.

8. Set the Record Selectors, Navigation Buttons, and Dividing Lines properties to No.
These settings will remove the indicated objects from the form when it is displayed in Form view.

9. Close the form and save it as **Main Switchboard**.

Skill Builder 9.2   Create Macros

In this exercise, you will set up several macros. One of the macros will set the value of the Order Date control on the Custom Packages form while the other macros will open forms.

1. Click the Macros button on the Objects bar and click the [New] button.

2. Set up the OpenForm and GoToRecord actions as shown in the following illustration. Make sure you set the Form Name argument to Customers for the OpenForm action. Also, change the Record argument for the GoToRecord action to New.

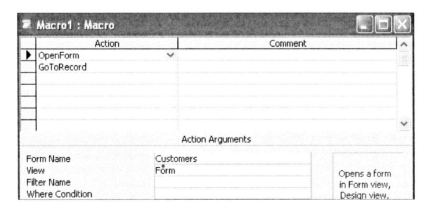

3. Close the macro when you have finished and save it as **Open Customers Form**.

4. Test the macro by choosing it in the Macros window and clicking the ▸ Run button.

5. Close the Customers form without entering data.

6. Set up another new macro as shown in the following illustration. Make sure you set the Form Name argument to New Trips for the OpenForm action. Also, change the Record argument for the GoToRecord action to New.

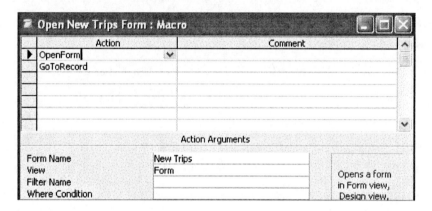

7. Close the macro when you have finished and save it as **Open New Trips Form**.

8. Test the macro to make sure it functions correctly.

9. Close the New Trips form.

10. Set up another new macro as shown in the following illustration. Make sure you set the Form Name argument to Custom Packages for the OpenForm action. Also, change the Record argument for the GoToRecord action to New.

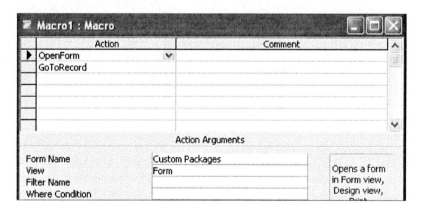

11. Close the macro when you have finished and save it as **Open Custom Packages Form**.

12. Test the macro to make sure it functions correctly.

13. Close the Custom Packages form.

14. Set up another new macro. Make sure you set the Action to Open Form and the Form Name argument to Main Switchboard.

15. In the same macro, set up the Close actions as shown in the following illustration. Make sure you set the Object Name argument to Custom Packages and the Save argument to Yes.

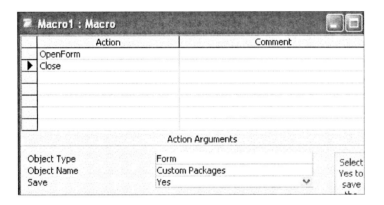

16. Close the macro when you have finished and give it the name **Back to Main Switchboard**.

17. Set up another new macro.

18. Follow these steps to choose the SetValue action and initiate the Expression Builder:

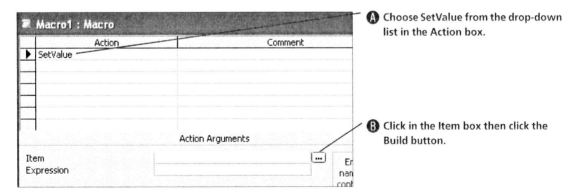

Ⓐ Choose SetValue from the drop-down list in the Action box.

Ⓑ Click in the Item box then click the Build button.

19. Follow these steps to build an expression that will specify the Order Date field on the Custom Packages form. In Skill Builder 9.5, you will use this macro to enter the current date into the Order Date field.

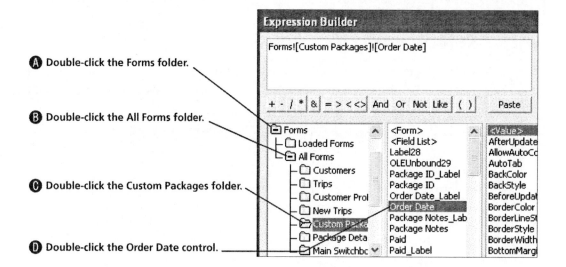

A Double-click the Forms folder.

B Double-click the All Forms folder.

C Double-click the Custom Packages folder.

D Double-click the Order Date control.

The expression Forms![Custom Packages]![Order Date] should appear at the top of the Expression Builder.

20. Click OK, and the expression should appear in the Item box.

21. Enter the expression **Now()** in the Expression box.

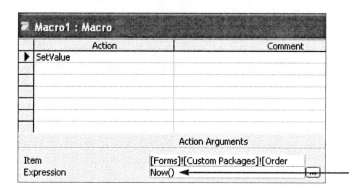

22. Close the Macro window. Choose Yes when Access asks you to save the macro and assign it the name **Set Order Date**.

Create Command Buttons

In this exercise, you will add command buttons to the Main Switchboard. Some of the buttons will initiate macros, while others will open reports in Print Preview mode. You will also add a button to exit Access.

1. Open the Main Switchboard form in Design view.

2. Follow these guidelines to add command buttons, labels, and rectangles to the form as shown in the following illustration:

   ■ Create the command buttons in the positions shown.

   ■ Assign macros to the command buttons shown in the Forms rectangle. In Skill Builder 9.2, you created a macro for each button.

   ■ Assign reports to the command buttons shown in the Reports rectangle. You can choose the indicated reports in the Command Button Wizard. Make sure you choose the Print Preview option in the wizard so the reports open in Print Preview mode.

   ■ Add the labels and rectangles to the form as shown. Also, adjust the size of the form and size and align the command buttons as shown.

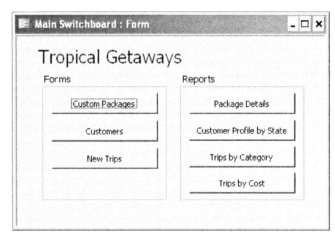

Create a Command Button to Exit Access

This button will close and exit Access:

3. Click the Command 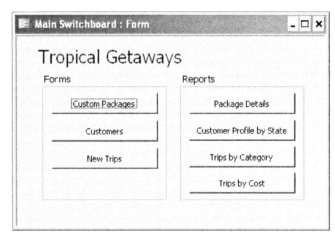 button on the toolbox then click below the rectangle you drew around the forms buttons.

4. Choose the Application category then choose the Quit Application action.

5. Click Next, choose the Text option, and type **Exit Access**.

6. Click Next, type **Exit Access** on the last screen, and click the Finish button.

7. When you have finished, switch to Form 📧 view and test the buttons.
   *The buttons should open the indicated forms and display the indicated reports in Print Preview. The Trips by Cost report will require you to enter a number in a pop-up box. Use the number **3,000**. Only trips with a cost greater than 3,000 will appear in the report. Don't test the Exit Access button at this time.*

8. When you have finished, close the Main Switchboard form and save the changes.

Skill Builder 9.4   Specify a Startup Form

In this exercise, you will specify the Main Switchboard as the startup form for the database. The Main Switchboard will be displayed as soon as the database is started.

1. Choose Tools→Startup from the menu bar.

2. Set the Display Form option to Main Switchboard and click OK.

3. Close the Tropical Getaways database.

4. Now open the Tropical Getaways database.
   The Main Switchboard form should be displayed.

Skill Builder 9.5   Assign a Macro to an Event and a Close Command Button

In this exercise, you will assign the Set Order Date macro to the On Click event for the Order Date control in the Custom Packages form. The macro will set the Order Date field to the current date whenever the Order Date control is clicked. You will also add a button to close the form and go back to the Main Switchboard.

1. Close the Main Switchboard form.

2. Open the Custom Packages form in Design view.

3. Click the Order Date control near the top of the form to select it.

4. Make sure the Properties box is displayed, choose the Event tab, and set the On Click event to Set Order Date, as shown to the right.

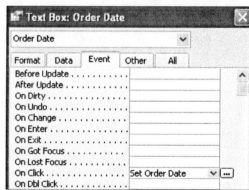

5. Create a command button at the bottom of the form and assign it to the Back to Main Switchboard macro you created in Skill Builder 9.2. Label the button **Return to Main Switchboard**.

6. Save the changes and click the Return to Main Switchboard button.

Skill Builder 9.6   Enter Data

In this exercise, you will enter a new record into the Custom Packages form. You will set the Order Date field to the current date by simply clicking the Order Date control.

1. Click the Custom Packages button on the Main Switchboard to display a new record.

2. Click the Order Date control and Access will set the date to the current date.

3. Choose Customer ID 3 from the Customer ID drop-down list.
   Access will display all of the customer information for Ted Wilkins.

4. Enter data into the remaining fields as shown in the following illustration. Your Order Date should be set to the current date (not the date shown).

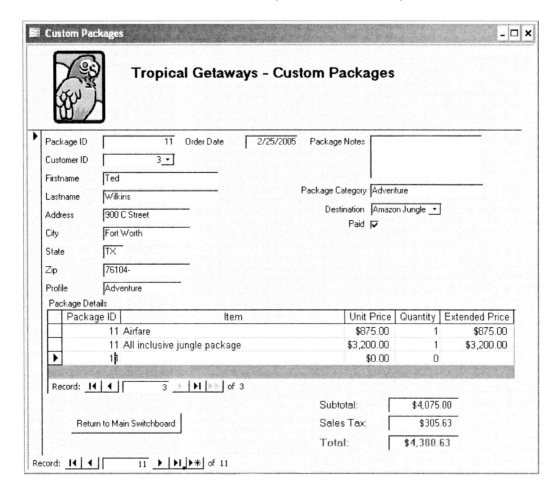

5. Click the Return to Main Switchboard button when you have finished.

6. Close the Tropical Getaways database by clicking the Exit Access button.

Assessments

Assessment 9.1   Create a Switchboard

In this exercise you will create a Switchboard for the Classic Cars database.

1. Start Access, and then open the Classic Cars database.

2. Follow these guidelines to create the Main Switchboard shown in the following illustration:

   ■ Create three macros that open the Events, Collectors, and Cars forms. Display new records in the forms.

   ■ Create command buttons as shown. The buttons in the Forms rectangle should initiate macros, while the buttons in the Reports rectangle should display the indicated reports in Print Preview mode.

   ■ Add labels and rectangles to the form as shown.

   ■ Remove the scroll bars, record navigation bar, record selector bar, and dividing lines from the form.

   ■ Assign the name **Main Switchboard** to the form.

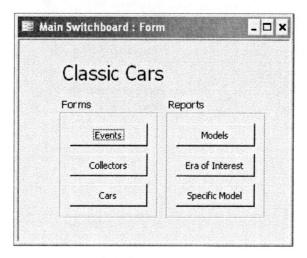

3. Set the startup options so the Main Switchboard is automatically displayed when the Classic Cars database is opened.

4. Create a macro that automatically sets the Event Date control in the Events form to the current date. Assign the name **Set Event Date** to the macro.

5. Set the On Click property of the Event Date control in the Events form to initiate the Set Event Date macro when the Event Date control is clicked.

6. Close all open forms and save the changes.

7. Close the Classic Cars database.

Assessment 9.2　Specify a Startup Form

In this exercise you will create macros and command buttons for the database.

1. Open the Classic Cars database and the Main Switchboard should automatically appear.

2. Follow these guidelines to create macros and command buttons on each of the forms.
   - Create macros for each of the forms (Events, Collectors, and Cars) that save and close the forms then open the Main Switchboard form.
   - Create command buttons on each of the forms to initiate the macros.
   - Create a command button on the Main Switchboard form that closes the Classic Cars database and exits Access.

3. Test your macros and your command buttons.

4. Click the Events button on the Main Switchboard.
   The Events form should open and a new record should be displayed.

5. Enter the data shown in the following illustration into the new record. You should be able to set the Event Date field to the current date by clicking the Event Date control. However, the date will differ from that shown in the illustration. Also, the collector's first name and last name can be displayed by choosing the indicated Collector ID in the Collector ID control.

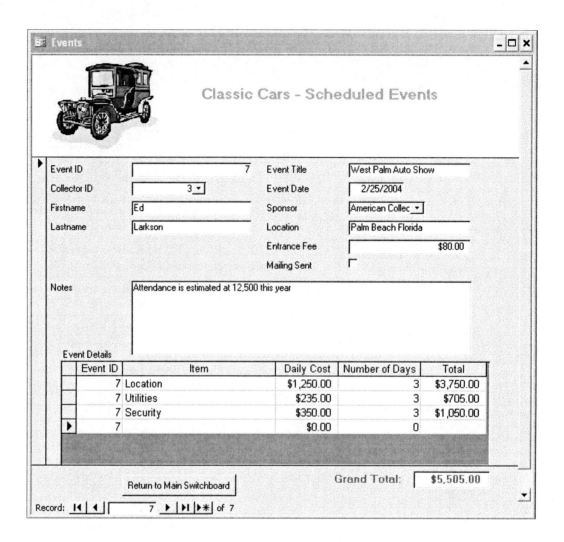

6. Click the Return to Main Switchboard button on the Events form when finished.

7. Click the Exit Access button you created to close the Classic Cars database when you have finished.

Critical Thinking

Critical Thinking 9.1   Create Switchboards

Linda Holmes wants an interface to the Holmestead Realty database that makes it easy for users to access important database information. She asks you to create a switchboard that provides access to the most important forms and reports in the database. Open the Holmestead Realty database and follow these guidelines to create a switchboard:

- Create a blank form to be used as the switchboard. Name the form **Main Switchboard**. Add a label with the text **Holmestead Realty** to the top of the form.

- Create a macro that opens the Contacts Data Entry form and displays a new record. Name the macro **Open Contacts Form**.

- Create a macro that closes and saves the Contacts Data Entry form and opens the Main Switchboard form. Name this macro **Contacts to Main**.

- Create another macro that opens the Listings Data Entry form and displays a new record. Name this macro **Open Listings Form**.

- Create a macro that closes and saves the Listings Data Entry form and opens the Main Switchboard form. Name this macro **Listings to Main**.

- Add a label for Forms on the left side and a label for Reports on the right side of the switchboard form. These labels will become headings for a Forms section and a Reports section.

- Create the following command buttons in the Forms section of the switchboard:

Command Button Name and Button Text	Instructions
Contacts Data Entry	Use the Open Contacts Form macro
Listings Data Entry	Use the Open Listings Form macro
Feels Like Home Data Entry	Use the Command Button Wizard to open the Feels Like Home Data Entry form

- Create the following command buttons in the Reports section of the switchboard:

Command Button Name and Button Text	Instructions
Contacts Phone List	Use the Command Button Wizard to open the Contacts Phone List report
Expiration Date List	Use the Command Button Wizard to open the Expiration Date List report
Hearthfire Invoice	Use the Command Button Wizard to open the Hearthfire Invoice report

- Create command buttons on the Contacts Data Entry form and on the Listings Data Entry form that run the macros to return to the Main Switchboard.

Critical Thinking 9.2   Format the Switchboard

Follow these guidelines to remove objects from the switchboard, organize the switchboard, and set the startup options:

- Remove the scroll bars, record navigation bar, record selection bar, and dividing lines from the switchboard.

- Organize the switchboard buttons, add rectangles, and change the font sizes and colors and other formatting options as desired.

- Change the startup options for this database to display the Main Switchboard at startup.

- Add a command button to the bottom of the form that closes Access.

Critical Thinking 9.3   Create SetValue Macros

Follow these guidelines to create a SetValue macro and to use it to simplify data entry:

- Create a SetValue macro that returns today's date in the Listing Date field of the Listings Data Entry form. Call this macro **Set Date of Listing**.

- Attach the macro to the On Click event of the Listing Date control in the Listings Data Entry form.

- Test the macro by entering the following new listing:

MLS #	Street #	Address	Price	Listing Date	Expiration Date	Commission Rate	Seller ID	Style
53102	70	Oakley Place	$125,000	Today	In three months	4.5%	3	Ranch

LESSON 10

Integrating Access with Word, Excel, and the Web

Access databases are the information banks for many organizations. Customer mailing lists, order data, and other types of information often reside in databases. Access's OfficeLinks tools make it easy to export data to Word and Excel. Word is often used to conduct mail merges using Access address data, while Excel is often used to analyze financial data. In this lesson, you will set up a mail merge between a Word form letter and an Access query. You will also use Excel to analyze financial data exported from Access. Finally, you will learn important techniques for maintaining and securing databases.

Microsoft Office Access 2003 objectives covered in this lesson

Objective Number	Skill Sets and Skills	Concept Page References	Exercise Page References
AC03S-1-12	Create a data access page	344–345	345–347, 357–358
AC03S-4-1	Identify object dependencies	348	349
AC03S-4-2	View objects and object data in other views	348	
AC03S-4-4	Export data from Access	342–343	342–344
AC03S-4-5	Back up a database	350	
AC03S-4-6	Compact and repair databases	350	351

Additional learning resources are available at labpub.com/learn/access03/

Case Study

The staff at Pinnacle Pet Care needs to conduct periodic mailings to its customers. Al Smith wants to take advantage of the powerful word processing features available in Microsoft Word to generate a mailing using the names in the Customers table in the Pinnacle Pet Care database. Al also sets up the Pinnacle Pet Care database so his staff can use the Customers table to effortlessly generate mailing labels from within Access.

FirstName	LastName	Address	City	State	Zip
Mark	Roth	760 Maple Avenue	Fremont	CA	94538-
Tony	Simpson	312 York Lane	Richmond	CA	94804-
Jason	Jones	2233 Crystal Street	San Mateo	CA	94403-
Jacob	Samuels	2300 North Pratt Str	Atlanta	GA	30309-

An Access query is merged with a Word form letter to create personalized letters.

November 19, 2003

««AddressBlock»»

«,«GreetingLine»»

We are pleased to inform you that our annual Pinnacle Pet Care Dog Show on March 15 at our facilities. You are cordially invited to enroll your dog in You also may bring as many guests as you like.

A letter is produced for each record selected by the query.

November 19, 2003

Mr. Mark Roth
760 Maple Avenue
Fremont, CA 94538

Dear Mr. Roth:

We are pleased to inform
on March 15 at our facilit
You also may bring as m

November 19, 2003

Mr. Tony Simpson
312 York Lane
Richmond, CA 94804

Dear Mr. Simpson:

We are pleased to inform yo
on March 15 at our facilities
You also may bring as many

November 19, 2003

Mr. Jason Jones
2233 Crystal Street
San Mateo, CA 94403

Dear Mr. Jones:

We are pleased to inform you that our annual Pini
on March 15 at our facilities. You are cordially in
You also may bring as many guests as you like.

Integrating Access with Word

Many businesses use Access databases as the bank for customer and order information. A properly designed Access database should make it easy for individuals and businesses to send form letters, generate mailing labels, and perform other mailing functions. You can also transfer reports, tables, and query datasets created in Access to Word.

Using Access and Word to Conduct Mailings

A typical mailing requires labels and personalized letters. Word has a Mail Merge feature that lets you generate personalized letters using the address information from a data source. An Access table or query can be used as the data source for a mail merge. You can easily set up mailing labels using Access's Mailing Label Wizard. Access is tightly integrated with Microsoft Word. You can use Word to set up a form letter then merge the form letter with a table or query in your Access database. The resulting letters will be personalized with your customers' names and addresses. The following illustrations discuss the process used to conduct mailings using Access and Word.

Step 1—In Access, choose the table containing the desired customer information.

FirstName	LastName	Address	City	State	Zip
Mark	Roth	760 Maple Avenue	Fremont	CA	94538-
Tony	Simpson	312 York Lane	Richmond	CA	94804-
Jason	Jones	2233 Crystal Street	San Mateo	CA	94403-
Jacob	Samuels	2300 North Pratt Stre	Atlanta	GA	30309-

Step 2— The Merge It with Microsoft Office Word OfficeLinks button is used to establish a Dynamic Data Exchange (DDE) link between the table and a Word document. Field codes and text are inserted into the Word mail merge document, as shown to the right. The document is then merged with the table to produce personalized letters.

Step 3—A table or query is also used as the basis for a mailing label report. If you use a query, mailing labels will be generated only for those records that meet the criteria specified in the query.

November 19, 2003

««AddressBlock»»

««GreetingLine»»

We are pleased to inform you that our annual Pi on March 15 at our facilities. You are cordially You also may bring as many guests as you like.

Jacob Samuels
2300 North Pratt Street
Atlanta, GA 30309

Jason Jones
2233 Crystal Street
San Mateo, CA 94403

Mark Roth
760 Maple Avenue
Fremont, CA 94538

Creating a Mailing List Query

At times you will need to select only certain records from Access tables for a mailing. For example, you may want to send a mailing to customers who have outstanding balances. You can use a query to gather those customers. You may also want to send a mailing to a group of customers who can't be categorized in any particular manner. In this situation, you must have some way of identifying the customers you wish to include in the mailing. You can accomplish this by adding a Yes/No field to the table from which you wish to choose records. The Yes/No box can be checked for the desired records. A query can then be used to choose only those records where the Yes/No field is set to yes (checked).

The Merge It with Microsoft Word OfficeLinks Button

The Merge It with Microsoft Office Word [icon] OfficeLinks button is available whenever a table or query is highlighted in the Access database window. This button starts the Mail Merge Wizard that guides you through the process of merging a table or query with a Word form letter.

Hands-On 10.1   Create a Word Mail Merge Document

In this exercise, you will set up a Word mail merge document that is linked to the Customer table in the Pinnacle Pet Care database.

1. Start Access and open the Pinnacle Pet Care database.

2. If necessary, close the switchboard, and then click the Tables button on the Objects bar.

3. Follow these steps to choose the Customers table and start the Mail Merge Wizard:

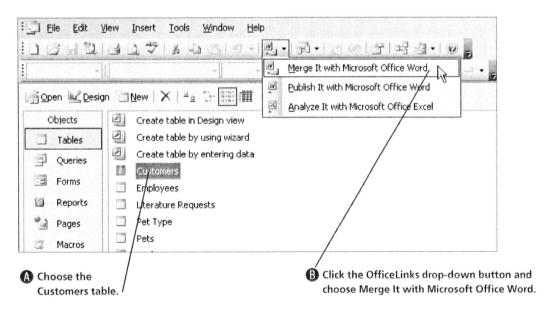

Ⓐ Choose the Customers table.

Ⓑ Click the OfficeLinks drop-down button and choose Merge It with Microsoft Office Word.

4. Choose the Create a New Document and Then Link the Data to It option in the first wizard screen and click OK.
Access will start Word and establish a dynamic data exchange link between the new Word document and the Customer table in Access. As you conduct a mail merge, the wizard provides step-by-step guidance in the Word task pane.

5. Maximize ▢ the Word window and tap Enter six times.
This will position the insertion point approximately 2" down from the top of the page. Most business letters begin at this point.

6. Choose Insert→Date and Time from the menu bar.

7. Choose the third date format in the Date and Time box and make sure the Update Automatically box near the bottom of the dialog box is checked.
Checking the Update Automatically box instructs Access to insert the date as a field. This way, the current date will be inserted in the document whenever the document is opened.

8. Click OK to insert the date then tap Enter four times.
At this point, you can continue following the Mail Merge Wizard in the task pane or take charge of the mail merge yourself using tools on Word's Mail Merge toolbar. Word 2003 offers enhanced mail merge tools that make setting up and conducting mail merges simple. In the remainder of this exercise, you will use tools on the Mail Merge toolbar.

9. Use the View→Task Pane command to close the task pane.

10. Follow these steps to insert an address block in your form letter:

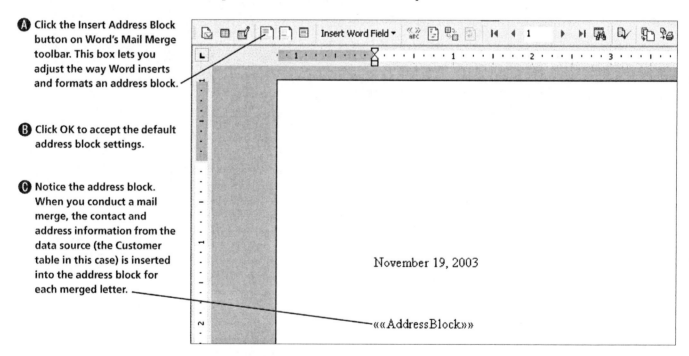

Ⓐ Click the Insert Address Block button on Word's Mail Merge toolbar. This box lets you adjust the way Word inserts and formats an address block.

Ⓑ Click OK to accept the default address block settings.

Ⓒ Notice the address block. When you conduct a mail merge, the contact and address information from the data source (the Customer table in this case) is inserted into the address block for each merged letter.

November 19, 2003

««AddressBlock»»

11. Tap Enter twice to create blank lines below the address block.

12. Follow these steps to insert a greeting line in the form letter:

🅐 Click the Insert Greeting Line button on Word's Mail Merge toolbar.

Insert Word Field ▾

Insert Greeting Line

November 19, 2003

««AddressBlock»»

««GreetingLine»»

We are pleased to inform you that our annual Pinnacle Pet Care Dog Show will be held on March 15 at our facilities. You are cordially invited to enroll your dog in the show. You also may bring as many guests as you like.

Please respond by February 28, so that we may reserve a spot for your pet.

Sincerely,

Cindy Marshall
Training Manager

🅑 Click the third drop-down button in the Insert Greeting Line box and choose the colon (:) format.

🅒 Click OK and the greeting line will be inserted.

🅓 Tap Enter twice and type the remainder of the letter shown here.

The form letter you just set up is linked to the Customer table through a DDE link, which will access the Customers table whenever the form letter is opened in Word. This way, the form letter will always receive fresh data from the Access database. The table data will be used to create personalized letters during the merge.

13. Save 🖫 the letter to your file storage location as **Customer Form Letter**.

⚠️ **TIP!** *If you are creating a form letter for an organization, you should consider saving it as a Word template. This way, you can use the template over and over as the basis for new form letters. Each form letter created from the template will be linked to the Access Customer table.*

14. Click the Merge to New Document 🗊 button (fourth button from the right end of the Mail Merge toolbar).

15. Click OK on the Merge to New Document box to merge all records.

16. Browse through the merged letters and note the four personalized letters.
A letter was generated for each record selected in the Customer table.

17. Close the merged letters without saving them.
Merged letters and other merge documents are rarely saved since they can be easily regenerated by conducting the merge again and because they typically require large amounts of disk space.

18. Close Word and, if necessary, save the changes to the Customer Form Letter document.

Setting Up Mailing Labels in Access

The button in the Reports section of the database window provides access to several report wizards and AutoReport tools. The Label Wizard can be used to set up mailing labels. The Label Wizard creates a report based on a table or query. The report is formatted to print on the mailing label paper stock you specify.

Hands-On 10.2 Create Mailing Labels for the Customers Table

In this exercise, you will set up mailing labels based on the Customers table. A mailing label will be generated for each record in the Customers table.

1. Click the Reports button on the Objects bar in the Access database window.

2. Click the button to display the New Report box.

3. Choose the Label Wizard, choose Customers from the table/query list, and click OK.

4. Follow these steps to choose a label format:

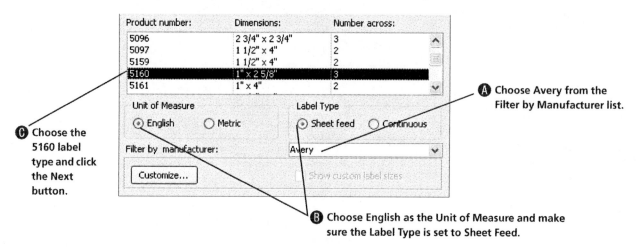

Ⓐ Choose Avery from the Filter by Manufacturer list.

Ⓒ Choose the 5160 label type and click the Next button.

Ⓑ Choose English as the Unit of Measure and make sure the Label Type is set to Sheet Feed.

5. Click Next again to bypass the font and color options screen.
The next wizard screen lets you arrange the fields on the labels.

6. Follow these steps to arrange the fields:

Ⓐ Choose Firstname on the Available fields list, and click the Add Field button.

Ⓑ Tap [Spacebar], choose Lastname from the Available fields list, and click the Add Field button.

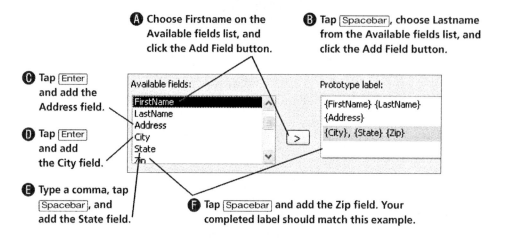

Ⓒ Tap [Enter] and add the Address field.

Ⓓ Tap [Enter] and add the City field.

Ⓔ Type a comma, tap [Spacebar], and add the State field.

Ⓕ Tap [Spacebar] and add the Zip field. Your completed label should match this example.

7. Click Next and the wizard will ask on which field you wish to sort.

8. Choose the Zip field and click the Add Field | > | button.

9. Click Next and type the name **Mailing Labels** in the last wizard screen.

10. Make sure the See the Labels as They Will Look Printed option is chosen and click the Finish button. Click OK if you receive a warning message.
Access will create the report, and the labels shown here should appear.

Jacob Samuels	Jason Jones	Mark Roth
2300 North Pratt Street	2233 Crystal Street	760 Maple Avenue
Atlanta, GA 30309	San Mateo, CA 94403	Fremont, CA 94538
Tony Simpson		
312 York Lane		
Richmond, CA 94804		

11. Click the Design view button.
This report is quite intricate and would require a substantial amount of effort to set up from scratch. Notice that the report includes the Trim function. It removes all blank spaces from a text string—except the spaces between words. This function can be quite useful when producing labels and other types of reports.

12. Close the report, and Mailing Labels should appear in the Reports section.
From this point forward, you can generate mailing labels by opening this report. Whenever this report is opened, a label will be generated for each record in the Customers table. Once again, the report is based on the Customer table. Keep in mind that recreating a mailing label report using the wizard is much easier than modifying a report that did not turn out the way you intended.

Copying Access Data to Word

You can copy Access data to Word in several ways:

- OfficeLinks—Use the OfficeLinks tool to copy reports, tables, queries, and forms to Word. Depending on the object chosen, you can publish, analyze, or merge the Access data.

- Copy and Paste—Use the Copy and Paste tools to copy selected data through the Office Clipboard to Word.

- Drag and Drop—Tile the Access and the Word window, and drag the database tables, reports, forms, or queries into a Word document.

Publishing Data to Word

The Publish It with Microsoft Office Word OfficeLinks button copies data from an Access table, query, form, or report into a Word document. You may want to have a report, table, query, or form in Word so you can email it to someone without having to send the entire database. You may want to be able to add these objects in Word to a larger report. In Hands-On 10.3, you will use the OfficeLinks tool to open a report in Microsoft Word.

Hands-On 10.3   Publish a Report to Word

In this exercise, you will use the OfficeLinks tool to save an Access report as a Microsoft Word document.

1. Click the Reports button on the Objects bar in the database window.

2. Choose the Visit Details Report then click the OfficeLinks drop-down button on the Access toolbar.

3. Choose the Publish It with Microsoft Office Word option.
   Access will open the report in Microsoft Word. It will be automatically saved to the default location, which is My Documents for most Microsoft Office applications.

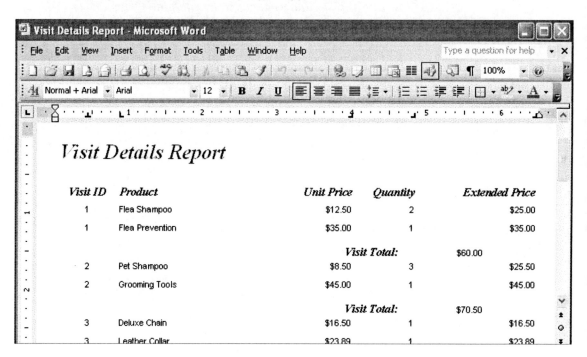

4. Close the report then close Word.

Using Drag and Drop to Export Objects to Word

A simple way to export queries and tables from Access to Word is to use the drag and drop method. To do this you must have both Access and Word open at the same time and arranged on the computer screen so you can see both windows. You simply locate the table or query you would like to use and, without opening the object, drag it from the Access window to the Word window.

 Hands-On 10.4   Drag and Drop a Table to Word

In this exercise, you will save a table in Word by dragging the table name icon from Access to a Word document.

1. Click the Tables button on the Objects bar in the database window.

2. If necessary, click the Restore [🗗] button in the upper-right corner of the Access window.

3. Open a blank document in Word.

4. If necessary, click the Restore button on the Word window.

5. Arrange the windows so you can easily see both.

6. Follow these steps to drag and drop the Customers table to the Word document:

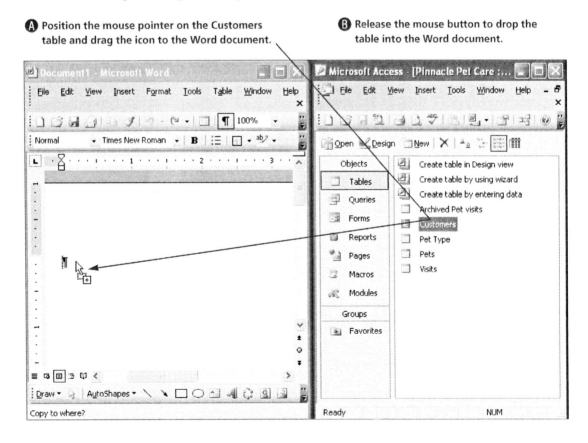

Ⓐ Position the mouse pointer on the Customers table and drag the icon to the Word document.

Ⓑ Release the mouse button to drop the table into the Word document.

7. Click anywhere in the highlighted table in the Word document to see how it looks on the page.

8. Exit from Word when you have finished, but do not save the document.

Integrating Access with Excel

You can export data from a table or query to an Excel spreadsheet.

Exporting Data to Excel

The most common ways to export data are to use Export, Copy and Paste, or Drag and Drop. The Export option is available from the File menu. Choosing the Export option opens a Save As dialog box in which you choose Excel as the file type. You can choose Save Formatted to preserve as much of the Access formatting as possible.

 Hands-On 10.5   Export the Pets Table to Excel

In this exercise, you will use the Export option to export an Access table to Excel.

1. Click the Tables button on the Objects bar in the database window.

2. Click on the Pets table to select it.

3. Choose File→Export from the menu bar.

4. Follow these steps to export a table to Excel:

Ⓐ Navigate to your file storage location.

Ⓑ Choose Microsoft Excel 97-2003 from the Save as Type drop-down list.

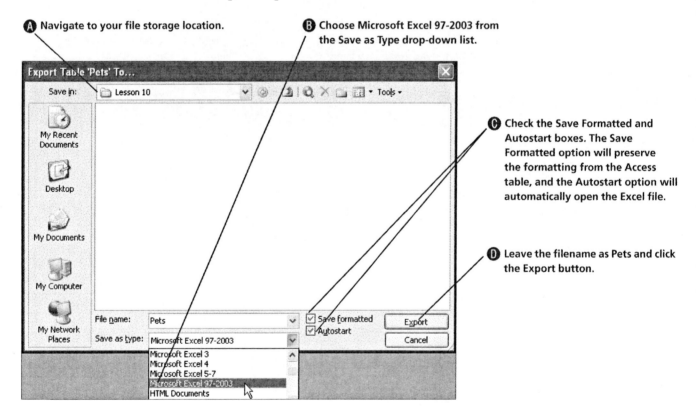

Ⓒ Check the Save Formatted and Autostart boxes. The Save Formatted option will preserve the formatting from the Access table, and the Autostart option will automatically open the Excel file.

Ⓓ Leave the filename as Pets and click the Export button.

5. View the exported table in the Excel file. Notice that it preserved the formatting from the Access table.

6. Exit from Excel when you have finished.

Publishing Data to Excel

Microsoft Office
Specialist The Analyze It with Microsoft Office Excel OfficeLinks button exports the table or query selected in the database window to Excel. The table or query field names become heading rows in the Excel worksheet. If you export a table, all rows from the table are output to Excel. If you export a query, the query is run and the entire recordset is exported to Excel.

Using Copy and Paste to Export to Excel

You can also open a table or run a query in Access, select and copy the desired data, and paste the data into an Excel worksheet. This can be useful if don't want to export the entire table or query recordset. However, if you want to export the entire table or recordset, the OfficeLinks button is probably your best choice. It will format the worksheet for you.

Subtotaling and PivotTables in Excel

Excel has a variety of powerful tools for analyzing data. Subtotals and PivotTables are two of these tools. Many organizations have order information and other types of numeric data stored in Access database systems. These data can easily be analyzed by exporting them to Excel and using subtotals, PivotTables, and other analytic tools. In Hands-On 10.6, you will receive a brief introduction to Excel's subtotaling feature. For complete coverage of all of Excel's tools, see *Microsoft Office Excel 2003: Comprehensive Course*.

 Hands-On 10.6 **Export Data to Excel and Use Excel Subtotals**

In this exercise, you will export an Access query to Excel using the OfficeLinks tool.

Export the Data

1. Click the Queries button on the Objects bar in the database window.

2. Choose the Query-Visit Details query then click the OfficeLinks ⬜ drop-down button on the Access toolbar.

3. Choose the Analyze It with Microsoft Office Excel ⬜ option.
   Access will run the query, start Excel, and output the recordset.

Subtotal the Data

The first step in the subtotaling process is to sort the data on the field you wish to subtotal. In the following steps, you will sort on the Product field then subtotal on that field.

4. Click in any cell in the Product column.

5. Click the Sort Ascending ⬜ button on the Excel toolbar.

6. Choose Data→Subtotals from the Excel menu bar.

7. Follow these steps to set up the subtotals:

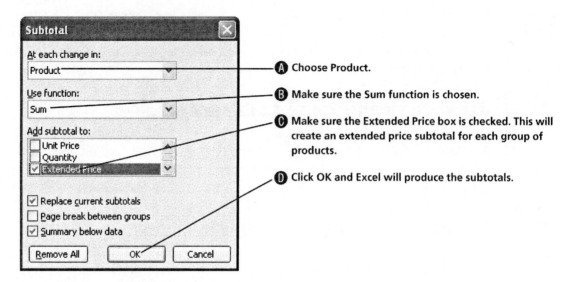

A Choose Product.

B Make sure the Sum function is chosen.

C Make sure the Extended Price box is checked. This will create an extended price subtotal for each group of products.

D Click OK and Excel will produce the subtotals.

Take a moment to examine the worksheet and notice that each product has a subtotal.

8. Feel free to experiment with subtotals. You can remove subtotals by displaying the Subtotals box with the Data→Subtotals command then clicking the Remove All button.

9. Exit from Excel when you have finished, but do not save the worksheet.

Working with Data Access Pages

Microsoft Office Specialist

A data access page is a Web page connected to an Access database. Data access pages function like forms, allowing users to enter and modify data. However, the benefit of data access pages is that they can be posted to an intranet or as Web pages on the World Wide Web. Therefore, users in various locations can access and modify data in an underlying database.

How Data Access Pages Work

Any user with permission to enter a data access page can edit or add records. These changes are reflected in the underlying Access database. A data access page also features a toolbar that allows users to sort and filter records. However, these actions affect only the sequencing of records displayed on the user's data access page—not in the underlying database. Because data access pages allow outside users to modify data, the use of these pages should be carefully considered before they are deployed. The following illustration shows the data access page you will create in Hands-On 10.7.

Literature Request Page

FirstName: Tonya

LastName: Dennings

Address: 235 Parker Road

City   Richmond

State: CA

Zip: 94803

Literature Requests 5 of 5

The data access page resembles a form with controls that display fields from an underlying access database.

A toolbar gives users limited control over the entry and display of records.

The Data Access Page Wizard

You use the Data Access Page Wizard to set up data access pages. You can also create or modify a data access page in Design view as you would with any other database object. When a data access page is created, a data access page object is created in the database and an HTML version of the data access page is created outside of the database. The HTML version is linked to the underlying Access database, allowing users on the World Wide Web to access the underlying database.

 Hands-On 10.7   Create a Data Access Page

In this exercise, you will use the Data Access Page Wizard to create a data access page. The data access page will allow customers to request literature from Pinnacle Pet Care over the World Wide Web.

Copy a Table

1. Click the Tables button on the Objects bar.

2. Choose the Customers table then click the Copy button on the Access toolbar.

3. Now click the Paste button, type the name **Literature Requests** in the Paste Table As box, and click OK.
   This creates a copy of the Customers table. In the next few steps, you will modify the structure of the new table.

Modify the Structure of the Table

4. Choose the Literature Requests table and click the Design button to open it in Design view.

5. Click in the Phone field and choose Edit→Delete Rows from the menu bar.

6. Click Yes on the warning box that appears to remove the row.

7. Now delete the Last Visit and Current Balance fields.
   You won't need these fields, since this table will be used as the basis for a literature request data access page.

8. Now add a Literature Sent field, setting the data type to Yes/No.
   Your completed table should match the example shown to the right.

	Field Name	Data Type
🔑	Customer ID	AutoNumber
	FirstName	Text
	LastName	Text
	Address	Text
	City	Text
	State	Text
	Zip	Text
	Literature Sent	Yes/No

9. Save the table and close it.

Use the Data Access Page Wizard

10. Click the Pages button on the Objects bar.
    The Pages section is where data access pages are displayed.

11. Double-click the Create Data Access Page by Using Wizard option.

12. Choose the Literature Requests table from the Tables/Queries list.

13. Add the Firstname, Lastname, Address, City, State, and Zip fields to the Selected Fields list.
    It isn't necessary to have the Customer ID and Literature Sent fields appear on the data access page. The Customer ID field is an autonumber field that simply identifies each customer record. The Literature Sent field will be used by the staff at Pinnacle Pet Care to mark prospective customers who have already been sent literature.

14. Click the Next button three times to display the last wizard screen.

15. Use the name Literature Requests, make sure the Modify the Page's Design option is chosen, and click the Finish button.
    The wizard will create the page and display it in Design view. Notice that the fields you chose are displayed on the page and a toolbar with various controls appears below the fields. Also notice the gray title box at the top of the page. You will enter a title in this box in the following step.

Modify the Page and Save It Outside the Database

16. Click the title box at the top of the page and type **Literature Request Page** as the title.

17. Click the Save 💾 button on the Access toolbar, and the Save as Data Access Page box will appear.
    This box allows you to save the data access page outside of your Access database. This way, the page is available for display on an intranet or the World Wide Web. Normally, you would give such a page a URL to identify its location. URLs are the names you see in Web browsers, such as http://www.labpub.com. However, you will simply save your data access page to your file storage location because you won't post it to a Website in this course.

18. Use the name Literature Requests and click the Save button to save the page to your file storage location.
    Access will display a warning message indicating that the name you used will not allow users to locate the page on an intranet or the Web.

19. Click OK to accept the name.

20. Now close your new data access page.

Use the Data Access Page

Notice that the data access page is available in the Pages section of the database. You could open this page and use it to edit data as you would use a form. However, you will open the data access page saved to your file storage location in the Internet Explorer Web browser.

21. Use Windows Explorer to navigate to your file storage location, in which you saved the Literature Requests data access page.
It should be identified as an HTML (Web) document.

22. Double-click the page, and it will open in an Internet Explorer Web browser window.
This is exactly how the page would look to a user accessing it over the Web.

23. Follow these steps to add a new record:

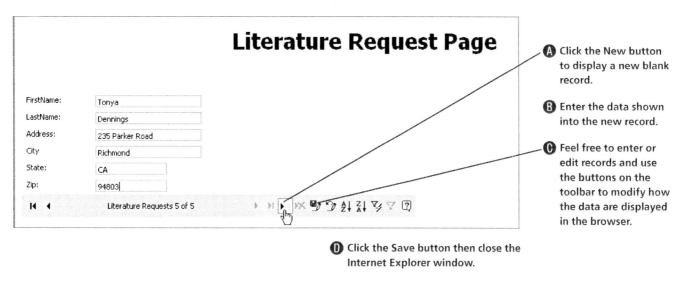

Ⓐ Click the New button to display a new blank record.

Ⓑ Enter the data shown into the new record.

Ⓒ Feel free to enter or edit records and use the buttons on the toolbar to modify how the data are displayed in the browser.

Ⓓ Click the Save button then close the Internet Explorer window.

Examine the Underlying Table

24. Switch to Access then click the Tables button on the Objects bar.

25. Double-click the Literature Requests table to display its datasheet.
The record you added, and any other changes you made in the data access page, should be reflected in the table. However, changes you made in the organization of the data in the data access page (such as the sort order) will not be reflected in the underlying table.

26. Close the Literature Requests table and continue with the next topic.

Saving Objects as Web Pages

Access 2003 lets you save tables, queries, forms, and reports as Web pages. You can easily publish any of these objects to the World Wide Web using the procedure outlined in the following Quick Reference table. There is no Hands-On exercise to accompany this topic. If you wish to publish one of these objects, you will need access to a Web server. Additional information on this topic can be found in Access's online Help.

QUICK REFERENCE: SAVING OBJECTS AS WEB PAGES

Task	Procedure
Save an object as a Web page	■ Choose the desired object in the Access database window.
	■ Choose File→Export and choose HTML Documents from the Save as Type list in the Export dialog box.
	■ Choose a location to save to and specify a filename.
	■ Check the Save Formatted box and click the Save button.
	■ Decide whether you want to use an HTML template (see online Help for more information on this feature) and click OK.

Maintaining Databases

Access databases are often the information banks for entire organizations. For this reason, it is important that databases be properly maintained. The following topics discuss the most useful techniques for maintaining databases.

Identifying Object Dependencies

Viewing a list of objects dependent on other objects is extremely helpful to maintaining a database over time and avoiding errors. For example, deleting a query can cause a problem in a report. In Access 2003 you can view a list of objects and their dependencies. You can also view a list of objects that use a selected object, or you can view the objects being used by a selected object. Dependency information is only shown for tables, queries, forms, and reports. To view the list of object dependencies, all objects must be closed.

Hands-On 10.8   **Object Dependencies**

In this exercise, you will view your object dependencies for the Pinnacle Pet Care database.

1. If necessary, close any objects you have open.

2. Choose the Customers table.

3. Choose View→Object Dependencies from the menu.

4. Choose OK on the warning box and study the following illustrations:

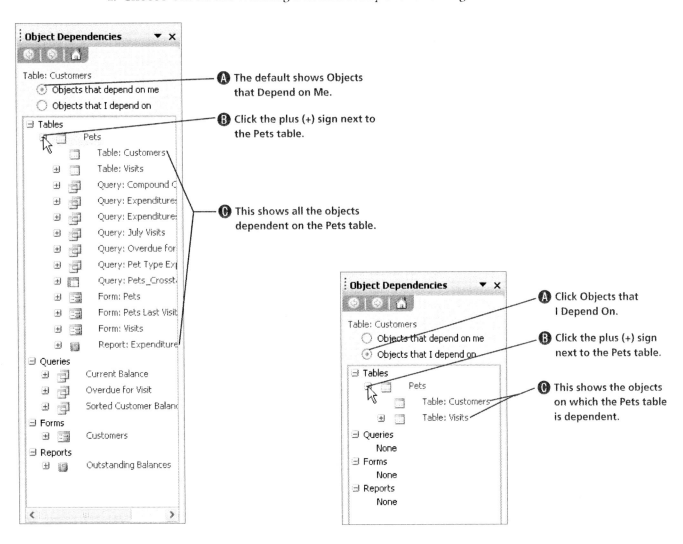

5. Close the Object Dependencies task pane when finished.

Backing Up and Restoring Databases

You should always make a copy of your database before making significant changes to its structure. Some procedures, such as modifying the design of tables or deleting tables, can result in lost data. It is also recommended that you periodically make a backup copy of your database in case it gets damaged.

Access assigns an .mdb extension to database files. For example, your Pinnacle Pet Care database has the name Pinnacle Pet Care.mdb. You can back up a database by making a copy of the .mdb file. You should store the copy on a different computer system or in an off-site location. If your original database becomes damaged, you can replace it with the backup copy.

You can also make copies of tables, forms, and reports using the Copy and Paste buttons in the database window. You may want to do this prior to making design changes to objects. If the design changes don't work out as planned, you can delete an object and replace it with the backup copy.

Compacting and Repairing Databases

Databases may become fragmented as you delete unwanted records and objects. This can reduce the performance of large databases that have many transactions. Compacting defragments a database, improves its performance, and reduces the size of the .mdb file. The compacting operation also repairs any internal problems encountered with the database. There are two ways to compact and repair a database. You can perform the operation while the file is open by clicking Tools→Database Utilities→Compact and Repair. Or, you can perform the operation while the file is unopened. In Hands-On 10.9 you will compact and repair an unopened database.

QUICK REFERENCE: COMPACTING AND REPAIRING AN UNOPENED DATABASE

Task	Procedure
Compact and repair a database	■ Start Access but do not open the database.
	■ Choose Tools→Database Utilities→Compact and Repair Database from the menu bar.
	■ Navigate to the .mdb file you wish to compact.
	■ Click the Compact button.
	■ Enter a name for the compacted database. You can enter the same name as the database you are compacting. If you use the same name, Access will replace your database with the compacted version. Otherwise, a new compacted copy of the database will be created with the name you specify.

Hands-On 10.9 **Compact and Repair a Database**

In this exercise, you will compact and repair the Pinnacle Pet Care database while it is unopened.

1. Close the Pinnacle Pet Care database but leave the Access window open.
   The Access program window should be visible.

2. Choose Tools→Database Utilities→Compact and Repair Database from the menu bar.

3. Navigate to the location of your Pinnacle Pet Care database file.

4. Choose the Pinnacle Pet Care file and click the Compact button.
   Access will prompt you to enter a name for the compacted database file it is about to create.

5. Choose your Pinnacle Pet Care file from the list and click the Save button.

6. Choose Yes when Access informs you that your original database will be replaced.
   Access will compact the database and replace your original database with the compacted version.

7. Choose File from the menu bar then choose the Pinnacle Pet Care file from the Frequently Used Files list at the bottom of the menu.

8. Feel free to browse the objects in your compacted database.
   You won't notice any changes in the database. If you had compacted a large, heavily used database, you would probably notice an increase in performance if you were to access data.

9. Close the database and continue with the end-of-lesson questions and exercises.

Concepts Review

True/False Questions

1. Word Mail Merge form letters can be linked to Access queries. TRUE FALSE

2. The OfficeLinks ![button] button is used to initiate the Mail Merge Wizard. TRUE FALSE

3. DDE is an acronym for Dynamic Data Exchange. TRUE FALSE

4. A data access page is a Web page connected to an Access database. TRUE FALSE

5. The Mailing Label Wizard can be used to set up form letters in Word. TRUE FALSE

6. The Mailing Label Wizard lets you choose from a variety of label formats. TRUE FALSE

7. The Analyze It with Microsoft Office Excel ![button] OfficeLinks button exports data to Excel and automatically subtotals the data. TRUE FALSE

8. Backing up a database defragments the .mdb file and reduces its size. TRUE FALSE

9. Viewing the list of dependencies can help avoid errors. TRUE FALSE

10. You cannot use the drag and drop method to export a query. TRUE FALSE

Multiple Choice Questions

1. Which button establishes a DDE link between an Access query and a Word form letter?
   a. ![button]
   b. ![button]
   c. ![button]
   d. ![button]

2. Which button is used to export data to Excel?
   a. ![button]
   b. ![button]
   c. ![button]
   d. ![button]

3. Which section of the database window should be active if you want to establish a DDE link between an Access object and a Word document?
   a. Tables
   b. Forms
   c. Queries
   d. Either a or c

4. Which of the following will potentially reduce the size of an .mdb file?
   a. Backing up
   b. Compacting
   c. Restoring
   d. All of the above

Skill Builders

Skill Builder 10.1   Modify a Table and Set Up a Query

In this exercise, you will add a Mailing List field to the Customers table in the Tropical Getaways database. You will also create a query that selects records from the Customers table only if the Mailing List field is checked.

Modify the Customers Table

1. Open the Tropical Getaways database and close the Main Switchboard form.

2. Click the Tables button on the Objects bar.

3. Choose the Customers table and click the ⬚ Design button.

4. Add a Mailing List field to the table and set the Data Type to Yes/No, as shown to the right.

Field Name	Data Type
🔑 Customer ID	AutoNumber
Firstname	Text
Lastname	Text
Address	Text
City	Text
State	Text
Zip	Text
Profile	Text
Mailing List	Yes/No

5. Click the Datasheet ⬚ view button on the left end of the Access toolbar.

6. Click the Yes button when Access asks if you want to save the table.

7. Check the Mailing List boxes for all records where the state is equal to TX as shown here.

Firstname	Lastname	Address	City	State	Zip	Profile	Mailing List
Debbie	Thomas	450 Crestwood Lane	Austin	TX	78752-	Adventure	☑
Wilma	Boyd	855 State Street	Richmond	NY	12954-	Leisure	☐
Ted	Wilkins	900 C Street	Fort Worth	TX	76104-	Adventure	☑
Alice	Simpson	2450 Ridge Road	Fort Worth	TX	76105-	Family	☑
Rita	Bailey	1625 Palm Street	Portland	OR	97240-	Family	☐
Cheryl	DeMarco	1250 Sandy Plains	Atlanta	GA	30062-	Singles	☐
Victor	Thomas	2300 Wilmont Street	Danvers	MA	01923-	Adventure	☐
Lisa	Simms	100 Westside Drive	Batavia	NY	14020-	Leisure	☐
Ted	Carter	250 Smith Street	Charlotte	MA	01507-	Family	☐

8. Close the table.

Create a Mailing List Query

9. Click the Queries button on the Objects bar.

10. Double-click the Create Query in Design View option.

11. Add the Customers table to the Design grid and close the Show Table box.

12. Set up the following query. Make sure to uncheck the Show box for the Mailing List field. Also, enter the word **Yes** in the Criteria box of the Mailing List field.

Field:	Firstname	Lastname	Address	City	State	Zip	Mailing List
Table:	Customers	Customers	Customers	Customers	Customers	Customers	Customers
Sort:							
Show:	☑	☑	☑	☑	☑	☑	☐
Criteria:							Yes

13. Run ⚡ the query to produce the following recordset:

	Firstname	Lastname	Address	City	State	Zip
	Debbie	Thomas	450 Crestwood Lane	Austin	TX	78752-
	Ted	Wilkins	900 C Street	Fort Worth	TX	76104-
	Alice	Simpson	2450 Ridge Road	Fort Worth	TX	76105-

14. Close the query and save it as **Mailing List**.

Skill Builder 10.2   Conduct a Mail Merge

In this exercise, you will set up a Word form letter. You will also merge the form letter with the Mailing List query.

Create the Mail Merge and Form Letter

 TIP! *Your Customers table does not currently include a prefix field for Mr., Mrs., and Ms. If desired, you can add a Prefix field to your table, include the Prefix field in the query you will set up, and use the Prefix field in your form letter as you did in the Pinnacle Pet Care database.*

1. If necessary, click the Queries button on the Objects bar.

2. Choose the Mailing List query and click the OfficeLinks 📑 ▾ drop-down button.

3. Choose the Merge It with Microsoft Office Word option.

4. Choose the Create a New Document option in the first wizard screen and click OK.

5. Maximize the Word program window.

6. Tap [Enter] six times and choose Insert→Date and Time from the Word menu bar.

7. Choose the third date format in the Date and Time box and make sure the Update Automatically box is checked.

8. Click OK to insert the date then tap [Enter] four times.

9. Click the Insert Address Block 📄 button on Word's Mail Merge toolbar.

10. Click OK to accept all of the default formats and insert the address block.

11. Tap [Enter] twice and click the Insert Greeting Line 🔲 button.

12. Choose the colon (:) format from the third drop-down list then click OK to insert the greeting line.

13. Tap [Enter] twice and type the following text into the letter:

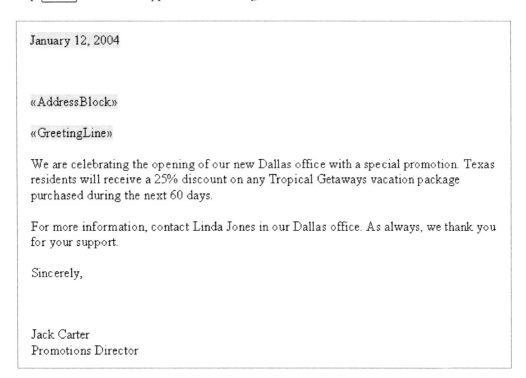

```
January 12, 2004



«AddressBlock»

«GreetingLine»

We are celebrating the opening of our new Dallas office with a special promotion. Texas
residents will receive a 25% discount on any Tropical Getaways vacation package
purchased during the next 60 days.

For more information, contact Linda Jones in our Dallas office. As always, we thank you
for your support.

Sincerely,



Jack Carter
Promotions Director
```

14. Save the document to your file storage location as **Tropical Getaways Form Letter**.

Conduct the Merge

15. Click the Merge to New Document 🔲 button on the Mail Merge toolbar and click OK to merge all records.
    A personalized letter should be addressed to each Texas resident.

16. Close the merged letters without saving them.

17. If you noticed a problem in your merged letters, make any necessary corrections and redo the merge.

18. When you have finished, close Word and save any changes you made to the form letter.

Skill Builder 10.3 Create Mailing Labels

In this exercise, you will set up mailing labels for the Mailing List query.

1. Click the Reports button on the Objects bar.

2. Click the 🔲 New button to display the New Report box.

3. Choose the Label Wizard, choose Mailing List from the table/query list, and click OK.

4. Choose Avery from the Manufacturer's list in the second screen.

5. Choose English as the Units of Measure and make sure the Label Type is set to Sheet.

6. Choose the 5160 product number and click Next.

7. Click Next again to bypass the font and color options screen.

8. Add fields and insert spaces and punctuation marks in the Prototype field box until your prototype label matches the example shown to the right.

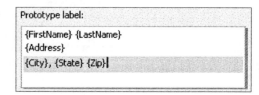

Prototype label:

{FirstName} {LastName}
{Address}
{City}, {State} {Zip}

9. Click Next and the wizard will ask on which field you wish to sort.

10. Choose the Zip field and click the Add Field ⟩ button.

11. Click Next and type the name **Mailing Labels** in the last wizard screen.

12. Make sure the See the Labels as They Will Look Printed option is chosen and click the Finish button.

13. If you receive a Data May Not Be Displayed message, click OK to accept the settings. *Access will create the report and the following labels should appear.*

Ted Wilkins 900 C Street Fort Worth, TX 76104	Alice Simpson 2450 Ridge Road Fort Worth, TX 76105	Debbie Thomas 450 Crestwood Lane Austin, TX 78752

14. Click the Close ☒ button at the top-right corner of the report.

Create a Data Access Page

In this exercise, you will create a data access page and apply a theme to the page.

Use the Data Access Page Wizard

1. Click the Pages button on the Objects bar.

2. Double-click the Create Data Access Page by Using Wizard option.

3. Choose the Customers table from the Tables/Queries list.

4. Add the Firstname, Lastname, Address, City, State, and Zip fields to the Selected Fields list.

5. Click the Next button three times to display the last wizard screen.

6. Use the name Customers and make sure the Modify the Page's Design option is chosen. Check the box to apply a theme and click the Finish button.

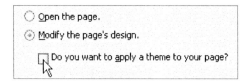

7. Choose the Blends theme, check the box for Vivid colors, and click OK.

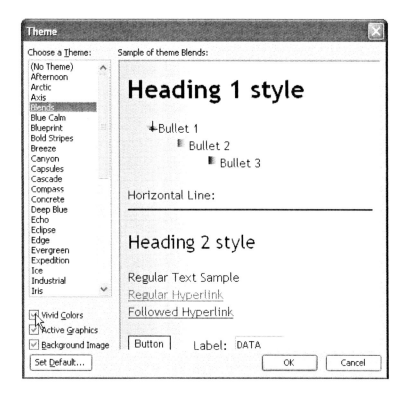

Add a Title and Save It Outside the Database

8. Click the title box at the top of the page and type **Customers** as the title.

9. Click the Save 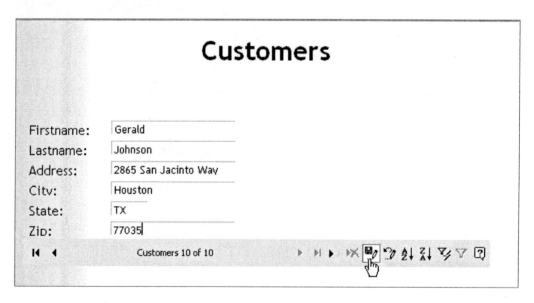 button on the Access toolbar, and the Save as Data Access Page box will appear.

10. Use the name Customers and click the Save button.

11. Click OK to accept the name and close your data access page.

Use the Data Access Page

12. Navigate to the Customer data access page.

13. Double-click the page and it will open in an Internet Explorer Web browser window. Now add the following new record:

Customers

Firstname:	Gerald
Lastname:	Johnson
Address:	2865 San Jacinto Way
City:	Houston
State:	TX
Zip:	77035

Customers 10 of 10

14. Close the Tropical Getaways database.

Assessments

Assessment 10.1   Create a Mail Merge

In this exercise, you will set up a form letter and mailing labels.

1. Open the Classic Cars database and close the Main Switchboard form.

2. Add a field named **Mailing List** to the Collectors table. Set the data type of the Mailing List field to Yes/No.

3. Switch to Datasheet view and save the changes to the table.

4. Check the Mailing List box for all records where the Era of Interest is 1950s or 1960s.

5. Close the Collectors table.

6. Create a query that produces the following recordset. Notice that the query chooses records from the Collectors table where the Mailing List field is set to Yes.

	Firstname	Lastname	Address	City	State	Zip
	Cindy	Johnson	4220 Edward Street	Northlake	IL	60164-
	Tammy	Olson	1200 Big Pine Drive	Moses Lake	WA	98837-
	Bob	Barker	6340 Palm Drive	Rockridge	FL	32955-
	Angela	Hall	159 SW Taylor St	Portland	OR	97205-

7. Close the query and save it as **Mailing List**.

8. Use the OfficeLinks ![OfficeLinks button] button to establish a DDE link between the Mailing List query and a new Word document.

9. Using Word, set up the following form letter. Use Word's Insert→Date and Time command to insert the date as a field that is automatically updated.

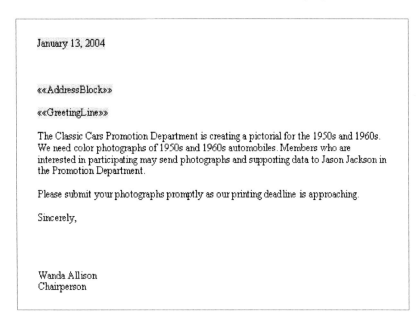

January 13, 2004

«AddressBlock»

«GreetingLine»

The Classic Cars Promotion Department is creating a pictorial for the 1950s and 1960s. We need color photographs of 1950s and 1960s automobiles. Members who are interested in participating may send photographs and supporting data to Jason Jackson in the Promotion Department.

Please submit your photographs promptly as our printing deadline is approaching.

Sincerely,

Wanda Allison
Chairperson

10. Save the form letter to your file storage location as **Classic Cars Form Letter**.

11. Merge the form letter with the Mailing List query choosing the All Records option.

12. Close the merged letters without saving them.

13. Close the form letter and save any changes.

14. Use the Access Label Wizard and these guidelines to produce the mailing labels from the Mailing List query:

   ■ Base the labels report on the Mailing List query.

   ■ Use the Avery 5160 label style and English units of measure.

   ■ Sort the labels by zip code.

   ■ Assign the name Mailing Labels to the report.

Assessment 10.2 Export a Table to Excel

In this exercise, you will export the Collectors table to an Excel file.

1. Click the Tables button on the Objects bar and choose the Collectors table.

2. Choose File→Export from the menu bar.

3. Save the file as an Excel file named **Collectors** to your file storage location, preserving the formatting from Access.

4. Close the Classic Cars database and exit from Access.

Critical Thinking

Conduct a Mail Merge

Linda Holmes wants to send a letter to property owners who have not taken advantage of the Feels Like Home service. Open the Holmestead Realty database and follow these guidelines to prepare the database for a mailing:

- Add a field named **Mailing List** with a Yes/No data type to the Contacts table.

- Place a checkmark in the Mailing list field for the Desmonds and the Stevens.

- Create a query named **Mailing List**. Add the Contacts table to the query. Include the Name, Address, and Mailing List fields from the Contacts table in the query. Do not show the Mailing List field in the recordset. Set the criterion for the Mailing List field to Yes.

- Use the Mailing List query as the basis of a mail merge with Word. Create a form letter in Word that introduces the Feels Like Home service to the property owners in the Contacts table. Your form letter should include the current date, an address block, a greeting line, a body, and a complimentary close.

- Save your letter as **Feels Like Home Form Letter**.

Now merge your letter to a new document. Review the merged letters and, if necessary, make corrections in the database or form letter. Once the merge functions properly, you can print the letters or just review them. Do not save them when you are finished.

Create Labels

Now that you have completed the letters, you need labels for the envelopes. Though you could type them, Access can create them with minimal effort on your part. Follow these guidelines to accomplish this:

- Use the Labels Wizard to create a new report using the Mailing List query as the basis of the report.

- Choose Avery 5160 labels. Use the default color and font options.

- Arrange the fields into the prototype label. Name this report **Mailing Labels**.

- Preview the report and print the labels if desired.

Critical Thinking 10.3 Manage Mailing Lists

A good mailing system must have a mechanism for easily choosing contacts to be included in a mailing. Follow these guidelines to set up such a system in the Holmestead Realty database:

■ Create an Update query for the Contacts table that updates all records with Yes in the Mailing List field to No. Save this query as **Update Mailing List**.

■ Add the Mailing List field to the Contacts Data Entry form. This will place a Yes/No checkbox for the Mailing List field on the form.

■ Add a command button to the Contacts Data Entry form that runs the Update Mailing List query. Call this command button **Uncheck Boxes**. Test the button to ensure that it functions properly.

■ Use the Feels Like Home Form Letter to conduct a mail merge using any three records from the Contacts table. Discard the merged letters when you finish and use the Uncheck Boxes command button to remove all contacts from the mailing list.

Critical Thinking 10.4 Export Data to Excel

Linda wants to analyze information from her Feels Like Home service. To accomplish this, she wants to export the data to Excel. Follow these guidelines to export data to Excel:

■ Use the Analyze It with Microsoft Office Excel OfficeLinks button to export the recordset from the Extended Cost query to Excel.

■ AutoFit all column widths in the Excel worksheet.

■ Sort the worksheet on the Service column in ascending order.

■ Subtotal the worksheet to see a sum of the extended cost for each change in service.

■ Discard the worksheet when you finish.

APPENDIX

Using File Storage Media

You may wish to use storage media besides the floppy disk referred to in most of the lessons. This appendix contains instructions for downloading and unzipping the exercise files used with this book, and an overview for using this book with various file storage media.

In This Appendix

The following topics are addressed in this appendix:

Downloading the Student Exercise Files

The files needed to complete certain Hands-On, Skill Builder, Assessment, and Critical Thinking exercises are available for download at the Labyrinth Website. Use the following instructions to copy the files to your computer and prepare them for use with this book.

Hands-On A.1   Download and Unzip Files

Follow these steps to download a copy of the student files necessary for this book:

1. Launch Internet Explorer.

2. Enter **labpub.com/students/fdmso2003.asp** in the browser's address bar and tap Enter.
   A list of books in the applicable series appears. If you don't see the title of your book in the list, use the links on the left side of the Web page to display the list of books for your series.

3. Click the link for your book title.
   A prompt to open or save a file containing the student exercise files appears.

4. Click the Save button.

5. Choose your file storage location and click Save.
   After a pause, the exercise files will begin downloading to your computer. Continue with the next step after the download is complete.

6. Click the Open button on the Download Complete dialog box. Or, open your file storage location and double-click the newly downloaded file if the dialog box closed automatically.

7. Click OK, and then follow the step for your file storage location:
   - **Floppy Disk:** Click the Browse button, choose the 3½ Floppy A: drive, click OK, and then click the Unzip button.
   - **USB Flash Drive:** Click the Browse button, navigate to your USB flash drive, click OK, and then click the Unzip button.
   - **My Documents Folder:** Click the Browse button, navigate to the My Documents folder, click OK, and then click the Unzip button.
   - **Network Drive Folder:** Click the Browse button, navigate to your assigned folder on the network drive, click OK, and then click the Unzip button.

8. Click the Close button after the files have unzipped.

Working with File Storage Locations

New technologies continue to expand the variety of available computer storage media. The 3½ inch floppy disk has been around since about 1983. That's incredibly ancient in the fast-moving field of computers. It's easy to use other storage media with this book. Potential alternative storage locations include:

- The My Documents folder
- A USB flash drive
- A folder on your local hard drive
- A folder on a network drive

Using Alternative File Storage Locations

Depending on the file storage media you select, some steps you perform in the exercises will differ from what you see illustrated. However, with a little practice you should find it easy to interpret the instructions for use with your file storage media.

Example: Using a USB Flash Drive

You are performing an exercise in which you create and save a new file. If you are using a USB flash drive, simply substitute the drive letter for your flash drive for the 3½ Floppy (A:) drive shown in the figure instruction.

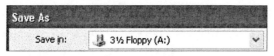

The storage location as it appears in the book   The storage location as you perform it on the screen

Using a Floppy Disk

If you use a floppy disk to store your exercise files, you should be aware of space limitations. This section explains how to keep track of the available space on a floppy diskette, and how to delete unnecessary files to conserve space.

Storage Limitations of Floppy Disks

As you work through the exercises in this book, you will create numerous files that are to be saved to a storage location. A floppy diskette may not have enough storage capacity to hold all files created during the course (particularly if you perform all of the Skill Builder and Critical Thinking exercises). Thus, you may want to use an alternate storage location for all files accessed and created during the course.

Checking Available Space on a Floppy Disk

If you choose to use a floppy disk as your storage location, you may reach a point at which the disk fills up and no additional files can be stored on it. However, if you regularly check the available space on your floppy disk, this problem should not arise.

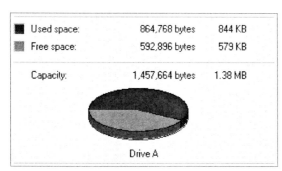

■ Used space:	864,768 bytes	844 KB
▨ Free space:	592,896 bytes	579 KB
Capacity:	1,457,664 bytes	1.38 MB

Drive A

Windows can display a pie chart of the available space on your floppy disk.

Freeing Up Space on the Floppy Disk

If your floppy disk runs short of space, you will need to selectively delete files from it. You should delete files from lessons already completed, freeing up space for exercises in the current lesson.

TIP! *Use the following procedure to check your available floppy disk space before you begin work on a new lesson. If you have less than 100 KB remaining on the disk, delete some files to free up space.*

Hands-On A.2   Check Free Space on a Floppy Disk

1. Open a My Computer window.

2. Right-click the 3½ Floppy (A:) drive and choose Properties from the context menu.
   Windows displays a pie chart with details on the used and available space on the floppy disk.

3. Examine the Free Space information and click OK.

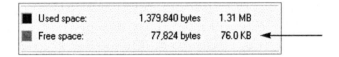

4. Follow the step for the amount of disk space remaining:
   - **Close** the Properties window. Close the My Computer window if there is more than 100 KB of space remaining on the disk. Skip the remaining steps in this procedure. You are finished and ready to proceed with the next lesson.
   - **Close** the Properties window. Continue with the remaining steps in this exercise if there is less than 100 KB of space remaining on your floppy disk.

Delete Unnecessary Files

5. Double-click to open the 3½ Floppy (A:) drive.

6. Choose View→List from the menu bar.
   The My Computer window displays your files as a compact list.

7. While holding down the Ctrl key, select files for lessons that preceded the one you are working on now and tap the Delete key on the keyboard. Choose Yes if you are asked to confirm the deletion of these files.
   Windows deletes the selected files.

8. Close the My Computer window.
   You now have plenty of space for your work in the next lesson.

TIP! *If you accidentally delete an exercise file needed for a later lesson, don't worry. You can repeat the procedure outlined in Hands-On A.1 to download and unzip the student exercise files as many times as necessary.*

Using a USB Flash Drive

A USB flash drive stores your data on a flash memory chip. You simply plug it into a USB port on any computer and Windows immediately recognizes it as an additional disk drive. USB flash drives typically are able store 32 megabytes (MB) or more of your data files. Large capacity USB flash drives can store 512 MB or more.

Most USB flash drives are about the size of your thumb and plug into any available USB port on your computer.

USB Flash Drive Letter

When you plug in a USB flash drive to a Windows computer, Windows automatically assigns it the next available drive letter. Windows uses drive letters to identify each drive connected to the computer. For example, the primary part of the hard drive is always identified as the C: drive. The CD/DVD drive is typically the D: or E: drive.

Devices with Removable Storage

This USB flash drive is the F: drive.

3½ Floppy (A:)   DVD/CD-RW Drive (E:)   Removable Disk (F:)

TIP! *Your USB flash drive may receive a different drive letter on different computers. This does not affect any files stored on the drive.*

Hands-On A.3 **Rename Your USB Flash Drive**

You may find it convenient to rename your USB flash drive to make it easier to recognize when you save or open files.

 TIP! *Some Windows systems may not give you renaming privileges for drives.*

1. Plug the USB flash drive into an available USB port.

2. Open a My Computer window.

3. Right-click your USB flash drive and choose Rename from the context menu.

 NOTE! *In the next step, Windows may display a prompt that you cannot rename this flash drive. You have not done anything wrong! You can use the drive with its current name. You may also want to try renaming it later using a different login.*

4. Type **FlashDrive** as the new drive name and tap Enter. Click OK if you receive a prompt that you do not have sufficient rights to perform this operation.
   If you were unable to rename the flash drive, don't worry. Renaming the flash drive is a convenience for recognition and has no other effect.

Using the My Documents Folder

Windows creates a unique My Documents folder for each login. This folder resides on the main system drive (usually the C: drive). The Office 2003 application programs provide a My Documents button in their Open and Save As dialog boxes to make navigation to this folder convenient.

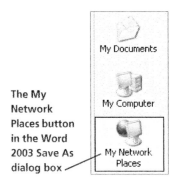

The My Documents button in the Word 2003 Save As dialog box

Using a Network Drive Folder

You may use a system connected to a network. There may be a folder on a network server computer in another location that is dedicated to storing your work. Usually, you will find this folder within the My Network Places folder of your computer. The Office 2003 application programs provide a My Network Places button in their Open and Save As dialog boxes to make navigation to this folder convenient. You may have to navigate deeper into the folder to locate your personal network drive folder.

The My Network Places button in the Word 2003 Save As dialog box

Index

operators for criteria selection, 101, 106–109
OR criteria in queries, 106, 108–109
orientation of pages, 23

P

Page Header/Footer, 277
Page Setup, 23
parameter queries, 135–136
pictures, forms design, 186–187
PivotTables in Excel, 343
primary key fields, 16, 37–38, 122
printing
    forms records, 71
    query results, 109–110
    reports, 74, 127
    tables, 20–23, 49
Print Preview, 21, 74
Properties button, forms, 174–175
Properties dialog box, 129
publishing data to Word/Excel, 340, 343

Q

queries
    action, 140–142
    calculated fields, 127–129
    criteria selection, 100–109, 132
    crosstab, 137–139
    Design grid for, 94–96, 103–104
    formatting and printing, 109–110
    mailing list, 335
    modifying properties, 129–130
    multiple tables, 133–135
    parameter, 135–136
    reports based on, 142–143
    running, 97
    select, 92, 134–135
    setup procedures, 92–94
    sorting results, 97–100
    statistical functions, 131–133
    subforms and, 223–225
    wizards for, 92, 137
Query Wizard, 92

R

ranges, specifying, validation rules, 50
records
    criteria for queries, 100–109, 132
    Datasheet view, 38–43
    definition, 10
    forms method, 66–72
recordset for queries, 92
Rectangle button, 198–200
referential integrity in table relationships, 123–125
relational databases, features of, 10
relationships between tables, 122–127
renaming objects, 77, 78
repairing databases, 350–351
replacing records, 41
Report Header/Footer, 277, 282
reports
    basic procedures, 73–77
    command buttons for, 306–307
    customizing, 276–286
    publishing to Word, 340
    queries and, 142–143
Report Wizard, 73–77
required fields, validation rules, 50
restoring databases, 350
restricting data entry, 173–175
rows and columns, resizing, 22, 228–230

S

saving
    blank databases, 8–9
    objects, 16, 17, 348
sections of forms, 177
select queries, 92, 134–135
setup procedures
    fields, 11–15
    queries, 92–94
    tables, 10
SetValue action and macros, 310
Show check box for criteria selection, 101, 102–103
Show Table button, 126
Simple Query Wizard, 137
Single Step macro mode, 303
sizing tasks
    form controls, 180–184
    subforms, 228–230